Essential Computational Thinking

Computer Science from Scratch

Ricky J. Sethi

Essential Computational Thinking

Computer Science from Scratch

Ricky J. Sethi

Bassim Hamadeh, CEO and Publisher
John Remington, Executive Editor
Michelle Piehl, Senior Project Editor
Christian Berk, Production Editor
Jess Estrella, Senior Graphic Designer
Greg Isales, Licensing Associate
Natalie Piccotti, Director of Marketing
Kassie Graves, Vice President of Editorial
Jamie Giganti, Director of Academic Publishing

Cover: Source: https://unsplash.com/photos/Dwheufds6kQ.

Printed in the United States of America.

For Rohan, Megan, Surrinder, Harindar, and especially the team of the two Harindars.

Acknowledgments

I would like to thank my current and former students for the feedback and help in crafting a clearer, more concise book than my meandering initial drafts. In particular, thanks to Kabir Chug and Bryce "Texas" Shurts for assisting with the reviews and administration of the text. I'd also like to acknowledge my Fitchburg State University colleagues for their feedback and encouragement, and particularly Kevin B. Austin, Natasha Kurtonina, Nadimpalli V.R. Mahadev, and John Russo for going the extra mile.

I'm grateful to all of the reviewers, especially Dmitry Zinoviev of Suffolk University, Frank J. Kachurak of Pennsylvania State University, and Siva Jasthi of Metropolitan State University, who so generously donated their time and expertise to help produce a much better and more correct book with their detailed and insightful feedback.

This book depends on quite a few open source resources and I'd like to acknowledge some that were indispensable to its development like `LaTeXTemplates.com`, `www.pexels.com`, `www.pixabay.com`, `venngage.com`, `htmltidy.net`, `repl.it`, and `generatedata.com`.

And last, but certainly not least, I'd like to thank my family, especially my mother for the constant encouragement and positive reinforcement; my father, for reading endless drafts and commenting thoughtfully and proudly on each one; my son, for letting me bounce ideas off him and making life a joy, in general; and my beautiful wife, for being a constant support and always helping edit drafts in a topic that's not only outside her area of expertise but also includes occasional sentences full of equations, the bane of her existence.

I should add that any errors which remain, and I'm sure there will be quite a few, are my sole responsibility. The book resource page, available at `http://research.sethi.org/ricky/book/`, will also contain the reams of errata as they're discovered.

Ricky J. Sethi
`http://research.sethi.org/ricky/`
January 2020

Preface

Why a book on CS0 from scratch?

Most of us write the books that we would have wanted to read and this is no different. As such, it follows a normal CS0 breadth-first approach but lays particular emphasis on computational thinking and related topics in data science.

My hope is this book will help build a theoretical and practical foundation for learning computer science from the ground up. It's not quite from first principles as this is not a rigorous text. But, following William of Occam's Razor, it is placed on a firm mathematical footing that starts with the fewest assumptions.

And so we delve into defining elementary ideas like data and information; along the way, we quantify these ideas and eke out some of their links to fundamental physics in an effort to show the connection between computer science and the universe itself. In fact, all the laws of physics can be represented as computable functions, and we can, in a very real sense, think of computer science as the most basic representation of the physical universe.

The eminent physicist John A. Wheeler went so far as to say, "...the universe is made of information; matter and energy are only incidental." I view the role of this book, at its theoretical core, to be to help explore, elucidate, and communicate this deep and perhaps surprising relationship between physics, information, and computation.

Target Audience

This book would be most appropriate for highly-motivated undergraduates who have a significant technical bent and a genuine interest in computer science. It is also appropriate for non-CS graduate students or non-CS professionals who are interested in learning more about computer science and programming for either professional or personal development.

So what kind of a background do you need to appreciate these various connections and learn some of the more advanced material? Although you should be quantitatively inclined, you don't need any specific background in mathematics. Whatever math we need, we'll derive or explain along the way. Things might look heinous at times but all the tools you need should be in here.

Book Organization

Computer science is a diverse field and, in **Part 1**, we explore some of its theoretical bases in a connected but wide-ranging manner with an emphasis on breadth, not depth. Some chapters might still pack quite a punch but, if students are interested in computer science, they should get an overview of the field in large measure, not necessarily in its entirety. Not only is computer science an enormously broad area but this book, to paraphrase Thoreau, is limited by the narrowness of my experience and vision to those areas that caught my eye.

For that matter, this book is not a comprehensive introduction to a particular programming language, either. By necessity, we are constrained to only meeting those parts of Python or Java that support our understanding of fundamental computational ideas. In general, computer scientists tend to be a language agnostic bunch who pick the most appropriate language for a particular problem and that's the approach in this book, as well. But we should still get a sense of the large variety of topics that underly our study of computer science, from the abstract mathematical bases to the physical underpinnings.

Once the theoretical foundation is laid in Part 1, we shift gears to a purely pragmatic exploration of computing principles. So, in **Part 2**, we learn the basics of computation and how to use our greatest tool: programming. These chapters should be short and approachable. Students will hopefully find them digestible in brief sittings so they can immediately apply the ideas they've learned to start writing substantial programs, or computational solutions. Computer science is an inherently empirical science and few sciences can offer this unique opportunity to let students actually implement and execute theoretical ideas they have developed.

In **Part 3**, we'll explore some relatively sophisticated computational ideas. We'll both meet powerful programming concepts as well as investigate the limits of computational problem solving. We'll also increase the tools in our toolkit by learning about object-oriented programming, machine learning, data science, and some of the underlying principles of software engineering used in industry. In addition, online supplementary chapters will address topics such as P vs. NP, Big O notation, GUI development, etc.

How to use this book

Depending upon student or instructor interests, **Part 1 can be considered completely optional** and skipped entirely. The most important aspects of Part 1 are summarized in Ch. 3 and, if you don't want to emphasize the theoretical underpinnings, you can safely choose to start directly with Part 2.

Similarly, in Part 3, you can pick and choose any chapters that interest you as each chapter in Part 3 is independent of the other chapters. For a typical semester-length course, I spend about 1-2 weeks on Part 1, cover all of Part 2, and pick topics of interest from Part 3 depending on the particular course.

You can also access supplementary information for the text at `http://research.sethi.org/ ricky/book/`, including complementary videos and auto-graded problem sets.

Nota Bene: This book uses standard bibliographical notation as is common in computer science literature so references are indicated by a number in brackets, like [XX]. It also uses **bold** and *italics* to define phrases and emphasize concepts inline. Finally, it contains call out boxes like IDEA boxes, NOTE boxes, etc., which are important points that should be highlighted separately or extend a concept without breaking the main narrative.[1]

Okay, that's enough build-up... strap yourself in and let's get started on our adventure!

---

[1] The same applies to footnotes, of course.

Contents

Theory: What Is Computer Science?

Basics: Algorithmic Expression

III Advanced: Data and Computation

Figures

Tables

Algorithms

Code Listings

I **Theory: What Is Computer Science?**

Contents

0. On the Road to Computation

> *In general we look for a new law by the following process. First we guess it. Then we compute the consequences of the guess to see what would be implied if this law that we guessed is right. Then we compare the result of the computation to nature, with experiment or experience, compare it directly with observation, to see if it works. If it disagrees with experiment it is wrong. In that simple statement is the key to science.*
> – Richard P. Feynman, *The Character of Physical Law*[1]

0.1   What Is Knowledge?

If you're like me, you're usually rushing out the door in the morning. Wouldn't it be nice to know if you need a jacket before you dash to your next class? You could check the weather channel but that doesn't give you the exact temperature in your particular neck of the woods, which can often vary significantly from the city center. So maybe you recruit some of your friends and place some temperature sensors all around campus to get a more accurate gauge of the temperature. This isn't a very realistic scenario but let's play along for a bit.

0.1.1   Step 1: Gather the Facts

The sensors you distribute might record temperature, humidity, and their GPS location. Suppose your friends go around every hour and record these values for you. How could you use the mass of notes your friends pile up at your doorstep every day, as shown in Figure 0.1?

---

[1] With the implied caveat that the initial guess you make is somehow falsifiable, as defined by Karl Popper. You can see Feynman's video of this quote at his Messenger Lectures on "The Character of Physical Law" at Cornell University in 1964 here: `http://www.cornell.edu/video/richard-feynman-messenger-lecture-7-seeking-new-laws`

3

Figure 0.1: The pile of sensor temperature values collected by your friends from all across campus.

As a first step, you might decide to organize all these disparate values in order to make sense of them. How should you go about organizing them? You could put them in a table or spreadsheet format. Let's say you decide to organize the values for each sensor based on the time your friends collected them.

Timestamp	Temperature	Humidity	GPS Location
4am	68°F	30%	Library
5am	71°F	31%	Library
6am	73°F	35%	Science Building
. . .	. . .	. . .	. . .

Table 0.1: Organized Sensor Values

You would end up with something like the table shown in Table 0.1. After organizing these values, you can already notice trends in the Temperature and Humidity columns: both seem to be increasing as the day wears on.

Now we're getting somewhere! Let's pause and see what we've done so far. We started by recording some **values**, which are the *quantitative* **observations** of the physical world.[2] Initially, we had a jumbled mess of values but, after *organizing* these values into a more appropriate structure, we end up with *data* that we can use to conduct some kind of analysis. We'll define this idea of data more precisely later but, for now, let's think about how we might use the **data**, which are the *structured representations* of the raw values.

0.1.2 Step 2: Contextualize the Data

We could, for instance, graph this data that we've collected in order to see if we can discover any trends over time in the dataset. If we plot the Temperature versus Time, we can clearly see a trend as shown in Figure 0.2.

We could then make a determination about whether it'll be cold enough for a jacket or not: if the predicted temperature at 8am is below a certain value, say 70°F, you might conclude that it is cold. Conversely, if the temperature is above that certain **threshold** of 70°F, you would conclude that it is not cold and, in fact, it's decidedly warm. This threshold is very subjective: 70°F might be hot for you but still considered freezing for your friend!

What have we accomplished so far? First and foremost, we have now succeeded in *transforming*

---

[2]We'll have more to say about a precise definition of the term value in Section 4.2.

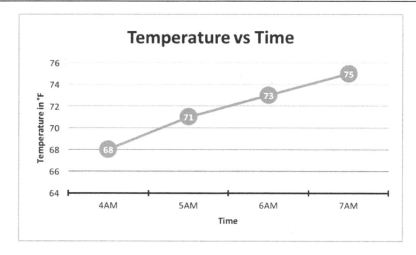

Figure 0.2: Plot of Temperature vs. Time

the observed values into data by finding a suitable **representation** for those values (in this case, as a table) and then using that data with a *rule* (in this case, a threshold) to get some insight about the world you're observing (in this case, that it's hot if the temperature value is above the threshold at 8am).

Giving the data a *context* like this transforms it into usable **information**. We'll once again hold off on quantifying this idea of information until later, when we meet Claude Shannon's theory of information and uncertainty and Leo Szilard's relating of information and energy. Nevertheless, we can continue on our adventure using just this intuitive concept of information as data that has been given a context of some sort to help *reduce uncertainty* and thus reveal meaning.

0.1.3 Step 3: Take Some Action!

The *transformation* of data into information makes it useful. You can now use that information to make *actionable decisions*. In this instance, we can use the trend in our graph from Figure 0.2 to *predict* that the temperature on campus would likely be above 70°F at 8am and conclude, using our threshold, that it's hot outside and, based on this information, decide to not wear a jacket.

We have thus managed to transform our information into *actionable knowledge*, the final decision to skip the jacket. This is an example of *rule-based knowledge* that we have codified into action. We can represent this process, the transformation of data to information to knowledge, as shown in Figure 0.3.

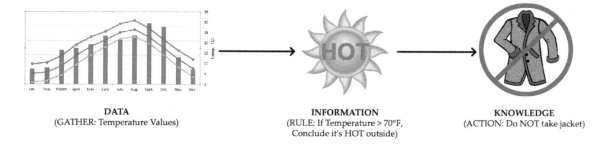

DATA
(GATHER: Temperature Values)

INFORMATION
(RULE: If Temperature > 70°F,
Conclude it's HOT outside)

KNOWLEDGE
(ACTION: Do NOT take jacket)

Figure 0.3: Transformation of Data to Information to Knowledge

Knowledge, then, can be thought of as structured or organized information that can lead to action in problem solving [1]–[3]. In the simplest terms, you can think of it as a collection of facts about some topic. This collection of information is often referred to as a *knowledge base* and is *modeled* or *represented* as a set of sentences.

The sentences in a knowledge base are usually expressed in a formal knowledge representation language in which each sentence represents some assertion about the world and the sentences can be used in logic-based reasoning systems to draw *conclusions* about the world. The logic-based systems can even incorporate fuzzy logic where the thresholds are not such stark dividers. [3]

Knowledge Generation Process

Our simple rule-based example above demonstrates this process: we collected raw observations of the world via sensors. We then transformed those raw values into data by structuring them into a suitable representation (e.g., a table). Next, we gave that data some context by using a threshold to draw a conclusion and predict whether each temperature value was hot or cold. We organized these facts about the warmth and time of day into a graph and used that to gain actionable knowledge which we used to make a decision about whether or not to wear a jacket at that time.

0.2 Declarative vs Imperative Knowledge

The knowledge used in such knowledge-based systems is curated using *knowledge management* techniques that define two types of knowledge: explicit and tacit. Explicit knowledge, also called know-what knowledge, is formalized and codified, e.g., in books and tables. Tacit knowledge, also called know-how knowledge, is less formal and refers to experience-based knowledge that can often be intuitive and hard to define formally. We'll see alternative representations of these in Section 10.1.1, as well.

These two types of knowledge, know-what (explicit) and know-how (tacit), can more generally be classified as either declarative or procedural. **Declarative knowledge** involves knowing *what* is true and is composed of statements of fact. For example, stating that the average temperature on campus at 7am was 75°F is a declaration of a fact but does not give us any information about how to actually *compute* that average.

On the other hand, **imperative knowledge**, also called **procedural knowledge**, involves knowing *how* to do something and is normally referred to as how-to knowledge which usually involves methods or recipes for deducing information. In this case, procedural knowledge would be the specification of a method or *procedure* for computing the average temperature on campus; for example, one approach might be:

1. Count the number of sensors that reported a temperature value at 7am
2. Add up temperature values reported from each sensor at 7am
3. Divide the sum of temperatures by the number of sensors

---

[3] The field of of *knowledge representation* further formalizes and organizes the information just as a data representation formalizes and organizes observed values. These representations are used in *knowledge engineering* to build *expert systems* using *problem-solving models* that are built into modules called *inference procedures* or *inference engines* [4].

0.3 The Key to Science

On the road so far, we've taken our quantifiable observations, the raw facts, and represented them in some structure. These structured observations are our data, in our case the table of temperature values. Information can be thought of as data which has been further placed in a useful context so as to reveal its meaning[4], in this case the determination of whether it was cold or hot. We used that conclusion to gain actionable knowledge and make a decision about whether or not we should take a jacket. That decision reflects our falsifiable prediction about the world; e.g., if we don't take the jacket and the temperature suddenly drops precipitously, our decision, based on our prediction of the temperature, would be falsified.

A Quick Recap

So giving the *raw facts*, the observations of nature, some *structure* transforms values into **data**. Then, giving some *context* to that data, or reaching some *conclusion* with that data, gives us **information**. That information reflects our *prediction* about the world. We can organize that information into a knowledge base and use some logic-based reasoning to derive a *decision* about the future, the *actionable* **knowledge**, from that information which we can subsequently falsify.

At its core, all fundamental science is about making predictions in the form of experiments: precise, quantifiable, falsifiable predictions. As Richard P. Feynman put it,

> "The fundamental principle of science, the definition almost, is this: the sole test of the validity of any idea is experiment."

So if science is about making predictions, how is it different from the predictions that astrologers make? The core distinction is in the kinds of predictions each makes. Most horoscopes, for example, will give you general predictions. These horoscopes will usually say things like, "you'll have a great day today." Scientific predictions, on the other hand, are precise, quantitative predictions; they don't say you'll have a nice day but instead they say you'll step outside your door at precisely 3:07pm and get struck by a meteor!

Admittedly, most predictions are not quite so dire and are usually more prosaic in nature. But **prediction** itself, which we can also call **experimentation**, is at the heart of **basic science**. We can think of basic science as that which focuses on the most *fundamental aspects of the universe*, matter, and energy. The examination of basic science has revealed an intimate relationship between such **fundamental science** and **computation**. In fact, *computer science can be thought of as the study of computation* so the first step might be to define computation in order to explore the relationship between computation and fundamental science.

---

[4] Raw facts or values based on observations of the manifestations of the universe are already a representation of sorts but here we have added a further level of *abstraction* in the structured representation of values as data. If we're so inclined, we can think of the data as a *meta*-representation that can be used to construct or describe or reason about the "lower-level" representation of the raw observations of nature.

0.4 Computer Science: The Study of Computation

The transformation of data $\Rightarrow$ information $\Rightarrow$ knowledge is essential for making actionable decisions. But if we step back and examine these transformations, a natural question arises: what the heck are these transformations or processes or procedures that manipulate and munge our representations of the world? We can start to think of these transformations of our representations of the observable universe as *computations*.

In fact, we can think of a **computation** as some process that transforms one representation of the world, our input, to some other representation of the world, our output. For example, the input might be a list of temperatures at each of the sensors distributed around campus at 6am and the output would be the average of all the sensors' temperature values. The process or method that transforms the input to the output would be the calculation of the average itself. We might thus say that the problem of computing the average of temperatures of all the sensors at 6am is a computable problem.

As it happens, an important component of fundamental science deals with those problems in the universe that are *computable*, a term we'll be defining precisely in just a bit. As David Deutsch says [5], "the laws of physics refer only to computable functions." This implies that, in a very real sense, all the laws of physics belong to this set of **computable functions**, even though computable functions themselves are only a small subset of all possible *mathematical* functions!

Computer Science: The Root of all... Science?

Since all the laws of physics can be represented as computable functions, we can, in a very real sense, think of computer science as the most basic representation of the physical universe. In fact, John A. Wheeler famously said, "... the universe is made of information; matter and energy are only incidental." Let's further explore this deep and perhaps surprising relationship between physics, information, and computation as we quantify the idea of computation.[5]

As a first step, let's think about precisely what we mean by the phrase "computable function". We can break that term up and take each in turn, starting by first defining a function.

0.5 A Review of Functions

Let's review exactly what the term function means. If you're already on an intimate basis with functions, please feel free to skip this section entirely. If functions are odd, nebulous entities for you, follow along below!

A **function** can be thought of as a *mapping* or a *correspondence* from one *set* of values, often called the **domain**, to another *set* of values, called the **range** (selected from a possibly larger *set* of possible numbers called the *codomain*), as seen in Figure 0.4. A **set**, for our purposes, is just a group of objects that is represented as a single unit.[6]

---

[5] In one sense, we could say computer science is about making predictions that are computable and tractable while physics is about making predictions that are also physically realizable. Information could then be thought of as the connection

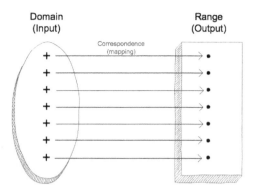

Figure 0.4: A Function is a Correspondence, or Mapping, between a Domain and a Range

The key to this correspondence is that each member of the domain is matched with one, and only one, member of the range, as shown in Figure 0.4. This correspondence is also called, quite unimaginatively, a **one-to-one** mapping since each value in the domain is paired with a single unique value in the range, as seen in Figure 0.5a.

In our temperature example, for a specific sensor, you can think of the Time values (e.g., 4am, 5am, 6am, etc.) as the domain and the Temperature values (e.g., 68°F, 69°F, 70°F, etc.) as the range. So for each Time value in the domain (let's say, 4am), you will have a specific value associated with it in the range (i.e., 68°F, as per Table 0.1). Since we won't always be dealing with Temperatures and Times, I'm going to switch to a more abstract example with simpler numbers as seen in Figure 0.5 so we can continue to explore functions as a more general idea.

A function can also have a **many-to-one** mapping, where more than one value in the domain might be mapped to the same unique value in the range, as shown in Figure 0.5b, where both 3 and -3 in the domain are mapped to the same unique value, 9, in the range. Please note, even in this mapping, each value in the domain is still matched only with a single value in the range; e.g., -3 is mapped *only* to 9, and not to both 9 and 4. However, different values in the domain may be matched to the *same* value in the range; e.g., -3 and 3 in the domain both map to 9 in the range shown in Figure 0.5b.

We can represent relationships between the domain and the range in a few ways: diagrammatically (in a cartoon as seen above or in a *graph*, as we'll see in the graphical representation below), as a *relation* (a set of ordered pairs), or in *functional notation* (using symbols).

0.5.1 Graphical Representation

A graphical representation of these two mappings is shown below in Figure 0.6, where we see the familiar Cartesian coordinate system with the abscissa labelled x (for the domain) and the ordinate

---

between the two. Information Theory is in fact central to physics, biology, etc.[6], [7]

[6] In mathematics, a **set** can most generally be thought of as an object that contains other objects. We can also think of a set as a collection of unique elements. An **ordered set** gives the elements an ordering, or a mapping to natural numbers, usually cardinal numbers; this ordering can involve a relation between every pair of elements, a *full ordering*, or just some pairs of elements, *partially ordered sets*. A **sequence** is an ordered set that allows for repeating elements while a **series** is the summation of an infinite sequence of numbers. A **vector** can then be represented as either a finite ordered set of indices (e.g., $(x_1, x_2, x_3, ...)$) or a finite sequence of values (e.g., $(3, 2, 3, ...)$), which can also be called an **n-tuple**, with the strong disclaimer that a vector and n-tuple are not the same thing. As you can see, none of these statements are precise mathematical definitions and there are subtleties, some the size of buses, that should be taken into account for any formal consideration of these terms.

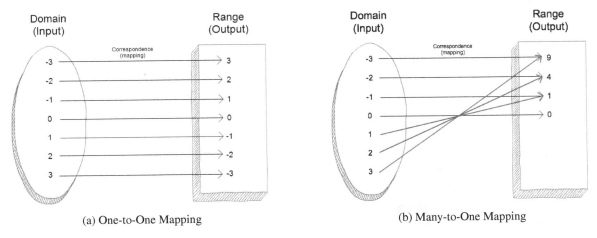

(a) One-to-One Mapping   (b) Many-to-One Mapping

Figure 0.5: One-to-One and Many-to-One Mappings

labelled y (for the codomain).

Figure 0.6a shows the graph corresponding to the same one-to-one mapping from Figure 0.5a while Figure 0.6b shows the graph corresponding to the same many-to-one relationship in Figure 0.5b.

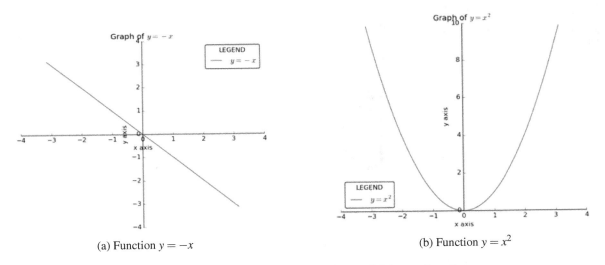

(a) Function $y = -x$ (b) Function $y = x^2$

Figure 0.6: Graphical Representations of the two functions

0.5.2 Relational Representation

A **relation** is a *rule* that associates each element of the domain with at least one element of the range.[7] It can be represented, somewhat confusingly, as a set of ordered pairs as shown below for the first and second relations:

$$(-3,3), (-2,2), (-1,1), (0,0), (1,-1), (2,-2), (3,-3) \tag{1a}$$

$$(-3,9), (-2,4), (-1,1), (0,0), (1,1), (2,4), (3,9) \tag{1b}$$

Once again, Equation (1a) corresponds to the one-to-one mapping from Figure 0.5a while Equation (1b) shows the relation corresponding to the many-to-one relationship in Figure 0.5b. Each term in these two equations is an ordered pair, like $(-3,9)$ in Equation (1b), where the first element, -3, is from the domain in Figure 0.5b and the second element, 9, is the corresponding value from the range, also in Figure 0.5b.

Not all mathematical constructs are functions; in fact, you can have relations other than one-to-one or many-to-one! For example, you might have a relation in which one element of the domain maps to more than one element of the range in an equally unimaginatively named **one-to-many** relationship. Any relationship that is not one-to-one, though, is not a function. In fact, the badly named constructs called multi-valued functions, which are **many-to-many** relations, are actually reverse/inverse mappings ~~and not functions~~.

0.5.3 Functional Representation

In addition to the graphical and relational representations, we can express these relationships in **functional notation**, in which we think of the function, or relation, as an opaque *black-box*, wherein you can't look inside the box to see the inner workings of how it's doing its processing, as shown in Figure 0.7.

INPUT (x) ⟶ OUTPUT (y)

Figure 0.7: A function f can be represented as a black box with input x and output y

In this approach, we think of the **input**, represented by the letter x, as a value from the domain and the result or **output**, represented by the letter y, as the corresponding number from the range. The function, or black box, is given a symbolic name; in this case, we called it f but we could just as well have called it *MyFunction* or ϕ.

In the same way, we gave a symbolic name to the input, x, and the output, y. These symbols, x and y, will be used by the function, f. Since their values can vary (i.e., we can provide anything as input and

---

[7]Often, you might hear the term *predicate*, as well. A predicate is a relation or function that returns a `true` or `false` value, also called a Boolean value, as opposed to a generic function which can return any kind of value. We'll meet Boolean values in a later chapter and explore this distinction in more detail then but the term predicate can be somewhat confusing as it has other meanings in math and computer science, as well.

the output might change depending upon that specific input), these *placeholders* are called **variables**.[8] Since the variable we decided to call x represents the input, it is often called the **independent variable** as the input isn't controlled by the function. The input is, however, changed or *transformed* by the function, f, and the symbolic name for the output, the variable we decided to call y, is referred to as our **dependent variable** since its value depends on the input. We'll have quite a bit to say about variables later on.

Since the function, f, is the black box that transforms the input, x, we can also represent this **process** as $f(x)$, which essentially means "*function of x*." The parentheses, "(" and ")", are used to demarcate the name of the function, f, from its input, x. So the entire process consists of some input plus some transformation, which, in anticipation of the next chapter, we could write as:

$$Process = Transformation_{\text{\_of\_the}} + Input \tag{2}$$

Using the above *symbolic representations*, we can write our two relations in functional notation as:

$$y_1 = f_1(x) \tag{3a}$$

$$y_2 = f_2(x) \tag{3b}$$

or, more familiarly, as:

$$y_1 = f_1(x) = -x \tag{4a}$$

$$y_2 = f_2(x) = x^2 \tag{4b}$$

Here, $f_1(x)$ represents the mapping in Figure 0.5a and $f_2(x)$ represents the relationship in Figure 0.5b. But we cheated a bit and actually peeked inside the black box to also *define* the two functions (Equations (3a) and (3b)) as $-x$ and x^2, respectively, as shown in Equations (4). Please note that we decided to add a subscript to both the functions (the f's) and the outputs (the y's) as we've been dealing with two different relations. However, we decided to not add a subscript to the input as we'll later use this device to distinguish between the terms parameter and argument as used specifically in computer science (as opposed to mathematics, in general).

0.6 Computable Functions

Now that we have a handle on functions, we can start to think about computable functions and what the term computable, or computation, might mean. **Computation** can be thought of as a method or **procedure** that transforms some *input information* into some *output information*. In the classical theory

---

[8]More precisely, we could say a variable is any symbol used to represent an unspecified element chosen from some set of elements.

of computation, we generally deal with processing some input string of generic symbols into some output string of generic symbols (these strings are technically a finite ordered sequence of symbols from a finite set of such symbols). Some of these transformations can be accomplished by using a *function* because that's what functions do: they **transform** some input into some output as we've seen above! [9]

Putting these two terms together, a **function** is said to be **computable** if, for some given input, the corresponding output can be calculated by using a finite mechanical procedure.[10] What is this finite, mechanical procedure? It's any **effective procedure**, defined as some method or approach that has a finite number of unambiguous, finite instructions; in addition, it must always halt after a finite number of steps and, when applied to a certain class of problems, produce the correct answer.

0.6.1 Computation and Algorithms

These effective procedures can be carried out by any agent, often called a **computing agent**; sometimes the computing agent is a human, sometimes a digital machine, and sometimes the universe itself.[11] When an effective procedure, also called an *effective method* or *effectively computable operation*, can calculate all the values of a function, it is called an **algorithm** for that function.

For example, we could have an algorithm for computing the average of any set of numbers. We can express this algorithm as simple instructions: add all the numbers and divide by the total number of numbers. We could also express this mathematically as $\sum_i \frac{T_i}{N}$. We applied this algorithm for solving the general problem of calculating averages to the *specific* case of calculating the average temperature of our temperature sensors in Section 0.1.3.

At a simpler level, you can think of an **algorithm** as a recipe or a sequence of step-by-step instructions. As can be seen above in the definition of an *effective procedure*:

1. each of the algorithm's steps should be finite and exact
2. the number of instructions should be finite, and
3. when the algorithm finishes, it should solve the problem

The word algorithm is a corruption of the last name of Abu Ja'far Muhammad ibn-Musa Al-Khwarizmi, a 9th century Persian mathematician. He wrote a book called *Kitab al jabr* [8], whose name was Latinized to Algebra since *al jabr* means a reduction of some sort. Al-Khwarizmi wrote another book in which he described a formal, step-by-step procedure for doing arithmetic operations, like addition and multiplication, on numbers that were written in the new base-10 positional number

---

[9]Computable functions are a subset of all the possible functions in mathematics. However, all laws of physics correspond only to computable functions, except for possible hypercomputational systems which posit there are some natural phenomena that cannot be simulated computationally. We will also look at this some more when we discuss the difference between Polynomial (P) and Non-Deterministic Polynomial (NP) problems.

[10]Computer science deals with mathematically computable functions but the term function is used slightly differently in *programming*, as we'll see in later chapters.

[11]An idealized computing agent should be able to accept an instruction, store and retrieve information from some memory, carry out the actions required by the instructions, and produce an output.

system that had just been developed in India. Over time, references to his work started to be called by his name which, in Latin characters, was written as Algoritmi. Eventually, his name was corrupted to Algorismi, and then to algorism, and then finally to *algorithm*, which is the word now used for those formalized, step-by-step procedures.[12]

■ **Example 0.1** One example of a simple algorithm might be doing dishes. If you were to describe the process of cleaning a pile of dirty dishes to a 5-year-old, you might describe the step-by-step process, or algorithm, as shown in Algorithm 0.1.

Algorithm 0.1: Algorithm for doing dishes

1 Grab a wash cloth
2 Add detergent to the washcloth
3 Turn on water
4 **while** *there are still dirty dishes left on the pile of dirty dishes* **do**
5   Grab a dish
6   Clean it with your wash cloth
7   Rinse it off
8   Dry the dish
9   Put it on the drying rack
10 **end**
11 Turn off water

■

Most algorithms are more complex, and precise, than this simplistic approach to cleaning dishes. Broadly speaking, an *algorithm* can be said to be a general method consisting of a finite sequence of steps that are performed in order to reach a desired result. In fact, an algorithm can be thought of as a general method to solve a whole family, or **class**, of related questions, as opposed to only one specific problem; e.g., we can have an algorithm for computing averages (of *any* set of numbers) and use that algorithm to compute the average in the specific case of the Temperature values gathered by our sensors. An *algorithm*, in this sense, **defines** what might be considered to be a *computation*.

Problem 0.1 Can you come up with an algorithm for a hungry friend instructing them exactly how to make a peanut butter and jelly sandwich? How would your algorithm be different if you were to draft it for your hungry 5-year-old nephew instead?

0.7   Talking in Tongues: Programming Languages

So far, we've figured out that *computation* deals with the *transformation* of input information into output information by an *effective procedure*. A *computable function*, we found, uses an *effective procedure* to calculate the output value. This effective procedure, called an *algorithm*, is expressed as a sequence of finite instructions that are carried out by some *computing agent*.

If the task at hand is physical, as in the cleaning dishes example, the computing agent that carries out the process can be a human. But if we were going to use a digital machine, like a modern personal computer, as the computing agent to help solve some of the more abstract problems, we'd need a way to express the algorithm, or *sequence of precise instructions*, in the language of the computer.

---

[12]In fact, even today, Al-Khwarizmi's name is spelled with many variations, including Al-Khowarizmi or Al-Khuwarizmi.

Some formal definitions

1. **Effective Procedure**: a procedure is said to be effectively computable if it can be carried out by a *computing agent* and consists of a finite number of exact, finite instructions or steps which always finish after a finite number of steps and produce the correct answer
   - An effective procedure solves some category of problems and can consist of multiple steps or just a single step
2. **Computable Function**: a function whose *output* can be calculated using an effective procedure on some given *input*
3. **Algorithm**: A well-ordered sequence of effectively computable, clearly defined steps that can be understood and carried out by a computing agent which can complete the operations successfully in a finite amount of time
   - Also known as a *computation*: an effective procedure that calculates the values of a function is called an *algorithm*

An effective procedure can be expressed in different forms, or representations. Each expression of the effective procedure is an algorithm if it calculates the value of some function. Some algorithmic expressions, or representations, are intended for human computing agents while other representations are intended for digital computing agents.

Just as a function can be expressed as either a graph or a relation, different algorithms can represent the same effective procedure for different computing agents. In one sense, you can think of an algorithm as a way to *translate* the effective procedure for a particular computing agent.

Most modern-day computers express instructions for their central processing unit (CPU) in a particular **programming language**. These programming languages tend to be much more specific, precise, and limited in scope when compared to natural languages like English. Like natural languages, they have a specific syntax and structure which must be followed precisely in order to direct the computer to carry out, or *execute*, the instructions in the algorithm. An *ordered set of instructions* in a particular programming language is called a **program** or **source code** or simply **code**.

We'll be talking more about the essential aspects of these programming languages later as we explore Java and Python, two popular programming languages. By way of preview, let's write a simple program in the Java programming language that just prints the phrase, "Hello World!" This Java program is shown in Listing 0.1.[13]

```java
1  public class HelloWorld {
2      public static void main(String[] args) {
3          System.out.println("Hello World!");
4      }
5  }
```

Listing 0.1: Canonical "Hello World!" program in Java

---

[13]This is an example of the so-called canonical "Hello World!" program which is the traditional first program you might write when you first learn a new programming language. If your program successfully prints out this phrase, that means you've mastered the mechanics of writing and executing, or running, a program in that language. And, if you're trying to impress your parents, you can now pad your résumé by listing this as a language you're "familiar with," although it would probably be more accurate to still say, "aware of".

This same "Hello World!" program can be written in Python, as well, as shown in Listing 0.2. As you can see, these different programming languages take different approaches to specifying a particular computational solution. Thus, one language might be more appropriate for a specific problem or perhaps a specific programmer's style. In the case of printing out the string, "Hello World!", the Python approach is much simpler and I'd likely pick that. But if I had to write an Android app, I'd probably pick Java.

```
1  print("Hello World!")
```
Listing 0.2: Canonical "Hello World!" program in Python

0.7.1 Going to Church-Turing

In the early 20th century, a lot of great minds were struggling with defining the notion of computation in a mathematical sense. People like Alonzo Church, Kurt Gödel, Emil Post, Alan Turing, and Haskell Curry[14] all came up with independent derivations or approaches for this concept.

One of the fathers of computer science, Alan Turing, described a hypothetical computing agent in 1936 that later came to be known as the *Universal Turing Machine* (Turing himself much more modestly called it a Logical Computing Machine or Universal Machine[15]). This imaginary machine followed the model of a ticker tape; a ticker tape was a machine that would print stock market information on paper tape. These ticker tape machines would generate reams and reams of paper tape; so much so, in fact, that people would toss the shredded paper tape out their windows during parades, thus giving us the ticker tape parade.

The theoretical Universal Turing Machine consisted of a simple tape head that could move over an infinite length of such a tape; the head could only carry out simple, primitive instructions like moving along, reading symbols from, and writing symbols to the tape. This straightforward machine was an *idealized* computing agent and *model* for mathematical calculations which formalized the notion of

---

[14]Curry credited and built upon work by Moses Schönfinkel and, implicitly, Friedrich Frege.

[15]A Universal Turing Machine is simply a Turing Machine which can simulate another Turing Machine. Turing had originally used this formal approach to reformulate Gödel's results on the limits of proof and mathematical computation. The simpler Universal Turing Machine approach was able to show the same results as the universal, arithmetic based formal language used by Gödel.

A Model of a Universal Turing Machine

algorithmic computation, systematic procedures that produce a solution to a problem in a finite number of steps.[16]

Up to this point, we had only met computation in an informal sense as a sequence of steps or process for manipulating data according to simple, finite rules. Turing **formalized** this notion of computation by providing a mathematical model for it: the Universal Turing Machine. Alonzo Church took a somewhat different approach to get at the idea of computation.

Instead of looking at "functions as graphs" (the way we did earlier when we thought of a function as a way to describe a relationship that maps a value from the domain to the co-domain), he looked at functions in the older sense of "functions as rules".[17] Defining a function in this paradigm meant specifying the rules for how that function should be calculated. Church used a version of this in which he expressed "functions as formulae," a system for manipulating functions as expressions. When preparing the manuscript, his typesetter accidentally used the Greek symbol λ in his equations and so this approach came to be called Lambda calculus, which is also the basis for functional programming.

People soon realized that all these different approaches to computation were *computationally equivalent* in that each approach could encode and simulate the other approaches and produce the same results. Church thought all of these equivalent formalisms embodied the same general notion of *computability* and his thesis was generalized to the **Church-Turing thesis**: if there exists an *effective procedure* or method for obtaining the value of a mathematical function, that function can be computed by a Universal Turing Machine.

Let's just pause for a bit and consider what this might be saying because, upon reflection, it might sound a little nutty: the Church-Turing Thesis says that **every** function that is computable, i.e., **every** computation and **every** single thing in the universe that is computable, can be described by a set of operations (an *algorithm*) expressed in some language for an appropriate computing agent.

The universality of this idea simply cannot be emphasized strongly enough: it essentially says that **everything** in the universe that is possible to compute can be computed by a Universal Turing Machine (or any of the equivalent formalisms for the idea of computation and computability).

 Studying the theoretical properties of such machines and processes separately, Alonzo Church and Alan Turing came up with the Church-Turing Thesis: the observation that a variety of seemingly different mathematical models of computation are actually *all equivalent* as long as you ignore the space and time complexity they might require (i.e., as long as you ignore the amount of scratch paper and time required to compute some mathematical function)!

In large measure, the entire theory of computation and, by extension, computer science, deals with the Church-Turing Thesis and effectively computable functions and finding the limits of which functions are computable. There have been several offshoots of this theory; one such variation, the Physical Church-Turing Thesis, addresses what can physically be realized by a computer in our universe; another,

---

[16]Turing had posited that if an *effective procedure* existed for obtaining the values of a mathematical function, that function could be computed by a Universal Turing Machine.

[17]We will revisit these ideas later when we discuss the difference between the functional and the imperative approach.

the Complexity-Theoretic Church-Turing Thesis, considers what can be efficiently computed. Indeed, the application of the Church-Turing Thesis has wide-ranging implications for the *universe itself* and implies that the universe might be equivalent to a Universal Turing Machine, as examined in digital physics, or perhaps a hypercomputer!

Transforming Information via Computation

Fundamental science is about making falsifiable *predictions* that are verified by experiment. We start with observations of nature; giving these raw facts some structure transforms *values* into **data**. Giving some *context* to that data, or reaching some conclusion with it, *transforms* data into **information**. That information reflects our *prediction* about the world. We can organize information into a knowledge base and use logic-based reasoning to derive a decision about the future, which is our *actionable* **knowledge** that we can subsequently falsify. *Computation* is the process by which we transform data into information and then into knowledge.

Uncomputable... that's what you are...

There are, of course, other possibilities, as well, and the bad news is that not all problems have *computational solutions*. The most famous of these is the *halting problem* designed by Turing. In this scenario, Turing considered a program that would print true if, and only if, it runs forever and showed that it is impossible to write such a program.

Computation, or *computability*, as we've built up so far, means the process of solving any problem that can be solved by some algorithm which manipulates symbols in the same way as a Universal Turing Machine. Our definition of an algorithm, however, still isn't completely formalized as we describe precisely, but not axiomatically, what we mean by an algorithm; even the term *effectively computable* depends upon the capabilities of a computing agent so if a computing agent is able to understand and execute an algorithm in a finite amount of time, then that algorithm is effectively computable for that computing agent.[18]

This means the Church-Turing Thesis can never be proved mathematically! Because it has not been formally proved, it is referred to as a thesis and not a theorem. The good news is that it has been extensively validated as there is an equivalent Universal Turing Machine for every algorithm that exists for all tasks that can be solved algorithmically. In addition, all other models for computing agents and algorithms have been proved to be equivalent to a Universal Turing Machine; i.e., the Universal

---

[18] This hearkens back to some of the attempts to formalize the notion of functions and computability in the 20th century, a la Kurt Gödel's formal definition of a class of general recursive functions, Alonzo Church's definition of functions on natural numbers in terms of the λ-calculus, and Alan Turing's definition of functions on natural numbers in terms of his abstract model of a simple machine. The Church-Turing Thesis states that these three formally defined classes of computable functions are equivalent and *assumes* these models are also equivalent to the informal notion of **effectively calculable**, a term used to describe functions that are computable by mechanical means. As a side note, the idea of relaxing the constraint of discreteness in these approaches is also tied to the idea of hypercomputation, as discussed later.

Turing Machine can do everything done by these other computational models upon processing their algorithms.

Conversely, this means that if we can find a problem that can be expressed as a symbol manipulation task which we can prove cannot be solved by a Universal Turing Machine, then the Church-Turing Thesis necessarily implies that the problem is **uncomputable** or *unsolvable*. To prove the problem cannot be solved by a Universal Turing Machine means that such a machine cannot exist and that no one will ever find one as nature itself prohibits its existence.

This might seem like a hyperbolic claim but, as Kurt Gödel showed in his incompleteness theorems, there are true statements about a formal system that cannot be proved to be true using that system. Although Gödel did this in the context of a formal system for ordinary arithmetic of natural numbers, his theorem motivated mathematicians to find some method for showing which statements are unprovable in a generalized formal system. These methods would require some computational procedure to process and recognize such statements.

So when mathematicians like Church, Post, Turing, etc., started to propose many different models for these computational procedures, along with an accompanying computing agent to carry out these procedures, their goal was to help provide a formal basis for mathematical proofs as that might help guarantee the correctness of a proof without relying upon ambiguous or unproven or subjective statements. The main advantage of formalizing this process of generating mathematical proofs is that it would allow for automating theorem-proving by providing a simple set of rules for some computing agent to follow.

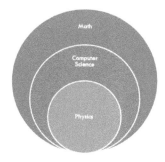

In fact, complexity theory analyzes the classes of problems that are computable and the ones that are un-computable. We could, in a way, think of physics as dealing with computable functions and think of mathematics as dealing with all functions, computable or otherwise. Computer science can then be thought to be the discipline that's concerned with determining which functions are computable or not and sits at the intersection of the other two disciplines. We'll pick this topic up again when we deal with the P vs NP problem later on. For now, though, let's continue our adventure by exploring the idea of computational thinking in detail in the next chapter!

The intersection of Math, Computer Science, and Physics.

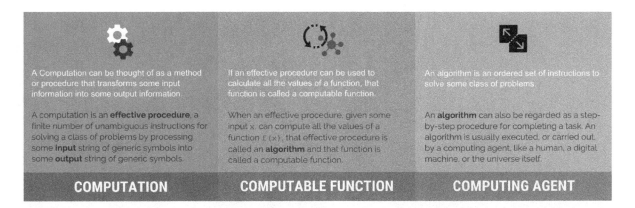

ESSENTIAL IDEAS IN COMPUTATION

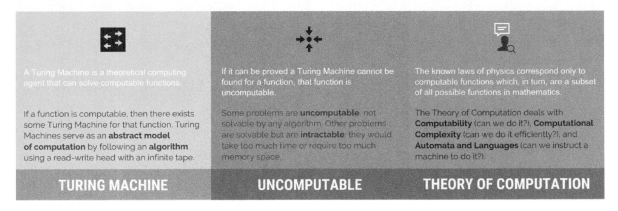

Figure 0.8: A **computation** is an effective procedure that transforms input information into output information. An **effective procedure** is a finite set of instructions for carrying out some unambiguous symbolic manipulation or transformation. If an effective procedure can calculate all the values of a function, it is called an **algorithm** for that function and that function is then considered a **computable function**. Algorithms, ordered sets of instructions to solve some class of problems, and computable functions are the basic objects in the **theory of computation**. A **Turing Machine** is a mathematical description of *any* algorithm in terms of a hypothetical machine with a simple read-write head and a tape of paper; a Turing Machine is *one* formalization of the *general* idea of an algorithm. In fact, **computation** itself can then be thought of as the study of algorithms or such formal models of algorithms.

1. Computational Thinking and Information Theo

> *We need to do away with the myth that computer science is about computers. Computer science is no more about computers than astronomy is about telescopes.*
> – Michael R. Fellows[1]

1.1 What Is Thinking?

The history of formal approaches to thinking in the Western world is usually traced back to the Hellenic culture. One of the most influential thinkers in the ancient Greek world was Socrates, the first moral philosopher. Socrates favoured using critical thinking to reason about questions using a dialectic method of inquiry in conversations.

So when you asked Socrates a question, rather than directly answering you, he'd ask you questions to lead you to the answers; often, he'd ask questions that led you to ask the question he was interested in discussing, as well. This approach, called the Socratic Method, was so irritating to some that it led the Athenians to sentence Socrates to death.[2]

Socrates was interested in finding out the true nature of moral and ethical ideas by looking at many examples of that idea and then generalizing from those examples. For example, if he was interested in figuring out the essential nature of a chair (he really wasn't), he might use this type of *inductive reasoning* to look at many examples of chairs and find those characteristics that are the same across all chairs.

---

[1]This quote is sometimes also attributed to Edsger Dijkstra and Ian Parberry; please see https://en.wikiquote.org/wiki/Computer_science for the juicy details.

[2]As you might suspect, this wasn't the real reason; Socrates was officially tried for "refusing to recognize the gods recognized by the state" and for "corrupting the youth" but I'm convinced, based on how students respond to my own implementation, it was due to the Socratic method.

Once you start to think about all the various things we might call chairs (stools? tripods? beanbags?), you might end up not coming to any real conclusion about the essence, or essential Idea, that was common to all chairs. Socrates' reasoning was similarly inconclusive but it did inspire his pupil, Plato, to start thinking more deeply about such Ideas or idealized Forms.

Plato decided that all these examples of chairs[3] were just pale imitations of some idealized chair that existed on another plane of existence. In fact, he posited there was an eternal world of Ideas and Forms that exists separate from our material world. This meant every material object, like our ever-present chair, was just an imperfect shadow of some Ideal Chair that existed in that other plane of existence. That Ideal Chair is perfect and eternal and every chair in our physical plane of existence is just a pale imitation of that Ideal Chair.

Plato used this type of *deductive reasoning* from these other-worldly Forms to gain insight about their reflections in our physical world. In his imagining, just as in Socrates', we are all born with an innate knowledge of these Ideas or Forms and can use critical reasoning to discover their reflections or implications.

Plato's student, Aristotle, wasn't as interested in a metaphysical plane of existence with idealized Forms. He strongly favoured using experience and physical perception to reason about the world. He used both *inductive reasoning* to gain knowledge about universal characteristics of objects by examining many examples (like Socrates) and then used *deductive reasoning* to take these derived universal principles and examine particular objects of that kind (like Plato).

Philosophy... it's the talk on a serial port...

Greek philosophy started around 610 BCE with Thales and Anaximander of Miletus and flourished through the Hellenistic period which ended around 30 BCE. It covered a wide range of human experience and thought but, arguably, culminated with three of the most influential ancient philosophers: a decorated soldier, a wealthy wrestler, and a dictator's son-in-law. They're usually better known as Socrates, Plato, and Aristotle, respectively.

Socrates was interested in logic and ethics and used the dialectic approach, in which two people with different opinions try to find the truth using argumentation. The Socratic Method in particular used questions to disprove the other person's point in order to highlight what they didn't know or what was not known. This approach involved using techniques like using questions to summarize what the other person was saying, asking for evidence, and challenging their assumptions or finding exceptions to their argument.

This kind of evidence-based reasoning not only informed Socrates' pupils, including Plato and Aristotle, but laid the foundation for Western thought, in general. This tradition continues in the process of finding computational solutions to (computable) problems.

1.2 Deductive vs Inductive Thinking

Finding a computational solution requires you to think computationally. In order to get a clear idea of *computational thinking*, we'll need to address both words that make up this term. We already know

---

[3]Despite my attempt to use a consistent example, I should add the disclaimer that the ancient Greeks were not obsessed with seating implements.

that *computation* is a method or procedure, called an *algorithm*, that transforms some input information into some output information. Let's now address the *thinking* part of computational thinking.

Thinking, in the context of computational problem solving, can be considered to be the ability to rationally draw inferences from statements, observations, and data using deductive, inductive, or probabilistic analyses [9]. That's quite a mouthful so let's take it one at a time.

Deductive reasoning involves drawing conclusions which necessarily follow from some body of evidence. It often includes constructing an *argument* such that if the premises are true, then the conclusion must necessarily be true.[4] We can also reason backward from this definition to infer, for example, that if the conclusion is false, then at least one of the premises must also be false.

Inductive reasoning is similar but an inductive argument *goes beyond* the available evidence to reach conclusions that are *likely* to be true but are not guaranteed to be true. Thus, in inductive inference, the conclusions are likely or plausible but (often) not certain to be true. This is because, in inductive arguments, the truth of the premises does not guarantee the truth of the conclusion. Often, inductive reasoning is used to build hypotheses which can then be checked via deductive reasoning.

Probabilistic inference, also incorporated in **abductive reasoning**, utilizes probabilities to assess the likelihood of the conclusion. It is based on *syllogisms*[5], a form of deductive reasoning, but incorporates probabilities in an intermediate step, as well.[6]

1.3 Thinking About Probabilities

As we can see, probability has snuck into our journey and, it turns out, probability is a central aspect of almost all investigations of nature. Let's talk a little bit about probability since it will be so germane to much of what we do later.

Probability can be thought of as a kind of *uncertainty* about or *likelihood* of some event occurring. Probability is one of the simplest mathematical theories and only has three basic rules known as Kolmogorov's Axioms of Probability.[7] In their delineation below, please feel free to ignore, for now, the mathematical formulas for probabilities, like $P(A)$, $P(A|B)$, etc., as we'll have plenty of time to familiarize ourselves with that mathematical notation later:

1. The probability itself is simply a value between 0.0 and 1.0 (inclusive)
   - This means probability is just a real number like 0.1 or 0.35. It's usually expressed as a percentage by multiplying this number by 100 so that 0.1 becomes 10% and 0.35 becomes 35% so you might say the probability of event A happening is 35%
     $$\Rightarrow 0 \leq P(A) \leq 1 \text{ and } P(A) = 0.35$$
2. The total probability is always 1.0 (or, if multiplied by 100, 100%)
   - This just means that if you're looking at some event, either it will happen or it will not happen; one of those things is guaranteed to be true. Put another way, the probability of A

---

[4]For our purposes, we can think of an **argument** as having mathematically well-defined procedures for reaching conclusions with certainty or necessity, based on the evidence that is presented.

[5]The most famous syllogism is, "All men are mortal. Socrates is a man. Therefore, Socrates is mortal." In probabilistic reasoning, you might change that to, "I believe all men are mortal. I think Socrates is a man. Therefore, in all likelihood, Socrates is probably mortal." Abductive reasoning is usually less formal and, given some observations, is called, "inference to the best explanation."

[6]Inductive reasoning also incorporates some aspect of probability as the truth of the premises does not guarantee the truth of the conclusion. This is why we can say the conclusion of a deductive argument is true if the premises are true but, for an inductive argument, we say it's strong (weak) if the probability of its conclusion given its premises is high (low).

[7]We could probably add in Countable Additivity or replace Additivity with it if the events are mutually exclusive, I suppose.

happening OR of A *not* happening is 1

$$\Rightarrow P(A \cup \neg A) = 1$$

3. The probability of an event A OR an event B happening is (the probability of A + the probability of B - the probability of A AND B happening together)

- $\Rightarrow P(A \cup B) = P(A) + P(B) - P(A \cap B)$

Kolmogorov's Axioms of Probability

1. The probability is a value between 0.0 and 1.0
2. The total probability is always 1.0
3. (The probability of event A OR event B happening) = (the probability of A) + (the probability of B) - (the probability of A AND B happening together)

1.3.1 Calculating the Probabilities

Probabilities are sometimes calculated by looking at frequencies.[8] Suppose I'm interested in figuring out the probability of getting snake-eyes (two 1's) at the Craps table in Las Vegas.[9] One way to do it would be to roll the two dice a whole bunch of times.

As you roll more and more dice, the frequency of snake-eyes in those rolls (i.e., how many times you roll a 2 compared to how many times you roll a $3, 4, 5, 6, 7, 8, 9, 10, 11$, or 12) will start to come close to the probability of getting a 2 if you roll any two random, unbiased dice thanks to the "Law of Large Numbers", which says that if you make a large number of observations, the results should be close to the expected value.

But there's a caveat: the frequency over a small number of rolls of the dice may be very different from the actual probability; the law of large numbers, unsurprisingly, doesn't apply when the numbers are small. Also, some events only happen once, like the 2016 election in the USA.

1.3.2 Samples and Populations in Statistics

These rolls of dice that we collected in estimating the probabilities can be considered to be a *sample*. In general, when we're reasoning or thinking computationally about a problem, we'll usually be examining a statistical **population**, which consists of all possible measurements or outcomes that are of interest in the problem context. A **random sample** is a portion of the population that is unbiased and representative of that population. A random sample is one in which every member of the population has an equal chance of being selected. When picking members of the population to include in the sample, we can use many sampling methods like Random Sampling, Stratified Sampling, Sampling With Replacement and Without Replacement, etc.

One of the goals of computational problem solving is to infer statistical properties of the population from the statistical properties of the sample. For example, we might want to determine the number of Independents in the population of all eligible voters in the USA. We might select a random sample of 1,000 eligible voters and find that 300 of them were Independents. From the sample, we might then infer that 30% of the entire electorate are also Independents.

---

[8]They can also be calculated using a Bayesian approach which we'll discuss later.

[9]If you're unfamiliar with Craps, don't worry; it's just a game played with dice and is one of the easiest ways to make and lose money in Vegas. For our purposes, the most important part is that it's played with two die, each of which can have a value between 1 and 6.

We often make claims about the population by providing a **confidence interval**, which is the range of values that contain the true value with a certain probability, called the confidence level. This confidence level is usually 95% or 99%. Confidence intervals are usually expressed along with a *margin of error*, which expresses the uncertainty in the measurement and is usually half the length of the confidence interval. In most surveys, the margin of error is expressed for the confidence interval at a 95% confidence level. So, for the above example, if we say, "30% of the US population are Independents with a 3% margin of error," we're really saying, "We are 95% confident that between 27% and 33% of the US population are Independents," where the confidence interval is between 27% and 33%, the confidence level is 95%, and the margin of error is 3%.

1.3.3 Conditional Probabilities and Sample Spaces

In probability, though, the similar sounding term, **sample space**, has a different meaning: a sample space is simply the set of all possible outcomes of an experiment. For our dice example, the Sample Space $= \{2, 3, 4, 5, 6, 7, 8, 9, 10, 11, 12\}$. We can calculate the probability of each outcome in the sample space, just as we did before for snake-eyes.

Suppose we roll our two dice and see that the first one is showing a 1 but can't quite make out the value on the second die. A question that might immediately come to mind could be, "I wonder what the likelihood is of getting a second 1 if I've already rolled a 1?" This is an example of **conditional probability**.

A conditional probability is the probability of an event A occurring (rolling snake-eyes) if another event B has already occurred (already rolled a 1 on the first die). This kind of conditional probability can be expressed as $P(A|B) = \frac{P(A \cap B)}{P(A)}$.

You can, once again, ignore the funky notation for now if it's unfamiliar to you. We'll be using this equation later to derive Bayes' Rule; this will lead us to discover Bayesian Analysis which is the underpinning of so many analyses, especially in statistics and machine learning. Being able to reason and think probabilistically, in general, is increasingly becoming an essential aspect of conducting any kind of systematic, scientific investigation.

1.4 Logical Thinking

We can even think about "reasoning with evidence" in this manner to be one way to characterize what we do in physics and computer science. Our present concern, though, is with reasoning or thinking about computational problems. Specifically, *computational thinking* requires thinking about a **process** for solving some problem that is computable. As we've seen in Section 0.5, a **function** is a process that takes some *input* and converts it to some *output*. The input can be considered to be the *data*, or *evidence*, and the output can be thought of as our answer, or *prediction*.

More broadly, computational thinking normally involves forming a *model* of some sort and reasoning with it in some way. So it's no wonder, then, that the model is usually mathematical and the reasoning is some kind of formal mathematical reasoning, like formal logic. But the model could also be graphical or linguistic or logical, depending on the kind of problem we're tackling and the resources we have available. Thus, the task of solving a problem is often reduced to finding a suitable **representation** of the model and a **logical process** to use that model in order to solve the problem.

1.4.1 Origins of Formal Logic

In general, **logic** is a way to reason about the world and discover answers. Its origins can be traced to the ancient Greeks, as we saw in Section 1.1.[10] The Greek approach to logic helped establish guiding principles for *assessing the validity* of arguments or statements.

In Section 1.1, we learned about Socrates and his approach of asking questions as a way to discovery. If two people had different opinions about a certain topic, Socrates would engage them in a conversation where he'd ask questions that forced them to think critically about that topic; this approach is often called the *dialectic* method of inquiry. So if you asked Socrates a question, he'd more likely than not respond by asking you more questions so you could discover the truth for yourself.

His pupil, Plato, also thought people could discover truths about the world and ideas by self-examination and inquiry; in fact, they both thought that universal knowledge was already inherently within people. But Plato thought our senses might deceive us sometimes and so the universal characteristics about things must exist separately from the thing itself, in the idealized world of Forms which can only be known through the mind. In fact, Plato was intensely concerned with inquiring into the nature of reality whereas Socrates was mainly interested in logic and ethics and not so much about the fundamental nature of the physical universe or metaphysics in that sense. As such, Plato sought to answer questions about this abstract nature of reality and its relation to the physical world we experience through our senses.

Aristotle, on the other hand, deviated from his teacher in this regard. Like Plato, he was also interested in the nature of reality but, like Democritus before him, Aristotle was a firm believer in the evidence he gained from his senses. He didn't care too much for alternate planes of existence and whatnot; instead, he argued that the Universal ideas both Plato and Socrates pursued were derived from experience and were already present in the material objects we examine. In this regard, Aristotle was interested in finding what was true and valid about the physical world we experience via our senses.

1.4.2   Propositional Logic and Argumentation

Logic, in general, deals with assessing the validity of assertions. In order to determine the validity, or truth, of a particular assessment, you have to establish the idea that an assertion can be evaluated as true or false. Building upon the work of Plato and Socrates, Aristotle observed how reason was used in conversations and was able to codify an approach for reasoning about the validity of statements.[11]

He helped establish a formal system for answering questions and laid the foundation for deductive logic based on True/False statements. Statements that are either True or False are called propositional statements and using logic to determine the validity of such statements is called propositional logic.[12]

But before you can reason about the things in the world, Aristotle thought that you have to be able to define what those things are; i.e., what kind of a thing it is or what is its essence or Substance.[13] Aristotle was thus specifically interested in propositional statements that would allow us to find the

---

[10]Logic itself has a rich history and was simultaneously developed and discovered in ancient cultures such as in India with Medhatithi Gautama, China with Mozi, Egyptian Geometry, Babylonian Astronomy, etc.

[11]The word logic is, in fact, derived from logos which Aristotle took to mean "reasoned discourse."

[12]Another way to think about it is that a statement that asserts a truth about the world is making a proposition about it which can be verified. There are, however, many kinds of logics, including syllogistic, predicate, modal, temporal, mathematical, probabilistic, intuitionistic, fuzzy, etc. Some of these are further related, like probabilistic and fuzzy logic, for example, as most statements are rarely true or false only but instead allow for multiple degrees of certainty. Such systems measure degree of belief or degree of membership in the given concept.

[13] Aristotle actually laid down three basic axioms, statements that are assumed to be true without requiring a formal proof, as the bases for his logical system:

- No statement can be both true and false (Law of Non-contradiction)
- Every statement is either true or false (Law of the Excluded Middle)
- An object is made up of its own particular characteristics that are a part of what it is (Principle of Identity)

categories to which things belong. His approach is usually called Aristotelean Logic or Syllogistic Logic and is based, unsurprisingly, on **syllogisms**.[14]

More formally, a *categorical syllogism* is an *argument* composed of two *premises* and one *conclusion*. Most people dislike arguments, thinking of them as involving bickering or fighting. But formal argumentation is a method of working through ideas or hypotheses critically and systematically.

An **argument** usually consists of a series of statements (called the **premises**) that provide reasons to support a final statement (called the **conclusion**). A *deductive* argument *guarantees* the validity of the conclusion while an *inductive* argument makes the conclusion more likely or *probable*.

In a syllogism, each of these statements (the two premises and one conclusion) are categorical statements where the first two (the premises) are true and the truth of the premises implies the truth of the conclusion. As Wikipedia, the font of all knowledge, puts it, a syllogism "is a kind of logical argument that applies deductive reasoning to arrive at a conclusion based on two or more propositions that are asserted or assumed to be true."

The most famous example of a syllogism is:
1. Socrates is a man.
2. All men are mortal.
3. Therefore, Socrates is mortal.

Each of these three statements is made up of a **subject** and a **predicate**. Just as in grade school grammar, a subject is the main *noun phrase* that controls the verb and a predicate is the *verb phrase* that describes or modifies some property of the subject. A predicate can be a single word, a group of words consisting of a main verb and helping verbs, or a complete verb phrase consisting of the main verb and all the words related to that verb. For example, in the first propositional statement above, "Socrates" is the subject and "is a man" is the predicate.[15]

Propositional logic extends Aristotelean logic to go beyond only dealing with the categories to which things belong. It is a more mathematical model for reasoning about whether propositional statements like logical expressions in general are true or false. We can represent individual statements with propositional variables, traditionally called p and q. We can then generalize propositional logic further to **predicate logic**, also called first-order logic, in which the predicates are functions of variables that return Boolean values, as we'll see in the next chapter. A predicate, in this context, describes the relationship between objects represented by these variables.

These logics, propositional and predicate, can also be represented symbolically. In propositional logic, an entire proposition is represented by a variable, typically a single letter like p, q, r, etc. Then, a logical operation can be used to combine propositions and create a compound proposition. These

---

[14] A syllogism is an example of a form of argument called *modus ponens*, "method of affirming", which simply says: If X is true, then Y is true. Y is true. Therefore, X is true. An example is the Socrates syllogism: If Socrates is a Man, then Socrates is Mortal. Socrates is a Man. Therefore, Socrates is Mortal. An alternative is *modus tollens*, "method of denying", which is at the heart of Karl Popper's falsification, the keystone of scientific proof, and says: Y is not true. If X is true, then Y is true. Therefore, X is not true. Leaning on Socrates again: Socrates is not a Dolphin. If Socrates can swim, then Socrates is a Dolphin. Therefore, Socrates cannot swim. I should add the disclaimer I have no idea if Socrates could swim or not but I'm relatively confident he was not a Dolphin.

[15] Since there is a distinction between a *simple predicate* and a *complete predicate*, the verb phrase can either describe a property of the subject (complete predicate) or be more narrowly defined as a relationship between the subject and object (simple predicate) as a linking verb. This terminology can get quite confusing in different fields. For example, in Aristotelean logic, the linking verb is often called a copula and the object the predicate. In the Resource Description Framework (RDF), the RDF triples are expressed as Subject-Predicate-Object as in "Jack-is a Friend of-Jill" where "Jack" is the Subject, "is a Friend of" is the predicate, a simple predicate in this case, which describes the relationship between the Subject and the Object (in this case, "Jill").

operations are represented by operators like $\land$ (AND), $\lor$ (OR), $\lnot$ (NOT), $\rightarrow$ (Implication/if-then), and $\leftrightarrow$ (Bi-conditional/If and Only If).

Statements and operators can be combined and the various combinations can be represented with a **truth table**, as below:

- p = "It is snowing."
- q = "The driveway needs shoveling."
- Truth Table for $p \land q$: "It is snowing AND The driveway needs shoveling":

		Compound Proposition $\overbrace{p \land q}$
p	q	
T	T	T
T	F	F
F	T	F
F	F	F

However, the formalism of propositional logic is somewhat limited and cannot even express the Socrates syllogism we've used as our running example! As such, predicate logic introduces formalism to express both the objects as well as the properties of those objects. It does so by introducing *variables* (like, x, y, z, etc.) to represent objects instead of entire propositions and *predicates* (like P, Q, etc.) to express the properties of the objects.

These predicates are then generalizations of propositions and are functions that return either True or False values only; thus, they become propositions when their variables are replaced with their actual values. All the logical operators from propositional logic carry over; in addition, we can add quantifiers like $\forall$ (Universal/For-All) and $\exists$ (Existential/There-Exists) to make propositional statements like: $\forall x P(x)$ which asserts that the predicate $P(x)$ is True for all x. We can, of course, still apply all the normal propositional logic operators to such quantified statements, as well, to make compound statements like: $\exists x (P(x) \land Q(x)) \equiv True$, which says that there exists an x such that both $P(x)$ and $Q(x)$ are True.

1.4.3 Declarative vs Imperative Statements

An argument is a way to reason from given information (the premises) to new information (the conclusion). The premises and conclusions, in our conception of formal logic so far, must be statements that then express information, in particular this information is either true or false. Such statements are called **declarative** statements. An example of a declarative statement, one that either states a fact or provides some information, is, "Socrates is a man."

This is different from statements that are either questions or commands and so don't express information. These kinds of statements, which are used to do something or give a command of some sort, are called **imperative** statements. An example of an imperative statement is, "Drink the hemlock!" These declarative and imperative statements are analogous to the declarative and imperative knowledge we met in Section 0.2.

Although the logics we've seen so far only involve declarative statements, it is entirely possible to develop a logic that includes imperative statements and, in fact, is the basis of many programming languages as we'll see soon when our adventure continues in the next section.

1.5 Computational Thinking and Computational Solutions

At the end of our last adventure, though, we learned that not all problems in the universe have a computational solution. The good news, though, is that if a function is computable, a Universal Turing Machine can be programmed to compute it. The Universal Turing Machine solves these problems by an *algorithm*, a *rule* for solving a mathematical problem in a *finite* number of precise, unambiguous steps. These algorithms can be expressed in any *language* that is appropriate for a particular computing agent. In dealing with digital computers, we can write these algorithms in a plethora of different programming languages, including Java and Python.

It turns out that if a programming language can be used to simulate a Universal Turing Machine, that language is said to be **Turing Complete** as it can then solve any computable problem in the universe as shown by the Church-Turing Thesis! All modern programming languages, like Java and Python, are Turing Complete. What this means is that any solution that can be programmed in one programming language can be programmed in any other programming language: they are all equivalent in their computational ability!

This implies that a *computational solution*, or **program**, written in Java can be translated or expressed in Python without loss of correctness.[16] For this reason, most computer scientists are language agnostics and choose whichever programming language is most appropriate for a particular problem since all languages are fundamentally equivalent in regards to their computational power. All you need to do is come up with a computational solution, or algorithm, for the problem at hand!

Listen to your heart... there *is* something else you can do...

How do you solve problems in your life, whether they're interpersonal or practical or physical? Most people start by just using their **intuition**, which they often characterize as following their heart or listening to their gut. As it turns out, the gut doesn't do a lot of thinking and the heart does even less.[17] Almost all of our thinking is in our brains and it often builds upon sub-conscious processing as well as our experiences.

Intuitive solutions are perfectly acceptable as long as they work and make accurate predictions reliably and consistently. Most of us, though, have more of a hit-and-miss record with intuitive solutions. Over time, people realized that systematic solutions to problems often yield more effective and consistent results.

As the early Greeks systematized those approaches to thinking which resulted in more consistent solutions to problems, **formal logic** became an accepted method for solving complex problems. A problem could then be modelled as an **argument**, a series of statements, or *premises*, and a *conclusion*; the *rules* that determined whether the conclusion was a reasonable consequence of the premises constituted the argument's **logic**. So logic is just a structured, systematic way of thinking or reasoning about an argument.

Natural philosophers like Galileo Galilei used empirical thinking, where the premises are based on data from the natural world, which led to a particularly effective iterative process for solving problems that is often called the **scientific method**. In fact, **computational thinking** can be thought of as a set of skills or ideas that are a generalization of that iterative methodology.

---

[16]What is a program? A translation of the algorithm into a language that can be interpreted and executed by a digital computer. A digital computer thus becomes the computing agent which carries out, or executes, that algorithm. E.g., our algorithm for finding the average in Section 0.1.3 can be thought of as $\sum_i \frac{T_i}{N}$, which we can then translate into the algorithm shown in Section 1.7.

[17] Surprisingly, the gut does have a hundred million or so nerve cells in the Enteric Nervous System (ENS) and also

1.5.1 Computational Thinking Overview

Computational problems, in general, require a certain mode of approach or way of thinking. This approach is often called **computational thinking** and is similar, in many ways, to the scientific method where we're concerned with making predictions.[18] We'll delineate the steps involved in Computational Thinking in much more detail in Section 2.9.

> **Definition 1.5.1 — Computational Thinking.** In order to make predictions using *computational thinking*, we need to define three things related to the problem and its solution:
>
> 1. Problem Specification: We'll start by analyzing the problem, stating it precisely, and establishing the criteria for solution. A *computational thinking approach to solution* often starts by breaking complex problems down into more familiar or manageable sub-problems, sometimes called **problem decomposition**, frequently using deductive or probabilisic reasoning. This can also involve the ideas of **abstraction** and **pattern recognition**, both of which we saw in our temperature sensor problem when we found a new representation for our data and then plotted it to find a pattern. More formally, we'd use these techniques in creating **models** and simulations, as we'll learn later on.
>
> 2. Algorithmic Expression: We then need to find an algorithm, a precise sequence of steps, that solves the problem using appropriate data representations. This process uses inductive thinking and is needed for transferring a particular problem to a larger class of similar problems. This step is also sometimes called **algorithmic thinking**. We'll be talking about *imperative*, like procedural or modular, and declarative, like *functional*, approaches to algorithmic solutions.
>
> 3. Solution Implementation & Evaluation: Finally, we create the actual solution and systematically evaluate it to determine its *correctness* and *efficiency*. This step also involves seeing if the solution can be **generalized** via automation or extension to other kinds of problems.

I should add a little caveat here: these rules for computational thinking are all well and good but they're not really rules, per se; instead, think of them more like well-intentioned heuristics, or rules of thumb.

These heuristics for computational thinking are very similar to the heuristics usually given for the 5-step scientific method[19] taught in grade school: they're nice guidelines but they're not mandatory. They're suggestions of ideas you'll likely need or require for most efforts but it's not some process to pigeonhole your thinking or approach to solution.

The best way to think about it might be in more general terms and harkens back to how Niklaus Wirth, the inventor of the computer language Pascal, put it in the title of his book, *Data Structures +*

---

interacts with the nervous system via gut hormones and microbiota, bacteria in the digestive system. Similarly, the heart has a few thousand ganglia, or clusters of nerve cells, but these neurons are mainly used for regulating cardiac function. So, as you might imagine, the vast majority of our thinking experience is in the brain.

[18]The term computational thinking was popularized by Jeanette Wing, who studied under John Guttag, in her landmark 2006 viewpoint paper [10].

[19] The scientific method is usually written out as something like:

1. *Observe* some aspect of the universe
2. Use those observations to inform some *hypothesis* about it
3. Make some *prediction* using that hypothesis
4. Test the prediction via *experimentation* and modify the hypothesis accordingly
5. *Repeat* steps 3 and 4 until the hypothesis no longer needs modification

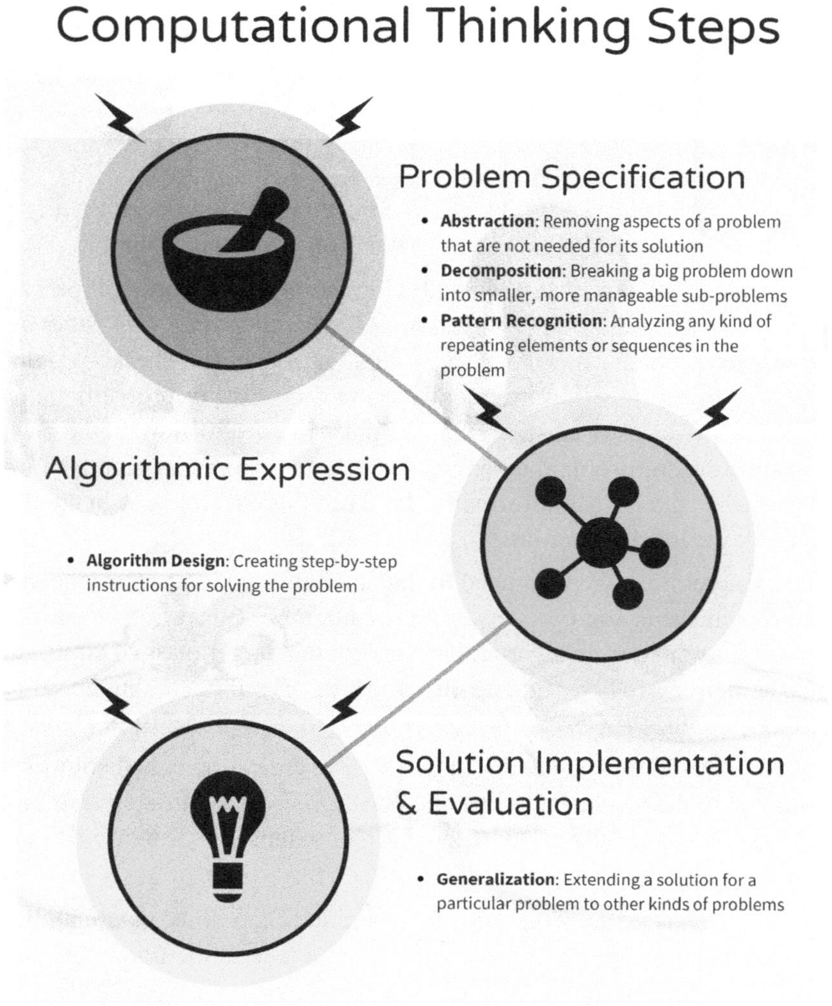

Computational Thinking Steps

Problem Specification

- **Abstraction**: Removing aspects of a problem that are not needed for its solution
- **Decomposition**: Breaking a big problem down into smaller, more manageable sub-problems
- **Pattern Recognition**: Analyzing any kind of repeating elements or sequences in the problem

Algorithmic Expression

- **Algorithm Design**: Creating step-by-step instructions for solving the problem

Solution Implementation & Evaluation

- **Generalization**: Extending a solution for a particular problem to other kinds of problems

Figure 1.1: **Computational Thinking is a set of techniques for solving complex problems** that can be classified into three steps: *Problem Specification*, *Algorithmic Expression*, and *Solution Implementation & Evaluation*. The skills involved in each step of the Computational Thinking Approach are above.

Algorithms = Programs. The title of the book suggests that both data structures and algorithms are essential for writing programs and, in a sense, they define programs.

We can think of **programs** as being the computational solutions, the solutions to *computable functions*, that we express in some particular programming language. We also know that an **algorithm** is an *effective procedure*, a sequence of step-by-step instructions for solving a specific kind of problem. We haven't met the term **data structures** yet but we can think of it as a particular *data representation*. Don't worry if this isn't completely clear yet as we'll be getting on quite intimate terms with both that and algorithms later on. For now, you can think of this equation as:

Representations of Data + Representations of Effective Procedures = Computational Solutions

$$(1.1)$$

At its core, the central aspect of all fundamental physical science is *prediction*, usually through experimentation as Feynman said in the quote earlier; if you're able to make repeated, precise, quantitative predictions, whichever model you use or mode of thinking you employ is working and should likely be re-employed. If it's a formal method, great; if it's something less formal, yet still structured and repeatable like the above equation, and leads to correct computational solutions, that's also fine.

Any structured thinking process or approach that lets you get to this state would be considered *computational thinking*. You can even think of it as an alternative definition of *critical thinking* or *evidence-based reasoning* where your solutions result from the data and how you think about that data:

$$\text{Data} + \text{How to Think about that Data} = \text{Computational Thinking} \qquad (1.2)$$

In this sense, being able to represent the data and then manipulate it is itself a computational solution to a computable problem! We'll look at the detailed steps involved in computational problem solving in a little bit.

Some formal definitions

Before we can formally examine the differences between the declarative and imperative programming languages, we'll need to define some basic programming concepts. We'll be discussing these ideas more deeply when we get into the guts of machines and programming later on.

- **Variable**: a variable is the name for a stored value that represents some fundamental characteristic of the system or function. This stored value is **mutable**, i.e., it can be changed by the function or computation or program. We've previously seen input and output variables for a function as well as the variables for Time and Temperature when we collected sensor data in the previous chapter.
- **State**: the state of a system or function can be thought of as the values for some set of variables that fully describe the system or function. Usually, the state at a position in time does not include anything about its history. The state of the system for our Temperature Sensor example might be determined by the location of each sensor and the temperature reading on each sensor at a certain time; the state would then be determined by the location, temperature, and time variables for each sensor.
- **Function**: Another way to think about functions is to characterize them as a structured method for transitioning from one state (the input set of variables) to another state (the output set of variables). This state transition is not a mutable stored value.

1.6 Two Fundamental Models of Programming

In our previous discussion, we described functions in two ways: one was as a mapping or relation between the domain and the range of that function and the other was a mathematical representation of the function in functional notation.

These two approaches can also be categorized, respectively, as *declarative* and *imperative* (sometimes called *procedural*), the same two categories of knowledge we saw earlier when we discussed *know-what* and *know-how* knowledge and when we discussed declarative vs imperative *statements* in formal logic in Section 1.4.3.

So another way to characterize the function is to directly utilize our procedural knowledge about that function. In the imperative or procedural approach to defining a function, we found a *procedure* for determining an output value from a set of input values. More specifically, we found that the values of *computable functions* can be specified by *effective procedures*, or *algorithms*.

As we saw above, these *computational solutions*, or algorithms, for *computable functions* can be expressed in some *programming language*, especially when we want to use a digital computer as the computing agent for that solution. Approaches to computation using programming languages can also be classified in this same way.

Thus, the two primary **models of computation** for programming languages are: *declarative* approaches to computation, which include **functional programming**, and *imperative* approaches to computation, which include **procedural programming** and **object-oriented programming**.

1.6.1 Declarative vs Imperative Programming Languages

A programming language can choose to provide either, or both, of these approaches to computation although most languages are predominantly one or the other.

Declarative programming languages define the program logic but not the actual control flow that determines how that solution is found. They can be reporting languages like SQL, for example. This declarative approach can be further extended to *functional programming*, which avoids the use of state and changeable data and instead approaches computational problems as functional transformations of data collections.

Imperative programming languages consist of statements that directly change the computed state. It can be further classified into the categories of *structured programming* and *procedural programming*, which we'll meet in more detail later.[20] Most modern languages like Java and Python are imperative languages that support both procedural and object-oriented paradigms.[21]

Referencing these formal definitions, we can think of declarative programming as a model of computation that is based on a system where relationships are specified by definitions or equations which specify what is to be computed, not how it is to be computed. In the declarative programming paradigm, variables can only ever have *one* value which cannot be changed during a program's execution (while a program is running). This approach is called a non-destructive assignment.

A Quick Recap

The **state** of a system can be thought of as the set of variables that give a complete description of the mathematical or physical system at a specific time. A real life system is much messier and more complex so you have to decide which variables form a complete description of the mathematical model of that system. The variables that completely describe the state of a system are called **state variables** and the set of all possible values of the state variables is called the **state space** of that system.

---

[20]On a more technical note, structured programming has subroutines and avoids the use of the simple tests used in `goto` statements and instead uses more abstract and complex control structures like `for` and `while`. Procedural programming in addition supports full modularization, including event-driven and object-oriented programming.

[21]We can think of declarative languages as specifying what to do and imperative programming specifying how to do it. This is similar to the two types of knowledge we saw earlier, know-what and know-how in Section 0.1.3.

Variables	Control Structures

`LIST_OF_SENSOR_LOCATIONS`
`RUNNING_SUM`
`TEMPERATURE`
`NUMBER_OF_SENSORS`
`AVERAGE_VALUE`
	`foreach`

Table 1.1: List of Variables and Control Structures in Algorithm 1.1

The imperative model of computation, on the other hand, uses well-ordered sequences of commands to modify variables by successive destructive assignments. They use three standard control structures to determine how the program carries out its set of instructions: either in **sequence**, one after the other; by **branching** or selecting between different series of options; or by **looping** or iterating over a series of instructions a certain number of times. We'll look at these three control structures (*sequence, selection,* and *repetition*) in much more detail later.[22]

1.7 Pseudocode

For now, let's see one representation of an algorithm that's not designed for a computer but rather for humans. In addition to programming languages like Java and Python, we can translate an algorithm into **pseudocode**, an English-like language that's not designed for any specific computer or programming language.

Let's see what all these variables and functions look like in pseudocode by designing an algorithm to calculate the average temperature at a certain time on campus from the notes collected in Figure 0.1. In order to calculate the average temperature, we have to add up all the temperatures on all the sensors and then divide that sum by the number of sensors.

The algorithm shown in Algorithm 1.1 is a method for calculating the average temperature at a certain time across all the temperatures. It uses some variables (like `LIST_OF_SENSOR_LOCATIONS`, `RUNNING_SUM`, `TEMPERATURE`, `NUMBER_OF_SENSORS`, and `AVERAGE_VALUE`) and control structures (like the `foreach` looping control structure), as shown in Table 1.1.

So the first thing we need is to get the `LIST_OF_SENSOR_LOCATIONS` that were recording temperatures at a certain time, say 8am. Then, in Line 1, we create a variable called `RUNNING_SUM` to hold the sum of all the temperature values. This is the variable that will hold the sum of all the temperatures. Each time we read a sensor value from the `LIST_OF_SENSOR_LOCATIONS`, we'll add it to the `RUNNING_SUM`. Since we haven't yet read any sensor values at Line 1, we'll initialize `RUNNING_SUM` to 0 in Line 1.

Next, in Lines 2 – 5, we loop over the `LIST_OF_SENSOR_LOCATIONS` and, for each `SENSOR` in the `LIST_OF_SENSOR_LOCATIONS`, we read the Temperature value (in Line 3) and then add that `TEMPERATURE` to the `RUNNING_SUM`.

---

[22]Declarative languages, like functional languages, don't have the looping control structure as not being able to change variable values would lead to infinite loops. Since functional programming cannot have loops, the only way to implement repetition is via functional recursion. Functional programming also treats functions as first-class components, which essentially means that they can be utilized everywhere other components, like variables, can be used.

After checking all the sensors in the LIST_OF_SENSOR_LOCATIONS, we then get the NUMBER_OF_SENSORS that were on that LIST_OF_SENSOR_LOCATIONS on Line 6. Finally, we calculate the actual AVERAGE_VALUE on Line 7 and, on Line 8, we print out that average value.

Algorithm 1.1: Algorithm for calculating average temperature

   Input: The LIST_OF_SENSOR_LOCATIONS from Post-It Notes

1 Set RUNNING_SUM = 0
2 **foreach** *SENSOR in the LIST_OF_SENSOR_LOCATIONS* **do**
3 | Set TEMPERATURE = The Temperature value read from the SENSOR
4 | Set RUNNING_SUM = RUNNING_SUM + TEMPERATURE
5 **end**
6 Set NUMBER_OF_SENSORS = Length of the LIST_OF_SENSOR_LOCATIONS
7 Set AVERAGE_VALUE = RUNNING_SUM / NUMBER_OF_SENSORS
8 Print the AVERAGE_VALUE

If all of Algorithm 1.1 made sense to you, you've got a handle on most of the basic ideas needed for any and all programming paradigms!

       The **state** of the algorithm can be considered to be the list of temperature values.

Problem 1.1 Would the average temperature value also be considered part of the state of the system? Why or why not?

1.7.1 Pseudocode Expanded: Now with Twice the Pseudo!

We can now expand the Algorithm to also incorporate the last two major constructs used in basic procedural programming: selection control structures and procedural units, also called procedures.

Nota Bene: This section is just for fun for now, where fun is, obviously, a very relative term. We won't define any of these terms, like selection control structures or procedures, precisely until later so don't worry if none of this makes sense right now. If it does make sense, all the better! The main purpose of this section is to give an intuitive feel and hopefully the expanded pseudocode algorithm will be as approachable as Algorithm 1.1.

Keeping with this informal theme, you can think of a **selection control structure** as something that lets you make a choice, often called an **if-statement**: e.g., "if I'm hungry, then I'll eat some pizza" is an example of a selection statement.

Similarly, we'll use a **procedural unit**, or **procedure**, by way of preview of a modular programming approach we'll explore in detail later; for now, let's parcel off some of the calculation steps into their own procedure, called HelperProcedure. HelperProcedure is defined on Lines 1 – 13 and then we can just call, or execute, that procedure separately on Line 14.

We'll shorten some of the variable names to make them descriptive but somewhat less verbose (e.g., we'll change RUNNING_SUM to SUM, etc.). We'll also include a selection control structure to ensure that the denominator is not 0. This might happen, for example, if there were no sensor values at all in the LIST_OF_SENSOR_LOCATIONS as you'd end up with an average value calculation of:

Algorithm 1.2: Algorithm for calculating average temperature using Procedures

Input:	The LIST_OF_SENSOR_LOCATIONS from Post-It Notes and initial AVERAGE

⋮

⋮

```
// First, Define the Helper Procedure which uses the INPUT
```
1 **Procedure** `HelperProcedure()`:
2   Set SUM = 0
3   **foreach** *SENSOR in the LIST_OF_SENSOR_LOCATIONS* **do**
4   Set TEMPERATURE = The Temperature value read from the SENSOR
5   Set SUM = SUM + TEMPERATURE
6   **end**
7   Set NUM_SENSORS = Length of the LIST_OF_SENSOR_LOCATIONS
8   // Make sure that number of sensors is not 0 to avoid division by 0
9   **if** *NUM_SENSORS equals 0* **then**
10   Set NUM_SENSORS = 1
11   **end**
12   Set AVERAGE = SUM / NUM_SENSORS
13 **end**

⋮

⋮

```
// This is the START OF THE PRORGRAM where we call the HelperProcedure
```
14 `HelperProcedure()`
15 Print the AVERAGE

$$AVERAGE \quad = \quad \frac{SUM}{NUM\_SENSORS} \quad = \quad \frac{0}{0}$$

This is a problem since dividing by 0 is undefined so we can use the selection statement to just force the denominator to be 1 and make that a valid, but perhaps inaccurate, average value (e.g., it's unlikely the temperature is actually 0 so you'd have to deal with this kind of **semantic** error, as we'll see in Section 3.5).

The algorithm shown in Algorithm 1.2 also creates the same variables and same control structures as Algorithm 1.1; however, Algorithm 1.2 also includes a procedure (`HelperProcedure`) that does all the grunt-work of the actual calculation.

This means that the guts of our program only consists of the last two lines, Lines 14 – 15!

We can already see some of the essential characteristics of algorithms and effective procedures in our two example algorithms. Each step is a finite, doable step and the algorithm, or program, consists of a finite number of these finite steps.

Most of the statements are executable, i.e., they do something. Some of them, the comments, are intended only as remarks for us and not the computing agent. The **comments**, in this case, are lines that start with //. The essential computation, though, is contained in the instructions on Lines 1 – 13 and Lines 14 – 15 of our program.

Problem 1.2 How might you deal with the kinds of semantic errors we noted above (where the Average Temperature is set to 0)?

Sometimes, **procedures are also called functions** but these *aren't functions in the mathematical sense* as they don't always have to have a return value, for example. Mathematical functions are more similar to the term functions as used in functional programming (please see Section 7.1 for more details).

1.8 Functional and Imperative Models of Computation

We've seen that two models of computation for programming languages are **functional programming** and **imperative programming**.

The **functional model** establishes some relation between the domain (the input) and the range (the output) of a function. This approach assumes that the function or computation always reads the input, processes it somehow, and then produces an output. Exactly how it processes it, the procedures it employs, are essentially irrelevant in the functional model of computation. All you have to do is **declare** the function that specifies what to do.

Looking in detail at the procedures, or sequence of commands or **imperatives**, that manipulate the *input data representation* to produce the *output data representation* leads us directly to the **imperative model** of computation. The imperative model of computation relies upon commands or statements called imperatives that map the program state *before* the statement is executed to a program state *after* the statement is **executed** or carried out by the computing agent.

If the *sequence of statements*, the **algorithm**, don't involve any non-deterministic steps (like rolling a random die), they will maintain a strict correspondence between the inputs and the outputs and always produces the same output data for a given set of input data. So if they both maintain the strict correspondence between inputs and outputs, what's the difference between these two models?

The most salient difference is that programs in the functional programming paradigm only specify *what* their outputs are, whereas programs in the imperative programming paradigm specify exactly *how* to compute the outputs. Some texts will even define Computer Science as the study of describing algorithms, constructing them, and comparing rival algorithms for computing the same function.

■ **Example 1.1** A simple example of the difference between the declarative programming and imperative programming paradigms is the common problem of answering someone who asks, "Where do you live?" In the *declarative*, or *functional*, programming paradigm, your answer might be, "I live at 137 Quantum Way, Beverly Hills, CA 90210." The *imperative* programming approach, on the other hand, might be something along the lines of, "Take a right on Heisenberg Way, go 1.5 miles, turn left onto Galileo Alley, go 0.5 miles but stay in the rightmost lane. Turn on your lights when you go into the tunnel and turn them off when you come out of it. Finally, turn right onto Quantum Way and pull into the third parking spot with the large sign saying 137 above it." ■

Problem 1.3 Can you express the above example as a pseudocode algorithm, similar to Algorithm 1.1 or Algorithm 1.2?

The advantage of the imperative model of computation is that it is much less restrictive than the functional model of computation since it covers any kind of manipulation of any data representation and it doesn't, in the general sense, require both specific inputs and outputs. All it requires is some data representation and a procedure or algorithm for using that representation.

The Big Lebowski

We can think of *imperative programming* as involving **procedures** that are a *collection of instructions*, or algorithm. These procedures don't always return a value, though. A function in mathematics, on the other hand, is something that maps specific inputs to specific outputs. As such, a **function** in the *functional programming* paradigm can be thought of as a *collection of instructions*, or algorithm, that also returns something, usually an *output* value of some sort.

1.8.1 Computation in General

Computation can then be broadly defined as the manipulation of some data representation by following some specific algorithm; but the strange thing is that the same computation, or mapping in the functional sense, can be carried out by many different permutations of algorithms, data representations, and computing agents.

In fact, algorithms themselves are representations since we can represent them as instructions for a human or as a program written for a digital machine to carry out. We can **translate** the algorithm, or procedure, from one language to another. When the computing agent needs to carry out, or execute, those instructions, it simply reads and follows the stored representation of the algorithm or program in a process called **interpretation**.

A Computational Universe

In this sense, computers can be thought of as devices that can store and interpret representations of algorithms and data, regardless of whether they are implemented in transistors, neurons, or quarks!

1.9 Information Theory

We talked about a function as transforming some input into the output. Both the input and the output contain information which the function processes and transforms.

These inputs and outputs are also encoded in some specific representation. In fact, the choice of a specific data representation can often affect our choice of corresponding algorithm to solve some problem. As a result, computer scientists often study the properties of different kinds of representations of data, or **data structures**.

Since we know we can transform data from one representation to another, we can start to abstract this process by ignoring the particular representation and instead think about the algorithm as manipulating the *information* in the input. But what is the information content of some particular data representation?

Is there more or less information content in another data representation? Can we somehow *quantify* this idea of information?

1.9.1 The Birth of Information Theory

This is just what occupied Claude Shannon, a mathematician at Bell Labs, in the 1940s. At the time, Bell Labs had a very liberal working policy: scientists were allowed to spend a significant portion of their time working on any problem that interested them as long as they kept their doors open for other scientists to drop by. Since Bell Labs was owned by AT&T Corporation, Shannon decided to take some of his free time and look at the meat and potatoes of their business: communication.

In particular, he realized that no one at AT&T had actually defined what it was they were communicating and what was at the very core of their extensive business enterprise: the information. Other people had, of course, thought deeply about this idea of quantifying information both at Bell Labs (like Harry Nyquist and Ralph Hartley) and outside (like Leo Szilard, Edwin James, and Leon Brillouin). But Shannon wanted to nail this down precisely and figure out the limits of communication. So, building upon some of this previous work, Shannon started work on a memorandum to analyze the transmission of information. Finally, in 1948, Shannon managed to fully quantify this idea of information in the context of communication channels and published his seminal paper, "A Mathematical Theory of Communication." [11]

1.9.2 First Rule of Communication Club: There Is No Meaning

The fundamental problem Shannon examined was how to send a message from a source to a receiver without any degradation of the message itself. In order to examine this transmission of messages, the first thing Shannon did was ignore the meaning of the message! This kind of **abstraction**, or ignoring of what are considered non-essential details for a specific approach to solution, is something we'll do quite often when we solve computational problems, as we saw in Section 1.5.1. As Shannon put it, the "semantic aspects of communication are irrelevant to the engineering problem". [11]

Instead, he tried to distill the problem down to its essential aspect which he finally conceptualized as selecting the actual message to be transmitted from the set of possible messages that could be transmitted. So how might this one message, *selected from the set of all possible messages*, suffer degradation when it's actually transmitted?

Let's start by looking at the same problem Shannon and Hartley had examined: suppose we had a very simple system that consisted of a transmitter, a wire, and a receiver. The person on the receiving end can receive three kinds of symbols[23]:

1. HIGH signal (a *spike up*)
2. NO signal (*no spike at all*)
3. LOW signal (a *spike down*)

This is shown in the original image from Hartley's paper [12], as shown in Figure 1.2. As Hartley points out, although these symbols might have some psychological meaning for the sender or receiver, we won't delve into those semantics. We're just concerned with the transmission of this sequence of symbols, which we call our message.

You can think of Figure 1.2(A) as showing the original signal as sent by the sender at the Transmitter. We can then think of Figure 1.2(B) as showing the signal after it has gone down the wire for quite a while. (C) is the same signal after it has gone down even more of the wire's length and, finally, (D) is

---

[23] You can also think of this as a telegraph system that sends Morse code. For more on Morse code, please see `https://en.wikipedia.org/wiki/Morse_code`

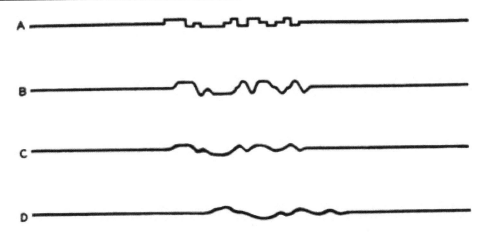

Figure 1.2: Signal degradation image directly from Hartley's paper

that same signal after it has traveled down the wire for perhaps a few miles. As you can see, the signal in (D) is unrecognizable from the signal in (A)!

What is the source of this degradation? As any continuous signal travels down any communication channel, there are small, unpredictable perturbations that creep into that signal. These small perturbations that arise due to the physical transmission of the signal down the wire are called *noise*.

If that signal encodes, or represents, a message, then the message itself gets corrupted! The degree of corruption, or degradation, of the message can be represented by a simple ratio, the **signal-to-noise** ratio. When the message is first sent from the receiver, as in (A), the message has very little noise so the signal-to-noise ratio is high. By the time the message gets to (D), however, the noise has increased greatly, due to the perturbations in the transmission of the signal down the wire, and the signal-to-noise ratio decreases significantly, thus garbling the final message received at the receiver end.

A unit by any other name...

Whenever we make a quantitative measurement, we usually express it in terms of some defined quantity. This lets us compare the measurements to an agreed-upon standard. For example, suppose I measure the distance between my desk and my chair and declare it to be 1 foot long. What do I mean by a foot? Do I mean my own foot or the much larger foot of my cousin, who stands a full head taller than me?

These kinds of discrepancies led people to standardize the measurements. Although the original standard may well have been the foot of some prominent personage, the foot is nowadays defined to be exactly $0.3048 meters$. Thus, if I say the distance is $1 foot$, someone on the other side of the world will know exactly what length I mean.

The unit in the term, *unit of measurement*, refers to the number 1 so that all measurements in terms of that unit of measurement will be multiples of that 1 unit. So $3 feet$ is $3 \times 1 foot = 3 feet$. In other words, all measurements are reported in terms of multiples of that unit. Once we quantify information, we need to express a standard unit of information, as well, so we can measure the amount of information we have. That is exactly what Shannon did when he quantified the idea of "information."

Encoding the Message

Hartley [12] had also tried to quantify the amount of information in a message without regard to its semantic meaning. The approach Hartley took was to quantify it by first finding the number of possible symbols, S, which, in our case above, are HIGH, NO, and LOW. For a specific message, made up of n symbols, Hartley characterized the quantity of information as:

$$H = \log_b S^n = n \log_b S \qquad (1.3)$$

If we set $n = 1$ in Equation 1.3, we end up with a single **unit of information** in this **representation**, $\log_b S$!

Log this way... add this way...

A logarithm is a way to allow multiplication to be performed via addition. A log can be thought of as the opposite, or inverse, of an exponential. The two important terms in a logarithm are the **base**, b, and the **exponent**, x, just as in exponentiation. For example, if I have the following exponent:

$$y = b^x$$

which raises the base, b, to the exponent or power, x, I can represent the **inverse** operation as the following logarithm:

$$\log_b(y) = x$$

Another neat thing about logs is that raising a number to a certain power lets you bring that power down as a multiple; this is probably easier to see in an equation than explain in words:

$$\log_b(y^A) = A \cdot \log_b(y)$$

This also implies that a multiplicaton by a *negative* factor, $-A \log_b(y)$, is the same as raising the number to a negative, or *inverse*, power, $\log_b(y^{-A})$.

Just as doing an operation, and then its inverse, gives us back the original, in the same way, doing a log followed by an exponentiation (or the opposite) gives us back the original:

$$b^{\log_b(m)} = m \text{ and } \log_b(b^m) = m$$

So how does this simple inversion allow us to do multiplication as addition instead? If you had to multiply the following:

$$\log_b(m \times n)$$

you could instead just **add** the following:

$$\log_b(m \times n) = \log_b(b^{\log_b(m)} \times b^{\log_b(n)}) = \log_b(b^{\log_b(m) + \log_b(n)}) = \log_b(m) + \log_b(n)$$

log calculations for a large number of values were historically recorded in voluminous log tables but today you're more likely to just type it into a calculator or a log calculator online.

If we then use log with the base $b = 10$, as in $\log_{10}$, the unit of information will be expressed in decimal digits; these units of information eventually came to be called the Hartley units and were our first measure of information. In fact, $H = \log_b S$, which is just Equation 1.3 with $n = 1$, is sometimes also called the **Hartley Function** or **Hartley's Information Entropy**.

$$H = \log_b S \qquad (1.4)$$

1.9.3 Shannon Information

Shannon decided to look at this problem more closely. He started by examining the transmitter and continued the process of *removing "semantic" meaning* from his examination of sending and receiving messages. So, rather than imagining a person sending a message, he thought about a mathematical process, a **stochastic process**, generating a string of symbols at the source. A stochastic process, in this case, is just some mathematical model of a system that produces a sequence of symbols based on some set of probabilities (probability rears its head once again!).[24]

If the set of possible symbols is again as before (i.e., HIGH, NO, and LOW), then the number of possible messages, if all of the symbols are equally likely, would be 3^n, where n is the number of symbols that make up our particular message and the set of all possible symbols, our alphabet, is made up of just 3 possible symbols (i.e., HIGH, NO, and LOW). So if our message consisted of just two symbols, there would be $3^2 = 9$ possibilities (like {HIGH,HIGH} or {LOW,HIGH} or perhaps {NO,LOW} for our 2-symbol message).

Shannon decided to take a somewhat different route here than Hartley. He started by imagining all the possible messages of a certain length he could make given a certain set of symbols (e.g., in our example with 3 possible symbols, we could make 9 2-symbol-long messages). Since he had removed all psychological meaning from these messages, a la Hartley, he figured all these 9 messages were *equally likely*.

He next asked the question, "Can we find a measure of how much 'choice' is involved in the selection of the event or of how uncertain we are of the outcome?" [11] In other words, how much "choice" is involved in picking one of these messages from the 9 possible messages to send down the pipeline? If you've been paying close attention all along, alarm bells must be going off for you now (I, of course, never was that good of a student so I never heard any bells while reading textbooks). This is exactly what all those *probabilities* we looked at earlier measure!

He decided to base his measure of the information that is "produced" when one message is chosen (from a finite set of possible messages) on the probability of that message occurring or being selected. The raw probability, however, wasn't mathematically convenient so he outlined three reasons for doing what Hartley had done earlier and used a logarithm function.[25] Since he was interested in finding out how "...uncertain we are of the outcome," he also inverted the probability, p, to end up with **Shannon's Information Function**:

$$\text{Information Function} = h(p) = \log_2\left(\frac{1}{p}\right) = -\log_2(p) \qquad (1.5)$$

---

[24]In particular, he modeled it as a Markov chain which, in his paper, he calls a Markoff process.

[25]As Shannon said, "If the number of messages in the set is finite then this number or any monotonic function of this number can be regarded as a measure of the information produced when one message is chosen from the set, all choices being equally likely. As was pointed out by Hartley the most natural choice is the logarithmic function."

This measure of information is calculated in base-2 rather than the base-10 of Hartley. Since Shannon was looking at the fundamentals of communication, base-2 was a convenient way to measure the amount of information if the device used was something like a flip-flop circuit, which only had two stable positions: ON or OFF, even simpler than our 3-position, or 3-state, system of HIGH, NO, and LOW above.

These kinds of devices with just two states, ON and OFF, can be represented using **binary digits**. A binary digit is a 1 or a 0 and can be represented in a base-2 positional system, as opposed to the base-10 of our normal *decimal digit* representations which use a base-10 positional system. So a binary positional system only uses 2 digits (a 0 or 1) but a decimal positional system uses 10 digits (0, 1, 2, 3, 4, 5, 6, 7, 8, and 9). We'll talk more about these positional representations in Section 2.3.1, as well.

Abstracting Information into Binary Systems

The idea of abstracting information in a system didn't originate with Shannon, of course. In 1801, the French weaver Joseph Marie Jacquard patented a mechanical loom that used perforated cards to control the weaving mechanism. The perforated cards had holes and blank spaces which controlled the movement of counterweights, thus allowing the wires to move in the pattern specified by the holes and spaces on the card.

The holes and blank spaces allowed Jacquard to **abstract** the information contained in any image or picture by using a **binary representation** of two symbols, a hole or a blank space, just like the flip-flops studied by Shannon! In fact, Leibniz had also advocated the use of a binary system in 1703.

A bit is *not* the same thing as a binary digit!

Even though the word *bit* is derived from the words *binary digit*, a bit and a binary digit are *not* the same thing in information theory. A binary digit is a specific *value*, a 0 or 1, that is assigned to a *binary variable*. A bit, on the other hand, represents the *amount of information*, $h(p) = \log_2(\frac{1}{p}) = -\log_2(p)$, carried by a symbol when the probability of seeing that symbol is $p = 0.5$ or 50% (this is the case when there are just two possible symbols, for example). If we plug this probability, $p = 0.5$, into our formula, we get the result that one bit of information is 1:

$$h(p = 0.5) = \log_2(\tfrac{1}{0.5}) = \log_2(2) = 1 bit$$

The amount of information, measured in bits, can be any real value. E.g., if the probability of seeing a symbol is $p = \frac{3}{4} = 0.75$, then the amount of information would be $h(p = 0.75) = \log_2(\frac{1}{0.75}) = 0.41 bits$

1.9.4 Information, Uncertainty, and... Surprise!

For now, we can think of **one unit of information** as the information carried by a symbol (or message) when the probability of seeing that symbol (of that event occurring) is $\frac{1}{2}$. In other words, one unit of information represents a choice between two equally likely possibilities. This unit of information is referred to as a **bit**, which John W. Tukey had recently coined as a portmanteau from **bi**nary dig**it**). Thus, Shannon's measure of information came to be measured in bits, which are also sometimes called *Shannons (Sh)* in his honour.

Nota Bene: A **bit** by definition is the *amount of information* needed to choose between two equally probable possibilities. Sometimes, a bit is also used as a short-hand to mean a **binary digit**, which is the value of a binary variable and can be a 0 or a 1. In some circumstances, the context will be the only way to determine which meaning is intended.

It's important to note that Shannon actually *defined information as a **decrease in uncertainty** at the receiver's end* [26] and posed 5 postulates for the information function, $h(p)$. This representation of information as $h(p) = \log_2(\frac{1}{p}) = -\log_2(p)$ can thus also be interpreted as a **measure of the amount of surprise** associated with observing some symbol from our set of possible symbols (or, alternatively, the surprise of some event occurring). The smaller the probability, p, the larger the surprise, $h(p)$.

Shannon's 5 postulates for information, $h(p)$

1. $h(p)$ is continuous for $0 \leq p \leq 1$
   (*Continuity*: just as for a normal probability)
2. $h(p) = \infty$ if $p = 0$
   (an event with 0% probability would result in an infinite amount of surprise)
3. $h(p) = 0$ if $p = 1$
   (an event with 100% probability has 0 surprise)
4. $h(p_i) > h(p_j)$ if $p_j > p_i$
   (if the probability of one event, j, is greater than another event, i, the surprise of that first event, i, is lower)
5. $h(p_i) + h(p_j) = h(p_i * p_j)$ if the two states s_i and s_j are independent[27]
   (*Additivity*: the information from two independent symbols is linearly additive)

It can be shown [11] that the only function that satisfies these five properties is $h(p) = -C\log_b(p) = C\log_b(\frac{1}{p})$ where b is some base, not necessarily base-2, and $C > 0$ is just a scaling factor or choice of unit of measure.

To get Shannon's Information Function, we set $C = 1$ since this gives a nice, simple 1 unit of "surprise" as a measure for information: $h(p) = \log_b(\frac{1}{p})$

---

[26] As we'll see later on, Shannon defined the Rate of Information Transmission as $R = H_{before} - H_{after}$, where H is his uncertainty function or entropy, as John von Neumann suggested in Section 1.10. Information is thus the reduction in uncertainty after subtracting what he called the equivocation or the "average ambiguity of the received signal," $H_y(x)$, the average rate of conditional entropy and this difference gives a sense of what he called the "missing information."

Interestingly, we can apply Shannon's Uncertainty Function, H, to the probability distribution of locations and momenta of a system of many particles. We can then use MaxEnt to find the distribution that maximizes H to get back the statistical physics result that, for a system of non-interacting particles, the distribution of locations is uniform and the distribution of the momenta is the Maxwell-Boltzmann distribution and is equivalent to Boltzmann's entropy, as we'll see later. Arieh Ben-Naim further showed that this equivalence is in the "sense that calculations of entropy **changes** between two *equilibrium states* of an ideal gas, based on this definition agree with the result based on Clausius entropy." In fact, David Layzer even went so far as to call Information, which was defined as the **difference** between Maximum Possible Entropy and Actual Entropy, the Arrow of Time.

Put another way, the rarer the message, the greater the information. The only caveat I'd add is to not extrapolate our idea of information to what Hartley called psychological aspects of information. As Mark Twain famously said, *"We should be careful to get out of an experience only the wisdom that is in it and stop there."*

1.9.5 Data → Information → Knowledge Revisited

We've previously talked about finding different representations of data and how we could translate from one representation to another with no loss of information. Now we can see why: we can encode any message into binary digits with no loss of information as defined above as long as the probabilities (or frequencies) of the symbols remains the same. The most impactful aspect of Shannon's seminal work consists in the implications of his simple formulation.

Digitizing information, converting it to a binary digit representation as a sequence of 0's and 1's, allows us to transmit messages without degradation by amplifying it using readers and amplifiers, also known as regenerative repeaters, instead of simple amplifiers.[28] Not only did Shannon find an approach to quantify information but he was also able to find the limits on the storage and transmission of that information. Shannon was thus able to explain the fundamental bounds on signal processing and communication operations such as data compression, including explaining why languages like English have to contain a certain amount of redundancy!

Earlier, we also saw that we can convert our observations of the physical world into data by finding a suitable *representation* for them. Giving the data a *context* of some sort *transformed* it into information. So how does Shannon's Information relate to the framework we developed in the last chapter?

For example, if we go back to the 3-symbol or 3-state system of HIGH, NO, and LOW, the data could be the observations of the symbols as they come down the wire. After observing a lot of symbols over a long time, we can transform those observations into tables sorted by each of the three symbols. Then, the observed frequencies for each of the three symbols would give us a sense of the probability for each of the three symbols. This probability, p, would be the **context** for the data and is directly related to the Shannon Information via $h(p)$!

A new kind of context...

The ability to change our representations of data without loss of information also allows us to digitize the message and utilize the full Shannon framework, as well. Once we have that, the **context** is simply the probability of each of the symbols and, hence, the probability of the messages.

So we can, in some sense, think of **information** as **data** that's been given some **context**. If that context is the *probability* of occurrence of the messages or the symbols that constitute the messages, we end up with *Shannon's Information measure*. If that context is some *logic-based* reasoning system, we

---

[27] Since the probability of two events occurring together is the product of their individual probabilities for independent events, this property also states that the information from both events occurring together (e_1 and e_2) is equal to the information from e_1 plus the information from e_2.

[28] Simple amplifiers will just increase the amplitude of a signal whereas a regenerative repeater will amplify, reshape, retime, and then retransmit a digital signal.

can use it to *argue* for some conclusion based on the evidence; that conclusion is then the information we can use as the basis for creating actionable knowledge.

Data → Information → Knowledge Defined!

In somewhat understated terms, we can then say that **data** is an *organized* sequence of symbols representing ideas or observations where the symbols might have some **value**, which is some meaning in some interpretation. **Information** is data that has some *context* which helps resolve uncertainty or answers a question of some sort and so reflects our prediction about the world. Finally, **knowledge** is an implicit (practical, know-how skills) or explicit (theoretical, know-what facts) understanding of formalized, organized information that can help solve some problem.

1.10 Shannon's Information Entropy

We can use this quantification of information, $h(p)$, to find the **average information per symbol** in a set of symbols with some *a priori* probabilities [11]. Shannon's information function is symbolized by a lower-case h while Shannon's uncertainty function, or Shannon's entropy, is symbolized by a capital H. If we take the sum of the information totals associated with each symbol, and weight each symbol's information by the probability of observing that symbol, we end up with Equation 1.6, which is called the **Shannon Information Entropy**, for N possible symbols.

$$
\begin{aligned}
H &= Cp_1 h(p_1) + Cp_2 h(p_2) + Cp_3 h(p_3) + \cdots + Cp_{N-1} h(p_{N-1}) + Cp_N h(p_N) \\
&= C \sum_{i=1}^{N} p_i h(p_i) \\
&= -C \sum_{i=1}^{N} p_i \log_2(p_i)
\end{aligned}
\tag{1.6}
$$

Here, we used the capital Greek sigma, Σ, as a shorthand to represent the Sum of numbers from $i = 1$ to $i = N$. If we again set the scaling factor, or choice of unit of measure, as $C = 1$, we end up with:

$$
H = - \sum_{i}^{N} p_i \log_2(p_i)
\tag{1.7}
$$

In this equation, p_i represents the probability of observing the *i*th possible symbol and H is given in units of bits per symbol, as well. This means that the entropy is the average information per symbol. If this is the case, in order for that average information per symbol to be high, the distribution of probabilities will likely have a large number of unlikely events in it. In other words, there is a lot of uncertainty in the distribution and entropy itself can be thought of as a measure of the spreading out of the probabilities. In fact, for a given distribution of states, entropy is maximized when the states are equiprobable and all have the same likelihood.

Alternatively, if we're looking at observing messages, rather than individual symbols, we can think of the probability, p_i, as the probability of the message, m_i, that is taken from the entire message space, or set of messages, M. If the messages are all equally likely, the p_i are all the same and Equation 1.7 reduces to **Hartley's Information Entropy**:[29]

$$H = \log_2 |M| \tag{1.8}$$

In this equation, the $|M|$ is the cardinality of the message space M. As we saw earlier, when base-2 is used for the logarithm, as in Equation 1.7, the unit of information entropy is called either the *bit* or the *Shannon*. If we were to use a different base for the logarithm, the resulting units have a different name. If we set the base to Euler's number e, and thus change the log to ln (or $\log_e$), the unit is called a *nat* (with $1 nat = 1.443 bits$) whereas setting the base to 10, or decimals, results in a unit called *Hartley*, as we saw before.

If we change C, we can have different units entirely as C is also a unit of measure factor. In fact, we'll soon change it to k_B which will allow us to connect our formulation to Thermodynamics. In some formulations, k_B is also set to 1 to make things more convenient. [13]

Shannon's information entropy is defined for a specific context, a specific probability of the symbols, and is equal to the *average amount of Shannon's Information provided by those symbols*. In the above case, we assume that each symbol has the same probability, p.

Shannon's information entropy can thus quantify the information content of a system; the larger the information entropy, the greater the information content calculated on the receiver's end as the unconditional entropy minus the conditional entropy, as we'll see later. In terms of the amount of surprise, we can think of H as an average of the surprise associated with all the possible observations.

We can also think of H as a **measure of the amount of uncertainty** associated with the value of a **random variable** when we only know the distribution of that random variable. We can then use information entropy to define other kinds of information. Just as information entropy is a measure of the amount of information in a single random variable, we can define **mutual information** as a measure of the amount of information that is in common to two different random variables, as we'll see later in Section 10.6.

In fact, Shannon's information entropy, H, can be used to help predict the efficiency limits on any binary encoding for a given set of symbols.[30] It also shows, via Shannon's source coding theorem, that the fundamental limit of the (lossless) encoding or compression of a message is such that a message cannot be compressed to have more than one bit of information, on average, for each bit of the message. In this way, Shannon's information entropy can even provide a lower bound on the most efficient encoding for compressing text in languages like English.

1.10.1 Entropy in Physics

In 1854, physicist Rudolf Clausius was wrestling with a different kind of efficiency, the efficiency of heat engines. A heat engine uses the temperature difference between two heat reservoirs to do work. Heat is the transfer of energy between two bodies which, in this case, are two reservoirs at two different temperatures.[31]

---

[29] If there are $|M|$ messages and each is equally likely, we get probabilities, $p_i = \frac{1}{M}$. This gives $H = -\sum_i^M \frac{1}{M} \log_2(\frac{1}{M}) \Rightarrow -M\frac{1}{M} \log_2(\frac{1}{M}) \Rightarrow -\log_2(\frac{1}{M}) \Rightarrow \log_2(M)$.

[30] For example, we can define efficiency as entropy divided by average number of bits per symbol used in code.

[31] Temperature is the average kinetic energy of the atoms of a physical system and is an intensive property of the system, which means it doesn't depend on how much of the substance you have. Heat, on the other hand, is energy that is transferred from one substance to another and is an extensive property of matter that does depend on how many atoms you have in the system. We'll also discuss work and energy further in Section 1.10.5.

Heat can be thought of as energy in transition, just like work, and involves the transfer of the internal energy, both kinetic and potential, of a system of particles. This heat energy is transferred via conduction, convection, and radiation and, in a **heat engine**, it's transferred via conduction from the hotter reservoir to the colder reservoir. As it's transferred, some of the heat energy can be used to do work in this full **cycle** of energy transfer from the hotter to colder reservoir. A **heat pump** works the opposite way: it uses work to transfer heat from the colder reservoir to the hotter reservoir.

The efficiency of a heat engine is defined to be the ratio of work done over input heat and tells us how much of the input energy ends up doing useful work. Maximum efficiency can be achieved when there are no losses to friction or other effects. This implies that the processes are reversible; if energy is lost to friction then the process is irreversible.

A Carnot engine is an idealized engine that uses this most efficient heat engine cycle, called the Carnot cycle; the Carnot engine is idealized because it has to be perfectly reversible and not have any losses to frictional effects, etc. All other engines are non-reversible and have a lower efficiency than this maximum.

Clausius characterized this thermodynamic irreversibility by defining a thermodynamic quantity that depends on the size of heat energy, Q, and temperature, T, involved in a heat transfer. He called this quantity **entropy**, S, after the Greek word, entropía, which means "in transformation," and defined the *change* in entropy (ΔS) to be:

$$\Delta S \geq \frac{\Delta Q}{T} \Rightarrow \frac{Heat}{Temperature} \tag{1.9}$$

The inequality, the **Clausius Thermodynamic Entropy**, becomes an equality only for a reversible process whereas, for an irreversible process, it is always the inequality. So, for an irreversible process, the entropy always increases and the change in entropy is positive. This implies that the total entropy of the universe always increases and is often called the Second Law of Thermodynamics.

Statistical Physics and Entropy

There is a strong connection between probability and thermodynamic entropy. Thermodynamic systems can be described either from a microscopic or macroscopic perspective. You can describe the *state* of a system from a microscopic perspective as its **microstate**, which is determined by the position and velocity of every particle in the system.

The **macrostate**, on the other hand, describes the state of a system using macroscopic properties like temperature, pressure, and volume of the set of particles in the system. All of these macroscopic properties are measurable but only give partial information about the system unlike the microstate, which gives complete information about the system of particles.

In 1877, the brilliant physicist Ludwig Eduard Boltzmann used atomic theory to define the entropy of a system of gases. He started by assuming that all microstates are equally likely where each microstate was a specific state for each of the particles of that system. Every time any particle changes its position or its velocity, you end up with a new microstate.

Castles in the air...

One way to think of this might be with a system made out of Lego's. Let's say you have a few thousand tiny little Lego's and you use them to build a really ornate castle. The outside of your castle consists of about 150 Lego's and all the rest go on the inside, making up the structure and volume of the castle. You can then think of the castle as seen from the outside as the **macrostate**: you can measure how tall it is and how much it goes around, for example. The exact layout of each and every Lego, including the ones that are hidden on the inside of the castle, is a description of one **microstate**. If you move even one Lego from inside the tower to inside the moat, you've changed to a brand new microstate. Just as with the physical case, many different microstates can correspond to the same macrostate. For example, if I move around the Lego's that are inside the tower, every move determines a different microstate but the macrostate, how the tower looks from the outside, might be unchanged.

In fact, given the inordinately large number of microstates, there will usually be a huge number of microstates that correspond to a particular macrostate with specific values of temperature, pressure, volume, etc.[32] So for a system with N different possible microstates consistent with some given macrostate, the individual probability for each equally likely microstate would be $p = \frac{1}{N}$. The entropy of a statistical thermodynamic system, called **Boltzmann's Thermodynamic Entropy**, can then be shown to be:

$$S = k_B \ln N \tag{1.10}$$

Another physicist, J. Willard Gibbs, came up with a formulation of the entropy in terms of the probability of each of the microstates as:

$$S = -k_B \sum_{i}^{N} p_i \ln p_i \tag{1.11}$$

The formulation in Equation 1.11, called **Gibbs' Thermodynamic Entropy**, is analogous to Shannon's Information Entropy in Equation 1.7. As we saw with Shannon's Information Entropy, if all the microstates are equally likely, you end up with Equation 1.10, just as the equally likely messages

---

[32]More than one microstate can correspond to a specific macrostate; the microstates are continuous and so you partition phase space into cells where each cell is considered to be a microstate, thus making them discrete and countable.

for Shannon's Information Entropy in Equation 1.7 gave us Hartley's Information Entropy in Equation 1.8![33]

The constant k_B in both of these equations is known as Boltzmann's constant and has units of heat capacity, just like classical entropy, as the logarithm itself is unitless. In fact, Gibb's Entropy is equal to the classical entropy calculated for heat engines by Clausius, $\Delta S = \frac{\Delta Q}{T}$, as shown by E.T. Jaynes [14]:

$$S = -k_B \sum_i^N p_i \ln p_i = \frac{\delta Q}{T} = \frac{Heat}{Temperature} \tag{1.12}$$

Unpredictability and Life, The Universe, and Everything...

In a way, you can think of **Shannon's Information Entropy** as a measure of *unpredictability* or **uncertainty** about a system. In fact, the most important consequence of Shannon's formulation of information was to show that what we had been calling entropy in thermodynamics or statistical mechanics or communication channels could be *generalized well beyond these fields*. Instead, that general concept could apply to **any** context where you can define probabilities for that system.[13]

Although we call this quantitative measure "information", remember that our "information" is stripped of all semantic meaning! It's essentially a mathematical *model* of some aspect of a system which we can then use to make **predictions** about the system. If these predictions are borne out, then we usually conclude that the mathematical model is very likely to describe the underlying physical reality and so "describes" something about the universe.

But really, concepts like energy, entropy, and information are all **abstractions**. As Feynman might say, they're **bookkeeping tools**: just a **bunch of numbers** we use to characterize some system, like we see in Section 10.6.2. Even force, mass, particles, waves, etc., at the fundamental level, are abstractions or **mathematical models**. These models have a collection of numbers associated with them, along with some rules for the model to follow. In other words, **Numbers + Rules About Those Numbers = Physical Theories**, which we use to predict various aspects of the world and how its components will behave.

1.10.2   Information Entropy and Physical Entropy

So where does all this get us? Well, so far, as shown by Jaynes, the classical entropy, Clausius' Thermodynanic Entropy, is related to a probabilistic description of the microstates of a system in Gibbs' Thermodynamic Entropy. This, in turn, has a formulation that looks just like the general formulation of Shannon's Information Entropy in Equation 1.6, where that pesky scaling factor or choice of unit of measure, C, is set to the Boltzmann factor, k_B, which gives us units of specific heat.

---

[33] You can easily get the Boltzmann entropy, S_B, from the Gibbs entropy, S_G for a system with microstates of probability p_i each, which is: $S_G = -k_B \sum_i^N p_i \ln(p_i)$. In equilibrium, all microstates associated with the equilibrium macrostate are equally likely so, for N equally likely microstates, we get probabilities, $p_i = \frac{1}{N}$. This gives $S_G = -k_B \sum_i^N \frac{1}{N} \ln(\frac{1}{N}) \Rightarrow -k_B N \frac{1}{N} \ln(\frac{1}{N}) \Rightarrow -k_B \ln(\frac{1}{N}) \Rightarrow k_B \ln(N) = S_B$, which is the Boltzmann entropy for a system with N microstates. There is a slight caveat that S_B is for an isolated, micro-canonical (where all microstates are equiprobable) system whereas S_G is for a canoncial system that *can* exchange energy with its environment.

This similarity in the two mathematical formulations is what led John von Neumann to recommend the term entropy for Shannon's measure of the average amount of Shannon's Information. In a personal message, Shannon, who had been struggling with finding a meaningful name for his new construction, was told by von Neumann to not call it **uncertainty**. He instead recommended:

You should call it entropy, for two reasons: In the first place your uncertainty function has been used in statistical mechanics under that name, so it already has a name. In the second place, and more important, nobody knows what entropy really is, so in a debate you will always have the advantage.

This famous anecdote was said to have occurred in 1940 at Princeton's Institute for Advanced Study and you can read various amusing summaries of this anecdote online.[34] But von Neumann might have had a deeper motivation for the nomenclature as he had already formulated his own version of Quantum Entropy in 1932!

Jaynes saw this connection as being more fundamental and went even further to suggest that Thermodynamic Entropy can be seen as an actual *application* of Shannon's Information Theory [15]. He was one of the first to realize that entropy essentially quantifies the amount of information about the *micro*state that we lose when we monitor the system *macro*scopically.

Another way to think about this is with the Lego's Castle analogy. In that analogy, we imagined that the castle's external appearance determined its macrostate and the detailed internal layout of each of the Lego's determined a single microstate. If you were to observe just the external macrostate, say a specific configuration of the castle's towers and moats, you wouldn't know exactly which internal Lego's were placed where.

Based on just the currently known macrostate of the castle system, the amount of information that's not available is related to knowing which particular microstate, out of the many different *micro*states that correspond to that same *macro*state, is the actual current microstate of the castle system. For example, the tower could have 10, 50, or 200 Lego's on the inside and the entropy would tell us how many are actually in there.

So Clausius' Thermodynamic Entropy is tied to Gibbs' Statistical Entropy via the missing microstate information. In fact, Shannon's Information Entropy talks about exactly this kind of information in the general sense, without being mired in Thermodynamics via k_B at all!

As it happens, in the Boltzmann formulation entropy, all microstates are considered to be equally likely; thus, the average amount of information is contained in the logarithm of the number of microstates, which is the same as applying Shannon's Information Entropy to equiprobable microstates!

---

[34]For example, you can find several transcripts here: `http://www.eoht.info/page/Neumann-Shannon+anecdote`

This means that thermodynamic entropy as derived by statistical mechanics is proportional, with the constant of proportionality being the Boltzmann constant k_B, to the amount of Shannon Information, $h(p)$, needed to define the aspects of the microstate that we can't define based solely on the macroscopic parameters of classical thermodynamics.

Different Entropy Formulations

INFORMATION ENTROPY

$$\text{Shannon's Entropy:} \quad H_S = -C \sum_{i}^{N} p_i \log_2 p_i$$

$$\text{Hartley Entropy:} \quad H_H = \log_b S$$

(1.13)

THERMODYNAMIC ENTROPY

$$\text{Gibbs' Entropy:} \quad S_G = -k_B \sum_{i}^{N} p_i \ln p_i$$

$$\text{Boltzmann Entropy:} \quad S_B = k_B \ln N$$

This leads to another significant interpretation of entropy as characterized by the second law of thermodynamics, which states that entropy cannot decrease in the universe. We can now think of that as the increasing impossibility of being able to define precisely on a macroscopic level the probabilities that determine the microstate at the microscopic level.

1.10.3 Demons Arise!

Determining what's precisely happening at the microscopic level occupied some of our greatest thinkers, including James Clerk Maxwell. Maxwell specifically examined a thought experiment, or *gedanken experiment* in Einstein's terminology[35], about an imaginary creature in a microscopic system that was designed to try to contradict the Second Law of Thermodynamics about increasing entropy.

The particular system he imagined was a box of gas molecules at a certain temperature, which is related to the average kinetic energy of the molecules. This means that some gas molecules will be moving faster than that average while others will be moving slower than that average. At this point, a wily demon sneaks in and places a little partition in the box, as shown in Figure 1.3.

The particles on either side of the partition will still have the same average kinetic energy or temperature. Now suppose the partition had a tiny door that was controlled by this demon: whenever the demon saw a particle approaching that was moving faster than a certain threshold, he'd open the partition and let it go to the right side of the box. Over time, all the fast moving particles would end up on the right side, which will now have a higher temperature than the left side, which contains all the particles that are moving slower than some threshold.

By forcing an ordering on the particles in the two partitions, the demon not only reduces entropy but also allows for heat to flow from a cold reservoir to a hot reservoir, thus violating all sorts of the

---

[35]Of course, Albert Einstein came after Maxwell and was, in fact, inspired by Maxwell's work.

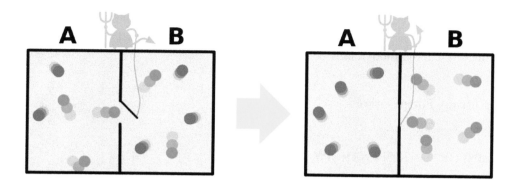

Figure 1.3: Maxwell's Demon at work

various aspects of the Second Law of Thermodynamics! In fact, you could even use the demon's work to create a perpetual motion machine that would take advantage of the temperature differential it creates. So how can we resolve this apparent paradox?

In 1929, Hungarian physicist Leo Szilard demonstrated that Maxwell's *gedanken experiment* did not actually violate the Second Law of Thermodynamics as the demon has to utilize energy in determining whether a particle is fast or slow. In particular, the demon had to have a way of making measurements and then storing and recalling the results. These measurements will increase the entropy by $k_B \ln 2$, which appears in the form of $k_B T \ln 2$ of heat; this increase in entropy will cancel out the entropy decrease!

Maxwell's demon: the link between thermodynamics and information

Leon Brillouin suggested there was no difference between physical entropy and information entropy. The point of connection between physical entropy and information entropy is in the fact that, in order to obtain information about a system, it must be measured. This act of measurement, in turn, increases the physical entropy of the universe by an amount exactly equal to the amount of information that was measured. So he thought of information creating entropy but also of entropy creating information and said:

"Every physical system is incompletely defined. We only know the values of some macroscopic variables, and we are unable to specify the exact positions and velocities of all the molecules contained in a system. We only have scanty, partial information on the system, and most of the information on the detailed structure is missing. Entropy measures the lack of information; it gives us the total amount of missing information on the ultramicroscopic structure of the system."[36]

This connection is exemplified by Maxwell's Demon and how it keeps track of particles: Szilard had said $k_B T \ln 2$ Joules of energy were needed for **getting** information about particles in a 1-particle system; Brillouin argued that **changing** 1 bit of of information requires $k_B T \ln 2$ Joules of energy; Landauer showed that **erasing** 1 bit of information costs $k_B T \ln 2$ Joules of energy.

---

[36]P. Jacquet: http://www.bibnum.education.fr/sites/default/files/Brillouin-analyse-english.pdf

The T comes in because of the relationship between entropy and heat energy, as shown in Equation 1.12. This then says that you need energy in order to acquire information and this is very weird!

While Szilard showed that $k_B T \ln 2$ Joules of energy were needed for acquisition of information in a one-particle system, French physicist Leon Brillouin suggested that **changing** one bit of information requires $k_B T \ln 2$ energy or $k_b \ln 2$ entropy.

Others made this connection even more explicit. Rolf Landauer and Charles Bennett both looked at the connection between information entropy and thermodynamics. Landauer published a paper in 1971 in which he explained that certain computing operations, as carried out by digital computers, necessarily resulted in an increase in entropy because they were not reversible. In particular, he argued that **erasing** 1 bit of information requires $k_B T \ln 2$ Joules of energy. The idea that erasing one bit of information increases physical entropy by $k_B \ln 2$ and generates $k_B T \ln 2$ Joules of heat energy is also known as Landauer's Principle or Landauer's Limit.

1.10.4   Connecting Information Entropy and Thermodynamic Entropy

Suppose you have a system where a particle can be in one of two equally likely states, each with probability $p_i = 0.5$. Initially, the system's Shannon Information Entropy (H) as seen in Equation 1.13 will be:

$$
\begin{aligned}
H_{initial} &= -C\sum_i p_i \ln(p_i) = C\sum_i p_i \ln\left(\frac{1}{p_i}\right) \\
&= C \cdot p_1 \ln\left(\frac{1}{p_1}\right) + C \cdot p_2 \ln\left(\frac{1}{p_2}\right) \\
&= C \cdot 0.5 \cdot \ln\left(\frac{1}{0.5}\right) + C \cdot 0.5 \cdot \ln\left(\frac{1}{0.5}\right) \\
&= \frac{1}{2} \cdot C \cdot \ln(2) + \frac{1}{2} \cdot C \cdot \ln(2)
\end{aligned}
\tag{1.14}
$$

$$
\Rightarrow H_{initial} = C \cdot \ln(2)
$$

We use ln instead of log for convenience since we can convert from one base to any other base by multiplying by an appropriate constant.

Following Shannon's formulation [11], if we set $C = \log_2(e)$,[37] we end up with Shannon's Information Entropy of:

$$
H_{initial} = \log_2(2) \Rightarrow 1 \text{ bit of Shannon Information}
$$

This means the system can, in its initial state, store 1 bit of Shannon Information.

We also saw that Shannon's Information Entropy is exactly the same as Gibbs' Entropy with $C = k_B$, as shown in Equation 1.13. So if we set $C = k_B$ in Equation 1.14 above, we end up with Boltzmann's Thermodynamic Entropy ($S_{initial}$) of:

$$
S_{initial} = k_B \cdot \ln(2)
$$

---

[37]Shannon just set $C = 1$ but we also add in a change of base from base-e to base-2 using a change of base: $\ln(2) = \log_e(2) = \frac{\log_2(2)}{\log_2(e)} \Rightarrow \log_2(2) = \ln(2) \cdot \log_2(e)$

Suppose we check the system after some time and find that the particle is actually in the first state and so it is not in the other state. That means $p_1 = 1$ and $p_2 = 0$. The Shannon Information Entropy for the final state is:

$$
\begin{aligned}
H_{final} &= C \cdot p_1 \ln(\frac{1}{p_1}) + C \cdot p_2 \ln(\frac{1}{p_2}) \\
&= C \cdot 1 \cdot \ln(\frac{1}{1}) + C \cdot 0 \cdot \ln(\frac{1}{0}) \\
&= C \cdot 1 \cdot \ln(1) = C \cdot 1 \cdot 0
\end{aligned}
\tag{1.15}
$$

$$\Rightarrow H_{final} = 0$$

The final state of this system can now store only 0 bits of Shannon Information. This means that the original 1 bit of Shannon Information has been **deleted**. The change in any variable is calculated as $\Delta Variable = Variable_{final} - Variable_{initial}$. So the change in entropies, both Shannon and Boltzmann, for deleting 1 bit of Shannon Information are:

$$
\begin{aligned}
\Delta H &= H_{final} - H_{initial} = 0 - \log_2(2) = -\log_2(2) \Rightarrow \text{Shannon Information Entropy} \\
\Delta S &= S_{final} - S_{initial} = 0 - k_B \ln(2) = -k_B \ln(2) \Rightarrow \text{Boltzmann Physical Entropy}
\end{aligned}
\tag{1.16}
$$

Using Equation 1.9, we see that the amount of heat energy required to delete 1 bit of Shannon Information is:

$$
\begin{aligned}
\Delta S &= \frac{\Delta Q}{T} \\
\Rightarrow \Delta Q &= \Delta S \cdot T \\
\Rightarrow \Delta Q &= -k_B \ln(2) \cdot T \Rightarrow \text{Amount of Heat released upon deletion} \\
&\qquad\qquad\qquad\qquad\qquad \text{of 1 bit of Shannon Information}[38]
\end{aligned}
\tag{1.17}
$$

Thus, any irreversible logical transformation of classical information will require at least $k_B \cdot T \ln(2)$ of heat per bit of Shannon Information; alternatively, the deletion of one bit of Shannon Information will result in heat production of $k_B \cdot T \ln(2)$ Joules, where T is the temperature of the storage medium, and increase in physical entropy of $k_B \ln(2)$. This result is known as Landauer's Princple or Landauer's Limit of energy needed to delete one bit of information and firmly makes the connection between information entropy and physical entropy![39]

---

[38] The negative ΔQ indicates this is exothermic, so it releases that amount of heat when 1 bit of Shannon Information is deleted. This was calculated from the perspective of the $Q_{reservoir}$ rather than Q_{system}. We also used the equal part of the inequality in Equation 1.9 as we can equivalently look at the $Q_{reservoir}$ and $Q_{res} = T\Delta S_{res} \geq -T\Delta S_{sys}$ and $\Delta S = -k_b \ln(2)$. From that perspective, the ΔQ is exothermic and deletion of 1 bit of Shannon Information gives off that amount of heat. Also, Q_{res}, the heat produced in the reservoir, is calculated in the quasistatic limit, which means a long cycle duration.

[39] In fact, Landauer went on to show in 1996 that information itself is physical since it has to be stored in physical systems and information itself, stored in units of bits, has to obey the laws of physics and the erasure of information requires some minimum heat dissipation.

1.10.5 The Universe Itself Is Informational

The implications of these connections is fundamentally staggering. In Section 0.7, we discovered that what was knowable in the universe is, at least so far, also computable. In Section 1.10, we have seen that what is doable in the universe, what the universe does at a most fundamental level, is computable, as well!

We saw that being **computable** meant that something was able to be carried out by a Universal Turing Machine. A Turing machine consists of certain processes, or **effective procedures**, in mathematics that could be carried out by following a set of rules. We looked at this as being something equivalent to:

$$\text{Computation} = \text{Data} + \text{Instructions to Transform that Data} \qquad (1.18)$$

The **data** are representations of fundamental **observations** and transforming them gives the data a **context**, which results in **information**. Information, we found, is a property of a *message* that is intended to be communicated between a system made of a sender and a receiver. It is an abstract idea that is encoded into some carrier and that reflects some **measure of uncertainty** about the system. We found the fundamental unit of information, the **bit**, can be thought of as the atom of communication.

These bits of information, it turns out, are related to physical entropy in thermodynamics and statistical mechanics. **Entropy**, in the physical sense, can be thought of as the *ability to exchange work and heat energy* and is something that increases in spontaneous transformations, as encapsulated in the Second Law of Thermodynamics. **Energy** is the ability to do work. **Work**, in turn, can be thought of as a Force times a Displacement of some sort; e.g., in mechanical work, it's mechanical force times mechanical displacement.

This idea of entropy not only designates the so-called arrow of time but, as physicists like Stephen Hawking and Jacob Bekenstein discovered, the entropy associated with a black hole can be thought to be contained within an imaginary spherical shell around that black hole. As the black hole's entropy increases, they found it did something strange: instead of increasing with the 3-d volume of the sphere, it increases with the black hole's 2-d surface area!

By studying the entropy, or information content of black holes, we've learned something about the information content of the universe itself. There is a finite amount of information that you need to describe everything that is going on in the universe.

We know how much information can fit inside a black hole and we've learned how much information a black hole carries. It turns out that information cannot get lost. We also know we can convert everything in the universe into a black hole and it would be finite since we could compress all information in the universe into that black hole. This information would record every single thing about the universe: information about every single microstate of every single system in the universe.

As physicist Raphael Bousso found, this number is about 10^{123} bits. This is the bound on information in the universe. In fact, following the holographic principle, the entire universe can be seen as two-dimensional information on the cosmological horizon!

Since entropy is so fundamental in the universe, it turns out that the universe itself is informational at its most elementary level. As we saw in the previous chapter, we manipulate this information in our computational solutions but we only deal with finite problems that are computable in the physical universe (in physics but not all of mathematics, in general).

So in a very real sense, we can then think of the universe itself as being computational! Instead of computation for Turing machines as we saw in Equation 1.18, we can think of computation in the

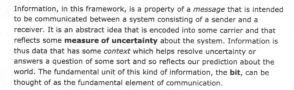

Data To Information

Fundamental science is about making falsifiable *predictions* that are verified by experiment. We start with observations of nature; giving these *raw facts* some *structure* <u>transforms</u> *values* into **data**. Then, giving some *context* to that data, or reaching some *conclusion* with that data, gives us **information**. That information reflects our *prediction* about the world.

Shannon's Information

In Shannon's Information framework, data can be thought of as an *organized* sequence of symbols representing ideas or observations where the symbols might have some *value*, which is some meaning in some interpretation. If the context that <u>transforms</u> data into information is the **probability** of occurrence of the messages or the symbols that constitute the messages, we end up with **Shannon's Information measure**. We can then transform one representation of data to another as Shannon's Information framework allows us to encode any message into binary digits with no loss of information as long as the probabilities, or frequencies, of the symbols remains the same.

Information, in this framework, is a property of a *message* that is intended to be communicated between a system consisting of a sender and a receiver. It is an abstract idea that is encoded into some carrier and that reflects some **measure of uncertainty** about the system. Information is thus data that has some *context* which helps resolve uncertainty or answers a question of some sort and so reflects our prediction about the world. The fundamental unit of this kind of information, the **bit**, can be thought of as the fundamental element of communication.

Information to Knowledge

More generally, we can organize information into a knowledge base, a repository of interlinked entities organized using a semantic model with constraint rules, and then use some logic-based reasoning to derive a *decision* about the future, which is our *actionable* **knowledge** that we can subsequently falsify. Knowledge is thus an implicit (practical, know-how skills) or explicit (theoretical, know-what facts) understanding of formalized, organized information that can help solve some problem.

Computational Transformations

Computation is the process by which we <u>transform</u> data into information and then into knowledge. *Computable*, in this context, means that such transformations can be carried out by a Universal Turing Machine. A Turing machine consists of certain processes, or *effective procedures*, in mathematics that could be carried out by following a set of rules.

A Computational Universe

Computing with these bits of information, it turns out, is related to physical entropy in thermodynamics and statistical mechanics. **Entropy**, in the physical sense, can be thought of as the *ability to exchange, or transform, work and heat energy* and is something that increases in spontaneous transformations, as encapsulated in the Second Law of Thermodynamics. **Energy** is the ability to do work and **work**, in turn, can be thought of as a Force times a Displacement of some sort; e.g., in mechanical work, it's mechanical force times mechanical displacement. Since entropy is so fundamental in the universe, we can say the universe itself is informational at its most elementary level and we can then think of the universe as being computational at this basic level.

Figure 1.4: Data to Information to Knowledge: Some essential ideas in the transformation of data to information and knowledge.

physical universe itself as:

$$\text{Computation} = \text{Data} + \text{Algorithms}_{\text{Computing Agent}}$$

$$\hookrightarrow \quad \text{Universe} = \text{States of Particles} + \text{Laws of Motion}_{\text{Particles}}$$

(1.19)

The physical universe is made of particles which have some state. As renowned physicist Leonard Susskind noted, the laws of motion are just the rules for updating the states of particles when you express the state of the system in terms of bits, usually in proportion to their corresponding degrees of freedom. You can then express the complete dynamical information of a system solely in terms of binary bits![40]

---

[40] We can represent the dynamical state of any system by some point in a phase space whose dimension is two times the number of degrees of freedom it has. A **phase space** usually consists of the generalized momentum versus the generalized position of all the particles in the system. It contains all the dynamical information about the system and is usually expressed via the **Hamiltonian** function, which determines the trajectory of the point in phase space and thus encapsulates the complete dynamics of the system.

The phase space is then divided into hypercubes where a representative phase space point can only occupy a single

The brilliant physicist John Archibald Wheeler, who was also Richard Feynman's doctoral advisor, had a penchant for coming up with pithy quotes that keenly capture deep insights about the universe. Not only did he coin descriptive terms like "black hole" and "wormhole" but he's famous for capturing the essence of general relativity succinctly in his saying, *"Spacetime tells matter how to move; matter tells spacetime how to curve."*

Similarly, Wheeler summarized the hints of emerging fields like Digital Physics by saying, *"it from bit"*, which suggests that all material, physical existence actually has an information-theoretic underpinning and that information is the essential aspect of the universe. In other words, *"the universe is made of information; matter and energy are only incidental."* He even went further to postulate,[41]

> "Every it–every particle, every field of force, even the spacetime continuum itself– derives its function, its meaning, its very existence entirely–even if in some contexts indirectly–from the apparatus-elicited answers to yes-or-no questions, binary choices, bits."

Shannon, in a sense, told us that bits could be decoupled from their physical implementation when he developed Shannon Information and Shannon Information Entropy. When Szilard, Landauer, et al., looked at the physical limits of number crunching, they found that computing can be thermodynamically reversible and the physics had to be put back in. Interestingly, some of the biggest names in physics and computing, including such luminaries as Richard Feynman, John Wheeler, Freeman Dyson, Konrad Zuse, Rolf Landauer, Paul Benioff, etc., met at the Endicott House in 1981 for the first Physics of Computation Conference and worked on such ideas as the physical limits of computation.

In fact, some of the questions that came out of it prompted computer scientists to look at physics: "How carefully should computer scientists listen to nature if they want to use its resources for computing?" as well as prompting physicists to look at computation: "And can physicists gain any significant insights by looking at physical processes as a kind of ongoing computation?" Feynman's keynote, Simulating Physics with Computers, even proposed a new device based on quantum mechanics, a quantum computer. But his perspective on computation, as expressed near the end of his keynote speech, might best summarize the need for computational thinking, as well:

> "...[T]he discovery of computers and the thinking about computers has turned out to be extremely useful in many branches of human reasoning. ... And all I was doing was hoping that the computer-type of thinking would give us some new ideas."

---

hypercube. This allows us to represent the entire dynamical information of the physical system in terms of a string of binary bits as, at each time step, the point will either be (represented by a 1) or not be (represented by a 0) in a particular hypercube. Thus the entire information contained in a physical system is simply the number of yes/no questions needed to fully specify the system in phase space. Finally, since phase space acts like an incompressible fluid, information in classical physics is always conserved. In fact, the laws of physics then consist entirely of only deterministic state changes as non-deterministic state changes would violate unitarity (a system having a unique future point and a unique past point) since all physical systems are reversible.

[41] The first quote is from Wheeler's famous paper "Information, Physics, Quantum: The Search for Links." Please see the following Scientific American article for more of the quotes: https://www.scientificamerican.com/article/pioneering-physicist-john-wheeler-dies/

2. Computational Problem Solving

> *When I am working on a problem I never think about beauty. I only think about how to solve the problem. But when I have finished, if the solution is not beautiful, I know it is wrong.*
> – R. Buckminster Fuller[1]

2.1 What Is a Model?

Our adventure started off by trying to predict whether or not we would need a jacket when we rushed off to campus. If you recall, we even went so far as recruiting our friends to embed sensors all over campus so we could stay comfy and cozy if we happened to venture out into the cold.

We then recorded temperature values and GPS locations at each of those sensors. As you start to examine the patterns and trends in the data, you might wonder if there are other values you should record from these sensors.

For example, should you keep track of the colour of the sensors? Some sensors might be yellow while others might be black. Knowing a little bit about black-body radiation, you know that a black-body is a perfect emitter <u>and</u> absorber of light.[2]   That means the ambient temperature around the black sensors will be ever-so-slightly higher than the ambient temperature around the yellow sensors. Should we account for this?

---

[1] At the risk of being presumptuous, I might have suggested changing the *wrong* to *incomplete*. But you can see the original quote here: https://simple.wikiquote.org/wiki/Richard_Buckminster_Fuller

[2] This is why people in the desert can get away with wearing black clothes; the black clothes will absorb all the incident radiation on the outside part *and* the heat radiated from the body on the inside part. If there are sufficient layers between the outer part and the body, the inner black layers can absorb your body heat and radiate it away to the wind so you can stay nice and cool in a very hot environment. In addition, thick black clothing is also slightly better at blocking UV radiation.

I don't know, it depends. If the problem you're tackling demands that level of *precision*, you'll have to account for it in your *model*. If the problem, on the other hand, is only concerned with nice, round temperature values, you can safely ignore any contributions to the ambient temperature by the darker coloured sensors.

Accuracy vs Precision

Let's say you're checking to see if a group of possible values matches some specific value. **Accuracy** is a measure of how close those values are to the actual value. So if the group of values you measure is $\{10.0, 11.0, 11.1\}$ and the actual, correct value is 10.003, these values are pretty close to the actual value and are relatively accurate but don't contain the correct number of significant figures.

If, on the other hand, the group of values were $\{78.101, 78.010, 78.111\}$, the values contain the correct number of significant figures and are all very close to each other but none of them are really close to the actual value of 10.003. These values would be **precise** but not accurate. Please see Figure 2.1 for the various permutations.

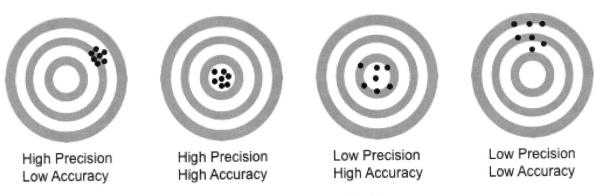

High Precision High Precision Low Precision Low Precision
Low Accuracy High Accuracy High Accuracy Low Accuracy

Figure 2.1: Accuracy vs Precision

2.1.1   Models and Abstractions

This process of not modeling certain details, like the colour of sensors, is called **abstraction**. Abstraction, in one sense, can be thought of as ignoring details that you deem to be unessential.

Suppose your friend, who is new to your campus, asks how to get from the Science Building to the Dining Hall. You might draw them a map which shows the Science Building and the Dining Hall. What else should you include on the map? Should you include the trees and grass? Probably not... but how about the walkways and roads? Depending on whether your friend decides to walk or drive, that would certainly be pertinent.

So in the final map you draw, you will decide to ignore certain details about the real campus and only include those details you deem to be relevant for the problem at hand. This approach of ignoring the non-essential details is the essence of *abstraction* and the map that you make would be the **model** you create of the real-world campus.

"All models are wrong, but some are useful."

That famous quote, attributed to the statistician George E.P. Box, encapsulates the idea of **abstraction**. This is a variation of the saying by the mathematician Norbert Wiener, *"The best material model of a cat is another, or preferably the same, cat."*

Both of these quotes point to the idea that a **model**, whether mathematical or computational or graphical or physical, is an abstraction of some real-world entity or phenomenon. Since a full examination of a real-world entity or phenomenon is usually too complex for us to describe and understand to the highest levels of granularity, we usually settle for solving an easier version of the problem in a *first approximation*.

As such, we place **constraints** on our model and abstract out non-essential details resulting in a simpler, but easier to solve and understand, model. But it's important to remember that all of these models are abstractions and not the actual underlying entity or phenomenon they represent. The model might be useful but it is imperative not to confuse the model for the actual thing.

As we create models and abstract out certain details, we place *constraints* on our model. This constrained model is usually much simpler than the real-world underlying entity or phenomenon, at least in the first approximation. As our initial model becomes increasingly validated, and our confidence in the underlying theory increases, we can start to **relax** some of those constraints and make the model more complex.

For example, in our temperature sensor model, we might start by only recording the temperature values and the GPS locations. Once we find this first-approximation model is nominally good at discerning a trend or pattern in the data, we can start to relax some of the constraints and make a more complex and possibly more precise model. So we could relax the constraint of ignoring the colour of the sensors, for instance. In addition, we might want to start recording the height of the sensors to see if the temperature variations with altitude make a difference or give us a better idea of the temperature distribution or (scalar) field.

The heart of the scientific method is still beating...

As we start to relax more and more of the constraints, the model gets more complex but the problem it solves starts to approach the real-world, underlying entity or phenomenon. Our incremental solutions start to incrementally solve this more complex problem by building on each smaller success. This incremental improvement in our knowledge and models is the heart of the scientific method!

The idea of incremental progress is captured well in a (hopefully funny but strikingly realistic) joke about a trapper who asks a physicist how best to trap a bear. The physicist, after a moment's reflection, responds, "Consider a spherical bear, in simple harmonic motion..." This is (perhaps) funny because a bear obviously is not spherical and doesn't exhibit simple harmonic motion. But, since we know how spherical objects behave in simple harmonic motion quite well, the physicist decides to model the problem similarly as a first approximation. One presumes the bear lived a long, healthy life while the physicist slowly refined the model to the necessary approximation for creating an effective bear trap.

2.2   Data Representations

A computational or mathematical model is often represented by a function of some sort. These models usually have associated inputs and outputs which are encoded in some specific representation. For example, if we're trying to calculate the average temperature across all sensors, we might find it easier to do that calculation using a decimal representation than, say, a binary representation or, even more masochistically, a Roman numeral representation.

The choice of data representation is often very important as it will dictate the particular algorithm we use to solve the problem. If I represent the temperature values in Roman numerals, I might have to do quite a few machinations in order to do simple addition.

Algorithm 2.1: Algorithm for adding $29 + 14 = 43$ using Roman numerals:

$\Rightarrow$ XXIX + XIV = XLIII

1 Convert any subtractive (e.g., IV) to its un-compacted version (i.e., IIII)

   $\Rightarrow$ XXIIIIIIIII + XIIII

2 Concatenate the two values together

   $\Rightarrow$ XXIIIIIIIIIIXIIII

3 Sort the symbols in order from left-to-right with the largest-value symbols on the left

   $\Rightarrow$ XXXIIIIIIIIIIIIII

4 Starting with the right end, combine groups of the same symbols that can make a larger-value and move the single larger symbol to the left

   $\Rightarrow$ XXXXIII

5 Add subtractives back in where possible

   $\Rightarrow$ XLIII

For example, an algorithm for doing addition using a Roman numeral representation of the data is shown in Algorithm 2.1. As you can see, this is a much more complex undertaking than simply saying $29 + 14 = 43$ when we represent the data in the Hindu-Arabic positional numeric system instead of the Roman numeral system.

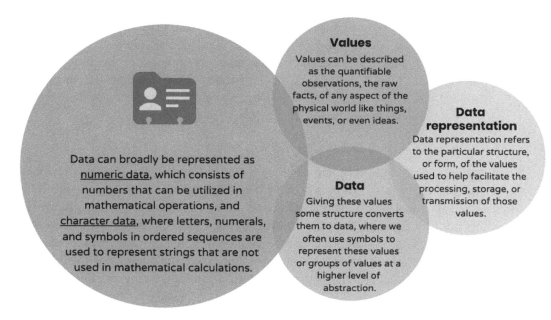

Figure 2.2: Values, Data, and Data Representation: Values, when given a certain context, become data. That context is the data representation, or structure, imposed upon the raw facts.

2.2.1 Data Structures

Just as we saw in Section 1.5.1, Niklaus Wirth said,

$$\text{Data Structures} + \text{Algorithms} = \text{Programs} \tag{2.1}$$

We reinterpreted this as:

$$\text{Representations of Data} + \text{Representations of Algorithmic Procedures} = \text{Computational Solutions} \tag{2.2}$$

Thus, the choice of data representation for a certain problem is intimately connected to the choice of algorithm for solving that problem. As a result, computer scientists spend a great deal of time studying the properties and consequences of different data representations, or **data structures**, as we'll see in a little bit.

From Observations to Data...

As we discussed in Section 0.3, *observations* can be thought of as recording the manifestations of the universe and when these observations are given a structure, these *representations*[3] can be thought of as *data*. Further giving the data a `context` transforms it into information.[4]

2.3 Number Representations

Since Shannon's Information is based on the binary representation, let's explore that number representation in some detail. Let's start by looking at the ordinary decimal system we use daily. The decimal number system we use is the Hindu-Arabic positional numeric system rather than the older Roman number system. A number is made up of one or more digits and each digit can be from $(0-9)$.

2.3.1 Positional Number Representations

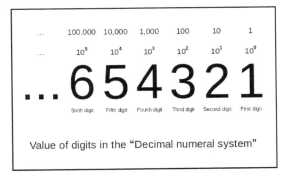
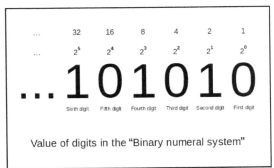

Figure 2.3: Positional Number Sysems

The decimal number system uses positional math where the position of a digit determines the value of the digit in the number, as seen in Figure 2.3. This is very different from the Roman numeral system where each digit has the same value regardless of its position, as we saw in Algorithm 2.1.

---

[3] As mentioned in [16]:

> The key to the interaction between abstract and physical entities in physics is via the representation relation. This is the method by which physical systems are given abstract descriptions: an atom is represented as a wave function, a billiard ball as a point in phase space, a black hole as a metric tensor and so on. That this relation is possible is a prerequisite for physics: without a way of describing objects abstractly, we cannot do science. We have given examples of mathematical representation, but this is not necessary: it can be any abstract description of an object, logical, mathematical or linguistic. Which type of representation has an impact on what sort of physics is possible: if we have a linguistic representation of object weight that is simply "heavy" or "light", then we are able to do much less precise physics than if we use a numerical amount of newtons.

[4] In a sense, you can think of this as when, say, electrons manifest from the electron field. In that case, you can think of the state of the electron as the data and the processing or transformation of the data being carried out by the particles. In this conception, physics can be thought of as the computational processing and transformation of information.

In the base-10 decimal system, the right-most digit, the 1st digit from the right, of any number has a value that's a multiple of $10^0 = 1$; the 2nd digit from the right has a value that's a multiple of $10^1 = 10$; the 3rd digit from the right has a value that's a multiple of $10^2 = 100$; etc.

For example, in the number 321, the 1 is in the 1's place, the 2 is in the 10's place, and the 3 is in the 100's place. When you add the values of all three digits, you end up with the number three hundred twenty-one: 321.

2.3.2 Computational Representations

When we looked at the theoretical Universal Turing Machines (UTM) as an idealized computing agent and mathematical model of computation in Section 0.7.1, we realized that a UTM needed some sort of alphabet, or set of symbols.[5]

This input alphabet can be any set of symbols like $\{a, b, c\}$ or $\{\uparrow, \downarrow\}$ or $\{0, 1, 2, 3, 4, 5, 6, 7, 8, 9\}$. As we saw in Sections 1.9.3 and 1.9.4, it turns out that a binary representation, $\{0, 1\}$, is sufficient to encode any message at all, as pointed out in Section 1.9.5.[6]

You can use this binary system to represent any number and, in fact, *encode any data*. So if we use a binary system with 1's and 0's, we could represent the number 13 using those 1's and 0's as the following string in that base-2 number system: 00001101.

Here, just like in the decimal representation, the right-most digit, the 1st digit from the right, 1, has a value that's a multiple of $2^0 = 1$ and is 1; the 2nd digit from the right, 0, has a value that's a multiple of $2^1 = 2$ and is 0; the 3rd digit from the right, 1, has a value that's a multiple of $2^2 = 4$ and is 4; the 4th digit from the right, 1, has a value that's a multiple of $2^3 = 8$ and is 8. All the other values in this number are 0 so when we add up the values we calculated above, we get $1 + 0 + 4 + 8 = 13$.

We could represent our binary system with $\{0, 1\}$ but we could just as well use any set of symbols since 1's and 0's are also just symbols. So we could represent our binary, base-2 number system with the symbols $\uparrow$ and $\downarrow$ instead, as in $\{\uparrow, \downarrow\}$! We would then represent the number 13 by the following string of up- and down-arrows: $\downarrow\downarrow\downarrow\downarrow\uparrow\uparrow\downarrow\uparrow$.[7]

So depending on the computing agent, we can use any numeric representation that would make the task of computation more efficient. For example, base-10 numbers work great for human computers who happen to have 10 fingers.

Problem 2.1 Some people posit that we use a decimal (base-10) positional system because we have 10 fingers. Suppose you lived instead in the world of The Simpsons, where people only have 8 fingers, rather than 10, as shown in Figure 2.4. What base would they have likely evolved to use? Can you represent the base-10 decimal number 8,357 in a base-Simpsons representation?

2.3.3 Physical Representations

But the digital computers that underly most of the hardware we use today rely on encoding all data as binary digits, in base-2. This works well because, at their core, these digital computers use transistors

---

[5]The UTM also needs a set of states, a transition table from one state to another, and a halting set in addition to an alphabet, which could actually be two different alphabets, one set of symbols for the input and one set of symbols for the tape.

[6]We could, if we wanted, use a unary representation, rather than a binary representation. A unary system is the same as using simple tally marks where a tally mark indicates 1. This is a limited system and to make it a true numeral system, you'd have to add in additional symbols and operators, like no tally mark indicating 0 and a cumbersome approach to multiplication. The binary representation seems to be the lowest-base n-ary number system that can represent numbers in logarithmic, rather than linear, space.

[7]This isn't quite as arbitrary as you might think and we'll see this again when we talk about Quantum Computing and the use of qubits and quantum particles with up- and down-spins, for example.

Figure 2.4: An (8-fingered) Homer Simpson contemplating the existence of (10-fingered) humans

and gates that deal with high and low voltages which we can then label as 1's and 0's to simulate the binary values in computational models.

Hardware, Software, and Firmware

Hardware normally refers to a digital computer which will be the physical computing agent used in our computational solution. The desktop on your desk (for us old fogeys, at least), the notebook on your lap, or the Smartphone/Snapchat/Instagram device that serves as your hub to connect to the world would all be considered hardware. Any of the physical, electronic devices that surround you would fall under this category. Almost all of these electronic devices use Integrated Circuits (IC) that contain billions and billions of transistors and gates to carry out the actual computation. These general ICs are used in components like the Random Access Memory (RAM) units and the microprocessors in the Central Processing Unit (CPU).

Software, on the other hand, is the ordered set of instructions that are realizable by the specific hardware computing agent. This is exactly what we called programs or source code or code in Section 0.7. Software is often stored on some digital medium like a flash drive and is loaded into the physical computer's RAM so that it can be executed by the operating system that controls the CPU on that machine. These programs can be written by anyone, including the operator of the computer, and can be changed and re-loaded and re-executed as many times as desired. Data is also stored on the same digital medium as these software instructions in the von Neumann computer architecture which we'll be discussing in just a bit.

Firmware is semi-permanent software that is not intended to change often as it is software that is embedded in hardware directly at manufacturing time, rather than loaded by a user, for example. The contents of the RAM memory are lost whenever a computer loses power, resulting in a loss of any software that has been loaded into the RAM. Firmware, on the other hand, maintains its state when hardware loses power since it is burned, or flashed, directly on the hardware in Read-Only Memory (ROM). A Field-Programmable Gate Array (FPGA) is similar in that it can be programmed after it has been manufactured and allows users to create their own digital circuits. You can create these circuit designs using some Hardware Description Language (HDL) like Verilog or VHDL.

This is similar to the {HIGH,LOW} 2-symbol language used by Shannon and Hartley, as seen in Section 1.9.3, where a HIGH voltage value is equivalent to a logical 1 and a LOW voltage value is equivalent to a logical 0. The exact values vary depending on the particular kinds of transistors used but usually some range of voltage values like 2.0V to 5.0V is deemed a HIGH voltage (or a logical 1 binary digit) while a voltage value like 0.0V to 0.5V is deemed a LOW voltage (or a logical 0 binary digit).

2.4 Digital Representations

Some computer scientists study hardware, the physical systems that underly the digital machines that surround us. The fundamental processing element of the Integrated Circuits (IC) in digital electronic computers is the **logic gate**, sometimes simply called the gate. A gate is an electronic device that takes one or more binary inputs and produces a single binary output, like Figure 2.6b.

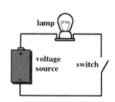

Figure 2.5: A simple electrical switch example

These logic gates are usually made using switches. A **switch** is exactly what you think of intuitively: it's an on/off device that allows current to flow through the circuit when it's closed and that stops all current flow when it's open, as shown in Figure 2.5 where we can see the schematic of a mechanical switch. Multiple switches are combined to make devices like AND gates, OR gates, XOR gates, etc. Examples of two such gates are shown in Figure 2.6.

In Figure 2.6a, electricity flows through this circuit, or AND gate, only if both the first **and** second switches are closed. In Figure 2.6b, electricity flows through this circuit, or OR gate, if *either* the top switch **or** the bottom switch is closed. If we represent an open switch with a 0 and a closed switch with a 1, we can say the OR gate outputs electricity, a 1, if either input is 1 or if both inputs are 1.

There have been many kinds of switches in the past: electromechanical relays, vacuum tubes, gas tubes, etc. Most modern logic gates are built using tiny electronic transistor switches. A **transistor** is a switch with no moving parts, a so-called "solid-state switch", that is composed of different semiconductors in the Complementary Metal-Oxide-Semiconductor (CMOS) approach used to design most digital circuit boards. Modern ICs contain billions of transistors on a single chip and are able to do trillions of operations per second.[8] These ICs are also sometimes called *chips* or *microchips* and

---

[8] You'll probably need a multi-core chip to achieve teraFLOP calculations per second.

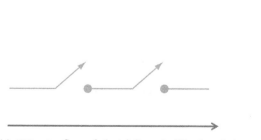

(a) AND gate: flow of electricity only if both switches are closed

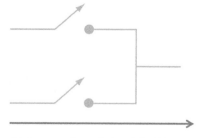

(b) OR gate: flow of electricity if at least one switch is closed

Figure 2.6: AND and OR circuits

multiple chips are connected together on a *circuit board*.

The number of transistors on a single chip, and hence the computing power of these microprocessors, have roughly doubled approximately every two years or so since 1965. This trend is sometimes called Moore's Law but it should more properly be called Moore's Observation as it's not a physical law at all. In fact, we're coming close to the limits of this observed trend as we reach the physical limits of computation.[9]

Boolean vs Binary: Round 1!
Nota bene: Boolean numbers are **not** the same as binary numbers! A binary number can contain any number of binary digits whereas a Boolean number can only contain a single binary digit.

The combination of multiple gates allows a physical implementation of all the binary mathematics that's possible for binary values. The 0 and 1 values of a binary number are represented by the physical position of the on/off switches. This allows us to physically implement all the algorithms that can be described by binary mathematics. In just a bit, we'll meet Boolean Algebra, the branch of mathematics that deals with binary values. Thus, the logic gates in ICs are able to physically implement all aspects of Boolean Algebra!

2.5   Boolean Algebra

George Boole (1815 – 1864) was a deeply religious man who had a mystical experience that motivated him to think about how the mind processes thought. He published *An Investigation of the Laws of Thought* in which he dealt with the basis of Aristotelean Logic and Probabilities by applying symbolic algebra to formal logic. In the introduction, he alluded to these lofty goals:

> *The design of the following treatise is to investigate the fundamental laws of those operations of the mind by which reasoning is performed; to give expression to them in the symbolical language of a Calculus, and upon this foundation to establish the science of Logic ... and, finally, to collect ... some probable intimations concerning the nature and constitution of the human mind.*[10]

Since Aristotelean logic was rooted in syllogisms, which we met in Sections 1.2 and 1.4, Boole decided to tackle such logical constructs using an objective mathematical structure, similar to the framework Descartes had laid for Euclidean geometry by representing geometric ideas as algebraic formulae in which you could manipulate symbols using formal rules.[11] To follow the example syllogism we gave earlier, Boole took the beginning of it, "All men are mortal", and replaced the nouns with variables and the modifiers and verbs with arithmetic operators. These variables, which came to be called Boolean variables, could only have two possible values, two binary values: TRUE or FALSE.

---

[9]Richard Feynman famously addressed this in his 1959 talk entitled, There's Plenty of Room at the Bottom, which also inspired the nascent field of nanotechnology. New approaches in physics and biology are looking for ways past the quantum blocks of further miniaturization.

[10]A very nice summary of these connections is here: `https://a16z.com/2017/03/21/` `logic-philosophy-computer-science-dixon-atlantic/` The one thing I might add to that is the contributions of Leibniz to formal logic and Boolean representations.

[11]This is also similar to what Shannon did for Information by stripping out all semantic content and giving it a mathematical underpinning.

Boole was able to develop a set of variables, operators, and rules for transforming those values that could be applied to the principles of logic and reasoning. We can then express these Boolean operators, like AND, OR, and NOT, using truth tables that use such Boolean variables, variables whose state can only have one of two possible values.

In this way, he derived an entire mathematical framework of logic that relied on only two kinds of values: TRUE and FALSE. He applied these formal laws of algebra to the principles of logic to create the field of Boolean Algebra. Since we can use any two symbols for these two base values, as we saw earlier, we can use symbols like HIGH and LOW or 1's and 0's; if we use the two binary numbers, $\{0, 1\}$, as our two base values, we end up with the mathematics of binary values.

This is exactly what inspired people like Tukey, Hartley, and Shannon, who realized this same Boolean Algebra could be used to analyze the relays, the on/off mechanical electrical switches, used in telephone switching circuits. Boolean Algebra can be used to describe the output state of not just relay-based systems but also the transistor-based ICs used in modern digital computers!

2.5.1 Boolean Algebra and Digital Circuits

The connection between Boolean Algebra and these digital circuits is also rooted in history. When Descartes first defined the formal rules for manipulating symbols representing geometric ideas, it allowed people to reason about abstract ideas without being constrained by their own spatial intuitions and language. This change in language or representation allowed people like Isaac Newton and Gottfried Wilhelm Leibniz to independently discover the calculus in the 17th century.

Leibniz went even further and postulated the development of a new language, called *Characteristica Universalis*, that could represent all possible mathematical and scientific knowledge. He also imagined a machine, called the *Calculus Ratiocinator*, that could use that language to perform logical deductions and settle any philosophical dispute by calculation.

Alan Turing was inspired by ideas like Leibniz's universal characteristics language and logic calculating machines when he started thinking about his mathematical models of computation, the so-called Universal Turing Machines we met in Section 0.7.1. In particular, he was looking at them in the context of the *Entscheidungsproblem* ("Decision Problem") as formulated by David Hilbert in 1928.

In the Entscheidungsproblem, Hilbert posed a challenge that asked if an algorithm existed which could determine whether an arbitrary mathematical statement is true or false. This was part of his larger program to formalize all of mathematics and required:

1. Formulation: Is mathematics complete? All mathematical statements should be written in a precise formal language with well-defined rules
2. Completeness: Is mathematics consistent? There should be a proof that all true mathematical statements can be proved in the formalism (along with Consistency and Conservation)
3. Decidability: Is every statement in mathematics decidable? There should be a clearly formulated procedure that can can definitively establish within a finite time (an algorithm!) the truth or falsehood of any mathematical statement (based on the given axioms)

That last item is the "Decision Problem" and it captured the attention of many famous mathematicians including Alan Turing, Alonzo Church, and Kurt Gödel. In fact, as we saw in Section 0.7.1, Gödel's First Incompleteness Theorem proved that, for any consistent system with a computable set of axioms that is capable of expressing arithmetic, it's possible to construct a proposition that cannot be proved from the given axioms (and neither can its negation). This means that any consistent logical system that encompasses arithmetic necessarily also contains propositions that are true but can't be

Table I. Analogue Between the Calculus of Propositions and the Symbolic Relay Analysis

Symbol	Interpretation in Relay Circuits	Interpretation in the Calculus of Propositions
X	The circuit X	The proposition X
0	The circuit is closed	The proposition is false
1	The circuit is open	The proposition is true
$X + Y$	The series connection of circuits X and Y	The proposition which is true if either X or Y is true
$X\,Y$	The parallel connection of circuits X and Y	The proposition which is true if both X and Y are true
X'	The circuit which is open when X is closed and closed when X is open	The contradictory of proposition X
$=$	The circuits open and close simultaneously	Each proposition implies the other

Figure 2.7: Shannon and Boolean Circuits: Shannon's mapping between symbolic logic and electrical circuits from his 1938 paper.

proven to be so!

The bad news didn't stop there for Hilbert's program: as seen in Section 0.7.1, both Turing and Church showed the answer to the "Decision Problem" was "No," although Church did it using the lambda calculus. Turing proved this result in his 1936 paper entitled, "On Computable Numbers, With an Application to the Entscheidungsproblem," in which he created a mathematical model of an all-purpose computing machine and showed that no such machine could determine whether or not a given proposed conclusion follows from given premises using a formal logical system.[12]

While Turing showed the connection between logic and computing, Claude Shannon was able to show the connection between electronics, logic, and computing, as well! Shannon's 1938 paper, "A Symbolic Analysis of Switching and Relay Circuits," showed how Boole's system of formal logic, a Boolean algebra consisting of True/False values only, could describe the operation of two-valued electrical switching circuits. Remember that Boolean logic, or Boolean algebra, is a form of propositional logic and relied upon just three fundamental operators (AND, OR, and NOT) to perform logic functions.

Shannon first showed that this Boolean algebra, and binary arithmetic, could be used to specify the design of logic circuits using electromechanical relays. He then further showed that arrangements of these relays, in turn, could be used to also solve Boolean algebra problems! This correspondence between the "symbolic study of logic" (Boolean algebra) and the relays and switches in the circuit is shown in Figure 2.7. This meant that any circuit can be represented by a set of equations based in Boolean algebra. This was the first time the logical operation, or layer, of a computing machine was separated from its physical operation, or layer.

As we saw in Section 2.4, the fundamental element of integrated circuits is the logic gate, which is based on an electronic switch (rather than the electromechanical switches and relays of Shannon's time). In fact, today's computer circuits are built upon such electronic gates that operate according to Boolean algebra to determine the value of the output signal. That output value is usually designated as a 1 or 0. These gates can also come together to store information in storage units called *flip-flops*.

---

[12]On an interesting side-note, the so-called Universal Turing Machines showed that the machine (the hardware), the instructions (the program), and the input (the data), were all combined in a single entity and further implied that any computing logic that could be expressed in hardware could also be expressed in software. But putting both the data and programs in the same architecture later came to be known as the von Neumann architecture, as we saw in Section 2.3.3.

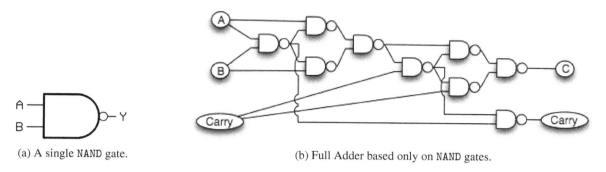

(a) A single NAND gate.   (b) Full Adder based only on NAND gates.

Figure 2.8: Full Adder circuit based only on NAND gates.

Although there are a few basic gates that correspond to the Boolean algebra operators (AND, OR, and NOT), compound gates like the NAND (NOT AND) gate are actually sufficient to build any computer circuit, including ones for arithmetic, memory, and executing instructions.

An example of both a NAND gate and an adder circuit that does arithmetic addition is shown in Figure 2.8. Modern computers usually have an Arithmetic Logic Unit (ALU), a key component of the Central Processing Unit (CPU), that consists of many such adder circuits strung together in order to carry out arbitrarily complex arithmetical operations. In fact, modern computer circuits can contain millions, some even billions, of these simple transistor gates.

2.5.2 Digital Logic Circuits

These simple transistor gates form complex digital logic circuits which come in two varieties: **combinational logic circuits** and **sequential logic circuits**. Combinational logic circuits are simple Boolean circuits whose output signals are a function of only the present input signals.

Sequential logic circuits, on the other hand, utilize flip-flops as their memory elements and use them to affect their final output, as well. Thus, sequential logic circuits depend on both the current input as well as the information from the history of past inputs that are stored in the flip-flops. In a way, we can think of the information stored in these memory elements as the **state** of the digital circuit.

Most complex digital logic circuits contain both combinational logic circuits as well as sequential logic circuits and use them to perform Boolean algebra on both the inputs as well as the stored data.

2.5.3 Theory of Computation

The relationship between Boolean algebra and digital logic circuits is extended in a *model of computation* known as Finite State Machines or **Finite State Automata** (FSA). These FSAs are abstract, mathematical models that are used for designing both digital logic circuits and algorithms. An FSA come in two flavours: a Deterministic Finite State Automaton (DFA) and a Non-Deterministic Finite State Automaton (NFA).

The states that are modeled in FSAs depend upon the system that's being examined. In essence, a **state** can be any well-defined condition that characterizes the system at some point in time. When dealing with abstract mathematical automata, we can delineate a finite set of states that are valid conditions for an arbitrary, abstract system; each of these states can be represented either as a separate function or as the set of values for one or more variables associated with the system.

Thus, a DFA is defined by a finite set of states, which are used to determine both the *initial* state, as well as the final *output*, or accepted, set of states of the system represented by the DFA. The DFA is controlled by an *input* set of symbols, called the *alphabet*, and also has a *transition function* that determines the next state based on both the current state and the input symbol. Although the DFA can only transition to a single, unique state each time it reads an input symbol, the NFA can transition to multiple states at once and does not require an input symbol to make a state transition. All NFAs can be converted back to a DFA, albeit with more states (sometimes, exponentially more states).

DFAs are also used in **formal language theory** where they help determine a valid language given the rules of the language, or **grammar**. In this context, we can think of a **language** as being made of some set of **strings**. The strings, in turn, are composed of some sequence of **symbols** that come from an **alphabet**, a set of symbols defined for that language. These strings are combined via some grammar for that language which consists of both a lexicon and a set of rules for creating valid *sentences*. The **rules** of the grammar describe the allowed ways to construct strings and valid strings are called **words** in that language. The **lexicon**, or *vocabulary*, of the language is made up of a set of pairs in which each pair has a word and a **category**; the category, in this case, is like the part of speech (e.g., noun phrase, verb phrase, adjective, etc.).

There are many different kinds of grammars and there is a corresponding kind of FSA for each of them. For example, a **context-free grammar**, one in which all the production rules only have a single, non-terminal symbol on the left hand side of each production, is recognized by a PushDown Automata (PDA). The set of all strings accepted by some DFA defines a **regular language**.

In fact, a Turing Machine can be considered to be a generalization of the DFA such that it includes a set of tape symbols, including the empty symbol, and it can also change the symbol on the tape as part of its transitions, in effect gaining a *memory*. A PDA is basically a FSA with a memory but it is less powerful than the general-purpose Turing Machine as it cannot simulate an infinite tape. In fact, because a Turing Machine helps define what is computable, an FSA and its various derivative automata can therefore also model computation in general.

In particular, since computation itself is a process, which can be modeled as a function as we saw in Sections 0.5 and 1.4, we can characterize any *model of computation* as the process by which some of set of inputs are transformed or mapped into some set of outputs using a particular algorithm. The **Theory of Computation** deals with such models of computation and how they can be used to compute some set of outputs efficiently. Thus, the theory of Computation deals with the theory of **Computability** (what is computable in the universe and what is uncomputable?), the theory of **Computational Complexity** (if we can compute something, can we do so efficiently?), and the theory of **Automata and Language** (what is the model of computation and how can it be used to solve problems using a given algorithm?).

2.6   What Is Information Processing?

Regardless of the particular model of computation or the data representation, the input and output contain a certain amount of "information", where I've put it in quotes to indicate a more generic meaning than Shannon's Information.[13] We can then think of the function or procedure more generically manipulating the information in the input rather than the components of the specific representation used for that input.

When we do this, we can think of computation as the pure transformation of information where the function or procedure processes the information from one form into another. In fact, this is the

---

[13]Since we can encode any discrete message into binary digits with no loss of information, as shown in Section 1.9.5, we can transform data without loss of information from one representation to another as long as the *context*, the probability of the symbols, stays the same.

conclusion we reached earlier in Section 1.5.1 when we said:

$$\text{Data} + \text{Process that Transforms that Data} = \text{Computational Solution} \quad (2.3)$$

The process that transforms the data is just the function or procedure we met earlier in Section 0.5, where we thought of functions as a black-box in functional notation. If we then state this equation in terms of information, we could rewrite it as:

$$\text{Information} + \text{Process that Transforms the Information} = \text{Computational Solution} \quad (2.4)$$

So we can think of computation as finding computational solutions which are composed of some information plus the processes that transform that information in some way. Different computer scientists concentrate on different aspects of this equation; e.g., some might concentrate on the processes that transform the information whereas others might be more concerned with how information flows and is processed or transformed in this computational system.

2.7 What Is Computer Information Systems (CIS)?

This difference in emphasis naturally leads to establishing different sub-fields within computation. Two of the main divisions could be said to be between **Computer Science (CS)** and **Computer Information Systems (CIS)**. We could then, in a sense, claim that Computer Science is mainly concerned with the processes that facilitate the transformations whereas Computer Information Systems is concerned more with the the flow and management of data or information in the system.

CS vs CIS

More generally, we might say that Computer Science deals with data representation and transformation in computational solutions while Computer Information Systems deal with data curation, data flow, and information management in a computational system.

What exactly would constitute an **information system**? It would be any system that:
- delineates the conditions needed for data collection and curation
- helps enable the transformation of Data $\rightarrow$ Information $\rightarrow$ Knowledge
- has the ability to effectively manage both data and information

These services could be provided by manual devices like a pen and paper but, nowadays, they're more likely to be computational systems that include both the hardware (the actual computing machines) and the software (like a DataBase Management System or DBMS), as well as the constraints on those systems as embodied in rules and procedures for a specific system or organization.

In fact, most of these information systems are usually embedded within an organization and so there are many business rules and processes that are encapsulated in them. When we say business rules, in this context, we almost always mean the rules for any large organization, not just a commercial enterprise. So these business rules apply for academic, governmental, and industrial organizations, as well.

Organizations are interested in making good decisions in order to grow their enterprise appropriately. The purpose of an information system is to facilitate good decision-making by ensuring the information, and its underlying data, are managed properly. CIS, in fact, often deals with business aspects of organizations, as well.

Many kinds of data might represent many different kinds of structured observations. As we start to collect the data, we might be able to group some of this data together. A collection of grouped data is likely related in some way and has internal relationships which might prove useful in considering how it could be transformed into information. The latent relationships in such a collection of data can be codified when the data is organized, perhaps in a relational DBMS.

CIS deals with data management and analysis, as well as the use and maintenance of the computational systems that allow for that processing. Maintaining and using the actual information systems and their components is usually encompassed in the field of **Information Technology (IT)**. IT is thus the application of computational systems to business processes.

CS, on the other hand, can be thought of as concentrating more on the computational processes and their implementation rather than the maintenance and use of the components of these computational systems. CS looks at the processes or, following the physical metaphor, how the universe does things. Part of that is the flow of data so there is quite a bit of overlap between CS and CIS. Although there isn't a clear division between these two fields, we can, in general, think of CIS as being more about the flow of data and CS as being more about the processes that transform and process the data.

What about Computational Thinking?

Computational Thinking, on the other hand, is mainly about data and how to think critically about that data and transform it. Thus, Computational Thinking is highly pertinent to all aspects of computation, both CS and CIS.

2.7.1 What Is Software Engineering?

No matter whether you're dealing with Computer Science or Computer Information Systems, the first step in finding a computational solution is to clearly define the problem. In fact, finding the **problem requirements**, and converting them into **problem specifications**, is a clearly defined process in software engineering that is often carried out by a **systems analyst**.

Engineering ideas were incorporated into software development by people like computer scientist Margaret Hamilton in the 1960s. As digital computers and programs became more ubiquitous in business settings, the need to make programs more efficient came to prominence. Since engineering principles proved to be successful in other disciplines, computer scientists decided to apply engineering principles to the development of software which resulted in the sub-field of **Software Engineering**.

Economics often motivates innovation and it's no different in computer science. We'll meet many fundamental aspects of Software Engineering as we dive into the various aspects of the Software Development Life Cycle (SDLC) and the Unified Modeling Language (UML) later on.

2.8 Programming Languages

To recap, all of physics consists of computable functions. Computable functions are those whose output can be calculated using an effective procedure as carried out by an appropriate computing agent. We then saw that if a function is computable, its final value can be computed by a a theoretical Universal Turing Machine, the computing agent. These theoretical machines can be implemented in actual physical devices like the modern digital computer.

Digital computers can be used as our computing agent to process or run or execute the effective procedures, which are then called the **software** instructions or **source code** for the digital computer. Since functions use data, the information in that data can be encoded using a binary representation. The digital computers are built using transistors, which can carry out Boolean Algebra operations as they're based on the on/off binary values of their switches, as well.

Since the computer program is an ordered set of instructions that should be carried out by the digital computer, our computing agent, those instructions have to be translated from the human programming language to binary, the language of the computer's on/off transistor switches. This process of translation is often called **compiling** or **interpreting** and the final binary instructions are called machine code, as opposed to the source code which is written in the human programming language.[14]

All software and data is stored as binary in a computer. In fact, the input data is also encoded as binary for use by a computer. Computation thus involves the manipulation of different representations of data by following some specified instructions or procedures. That same computation can usually be carried out by different equivalent procedures, data representations, and computing agents.

What might not be immediately apparent is that the procedures or instructions encoded in the software programs are represented as text in the appropriate programming language. But this textual content itself can be encoded in any other representation, as well! These representations of the software programs can then be stored together with the representations of the input data in the computer's memory.

The von Neumann Architecture

The von Neumann Architecture, unsurprisingly attributed to the mathematician John von Neumann, described just this design architecture in 1945 when he proposed that a computer should have some space for memory that can store both the data and the instructions that process that data in the same storage space.

Today, any stored-program computer, one which stores the computer program instructions in electronic memory, is said to follow the von Neumann architecture if it cannot fetch both the instruction and the data from the same memory at the same time as they both are stored in the same place and share the same *bus*, or communication pathway.

There are other architectures, like the Harvard architecture, but the von Neumann architecture is by far the most popular in digital computers (analog computers are another matter altogether, of course[15]).

---

[14]We will talk about this process in more detail in the next chapter when we discuss their sub-components like tokenizers and parsers, translation to binary machine language for the logic gates, and then having that data sent back up again.

[15]Analog computers are usually much faster than their digital counterparts and work by representing variables and constants

2.8.1 Programming Language Generations

As we've seen, computer programs are just ordered sets of instructions expressed in some programming language. Each instruction in the computer program is translated from source code into machine code, the binary language of the CPU. Programmers write the source code that is converted by either a compiler or an interpreter into binary instructions that the CPU can then execute. All data is also stored in a computer using binary, as specified in the von Neumann architecture.

Machine code, also called machine language or simply `binary`, is the binary representation of the instructions and is called a *First Generation Language*. Since the 1's and 0's of a binary representation are essentially incomprehensible to a human, scientists developed a higher-level, more abstract and human-friendly, language. That language, a *Second Generation Language*, is called `assembly`, although some might argue its odd mnemonic codes aren't much friendlier than `binary`.

So, as computers and their associated software programs became more ubiquitous and useful in different enterprises, software engineers realized they needed to make the development of computer programs more accessible to people other than those wearing white lab coats with long, complex titles. This led to the development of *Third Generation Languages*, also called **high-level languages**, like Java, C++, Python, etc.

For example, 0010 0001 0000 1000 0000 0000 0000 0001 is an instruction to add 1 in a low-level `binary` language for MIPS ISA while `addi $8, $8, 1` is the same add instruction in an assembly language. But a high level language like Python expresses that instruction much more intuitively as `x = x + 1`.

Scientists and engineers have continued developing higher-level, more abstract programming languages in Fourth and Fifth Generation Languages.[16] *Fourth Generation Languages* are non-procedural languages like query and reporting languages (e.g., SQL) or application generators and decision support systems languages. These languages work on collections of information rather than individual bits and so languages like Python are sometimes also included here.

Finally, some *Fifth Generation Languages* use natural language while other Fifth Generation Languages remove humans from the loop altogether by using constraints given to the program rather than using a human-generated algorithm. This generation of languages would include declarative and logic-based languages like Prolog, as well. Computer scientists are, for the most part, language agnostics and pick whichever programming language is most appropriate for the problem at hand.

2.9 Computational Thinking Defined

But before we implement our solution in a particular programming language, we have to define an algorithmic solution for the problem we're examining. Let's look at how to actually find such a computational solution!

We'll use these steps in evaluating every problem that we meet from here on out. The individual steps will be customized as different problems will require different detailed approaches.

In this approach, we can also think of the Principles as the *Strategy*, the high level concepts needed to find a computational solution; the Ideas can then be seen as the particular *Tactics*, the patterns or methods that are known to work in many different settings; and, finally, the Techniques as the *Tools* that can be used in specific situations. All of these are needed to come up with the eventual computational solution to the problem.

---

with voltage. These quantities can then be manipulated by electronic circuits to perform mathematical operations.

[16]This labelling of programming languages as belonging to different generations was all done retroactively. When people first used `binary` or `assembly`, they didn't do it knowing there were easier, more abstract, representations available!

Computational Thinking Steps

Computational Thinking is an iterative process composed of three stages:

1. **Problem Specification**: analyze the problem and state it precisely, using abstraction, decomposition, and pattern recognition as well as establishing the criteria for solution
2. **Algorithmic Expression**: find a computational solution using appropriate data representations and algorithm design
3. **Solution Implementation & Evaluation**: implement the solution and conduct systematic testing

Details of the Computational Thinking Approach

Let's list the details of the various computational thinking **principles** and the accompanying computer science **ideas** and software engineering **techniques** that can come into play for each of these three steps. Please note, this is just a listing and we'll be talking about all these principles, ideas, and techniques in more detail in the next few chapters.

1. Problem Specification
   - Computational Thinking *Principles*: Problem Analysis and Abstraction
   - Computer Science *Ideas*: Model Development using decomposition and pattern recognition
   - Software Engineering *Techniques*: Problem Requirements, Problem Specifications, UML diagrams, etc.
2. Algorithmic Expression
   - Computational Thinking *Principles*: Computational Problem Solving using Data Representation and Algorithmic Development
   - Computer Science *Ideas*: Data representation via some symbolic system and Algorithmic development to systematically process information using modularity, flow control (including sequential, selection, and iteration), recursion, encapsulation, and parallel computing
   - Software Engineering *Techniques*: Flowcharts, Pseudocode, Data Flow Diagrams, State Diagrams, Class-responsibility-collaboration (CRC) cards for Class Diagrams, Use Cases for Sequence Diagrams, etc.
3. Solution Implementation & Evaluation
   - Computational Thinking *Principles*: Systematic Testing and Generalization
   - Computer Science *Ideas*: Algorithm implementation with analysis of efficiency and performance constraints, debugging, testing for error detection, evaluation metrics to measure correctness of solution, and extending the computational solution to other kinds of problems
   - Software Engineering *Techniques*: Implementation in a Programming Language, Code Reviews, Refactoring, Test Suites using a tool like JUnit for Unit and System Testing, Quality Assurance (QA), etc.

2.9.1 Computational Thinking Skills

The first step of the computational solution, **Problem Specification**, relies upon some essential computational thinking skills. Although computational thinking isn't a formal methodology for reasoning, it does encompass some basic skills that are useful in all fields and disciplines. They constitute a way of reasoning or thinking logically and methodically about solving any problem in any area! These essential skills are also the buzzwords you can put on your résumé or CV so let's delve into an intuitive understanding of the more important ones, especially *decomposition, pattern recognition,* and *abstraction,* as well as its cousin, *generalization.*

Decomposition is simply the idea that you'll likely break a complex problem down into more manageable pieces. If the problem is some complex task, you might break it down into a sequence of simpler sub-tasks. If the problem deals with a complex system, you might break the system down into a bunch of smaller sub-components. For example, if you're faced with writing a large, complex paper, you might choose to tackle it by decomposing the paper into smaller sub-sections and tackling each of those separately.

Pattern recognition is the idea of spotting similarities or trends or regularities of some sort in a problem or some dataset. These patterns that we might identify help us make predictions or find solutions outright. For example, if you're driving on the freeway and you notice cars bunching together in the left lane down the road, you might decide to change into the right lane. Or if you see a consistent trend upward in a stock for a number of months, you might decide to buy some shares in that stock.[17]

Abstraction is the idea, as alluded to earlier, of ignoring what you deem to be unessential details. It allows us to thus *prioritize* information about the system under examination. We can use this idea of abstraction to do things like make *models,* such as the map to represent the campus mentioned before. Another example of abstraction might be creating a summary of a book or movie. We can also **generalize** to form a "big picture" that ignores some of the inessential details.

Generalization like this allows us to identify characteristics that are common across seemingly disparate models, thus allowing us to adapt a solution from one domain to a supposedly unrelated domain. Generalization can help us to *organize* ideas or components, as we do when we classify some animals as vertebrates and others as invertebrates. In addition, being able to identify the general principles that underly the patterns we've identified allows us to generalize patterns and trends into *rules.* These rules, in turn, can directly inform the final *algorithm* we'll use in the second step of constructing the computational solution.

2.9.2 Algorithmic Expression: Computational Problem Solving

The second step of the computational solution, **Algorithmic Expression**, is the heart of computational problem solving. So far we've learned that computer science is the study of *computational processes* and information processes. **Information** is the result of processing **data** by putting it in a particular **context** to reveal its *meaning.* Data are the raw *facts* or observations of nature and **computation** is the manipulation of *data* by some **procedure** carried out by some *computing agent.*

This conversion of Data to Information and then Knowledge can be done via computational problem solving. After defining the problem precisely, it involves these three steps:

- **Data**: structure *raw facts* for evidence-based reasoning
- **Representation**: create a *problem abstraction* that captures the relevant aspects of the system
- **Algorithm**: delineate a *systematic procedure* that solves the problem in a finite amount of time

---

[17] Disclaimer: correlation does not equal causation; even if you spot a pattern, you might want to confirm or validate that prediction with other analyses before actually putting your money where your pattern is.

Algorithmic Expression, Step 2 in the *Computational Thinking Approach* above, can also be called **Computational Problem Solving**.

Computational Problem Solving involves finding an appropriate **representation** of, or context for, the data, and using that representation in an **algorithmic**, step-by-step procedure that solves the problem once the problem is clearly defined.

The contextualization of data can be considered a first approximation of information and the solution transforms the data to information and then actionable knowledge. This can be seen in Figure 2.9, which shows the **information processing** workflow.

One way to think about information is data in some **context**. If that context is the probability of occurrence, we end up with Shannon's Information measure, as discussed in Section 1.9.5. If we put data in the context of some logic-based reasoning structure, we can reach some conclusion based on the evidence; this conclusion becomes our usable information that can form the basis of actionable knowledge. We can also codify this information in some knowledge-based system that is curated using knowledge management techniques.

One way to show a particular problem can be solved is to actually design a solution. This is done by developing an algorithm, a step-by-step procedure for achieving the desired result, using algorithmic thinking. If you can find an algorithm to solve the problem, then it is computable and you're set! But if you cannot find an algorithm to solve it, that doesn't mean the problem is not solvable, as we'll see when we talk about P vs NP problems later on.

Of course, there are some mathematical problems that are not computable. **Formal Analysis** is the process of examining algorithms and problems mathematically, and, as we saw in Section 0.7.1, Gödel's incompleteness theorems says there are some problems in the universe that are not solvable mathematically. In fact, some seemingly simple problems are **uncomputable**, not solvable by any algorithm!

Other problems are solvable but are **intractable**: they would take too much time or require too much memory space in order to solve them in any practical way. Such intractable problems, problems that are too complex to be solved analytically, can be examined **empirically** instead by implementing a system and studying its behaviour.

The majority of the computational problem solving process is spent in the design and analysis of the data representations and final algorithm, which is Step 2 in Section 2.9 above. The actual programming of the algorithmic solution in an appropriate programming language, called **Solution Implementation & Evaluation**, is only the final part, Step 3, of the Computational Thinking approach and what we'll explore in the next chapter!

Figure 2.9: Information Processing Workflow

Strategies for Computational Problem Solving

The best scientists in the world are babies: they observe the world, formulate hypotheses, and constantly test their hypotheses via experimentation. For example, they might start off by seeing a very tempting three-pronged hole in the wall and formulate the hypothesis that sticking your wet finger in that hole will be a lot of fun. After being duly shocked, successful babies modify their hypothesis and no longer stick their fingers in those inviting holes in walls. If you are reading this, congratulations, you were a successful baby, as well.

Over time, we intuit the lessons we learned but often forget the kind of scientific thinking that led us to those initial conclusions. One of the goals in delineating the computational thinking approach is to help re-discover and formalize how we think about solutions so we can generalize it to unseen problems in a systematic manner.

We can then apply that same structured thinking approach to new problems with which we might be wrestling. Along the way, we'll also come up with some strategies we can employ to aid and structure that innovative thinking. One approach to classifying the various problem solving strategies would be dividing them up into the following three categories:

- **Brute Force** Approaches that employ **Ad Hoc** Thinking:

  When we first face a new problem, we can delineate the initial state (the givens) and the final state (the goal) as precisely as possible. Once we have that, we can start to examine the various paths through the problem space that would solve the problem. Often, if the problem is simple enough, we can just take a **brute-force** approach where we do an **exhaustive search** of all the possibilities via *trial-and-error*.

  This kind of **hacking** is often easy to implement and will likely find a solution. But if the problem is sufficiently complex, it can quickly become **intractable**. We can even try a forward or reverse approach: i.e., we can either look for solutions that go from the *givens to the goal* or reverse the process and go from the *goal to the givens*. The *goal to the givens* strategy is most useful either when there are a large number of initial states or when there are a small number of possibilities for the final state.

  For example, if we're trying to solve a maze, we can determine the initial state (the givens) as the starting point of the maze. We can determine the final state (the goal) as the ending point of the maze. Then, we can go from givens to goal by starting at the entrance to the maze and hacking our way through the maze. We could also reverse the process and start at the goal and work our way backwards. This can work great as long as the maze is simple enough but, as soon as it gets sufficiently complex, you'll invariably be lost until the Minotaur ends your adventure. For these more complex problems, we can use more structured approaches that either take a deductive or inductive approach.

- **Deductive** Approaches that employ **Analytical** Thinking:

  Deductive approaches to solution involve laying out the evidence or resources for some problem domain in a logical structure and then examining that structure to determine to which solution it points. These kinds of approaches are often called *analytical* approaches and they can be classified as either **top-down** decomposition or **bottom-up** construction. Detectives and lawyers sometimes employ such deductive approaches; e.g., Sherlock Holmes will often take a bottom-up construction when he's trying to figure out who was the killer whereas Perry Mason will take a top-down approach to trap the killer once he's figured out whodunnit (and how).

  Top down analytical approaches start by defining the problem and the goal and then decomposing the problem into smaller and smaller sub-problems. The assumption is that eventually these sub-problems will be simple enough to solve easily and then re-combine into a final solution for the original problem. In the maze problem, this would be analogous to determining the goal and working your way backward to intermediate goals.

Bottom up approaches, on the other hand, start with the resources or skills that are available to solve a problem and construct a "super-resource" by combining and reusing simpler resources or skills. This requires that we have a very good idea of what resources or skills are available before we embark upon finding a solution. This approach can also be seen in the maze problem where this would be analogous to delineating the skills that are needed to maneuver in a maze; things like going left until you hit a dead-end or being able to go left or right. You can then combine these different skills or resources in the correct combination to make your way to the final goal. We will also see this strategy in the taxi cab problem, which we'll meet when we discuss different distance metrics in later chapters.

- **Inductive** Approaches that employ **Analogical** Thinking:
  Finally, we can also take an inductive approach via reasoning by analogy. This kind of analogical thinking is exemplified by the British economist and philosopher John Stuart Mill's Methods, a set of five patterns of inductive inference for evaluating causal relationships, published in *A System of Logic* in 1843. For our purposes, the methods that are most relevant are the Method of Agreement and the Method of Difference.

  These kinds of methods are used by lawyers when they argue a case by comparing it to other cases from the past which were similar or dissimilar to the current circumstances. In fact, such inductive approaches were also used by Aristotle in his elucidation of categories; today, software engineers use these methods in the modern computational equivalent of **object-oriented** programming (OOP) where you try to find *classes* of *objects* that you can reuse or extend. A class, in the computational sense, specifies the **properties** and **behaviours** of some set of objects that are categorized, or classified, together. We'll examine OOP in much more detail in a bit.

2.10 Problem Space and System State

The computational approach to problem solving depends upon a well-defined problem and a sequence of precise, unambiguous steps (the algorithm) for solving the problem. A well-defined problem specifies the *givens* (which can be the input or the **initial conditions**), the *goals* (also called the outputs), and the *resources* (includes the means or methods required to accomplish the tasks or steps of the algorithm).

A *systems analyst* can clarify and, hopefully, quantify the goals, givens, and resources and also determine the representation of each. As we've seen, the choice of representation can significantly impact the choice of solution, or algorithm. Different representations can have different expressive powers, reveal different features of the problem, or suggest different routes to solution. In computational applications, a mathematical representation or notation sometimes makes the most sense, expressing the problem (and solution) precisely and concisely.

Similarly, the algorithm has to consist of precise, unambiguous steps. An algorithm can sometimes be expressed in a **problem space**, especially when it deals with a mathematical problem. A problem space, in this context, is the *set* of all the states of a system. A specific **state** of the system is a record of the values of all the elements of the problem under examination.

Let's look at the task of making a peanut butter and jelly sandwich once again: the *elements* of the problem in this case might be the bread, peanut butter, jelly, utensils, and whether you want to keep the crust or not. A particular *state* of the PB&J system before you make the sandwich might then consist of:

State_Number	BREAD	PEANUT_BUTTER	JELLY	KNIFE	CRUST
S1	20	700g	600g	clean	no
S2	18	690g	595g	dirty	no

Table 2.1: State Table for PB&J System

- the number of bread slices: 20
- the amount of peanut butter: 700grams
- the amount of jelly: 600grams
- a usable butter knife: clean
- answer to keep the crust? no

After you make the sandwich, the state of the elements might become:
- the number of bread slices: 18
- the amount of peanut butter: 690grams
- the amount of jelly: 595grams
- a usable butter knife: dirty
- answer to keep the crust? no

We can delineate the initial and final states of our PB&J system as shown in Table 2.1. We can thus represent the *initial state* of the PB&J system as:

S1 = [20, 700, 600, clean, no]

and the *end state* as:

S2 = [18, 690, 595, dirty, no]

where each state consists of the following *set*, or *vector*, of *elements*:

[BREAD, PEANUT_BUTTER, JELLY, KNIFE, CRUST]

The problem space would then consist of just these two states, S1 and S2:

{S1, S2}

In general, though, a **problem space** consists of many possible states and a **solution** can be represented as some **path** from the initial state (which represents the givens) to the end state (which represents the goal state). We can often represent the complete **state space** of a problem as a **state space graph**. We can then traverse this graph in a **depth-first** or **breadth-first** manner in order to find the solution to our problem.

We can apply this kind of reasoning not just to making peanut butter and jelly sandwiches but to any general problem, from playing card games to computing the distribution of galaxies. Let's look at the slightly simpler problem of card games next!

Turing Machine Example

As we saw in Section 0.7.1, a Turing Machine is a generic symbol manipulator that has a tape head and a (possibly infinite) tape with squares for symbols.

The tape head can only do a few things:
1. **Read** the symbol on the current square
2. **Write** a symbol to the current square
3. **Move** from one square to an adjacent square (either left or right)
4. **Change** its internal state from one state to another
5. **Halt** when its program, the sequence of instructions, is done

Steps 3 and 4 above are a form of memory for the Turing Machine as they allow it to keep track of what it has just read (Step 3) and what it should do in response to that (Step 4). As we saw earlier, the tape the Turing Machine uses is also a form of memory. The (possibly infinite length) tape consists of a bunch of cells where each cell can either be blank or have some symbol on it. The particular symbol it might have depends on the problem the Turing Machine is trying to solve.

Let's imagine a scenario where we're playing a card game that converts all diamond cards to spade cards. So we might have a segment of the input tape with some diamond cards and, once our Turing Machine is done, that segment of tape should have only spade cards, as seen below:

$$[\diamond, \diamond, \diamond, \diamond, \diamond, \square] \longmapsto [\spadesuit, \spadesuit, \spadesuit, \spadesuit, \spadesuit, \square]$$

So each cell on the Turing Machine tape for this game can only have one of three symbols, where two of them represent two suits from a standard card deck (i.e., only diamonds and spades, we'll ignore the other two suits to simplify the problem somewhat) and the third symbol is a blank (to indicate there is no symbol in that particular cell of the tape).

The possible symbols that can be in a single cell of the tape, in this case, are:
- None ($\square$)
- Diamond ($\diamond$)
- Spade ($\spadesuit$)

We can then represent the different states of a Turing Machine with the following set, or vector, just like in the PB&J system we saw earlier:

[CURRENT_STATE, CURRENT_SYMBOL, MOVE, WRITE, NEXT_STATE]

Let's assume the Turing Machine we want to construct should go through and convert all diamonds to spades. So it should scan through the tape and, when it finds a diamond, it should change it to a spade. When it reaches the end of the current diamond/spade sequence, it should go on to the next diamond/spade sequence.

CURRENT_STATE then refers to one of the possible states of the system which, in this case, are:

- *Check_Suit*: in this state, the tape head checks the current symbol and, if it's a $\diamond$, it over-writes it with a $\spadesuit$, and then goes on to the next state. However, if the current symbol is a $\spadesuit$, then it leaves the symbol alone and instead moves to the right and goes to the Check_Stop state.

- *Check_Stop*: in this state, the tape head checks the current symbol and, if it's a ♠, it moves to the right. However, if the cell was empty (i.e., the symbol is None, □), it switches to the HALT state.

- *HALT*: in this state, the tape head checks the current symbol and, if it's blank (i.e., the symbol is None, □), it moves to the right of the tape and enters the Check_Suit state.

These different states, and how you can transition from one state to another, can be represented in a State Transition Table as shown in Table 2.2.

So if we take the example of a 5-card poker hand that has all diamonds, our input tape might look like so:

$$[\Diamond, \Diamond, \Diamond, \Diamond, \Diamond, \square]$$

Our Turing Machine can then convert all ◇'s to ♠'s using the following **program**, or *sequence of state transitions*, in our Turing Machine:

$$\{S1, S2, S3, S1, S2, S3, S1, S2, S3, S1, S2, S3, S1, S2, S4, S5\}$$

The above program would change the input tape to result in the following:

$$[\spadesuit, \spadesuit, \spadesuit, \spadesuit, \spadesuit, \square]$$

Finally, we can see that our definition of *computable functions* uses this same machinery: i.e., we can then say that some function, $f(x)$, is **computable** if we can construct a Turing Machine, with its input tape initialized to the string x, such that, when it finishes its program, it writes the string $f(x)$ as its output. Since Turing Machines are **general symbol manipulators**, we can use any set of symbols to represent our values; for example, if x and $f(x)$ are integer values, we can represent those integer values as binary strings or decimal strings or really any other consistent representation.

Thus, any function that is computable has a corresponding Turing Machine representation; inversely, there are functions that are **uncomputable** or *unsolvable* as no Turing Machine exists to solve them. Since a Turing Machine is synonymous with the term *algorithm*, we can then say that there are some functions that are not solvable as there is no algorithm for solving those problems!

Number	CURRENT_STATE	CURRENT_SYMBOL	WRITE	MOVE	NEXT_STATE
S1	Check_Suit	Diamond	Spade	No	Check_Suit
S2	Check_Suit	Spade	No	Right	Check_Stop
S3	Check_Stop	Spade	No	Right	Check_Suit
S4	Check_Stop	None	No	No	HALT
S5	HALT	None	No	Right	Check_Suit

Table 2.2: State Transition Table for a simplified Turing Machine to replace all Diamonds with Spades. Each row represents a possible step, or state transition, from the CURRENT_STATE to the NEXT_STATE.

Problem 2.2 Can you trace out the program above to see how it changes each cell? Once you do so, how many operations, or state transitions, are carried out on each input cell, including the final blank cell ($\square$)?

Problem 2.3 Can you come up with a Turing Machine state transition table and its corresponding program that takes the same input tape and converts it to an alternating sequence of diamonds and spades? I.e., your tape should go from the original input to the new output as seen below:

$$[\Diamond, \Diamond, \Diamond, \Diamond, \Diamond, \square] \quad \longmapsto \quad [\Diamond, \spadesuit, \Diamond, \spadesuit, \Diamond, \square]$$

2.11 Computational Thinking in Action

Okay, enough theory, let's look at this in the context of a real problem by revisiting our temperature sensor problem from Section 0.1. Let's see the three steps of Computational Thinking in action.

Step 1: Problem Specification

We started off by first defining the problem: determining if it was cold enough to warrant taking a jacket to school. We then distributed the sensors and started collecting the raw facts, the GPS and temperature values. This involved ignoring things about the sensors like their colour, their height, etc.; this is the process of *abstraction* where we don't model details that we deem to be irrelevant.

The problem abstraction is one of the first steps in defining the problem clearly and stating both the *requirements* and the *specifications*. We'll discuss the difference between the two when we delve into software engineering ideas in more detail. But for now, the problem we finally stated was to ask if we need to wear a jacket when we go to our class this morning.

Step 2: Algorithmic Expression

As a first approximation, we organized the raw facts into a table; by giving the gathered facts this structure, we transformed them into **data**. That data was then transformed into **information** by giving it a context; the particular *context* we gave it was in a logic-based reasoning system that utilized a threshold to *predict* whether it was hot or not.

We then further processed that information into an actionable decision by using this rule-based **knowledge** to decide whether we would need a jacket or not. The decision rule, which used a threshold to decide if a jacket was necessary, is the *procedure*, or *algorithm*, we designed to solve this problem. This computational process and overview is outlined in Figure 2.10.

Step 3: Solution Implementation & Evaluation

Finally, we need to instruct the *computing agent* to calculate the result using the algorithm we designed. We would normally do this by *implementing* the solution instructions in some language that was appropriate for the computing agent. In this case, we were the computing agent and so we gave the data a different representation by plotting the values in a graph which we used to extrapolate a temperature value for 8am.

You could, at this point, ask whether this is the most efficient or feasible way to go about solving the problem. Is your extrapolation justified? Is there an easier way to go about the process rather than the laborious task of gathering temperature values from all over campus using an army of your friends? Could your friends each implement this solution easily using their own friends? How about all the students at all the other universities? Questions like these will help you evaluate your solution and

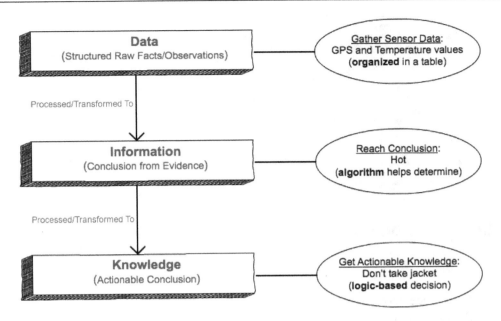

Figure 2.10: Data Processing Workflow for Temperature Problem from Section 0.1

assess how well your algorithm might generalize to this class of problems and whether it would scale to all the other students and universities, as well.

Problem 2.4 You sank my... marble!?

Here's a variation of the more familiar battleship game: suppose I place a single marble in one of 8 boxes. The goal is to find in which box the marble is located! Play this game with a friend twice where you'll employ a simple strategy in the first iteration and a different strategy in the second go at it. The first strategy is to guess random boxes. The second strategy is to ask which half the marble is in.

What happens after 5 times with each strategy?

What would happen if you increased the number of boxes?

Bonus: How about if you increased the number of marbles? Now what about if you increased both?

Problem 2.5 Suppose a computer scientist has discovered a rule of nature when observing nearby stars. The rule deals with a sequence of three numbers, each of which deals with the luminosity of the stars. The first such discovered sequence was:

$$\{3, 9, 81\}$$

Can you guess the rule by proposing three additional sequences, where each sequence also has three numbers that follow your rule? To confirm your rule, please check the footnote and see if you were right![18]

---

[18]The rule was actually just three increasing numbers although you might be forgiven for thinking it was squaring each subsequent number or some other rule. This is just to show that not only can multiple rules apply for a particular sequence of numbers but you also have to consider how you might verify or validate the underlying rules. Can you propose a method or algorithm to help validate when the rule you have conjectured is the correct one or not?

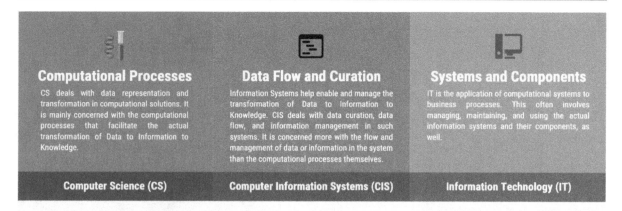

Computational Processes and Computational Systems

Figure 2.11: Difference between Computer Science (CS), Computer Information Systems (CIS), and Information Technology (IT), three of the sub-fields of computation.[19]

• CS deals with data representation and transformation in computational solutions. It is mainly concerned with the computational processes that facilitate the actual transformation of Data to Information to Knowledge. Information Systems help enable and manage the transformation of Data to Information to Knowledge.

• CIS deals with data curation, data flow, and information management in such systems. It is concerned more with the flow and management of data or information in the system than the computational processes themselves. Computational systems include both the hardware (the actual computing machines) and the software (like a DataBase Management System, or DBMS), as well as the constraints on those systems as embodied in rules and procedures for a specific system or organization.

• IT is the application of computational systems to business processes. This often involves managing, maintaining, and using the actual information systems and their components, as well.

---

[19] Other confusing terms are: Information Science, which deals with defining information and its properties, including examinations of information flow and processing, as well as optimizing information storage, accessibility, and usability; Information Theory, which usually refers to a derivative of Shannon's Information Theory; and Informatics, sometimes also confusingly called Information Science, which deals with things like text analytics and knowledge management and representation.

3. Computational Thinking and Structured Programming

And now I see with eye serene
The very pulse of the machine.
– William Wordsworth, "She Was a Phantom of Delight"[1]

3.1 Review of Computation

If you skipped Part I, or zoned out while skimming it, this section is for you. When last we met, we learned about Alan Turing's Universal Machines. This was our first step in trying to understand what it means for something to be **computable**. We found that a specific task can be said to be computable if we can enumerate a *sequence of instructions*, or **algorithm**, that can be carried out by some *computing agent* in order to complete the task.

Turing proposed a theoretical class of machines to serve as computing agents in order to develop a formal, mathematical notion of **computation**. Originally called `a-machines` or `automatic machines`, we now refer to them as Universal Turing Machines or, more simply, Turing Machines. In 1936, Turing showed that his hypothetical mathematical machines could solve *every* mathematical problem as long as there was an algorithm for it. Turing Machines were imagined to be very simple devices which only had a tape head, with some internal controller and memory, and an infinitely long tape on which it could read or write symbols under the control of some **program**, or *ordered set of instructions*.

3.1.1 Modern Digital Computers

All modern digital computers are Turing-complete and can do everything a Turing Machine can do. Modern computers are multi-purpose machines that use programs to accomplish certain tasks. In this

---

[1] Quoted in "VMS Internals and Data Structures", V4.4, when referring to software interrupts.

sense, all modern computers can simply be thought of as machines that are able to store and manipulate information under the control of some changeable program, just like the Turing Machines.

So what is a **changeable program**? Programs are algorithms, the detailed, step-by-step ordered set of instructions that tell a computer exactly what to do. If we change the program, the computer will then change what it does. And if you need to perform two different tasks (e.g., calculating a sum and writing a thesis), you don't need to get two different specialized machines (i.e., a calculator and a typewriter) as you had to in the past. Instead, you can use a general-purpose computer and just change the program to the one that's appropriate for each task. The programs that are run change but the machine stays the same!

Thus, there are three main aspects of modern digital electronic computers:

- Computers are devices for *manipulating information* derived from the input **data**.
- **Programs** are the *instructions* that a computer carries out or executes. These instructions are also called the **algorithm**, which is the *computational solution* to some computable problem.
- Computers operate under the control of a **changeable program**. They follow the *von Neumann architecture* and store both the data and the programs in the same memory space.

3.1.2 Evolution of Computers

These modern digital electronic computers were preceded by many different kinds of mechanical and electromechanical computers. The earliest computers, in fact, weren't machines at all; they were people who did computations. Even as late as the 19th century, you could still find ads in newspapers looking to hire human computers[2] and, in fact, the term persisted until the middle of the 20th century, where it was even applied to the female mathematicians that worked for NASA.

Humans also started to invent devices to help compute the result of complex and arduous calculations. Although many ingenious calculating devices were invented throughout human history, from the *Mesopotamian Abacus* to the Incan *Quipus*[3] to German mathematician Gottfried Wilhelm Leibniz's *Stepped Reckoner*, none of these devices used memory or were capable of operating without human intervention at every step. All this changed when the French merchant Joseph-Marie Jacquard invented the **programmable loom** in 1804. A loom is a device used to make fabric by weaving yarn or thread. A loom would hold the longitudinal warp threads in place so the weaver could interweave the filling threads. Most people used a handloom of some sort until the power loom was invented in the 18th century.

Jacquard invented a device that could be fitted to these power looms to help with the complex and tedious task of manually producing tapestries and patterned fabric. Jacquard's programmable loom could be operated without intervention by a human operator at every step and used *metal punched cards* for memory. These interchangeable metal cards with holes punched in them were used to represent different thread patterns thus allowing for the automatic and reproducible production of intricate woven fabrics. The loom was programmed using a chain of these punched cards where each punched card encoded one row of the overall design. These patterns of holes and non-holes are the same kind of binary representation that can be utilized in Boolean logic!

---

[2]Using the term computer to mean someone who computes dates back to the early 1600s: https://en.wikipedia.org/wiki/Human_computer

[3] In addition to the South American Quipu or *Khipu*, some of which might even have used vines, there were similar knotted string accounting systems used in ancient China and Hawaii. The Chinese of course also had the abacus, as did the Mesoamerican Aztecs who used maize kernels in a version called *Nepohualtzitzin*. Even the Romans used counting boards and the Greeks further developed complex machines like the *Antikythera* mechanism, which might be considered a mechanical analog computer as it used physical gears to carry out astronomical calculations.

A Punchy Historical Detour...

This same idea of using patterns of holes and non-holes was also used to encode musical compositions. As mentioned in Charles Fowler's *The Museum of Music: A History of Mechanical Instruments*, using a binary representation to encode musical information dates back to the 9th century Persian scholars, the Banu Musa. The Banu Musa invented a water organ that used interchangeable cylinders with raised pins on their surface, where the raised pins would represent the on/off states.

Over the years, many musical instruments and automata of various kinds, including musical boxes, clocks, and dolls that were powered by either water or sand or weights or springs or electricity, have used such encoding mechanisms with wooden barrels or perforated metal disks to encode binary information. By the 1670s, organs used wooden barrels with pins to play musical pieces automatically, eventually leading to mechanical organs and player pianos which used sheets perforated with holes to represent music.

In 1725, the French textile worker Basile Bouchon, inspired by such musical machines that were controlled by pegged cylinders, created a device to control a loom using perforated paper. His assistant, Jean-Baptiste Falcon, improved upon this initial invention but Jacques Vaucanson, in 1745, extended it to design the first fully automatic loom. His designs were further extended and perfected by Jacquard in his highly successful loom.

In 1832, the punch cards used by Jacquard also inspired the Russian inventor Semyon Niko-laevich Korsakov to use punched cards for storing arbitrary information as well as allowing for mechanized searches through large information stores, mainly of homeopathic medicines in his examples. You can learn about this fascinating bit of information technology history here: http://history-computer.com/ModernComputer/thinkers/Korsakov.html.

Twenty years after Jacquard, the English mathematician Charles Babbage used the punched-card idea to design his *Difference Engine* in 1822. The Difference Engine was a steam-powered mechanical calculator for automating the computation of polynomial functions, which are known to be good approximations of many useful functions, by using the "method of finite differences" to calculate the polynomial values without doing multiplication. In 1833, Babbage expanded upon the Difference Engine and designed the **Analytical Engine**, a programmable computer that also used metal punched cards for input and printed output on paper.

Although the Difference Engine was a special-purpose calculator, the Analytical Engine was a *general purpose* computer. This general-purpose machine could perform any mathematical operation in theory. The Difference Engine had a built-in sequence of steps which couldn't be modified; the Analytical Engine, on the other hand, enabled a person, eventually called a *programmer*, to modify the sequence of instructions the machine could execute via punched metal cards. Just like in Jacquard's loom, different patterns of holes in the cards would lead to different *mechanical* behaviours. By mechanizing the logical control, Babbage's machine could solve *any* formal problem by carrying out any *mathematical* operation!

Like modern computers, the Analytical Engine contained an arithmetic processing control unit for fetching and executing instructions (called the *mill*), a readable/writeable memory for holding data and programs (called the *store*), and input/output devices (the punched metal cards). It also used *stored programs* to modify its behaviour by modifying two boxes of the punched metal cards where one box was for the data, or variables, while the other box held the sequence of instructions, or program, for the machine. Babbage even imagined maintaining stores, or libraries, of the programs and data which could be reused easily.

In addition, the Analytical Engine even had a conditional branching statement, thus making it Turing complete. This allowed the program, or sequence of instructions, to *branch* to different options depending upon some condition. Not only did this branching allow the possibility of *choosing between alternate actions*, it also allowed the programmer to *repeat* some set of actions, as well.

Although Babbage died before the Analytical Engine could be completed, its innovative design was popularized by the writings of the English mathematician and writer Lady Augusta Ada King-Noel, Countess of Lovelace and daughter of the great English poet, Lord Byron. Her Notes also contained a step-by-step sequence of instructions (an algorithm!) that could be carried out by the machine in order to compute Bernoulli numbers.

The algorithm written in her Notes is considered to be the first computer program and Lady Ada Lovelace is recognized as the world's first programmer, which led to a language, **Ada**, being named in her honour. In fact, despite never having seen the machine actually built, she not only envisioned this kind of machine being able to solve any abstract mathematical problem that was solvable but even being applied to the composition of music, images, and non-mathematical applications by having the instructions and data represent images and sounds instead of numbers!

The next computer developed by the human race used *electromechanical relays*, which are just simple mechanical switches used to control the flow of electricity in circuits, and was invented by the German engineer Konrad Zuse in the 1930s. Although it was also a general-purpose programmable computer, similar to the Analytical Engine, it was originally supposed to use vacuum tubes instead of electromechanical relays. Vacuum tubes can amplify, switch, and modify signals by controlling the flow of electrons without any moving parts.

However, since Zuse didn't have sufficient financial resources living in Germany in World War II, he ended up using electromechanical relays instead. Unfortunately, the Nazis kept his work secret and his models (e.g., the **Z1, Z2, Z3,** etc.) were destroyed during the bombing of Berlin. Other electromechanical relay based computers were built in the US by people like John Atanasoff (eventually leading to the *ABC*, which was not programmable and so not Turing-complete), George Stibitz (the *Model V*, which was programmable), and Howard Aiken (the *Harvard Mark I*, which was also programmable). The Harvard Mark II led to the first computer bug being discovered by Admiral Grace Hopper, as we'll see later on.

The next generation of computers did, however, use vacuum tubes and the first electronic, general-purpose digital computer was the room-sized computer called the **ENIAC** (the Electronic Numerical Integrator and Computer) by the physicist John Mauchley and electrical engineer J. Presper Eckert. The brilliant mathematician Alan Turing helped design the **COLOSSUS** at roughly the same time in England. The mathematician John von Neumann was also involved with the ENIAC and formalized the idea of storing programs in the same memory along with data to help simplify the tedious task of programming via switches and cables.

Of course, both Babbage and Turing had suggested these ideas earlier but von Neumann's insight helped avoid having to unplug and replug hundreds or thousands of wires into boards every time a programmer wanted to perform a different computation. Von Neumann also recommended representing memory in binary and even suggested using the conditional control transfer machine instruction to invoke subprograms by storing the machine's current state in memory.

This architecture, which has come to be called the von Neumann architecture, was used in the ENIAC's successor, *EDVAC*. All modern digital computers, including our current transistor-based computers, use this von Neumann hardware architecture which consists of a Central Processing Unit (CPU), a memory which holds both programs and data, and an input/output system!

3.1.3 What Is a Computer Program?

In modern computers, programs are the **software** that control the **hardware**, the physical machine. The central processing unit (CPU) is the brain of a computer and carries out all the basic operations on the input *data*. At its core, the CPU is made of switches and gates using transistors and does very simple operations like arithmetic operations that test to see if two numbers are equal using the Arithmetic Logic Unit (ALU). The power of a computer derives from its ability to do these simple operations very fast and very accurately.

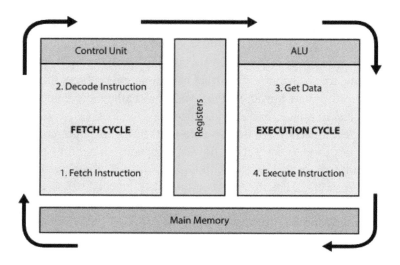

Figure 3.1: The Fetch-Execute Cycle in the CPU consists of Fetching the next Instruction; Decoding that Instruction and Getting the corresponding Data; and finally Executing that Instruction

The CPU can directly access information that is stored in its main memory, as seen in Figure 3.1. The main memory is usually called Random Access Memory (RAM) and is very fast but volatile.[4] Memory itself is divided into cells where each cell can store a small amount of data. Each cell in memory also has a unique address that can be accessed using a bunch of wires called the **address bus**; the address bus is uni-directional and can only carry data from the CPU to the main memory. As we saw in Section 2.8, there is another bus called the **data bus** which carries the data from the CPU to the main memory and vice versa and so is bi-directional. Each wire in the bus can send a high-voltage to represent a 1 and a low-voltage to represent a 0 so that it can transmit binary digits. There is one additional wire, called the **command wire**, that goes from the CPU to the main memory and sets the mode of the memory to either read or write, depending on the operation dictated by the CPU.

Since the RAM itself is made of electrical components, if power to the machine ever goes away, the contents of this main memory are lost. Secondary memory provides greater persistence and allows for more permanent storage on different media like magnetic media (e.g., hard drives, tape drives, etc.), optical media (e.g., CDs, DVDs, etc.), and non-volatile transistor-based semiconductors (e.g., USB

---

[4]In RAM, data can be accessed at random rather than sequentially, as in hard drives. RAM also needs power to keep the data persistent; this is different from Read Only Memory (ROM) which is a non-volatile storage medium.

flash drives). Data can be moved from RAM to secondary memory (and vice versa) via a local, internal bus, as well.

Programs are the instructions that are carried out by the CPU, our computing agent. Since a CPU consists of simple on/off switches, all program instructions are eventually translated to binary, the actual on/off values to be processed by these circuits of switches. The programs are *carried out*, also called **run** or **executed**, by the CPU using the **Fetch-Execute Cycle**. This involves repeating the following steps until the computer is powered off:

- Retrieve, or fetch, the next instruction from memory
- Decode the instruction to see what it represents and Get the corresponding data
- Carry out, or execute, the appropriate action

The instructions that are executed by the CPU constitute the program that's written by the programmer to solve some problem.

3.2 Computational Thinking Basics

The process of creating these programs, the software, is called programming. Programming is a fundamental tool in the computer scientist's toolkit. It's one of the most powerful tools for solving computational problems. Writing these programs, these computational solutions, requires us to think computationally.

Computational thinking can be thought of as involving three steps that are used iteratively to help solve the problem at hand:

1. **Problem Specification**: analyze the problem using abstraction, decomposition, and pattern recognition; state the problem precisely; and establish the criteria for its solution
2. **Algorithmic Expression**: solve the problem using algorithmic thinking, which involves designing an algorithm with an appropriate data representation
3. **Solution Implementation & Evaluation**: implement the algorithmic solution and systematically test it for correctness and efficiency

We'll use this computational thinking approach to help design and implement our computational solutions as programs for computers.

3.3 Minimal Instruction Set

In the end, these programs are **executed**, or carried out, by the CPU at the heart of modern digital computers. Turing's hypothetical machines also showed us that all modern computers have the same power as long as they have the appropriate programming. That means, given sufficient resources of memory and time, every computer can do all the things any other computer can do.

All that power is encapsulated by the simple functionality of a hypothetical Turing Machine[5], which can only do three things:

1. Write or Delete a symbol
2. Move the tape head Left or Right
3. Go to a new state or stay in the same state

---

[5]Nota Bene: we don't actually use Turing Machines as they are only hypothetical machines and do not exist in reality. But a real physical machine like a modern digital computer can do all the things a theoretical Turing Machine can do.

That's it! That's all that a machine needs to be able to do to solve any problem that is solvable by any computer. That means any machine with this kind of *minimal set of operations* can **calculate anything that *is* computable**.[6]

Turing Machines are hypothetical machines so when you have an actual, physical computer, that minimal set of operations increases slightly, depending on the kind of computer with which you're dealing. The set of all operations that the CPU of a physical machine can carry out is called its **instruction set**. The CPU is, in turn, controlled by a program, which is simply the ordered set of instructions needed to solve some problem; all the program's instructions are eventually broken down into combinations of the operations that constitute the CPU's instruction set which are then carried out, or executed, by the CPU.

Just as we have a minimal set of operations for a Turing Machine, it turns out we can define a minimal set of instructions, or **minimal instruction set**, for a real, physical machine, as well. That means *all* computer programs can be written using various combinations of just this minimal set of instructions! The importance of this statement deserves some additional emphasis: all possible programs that could *ever* be created can be written in terms of just this minimal set of instructions. For a specific approach to a certain class of computers, that minimal set of instructions consists of only five instructions. Thus, all computable functions ever can be computed with just these five instructions!

So what are these five instructions and what kind of a computer do you need to utilize them? Suppose you have a CPU with a separate, internal memory space, called a **register**, that can store a single value. Let's call this memory space, or register, the **accumulator**. You could re-write any computer program to instead be written using just the following five instructions.[7] This means that all programs ever written can be reduced to a combination of just these five instructions for this kind of a computer!

1. LOAD A: load data contents at RAM address A into the accumulator
2. STORE A: store the accumulator's data contents to RAM address A
3. INC: increment the accumulator's value
4. DEC: decrement the accumulator's value
5. BRZ X: branch program execution to address X in RAM if the accumulator value is zero

These instructions are in an Assembly language, which is not very intuitive and is thus not used extensively nowadays. Instead, today we tend to use more user-friendly, high-level languages like Python! Most high-level programming languages provide a much richer set of possible instructions that are more abstract and easier for humans to understand. But we can think of the task of programming as the process of expressing a computational solution as a sequence of instructions in a high-level language like Python. Each of those instructions can, in turn, be broken down into smaller and smaller sub-tasks until the individual sub-tasks are simple enough to be expressed as a sequence of instructions in an instruction set that is appropriate for the particular CPU. Let's jump right in and see how we can write programs in Python and run, or execute, them on an actual CPU.

---

[6]As we'll see later when we delve into P and NP problems, not everything knowable is computable.

[7]These would be single-cycle instructions in a Reduced Instruction Set Computer (**RISC**) architecture as opposed a Complex Instruction Set Computer (**CISC**) architecture or the so-called One Instruction Set Computer (**OISC**). Another way to think of these is that CISC processors favour richer functionality in the hardware whereas RISC processors minimize hardware complexity and push more work onto the software. There are also variations on this that can be based on anything from two to eight instructions.

3.4 Getting Started with Python

Let's start off by installing Python and getting the lay of the land in terms of the mechanics of writing a program in Python. Once we get our hands dirty, so to speak, we'll step back and review some of the fundamental ideas of programming like statements, expressions, etc. and even implement the algorithm for calculating the average temperature value we met way back in Section 1.7.

3.4.1 What Is Python and Where Do I Get It?

Python is one of the most popular programming languages today. Not only is it used ubiquitously in applications like data science and machine learning, but it is also used extensively in various pedagogical settings due to its ease of use and low learning curve.

Editors, Interpreters, Debuggers, Oh My!

So what exactly does an Integrated Development Environment (IDE) give you? As you can see in Figure 3.2, which shows an example image of the NetBeans IDE in action, most IDEs give you:

1. **An Editor**: An IDE usually includes a window that behaves like a regular editor, which is just a program that lets you write and edit text (in this case, the text is your source code, your instructions in some programming language like Python).
2. **A Translator**: This translates your instructions, or code (e.g., in Java or Python), into machine language so the CPU can understand and execute them. It usually comes in two flavours: an interpreter or a compiler. An *interpreter* is kind of like an over-eager doggy, always ready to play catch or follow your next instruction, and, as soon as you give it a command, it immediately goes out and does it without waiting to see what the next one might be! Its cousin, a *compiler*, is more like a calm, trained helper dog who patiently waits for all your instructions before carrying them out in a batch.
3. **A Debugger**: When you write code, you're guaranteed to get tons of errors, which are also called bugs. We'll be talking about the various kinds of errors later but, rest assured, the IDE will help you catch some of these errors and remove any bugs from your program using the debugger.

You can install Python on your computer relatively easily but the exact process will vary depending upon whether you're using a Windows, Linux, or MacOS computer. Both Linux and the MacOS should come with Python pre-installed, although its Integrated Development Environment (IDE) likely isn't installed by default. You can download the default IDE from the Python Software Foundation's website at https://www.python.org/downloads/.[8] In this book, we'll only use Python 3.x as opposed to Python 2.7, which is the older version that is still quite ubiquitous and somewhat less secure.

With either version, the IDE for Python gives you three things: an editor, an interpreter, and a debugger. The default IDE included with the Python download is called IDLE. The inventor of Python, Guido van Rossum, was a fan of the comedy troupe, Monty Python, and named the IDE after one of its players, Eric Idle.[9]

---

[8]If you don't want to install anything on your own machine, you can use one of a plethora of online Python interpreters listed here: http://www.sethi.org/tutorials/references_java.shtml#online-compilers

[9]In fact, large parts of early Python development were done under the influence of mass quantities of beer and stroopwafels: https://mail.python.org/pipermail/python-dev/2004-September/049041.html

3.4.2 "Hello World" in Python

If you install the default IDLE IDE, you'll find it looks more like what's shown in Figure 3.3, which shows the Python *shell* in Figure 3.3a and the Python *text editor* in Figure 3.3c, than the more feature-rich NetBeans IDE we saw earlier in Figure 3.2. When you first launch IDLE, you'll see the Python shell, which is essentially an interpreter, like the little doggy that's eagerly waiting for your very next command. You can enter any commands for the Python interpreter at the **prompt**, the three chevrons: >>>.

Let's type the code, or instructions, shown in Listing 3.1 directly at the prompt in the Python interactive shell. Nota bene: when you do type in the code, please make sure you don't type in the prompt (the three chevrons, >>>) and only type in the code, itself: print("Hello World!")

```
>>> print("Hello World!")
```
Listing 3.1: "Hello World!" program for the Python shell

Once you do that, you can press enter and you should see the result, Hello World!, printed out below your command as shown in Figure 3.3b. The interactive shell will execute every instruction as soon as you type it in.

If you'd prefer to have your program run in a batch so that the entire program, all your instructions for the complete computational solution, is run in one go rather than typing-and-running a single instruction at a time, you can instead write your program in *script* mode. In this approach, you can

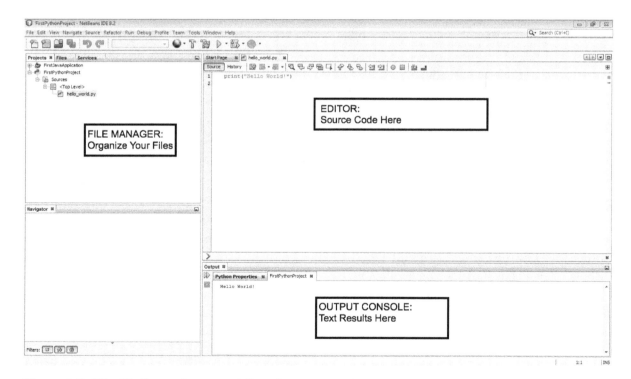

Figure 3.2: The NetBeans Integrated Development Environment (IDE), consisting of an Editor and Output Console. It usually also has a Debugger (not pictured above) and can work with multiple languages, like Python, Java, etc.

type your entire program, also called your **script**, into IDLE's text editor. In order to do so, you can choose File > New File to open a new Text Editor as shown in Figure 3.3c. You can then type in your code there as shown in Listing 3.2. As you no doubt suspect, most programs we write won't consist of a single line of code, or instruction, like these initial sample programs we're using to learn our way around the IDE.

```
1  print("Hello World!")
```
Listing 3.2: "Hello World!" program for the Python Text Editor

You can now save your file anywhere, just be sure to add the .py extension, especially if you're on a Windows system. Once you've got all that squared away, you can run it by choosing Run > Run Module.

Assuming you didn't make any mistakes, you should see the same output, Hello World!, in the Python interactive shell window. If you misspelled something or missed one of the steps above, you likely ended up with a dreaded error!

3.4.3 Error, Error... Does Not Compute!

But, following the sage advice of Douglas Adams, "DON'T PANIC!" Errors, or as they're better known in computer parlance, **bugs**, are a frequent annoyance that can actually prove quite helpful.

Since the ordered set of instructions, or algorithm, which specify your computational solution are designed to be carried out by the digital computer that serves as our computing agent, we have to ensure the instructions are precise enough to translate into an accurate sequence of gate and circuit activations. Since the CPU is just a bunch of simple circuits, any mistakes can wreak havoc with our computational

(a) Python IDLE Shell   (b) Python IDLE Shell with output

(c) Python IDLE Text Editor with "Hello World"

Figure 3.3: Python IDLE Shell and Text Editor

solution. In our context, this means that we might get no answer or, even worse, a wrong answer when we run, or execute, our program. So one of the main tasks that occupies most software engineers is tracking down and fixing these bugs, a process we fondly call **debugging**.

A Buggy History...

In 1947, the mathematician and computer scientist Grace Hopper was working on Harvard's Mark II electromechanical computer when she noticed an error in its execution. Upon examination, she found that a moth had gotten stuck in one of the relays, the electrical switches, inside the machine. Being a good scientist, she dutifully recorded the first bug in a computer program in her research notebook:

Although her notebook, this anecdote, and the remains of that unfortunate moth are now officially in the Smithsonian Museum of American History, the term *bug* has an older history in engineering, dating back to at least the 1880s (in fact, even the actual moth was found by other engineers although it was recorded by Admiral Hopper herself). The term *debugging*, however, seems to have come into prominence starting in this time period.[10]

3.5 Syntax, Semantic, or Logic Errors

Before we can fix these potential errors, we have to figure out what kind of errors we might have. There are three broad kinds of errors we encounter in software development:

1. **Syntax Errors**: these are errors in following the ***rules*** of the language, like misspelling words, forgetting punctuation, etc. In English, a convoluted example would be, "THE dog bit, the mahn." These are usually caught, often rather annoyingly, by the translator (either the compiler or the interpreter) every time you try to run your code. These are also the easiest to correct and often the IDE will even offer to fix them for you.

2. **Semantic Errors**: these are issues with constructing the statements of a language in a ***prohibited*** or improper manner. In English, it might be a typical conversation with Yoda, "Bit me the dog did." In software engineering, they come in two flavours: *dynamic* (e.g., disallowed operations like dividing by 0 or trying to access invalid data like an out of bounds array index) or *static* (e.g., trying to use a variable without assigning it a value).

---

[10]Please see this article: https://www.wired.com/2013/12/googles-doodle-honors-grace-hopper-and-entomology/

3. **Logical Errors**: these occur when the statements are fine but the result is ***incorrect*** or unexpected (e.g., printing the sum when you intended to print the average). The only way to find such errors is by testing. In English, this is what might happen in a journalism class when you might have intended to say, "A dog bit a man" but end up creating the headline, "A man bit a dog." In computing, companies like Microsoft often call these a Beta Release of their software.[11]

These errors can *occur* either at **compile-time** (syntax and static semantic) or at **run-time** (dynamic semantic and logical). Runtime errors are also sometimes referred to as **exceptions** and we'll see later how we can use **exception handling** to take care of such exceptional situations.

The important takeaway in this is to not get frustrated when you see errors. Most errors are syntactical errors so that means the translator is helping you by catching any imprecision in your instructions for the CPU. Not only is that a good thing unto itself but *everyone's* code usually contains some kind of error at first; in fact, the more complex the solution, the greater the likelihood of errors creeping in regardless of who is doing the programming. The toughest errors, as you might well imagine, are the logical errors since the only way to find them is to create an appropriate test. But as the computer scientist Edsger W. Dijkstra famously said:

 Testing shows the presence, not the absence, of bugs.

These bugs can, in fact, be incredibly persistent: some take literally decades to discover as the appropriate test wasn't created or discovered in that amount of time. For example, Bill Joy, co-founder of Sun Microsystems, wrote a program called head that, under a certain set of conditions, would crash but that particular set of conditions went undiscovered for 15 years![12]

3.5.1 Debugging

Once you've identified the bugs, the next step is to get rid of them by debugging them. This isn't an easy undertaking as the sources of the most significant errors aren't usually apparent. The syntactical errors, as we mentioned earlier, are the easiest to find and eliminate since the translator (either the compiler or the interpreter) will usually give you a heads-up on those. If appropriate for your language of choice, the static semantic errors will also be flagged by a compiler. The tough ones are the dynamic semantic and logic errors, both of which are only detectable at run-time.

A lot of languages, like Java, will give you clues about dynamic semantic errors and force you to handle these exceptional situations. But the only way to discover the logical errors is by becoming a bit of a detective yourself. Testing your program will give you clues as to which parts might have logical errors. Then, you can investigate what might have led to the error in your program. You can use the **debugger** that's included in most IDEs, including in IDLE, or you can manually insert statements that output the current *state* of the program in an effort to get a handle on what went awry.

---

[11]In the interest of avoiding any potential lawsuits, please note that this is a PJ (poor joke). On a more serious note, though, static program analysis can also be used to catch some subsets of logic errors.

[12]Please see here for the gory details: https://www.csoonline.com/article/2927441/application-security/ 11-software-bugs-that-took-way-too-long-to-meet-their-maker.html#slide12

One small step...

One of the best software engineering tips might be to make small modifications and check often. That is, as you write your program, make **small changes** each time and run it after making each change so you don't introduce any new errors that you have to track down after typing in 378 lines of code. This technique also serves you well when debugging or trying to *fix your code*: introduce **small corrections** and check to see if they make a positive difference before persisting further in that direction. The essential idea is to make sure the **state** of your program is valid at every step and you have a functional, working program at each step.

3.6 State of a Computational System

In Section 2.5, we saw that we could model any computational system as a *process* which takes some input and computes some desired output. The *state* of a computational system, as we saw in Section 2.5.2, can be specified for a digital circuit as the information stored in its memory elements or for a general mathematical system as the values for one or more of its variables. We also met the idea of a state and its associated variables in Section 1.6.

In our case, this process is some program we might write in a programming language and run on a modern digital computer. As we started to think about programming languages, we saw, in Section 2.5.3, that a formal language has a vocabulary, or lexicon, and a set of grammatical rules for constructing valid sentences, or statements. In the same way, a programming language has a specific vocabulary and a specific grammar for instructing the CPU, the computing agent, how to perform a particular task.

The vocabulary of a programming language consists of some **reserved words**, also called **keywords**, that it understands and a particular syntax for creating and organizing the instructions using those keywords. The program we write is just the specific implementation of our abstract algorithm, the step by step instructions, for solving some computational problem written in that particular programming language.

We can think of the algorithm as a sort of recipe and, just like in a cooking recipe, an algorithm can have variables, corresponding to the ingredients in a recipe, as well as statements, corresponding to the directions in a recipe. The directions in a recipe usually utilize or manipulate the ingredients in the process of transforming the input to the desired output. The *state* of the recipe at any point in time can be represented by the values of the ingredients (e.g., the cake is half-baked).

In the same way, your program can create variables, symbols for representing some data that's stored in the main memory of the computer, which it can utilize or manipulate as it carries out the instruction statements in an algorithm. The values represented by the program's variables at a specific point in time thus constitute the **state** of the program at that time, as well.

3.7 Natural vs Formal Languages

Although the high-level programming languages we use to write our programs can sometimes look very similar to human languages, they are very different. Human languages that evolve without the imposition of any specific design, like English, are called *natural languages*. These differ from *formal languages* which are artificial, invented languages that are designed by people for a specific purpose. For example, chemists might use a specific language to represent chemical shapes and structures. We met some of the rules for formal languages in Section 2.5.3 where we learned that computation can be expressed using programming languages that are designed to follow these same mathematical rules.

Programming languages can broadly fall into two main categories, **imperative** and **declarative**, similar to what we saw in Section 1.6. Imperative programming languages use an explicit sequence of statements to do something or give a command of some sort.

As we saw in Section 1.4.3, statements can be either *declarative* or *imperative*. Declarative statements indicate what we want and what is true. Imperative statements, on the other hand, are either questions or commands. Since we're only dealing with imperative programming languages, as opposed to functional languages which are declarative, our statements issue commands that are carried out, or executed, by the interpreter in Python. An example of a command we used earlier is the `print()` command in Listing 3.2.

Imperative programming languages, like C, C++, Java, etc., can be further classified as:

1. **Structured**: structured programming uses **control flow structures** over goto statements to avoid problems like creating "spaghetti code".
2. **Procedural**: procedural programming is based on the **modular** programming idea of dividing your program into individual elements called *sub-routines*, usually *procedures* or *functions*, named blocks of code with optional inputs and outputs, as seen in Section 7.1.
3. **Object-Oriented**: object-oriented (OO) programming **encapsulates** the *behaviour* and *state* data in an object with the actual computation being carried out by sending *messages* between objects. There is a subtle difference between modular programs and OO programs as modular programs can be purely procedural and rely upon either functions or classes but OO programs use a class-based representation as their primary model, as seen in Section 8.2.

Declarative programming languages, like SQL, Prolog, etc., on the other hand, specify the desired result but don't delineate an explicit procedure for how to compute it, more in line with a calculus than an algebra, for example.[13] We can think of these approaches as consisting of programming commands or mathematical assertions.

Functional programming languages, like Haskell, Ruby, etc., are usually considered a subset of declarative programming languages and are characterized primarily by not having any mutable data. They follow the *no side-effects* approach where the only result of a functional program should be the value that's computed but nothing else should change during the computation, including the variables and the state. One other quick point that might not make sense till we get to the functions chapter in a little bit but most functional programming paradigms also treat functions as "first-class elements," which just means that functions can be treated like variables and can be the values of data structures, or used as arguments, or used within control structures directly.

Although there are significant differences between formal and natural languages they both share some commonalities, as well. For example, they each are composed of **tokens**, which are the basic

---

[13]That might be more in the sense of modern, or abstract, algebra which is concerned with structure whereas calculus is not.

elements of the language. For natural languages, tokens might be the normal words we use when we talk to each other. For languages used in chemistry, they might consist of the chemical elements. For most programming languages, they are usually things like numbers, words, operators, delimiters, etc. As we saw with formal languages, they each also have a certain structure, an allowed syntax, and some sense of semantics, as well.

But formal languages, and programming languages, are distinguished from natural languages in that they cannot deal well with ambiguity. For example, in English, you might understand the phrase, "raise the roof," as an idiom in a social context or a directive in the context of a construction job. Sentences, or statements, in programming languages have to be *unambiguous* and *precise*.

Unlike natural languages, this means that each statement in a formal language has to have a unique meaning regardless of the context. This also helps reduce the *redundancy* in formal languages as compared to natural languages.

So you can't just tell a computer, "Give me a buck!" Computers take things literally and don't understand idioms or metaphors. A computer, upon hearing that sentence, just might try to get you a male deer.[14] Instead, you have to be literal in all instructions sent to the CPU as all it understands is the 1's and 0's of the digital logic circuits that compose its guts.

Talking about our Generations...

As we saw in Section 2.8.1, there are different generations of programming languages. A First-Generation Language is the machine language that is unique for each different kind of CPU and is the only kind of language the computer really understands. Second-Generation Languages are the assembly languages that replace binary digit codes with mnemonic keywords. Third-Generation Languages are the high-level computer languages with syntax and keywords that are almost English-like and designed to be used by people.

These include the languages we'll be studying like Python and Java. We'll use these high-level programming languages to write our programs, the instructions the computer will follow to solve our computational problem. Because these languages are still not completely natural, software engineers often refer to the program as their **code** and the process of writing an algorithm in a programming language is usually called *coding*. In the end, our high-level programs have to be translated to low-level languages like assembly or machine language in order for the CPU to understand them.

3.8 Translating Your Programs

When people speak different languages, there are a couple ways to communicate ideas, other than frantically waving your arms. One approach might be to hire an interpreter, someone that will listen to every sentence you say and immediately translate it to the other person's language. Another approach might be for you to write down all that you want to say and then have someone translate the entire note and give it to the other person. An interpreter immediately translates what's said but it slows down the

---

[14]Thankfully, we're still a few years away from computers actually being able to do this when they misunderstand you. We can, however, use programming to do Natural Language Processing (NLP) which can decode human idioms into something the computer can understand and interpret so it might just give you that $1 bill, or whatever denomination is appropriate for your locale.

communication of ideas as the speaker has to pause while each sentence is translated; a translation of the entire note takes a long time initially but then is much faster to read in one go by the other person.

In the same way, all programs written in a high-level, English-like programming language eventually have to be converted into a low-level machine language that the CPU can understand and execute. In fact, each different brand of CPU has it's own unique machine language which makes the task of translating from a high-level language to a low-level language somewhat tricky.

In general, there are three main paradigms we can use to translate a program from a high-level language like Python or Java to a low-level language so that we can execute it. We can do so by using a:

- **Compiler**: this is when the entire program written in a high-level programming language is translated, using a tokenizer and (usually) a parser, into low-level code, first into assembly and then into machine language (also called object code) for the particular processor you're using. Those object files are bundled into an executable by a linker which can attach them to any needed libraries. When you want to finally launch the newly-compiled program, a loader kicks into gear to load your instructions into the CPU's main memory so it can then start executing those instructions.
- **Interpreter**: a traditional interpreter takes a single instruction in a high-level programming language and immediately performs the requested actions. This can sometimes involve doing the same steps as in a compiler where some high-level instructions might need to be converted to machine language, as well.
- **Virtual Machine Interpreter**: In this scheme, both a compiler and an interpreter are used. A compiler, in this case, doesn't translate to machine language for the physical machine but rather to machine language for a virtual machine that only exists in software (i.e., it's some program that simulates a physical machine). The object code for this virtual machine is usually called bytecode and the bytecode, in turn, is interpreted by a Virtual Machine and the appropriate actions (or opcodes) are executed to produce output, as shown in Figure 3.4.

The advantage of this approach is that it allows a program converted to bytecode to be executed

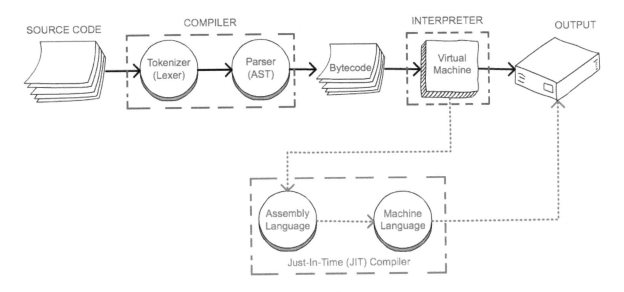

Figure 3.4: Python Virtual Machine and Compiler

on any physical machine that can run the virtual machine for that language. For a traditionally compiled program, every time you want to run it on a different hardware platform (e.g., MacOS vs Windows vs Linux), you would have to re-compile the program for the new platform. Interpreted programs, on the other hand, can run on any platform that has the appropriate interpreter since they're not compiled ahead of time.

As you might imagine, an interpreted program is often slower than a compiled program since it has to be interpreted each time it is run. As such, some interpreted languages also allow for Just-In-Time (JIT) compilation where the bytecode is converted into executable object code for the physical machine.

The Python shell is a way to interact with the Python interpreter. You can access the Python interpreter in either shell mode or script/batch mode. The Python shell might more accurately be called "interactive shell" rather than just shell.

3.9 Playing with Python

All right, let's dig in and start playing with Python a bit before we explore some of the more advanced ideas in the next few chapters. Assuming you have IDLE up and running, as in Figure 3.3, we can start seeing what Python can do. We've already learned how to say hello to Python in Section 3.4 using the `print()` command so let's see what else we can do with it.

We could, if we wanted, use Python as an overpowered calculator:

```
>>> 3 + 2
5
>>> 3 - 2
1
>>> 3 * 2
6
>>> 3 / 2
1.5
```

We can have it do simple arithmetic as above. If we need more complicated math functionality, we can import the math **library**. One of Python's biggest strengths is the various libraries, also called **modules**, that are available with Python. These modules contain commands or functions that other people have already written for us and all we need to do to use them is **import** that library or module:

```
>>> import math
>>> math.sqrt(16)
4.0
>>> math.sin(60)
-0.3048106211022167
```

Here, we imported the math module and, once we'd imported it into the Python shell, we were able to use it to invoke its `sqrt()` command and its `sin()` command. As you can tell with these examples, and the `print()` command, Python also follows the *functional notation* we met in Section 0.5 where the name of the function (like `print` or `sin`) is followed by the opening and closing parentheses, "()".

You might have noticed that the actual call to the sine function in Python wasn't `sin()` but rather `math.sin()`. We can think of the `sin()` function as living in the `math` module so when we want to use, or **invoke**, the `sin()` function, we have to use its full name or full location as `math.sin()`. The

period or full stop that separates the name of the module (math) from the **call** to the function (sin())
has a special name, the **dot operator**. The dot operator can be used to access any function or variable
in a module or object and is very powerful, as we'll see when we get to the chapter on classes. Because
the print() function is part of the base Python language and doesn't live inside another module, we
could *call* or *invoke* it directly without needing to qualify its location.

There are tons of other commands available in both the math module and the base Python language.
Sometimes, though, you might not remember where a particular function lives. When that happens,
Python lets you know right away:

```
>>> math.abs(-500)
Traceback (most recent call last):
  File "<stdin>", line 1, in <module>
AttributeError: module 'math' has no attribute 'abs'
>>> abs(-500)
500
```

We thought the math library had the abs() absolute value command but, when we tried it, Python
let us know that the math module did not have an attribute named abs. Since the abs() command is
part of the base language, we were able to call it directly on the next line to find the absolute value of
-500.

Similarly, if we had messed up typing in the print() command we've used before, Python will let
us know that something went awry:

```
>>> print("Hello World!")
Hello World!
>>> print("Hello World!
  File "<stdin>", line 1
    print("Hello World!
                      ^
SyntaxError: EOL while scanning string literal
```

We printed out the string "Hello World!" in the first two lines above but, when we tried to
do it again, we forgot to enter the closing quote and closing parenthesis. Python immediately let us
know there was an issue with our syntax with the warning, "SyntaxError: EOL while scanning
string literal".

3.9.1 Python and Mathematics

Python syntax very closely reflects standard mathematical syntax. As such, you can almost type
mathematical statements just as they are directly into the Python interactive shell. For example, in
mathematics, if you wanted to create a variable x and assign it a value of 5, you might say, x=5. This,
and other mathematical operations, carry over identically in Python:

```
>>> x=5
>>> print(x)
5
>>> y=x*5
>>> print(y)
25
>>> hypotenuse_squared = x*x + y*y
>>> print(hypotenuse_squared)
650
```

In fact, as you can see by the last statement in the listing above, we aren't constrained to short, non-descriptive names for variables as we are by convention in mathematics. So instead of calling our hypotenuse something uninformative like z, we can instead choose to call the variable by the much more descriptive name, `hypotenuse_squared`.

3.10 An Example Using Computational Thinking

We can easily extend this to solve the problem we started at the beginning of the book in Section 0.1.1, namely, computing the average of a bunch of temperatures. Let's follow the three Computational Thinking steps we learned in Section 3.2 and develop an initial computational solution for this problem:

1. **Problem Specification**: Compute the average value of three temperature values

2. **Algorithmic Expression**: Store 3 temperature values in separate variables and use them to compute average Temperature using our mathematical model as the algorithm: $\overline{T} = \frac{\sum_{i=1}^{3} T_i}{3}$

3. **Solution Implementation & Evaluation**: Implement this algorithm in Python and test with the following input values and results:

Temperature #	Temperature Value
1	68
2	71
3	73

Average of above 3 temperatures = 70.666667

Now we're ready to implement our solution in Python by creating the following program as seen in Listing 3.3.

```
1  >>> temperature1 = 68
2  >>> temperature2 = 71
3  >>> temperature3 = 73
4  >>> number_of_temperatures = 3
5  >>> average = (temperature1 + temperature2 + temperature3)/number_of_temperature
6  >>> print("Average temperature:", average)
7  Average temperature: 70.66666666666667
```

Listing 3.3: First attempt at computing the average temperature

In Listing 3.3, we needed to know exactly what the temperature values were and how many we had. As you might imagine, Python gives you a lot of power and flexibility so that you don't have to provide all this explicit information ahead of time. We're going to discover all the functionality Python offers to let us wield that power in the next few chapters.

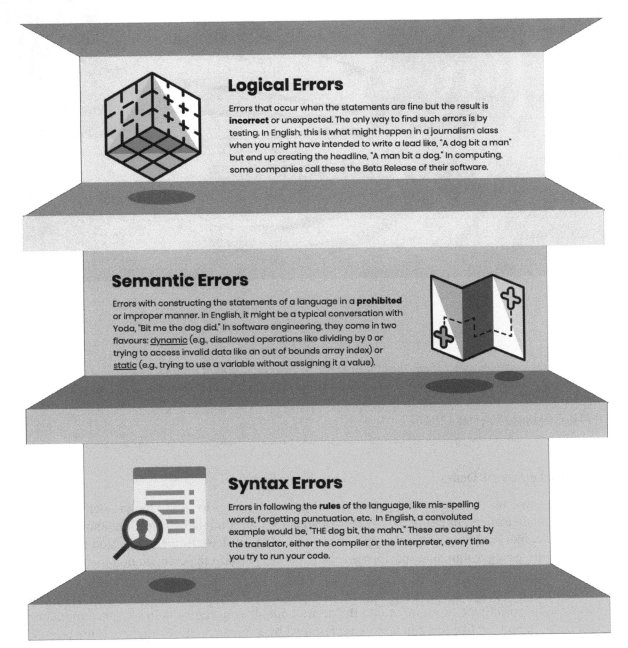

Figure 3.5: Different Kinds of Errors: Syntax, Semantic, and Logical errors occur at either **compile-time** (syntax and static semantic) or **run-time** (dynamic semantic and logical). Semantic and logical errors are also sometimes referred to as **exceptions** and we can use **exception handling** to take care of such exceptional situations. Most languages use exceptions for both compile-time and run-time errors. In languages like Java, exceptions that occur at compile-time are called **checked** exceptions whereas run-time exceptions are called **unchecked** exceptions. In languages like Python, C++, and C#, the compiler does not force the programmer to deal with exceptions so all exceptions are unchecked.

4. Data Types and Variables

I would have you imagine, then, that there exists in the mind of man a block of wax... and that we remember and know what is imprinted as long as the image lasts; but when the image is effaced, or cannot be taken, then we forget or do not know.
– Plato, Dialogs, Theateus 191[1]

4.1 Different Types of Data

Our story so far: we have some computable problem that we want to solve; the problem might be something mathematical, like solving a system of equations, or it might be something more abstract and symbolic, like searching and replacing some text in a file. We have further delineated a sequence of instructions, or algorithm, that specifies precisely how to perform the computation that will solve this problem.

We can then implement our computational solution as a program, which explicitly describes the process for converting the given input into the desired output as a step-by-step sequence of precise instructions. A process like this can also be represented by a function, an abstraction of the process, and the input can be characterized as some kind of data that is transformed by the function.

The world, in fact, has many different kinds of data we might want to model in our computational solutions: the kind of data, or its category as Aristotle might have said, is its **type**. Different types of data have different characteristics. For example, numeric data looks and behaves very different from alphabetical, string data. More formally, we can say the type of data tells us both the kinds of values that data can have as well as the kinds of operations allowed on those values.

Examples of different types of data you might encounter in a programmatic context include numeric data, boolean data, textual data, etc. Each of these various types of data can do different things; i.e.,

---

[1]Quoted in "VMS Internals and Data Structures", V4.4, when referring to image activation and termination.

the values of these different kinds of data can be used or modified via different kinds of operations. For example, you can do arithmetic operations on numeric types but these arithmetic operators (like addition, subtraction, multiplication, division, exponentiation, square root, etc.) might not be defined for textual data. Textual data, on the other hand, might have certain operations (like splitting a text string in half) that doesn't make sense for Boolean types of data.

4.2   Data Type = Values + Operations

A **data type** is thus defined by the kinds of values it can represent as well as the kinds of operations you can do on those values. These values can be combined in **expressions** and those expressions combined further into **statements**. Statements, in turn, constitute the instructions which make up your program. Each programming language also specifies the *grammar* and *syntax* for combining statements into valid instructions.

In fact, every programming language defines a set of symbols, its *alphabet*, and certain rules for creating allowed combinations of symbols; let's refer to these legal combinations of symbols as words. Words can be raw values, which are also called **literals** in Python, or they can be built-in commands, also called **functions**. You can further use the allowed symbols to create your own **variables**, which aren't built into Python but are unique to your specific program only. The language also has a unique set of keywords that it knows and understands out of the box. For Python, you can see the full list of reserved words, or built-in keywords, by checking the `kwlist` variable in the `keyword` module, as seen in Listing 4.1.

```
1  >>> import keyword
2  >>> keyword.kwlist
3  ['False', 'None', 'True', 'and', 'as', 'assert', 'break', 'class',
4  'continue', 'def', 'del', 'elif', 'else', 'except', 'finally', 'for',
5  'from', 'global', 'if', 'import', 'in', 'is', 'lambda', 'nonlocal', 'not',
6  'or', 'pass', 'raise', 'return', 'try', 'while', 'with', 'yield']
```
Listing 4.1: Reserved words or keywords in Python

In one sense, we could say that Python therefore has three kinds of fundamental **elements**:

1. **Literals**: these are elements that have a raw **value** of some data type, like a *numeric* or *string* value; some literals we've seen so far are numbers like 3 and 2 and strings like "Hello World!".
2. **Variables**: just like in mathematics, variables store values; think of them as a **symbol** or name that represents that *stored value*. Examples of variables we saw in the last chapter are x and `temperature1`.
3. **Functions**: also called **commands**, which do things and sometimes return a value they've computed; an example of a function we've already used is the `print()` function which just prints out some value to the screen or console.

There are additional elements like **control structures** (e.g., the `if` and `while` structures) and **classes/objects** but, for now, we'll concentrate on just these three elements.

A **value**, in our context, can be thought of as the representation of some symbol that can be manipulated by some algorithm. In mathematics, a *value* is considered to be any mathematical object that can be used to count, measure, or label, like a number. An equivalent definition might be: "A value is a member of the set of possible interpretations of any possibly-infinite sequence of symbols."[2]

Some of the data types that we use quite frequently in Python are:

- **strings** (*string literals*: `str`) - a sequence of characters surrounded by quotation marks,
- **integer numbers** (*numeric integer literals*: `int`) - a sequence of digits,
- **real numbers** (*numeric floating point literals*: `float`) - a numeric literal that contains a decimal point

In addition to these, we'll also see things like booleans, lists, tuples, dictionaries, etc. If you're uncertain what the type of some value is (e.g., is it an integer or a floating point number?), you can use Python's built-in function called `type()` to help you out:

```
>>> type("Hello, World!")
<class 'str'>
>>> type(5)
<class 'int'>
>>> type(3.1415)
<class 'float'>
```

Sometimes, things can get a little tricky. E.g., we know that 3.14 is a float but is "3.14" (note the surrounding quotes!) also a float? The good news is that computer science has an inherent empirical component so we can experiment and find out!

```
>>> type("3.14")
<class 'str'>
```

Because the value is in quotes, Python thinks of it as a string, as opposed to the bare value which it interpreted as a floating point value. Needless to say, Python also has trouble with the meaning of non-numbers so it doesn't understand things like commas or dollar signs in numeric values.

In fact, all these values are, in the end, encoded as bit patterns in binary in the computer's memory. This is because, at their core, computers store this information in digital logic circuits which use high and low voltages to represent the two binary states. You need a lot of bits to store meaningful data and information.

As such, different sequences of bits are given different names depending on their unit sizes. For example, 8 bits bundled together are called a **byte**. These bytes are used to represent all the values in a

---

[2] Stackoverflow is an excellent communal source of information for software engineers and is responsible, in part, for saving the last few bits of hair I have left: `https://stackoverflow.com/questions/3300726/what-is-a-value-in-the-context-of-programming`

computer. This means that even alphabetical characters are represented as numbers in the computer. The American Standard Code for Information Interchange (**ASCII**) standard was established for giving each character a unique numeric 1-byte code. Since a byte was made up of 8 bits, this allowed us to encode $2^8 = 256$ different symbols.

For example, the upper-case English letter, 'A', is represented by the code, or number, 65, while the lower-case 'a' is represented by the code 97. Depending on the context, when the computer sees the number 97, it can interpret it as either the numeric value, 97, or the character, 'a'. Regardless of the context, though, the decimal number 97 is stored internally by the computer as the binary number 01100001.

In fact, the situation is even more confusing as instructions are also stored as binary numbers since almost all computers follow the von Neumann architecture we first met in Section 2.8. Thus, the computer has to figure out if a particular binary number, like 01100001, represents an integer, a character, or an instruction before it can actually use it! The *context* is given by the software that's currently accessing that data in memory which decides exactly what kind of structure to impose on that particular binary data.

These kinds of contextual issues haunt humans, as well. For example, if I told you, *"There are only 10 kinds of people in the world: those who understand binary and those who don't,"* how did you decide to interpret the number 10 in that context, as a decimal number or as a binary number?

Although that was sufficient early on, it proved too limiting when you wanted to encode characters from different languages like Mandarin or Hindi. This ASCII code was then extended to **Unicode** which uses more bytes to represent characters; e.g., **UTF-32** is the Unicode Transformation Format that uses 4 bytes to represent each character and can thus encode $2^{32} = 4,294,967,296$ different characters or symbols!

4.3 Variables and Expressions

Similar to variables in mathematics, variables in a programming language like Python are a symbol or name, often called an **identifier**, for some value.[3] Valid identifiers for variables in Python have to follow the following rule: they can be an arbitrarily long sequence of letters, digits, or underscores (_) as long as they begin with a letter.

The value represented by a variable is stored at some location in memory. This stored value, as pointed out in Section 1.6, is *mutable* and can be changed by the program. We can change the stored

---

[3]Python differs from **strongly-typed** languages like Java in that its variables are **dynamically-typed**, or duck-typed. In a strongly-typed language like Java you have to specify the type of the variable when you first declare it but, in a dynamically-typed language like Python, you don't have to declare the type of a variable ahead of time and only have to worry about the type of value it holds when you actually use it. If it quacks like an integer and walks like an integer, it must be an integer.

value by issuing a statement that assigns a value to a variable; such a statement is called an assignment statement and it uses the **assignment operator** (=) to make the actual assignment:

```
>>> x=5
```

An **operator**, in mathematics, is any symbol that represents some operation, like addition, multiplication, exponentiation, integration, etc. More generally, we can think of these operations as some transformation or function that maps one set of elements to another set of elements or between two function spaces. These operators usually act upon one or more mathematical objects which are called the **operands**.

Floating Point Mess...

Representing real values in a binary format is especially troublesome. Even in a decimal format representation, we cannot express the exact value of expressions like $1/3$ as it is an infinite sequence and so we *approximate* it as the decimal number $0.3\bar{3}$. This is because 3 is not a prime factor of 10, the base in decimal. Similarly, 0.1 cannot be represented exactly in binary as 1 is not a prime factor of 2, the base in binary.

Floating point representations in binary are further plagued by rounding errors and both floating point underflow and over-flow. In general, when you deal with floating point numbers represented in binary, you would be well-served to define some ε, a small *approximate* value that's acceptable in that context, and use that for comparison of any subtractions, divisions, or multiplications.

In a programming context, operands are usually numerical, text, or Boolean values that can be manipulated or checked by operators; they can be anything that evaluates to a value like variables, operators, and calls to functions. Operators in computer science also work the same way as in mathematics and are basically symbols that represent particular actions. For example, the assignment operator (=) is a binary operator that has two operands: a left operand, which is always a variable, and a right operand, which is always a value, as in the example shown in Listing 4.2.

The assignment operator in computer science, =, is equivalent to the defined-as operators[4] in mathematics, $\equiv$ and $:=$, whereas the mathematical equality relational operator, =, which checks the equality of two quantities is represented as == in most programming languages (e.g., Python uses == as the equality relational operator but languages like BASIC and Pascal use = instead).

In Listing 4.2, the first statement, x=5, uses the assignment operator, =, to assign the value 5, the right operand, to the variable called x, the left operand. In the second statement, we have another assignment statement: in this case, the left operand is the variable y and the right operand has to be

---

[4]Please see this reference from Wolfram Mathworld: `http://mathworld.wolfram.com/Defined.html`

```
1  >>> x=5
2  >>> y=x*5
3  >>> x=x+5
```

Listing 4.2: Operators and Operands in Python

a value; since the right hand side is an *expression*, we have to **evaluate** that expression and find its corresponding value first. This involves figuring out the value of the variable x.

The easiest way for the interpreter or compiler to find the value of any variable is by consulting a **symbol table** of sorts. We can, in a first approximation, think of a symbol table as a simple way to keep track of the names of variables, their corresponding stored values, and perhaps the address in memory where those values are stored. To keep things simple, let's just look at a symbol table that only has the names and associated values of all the variables, as shown in Table 4.1.

Name	Value
x	5
y	25

Table 4.1: A simple symbol table with only the names and values of the variables used in Listing 4.2 for the first two statements

As we can see, in order to evaluate the expression on the right hand side of the 2nd statement in Listing 4.2, we have to first figure out the value of the variable x. The interpreter, in this case, can just look up the value of x in Table 4.1, which is 5.

It then evaluates the expression on the right hand side which itself is made up of another operator, the multiplication operator (*), which is also a binary operand. The left operand is the value of x, 5, and the right operand is also 5, so it multiplies the two operands and returns the resulting value, 25. That value, 25, is then assigned to the variable y, which is the left operand of the assignment operator (=), and that value is recorded for it in the symbol table in Table 4.1.

Whew! That was (more than) a little verbose but it's good to go through the first example in detail. This level of verbosity might prove helpful in examining what happens in the 3rd statement in Listing 4.2, as well: x=x+5. This statement is another assignment operation and uses the assignment operator, =, to assign the value of the right hand side to the variable on the left hand side.

This notation might look a little odd, though, as x appears on both sides of the equation with the assignment operator. This is actually equivalent to the mathematical equation shown in Equation 4.1 in which we imagine there to be an implicit time step *t*.

$$
\begin{aligned}
x &= x+5 &\Rightarrow& \text{ In Programming} \\
x_{t+1} &= x_t+5 &\Rightarrow& \text{ In Mathematics}
\end{aligned}
\tag{4.1}
$$

In a programming context, this means that the same variable, x, can appear on both the left- and right-hand sides of that equation. The assignment operator works in the usual way: it assigns the value of the expression on the right hand side (x+5) to the variable that is the left operand, x. In order to evaluate the value of x+5, it looks up the value of x in Table 4.1. It then replaces the call to x with its value, 5, which is then used by the addition operator. The + operator is also a binary operator and it adds the left operand, 5, to the right operand, 5, returning a value of 10.

This value, 10, is then assigned as the value of the variable x, the left operand of the assignment operator and the symbol table is updated to reflect the new value, as shown in Table 4.2.

Name	Value
x	10
y	25

Table 4.2: Final symbol table for Listing 4.2 after the third statement is executed

A partial list of operators in Python is shown in Table 4.3. These operators follow the usual mathematical order of precedence. Just like in mathematics, you can also override the order of evaluation of any of these operators using parentheses, "()", as in the expression "3*(5+5)" which, without the parentheses, would result in 20 instead of the correct value with parentheses of 30.

Operation	Symbol	Meaning
Exponentiation	**	5 ** 2 == 25
Multiplication	*	2 * 3 == 6
Division	/	14 / 3 == 4
Modulus/Remainder	%	14 % 3 == 2
Addition	+	1 + 2 == 3
Subtraction	–	4 – 3 == 1
Less Than	<	less than
Less Than Or Equal	<=	less than or equal to
Greater Than	>	greater than
Greater Than Or Equal	>=	greater than or equal to
Equal	==	equal
Not Equal	!=	not equal
Not Equal	<>	another way to say not equal

Table 4.3: Partial List of Python Operators

Finally, Python also provides functions to convert one data type to another. In particular, it provides the `int()`, `float()`, and `str()` functions that can convert to the integer, floating point, and string data types, respectively. A sample use of these conversions is shown below:

```
>>> int(3.14)
3
>>> int(3.9999)          # Does not do any rounding off
3
>>> int("45")            # Parse a string to produce an int value
45
>>> int("3.14 feet")
Traceback (most recent call last):
  File "<stdin>", line 1, in <module>
ValueError: invalid literal for int() with base 10: '3.14 feet'
```

As you can tell by the last entry, if you try to do an invalid or undoable conversion, you'll get a `ValueError` from Python's interactive shell. The formal name for changing the type of a variable is called **typecasting**; in the listing above, we typecast the string value, ''45'', to an integer value using the `int()` method: `int(''45'')`.

In the listing above, I also snuck a new kind of control character in Python: the #, which is variously called the number sign, the hash mark, or the pound sign. The hash mark indicates the start of a **comment** in Python, which is just an internal note intended for the software developers. Python ignores everything after the # symbol as nonsense that's only useful to the programmer but of no consequence to the all-important CPU that's working hard in the guts of the computer.

4.3.1 Expressions and Statements

In mathematics, you can combine variables and constants, as well as other mathematical symbols like operators, functions, brackets, etc., according to certain rules. These combinations are called **expressions** and, when you assign values to the variables and carry out the operations designated in the expression, you end up with a **value** for that expression.

That's quite a mouthful so let's look at an example; here is a mathematical expression:

$$x^2 + y^2 \tag{4.2}$$

If we assign the value 3 to x and the value 4 to y for the variables in Equation 4.2, we get $3^2 + 4^2$ which evaluates to the value 25. Thus, we can think of an expression in computer science in almost the same way: an *expression* is any legal combination of operands and operators that represents a value or, as we might say in programming, evaluates to a value or produces a value.

A **statement** uses a value to issue an instruction that the Python interpreter can execute. So far, we have seen a few statements like `print()`, `import`, assignment, etc.[5] There are many more kinds of statements and the kinds of things we can do with them will increase exponentially when we discover the statements corresponding to control structures like `if`, `for`, `while`, etc. For now, let's take some of the statements we've seen, and a couple more, and combine them to do something useful.

4.4 Input/Output

A few basic statements are essential in most programs you'll write. In fact, just about every program will require some way to get input from the user and relate output back to the user. Most operating systems give you access to three standard ways of communicating with the user of your program: the Standard Input (stdin), Standard Output (stdout), and Standard Error (stderr) *streams*.

These streams are abstractions of the **buffers**, the areas of computer memory, that are used when reading or writing data from input and output devices. For example, if you want to read data from the keyboard, the sequence of bytes entered by the user is sent to the keyboard buffer and, when they press the `enter` or `return` key, that entire sequence of bytes is returned by the input function as a single value. We can use these streams to get input from the user or from files, send output to the user or to files, and send error messages to the user or to files.

---

[5]Technically, `print()` is a function in Python 3.x and not a statement as in Python 2.7. But, since functions are expressions and expressions are statements, I can afford to be a little loosey goosey, which is, of course, a technical term.

Smooth Operating Systems

An **operating system (OS)** is a software component consisting of a collection of programs and libraries that sits between a computer's hardware and the other software that runs on it. An OS manages all the software and hardware on the computer and provides the common system level programs called services or daemons. It also serves as the interface between the computer and the end user, either via a Command-Line Interface (CLI) or Graphical User Interface (GUI) or both. Some popular operating system variants are MacOS, Windows, and Linux (which has many flavours of its own!).

In Python, we can get input from the user by connecting to stdin using the built-in `input()` function. The `input()` function can get data from the user's keyboard, a file, or any other input device connected to the computer. Data that the `input()` function receives is usually stored in a variable before it's used in some computation.

Here is an example of how to ask, or **prompt**, the user for their name and store their name in the variable called `username`:

```
>>> username = input("Please enter your name: ")
Please enter your name: Ricky
```

The phrase that's printed by the interactive shell (`Please enter your name:  `) is often called the prompt as it prompts the user for what kind of input is expected from them. As you can see above, I entered `Ricky` using my keyboard in response to the prompt.

We can then use the `print()` function to send output to the user's monitor. We can also use the `print()` to output data to a file or other device although Python provides other functions to commands for this functionality, as well. Let's extend the previous example to both get the name from the user and then also greet them by name:

```
>>> username = input("Please enter your name: ")
Please enter your name: Ricky
>>> print("What a coincidence, my name is also "+ username +"!")
What a coincidence, my name is also Ricky!
```

The one caveat in all this is that the `input()` function always returns the value entered by the user as a string value. So even if the user enters their age as the number 20, it is actually returned as the string ''20''! So if you wanted to do any kind of mathematical operation on that value, you would first have to convert it to an integer by typecasting it as we saw in Section 4.3.

Finally, as you can see above, the + operator, which does arithmetic addition when applied to integers, does **concatenation**, or linking together, when applied to strings! In particular, it combined the string, ''What a coincidence, my name is also '', with the string value stored in the variable `username`. The ability to have a single operator or function do different things in different *contexts* is also an example of **overloading**, which we'll meet in more detail later.

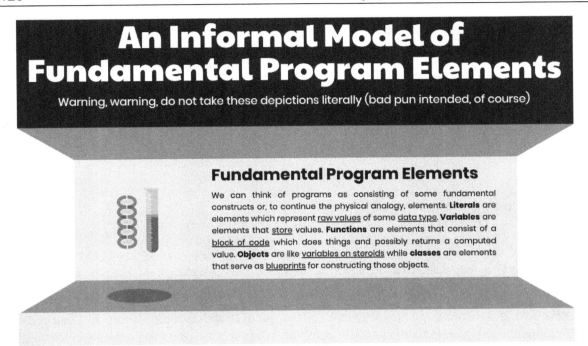

Figure 4.1: An Informal Model of Fundamental Program Elements: most programs consist of elements like *literals*, *variables*, *functions*, *objects*, and *classes*. Program **statements** are made up of **expressions** which contain elements. In addition, programs utilize **control structures** to determine the *flow of execution*, the order in which statements are executed. Three fundamental control structures, **sequence**, **selection**, and **repetition**, are sufficient to specify any programmatic solution. These control structures are implemented as statements; e.g., the selection control structure is implemented using the `if` statement in most programming languages.

4.5 An Example Using Computational Thinking

Now let's take all these basic ideas and combine them to do something (somewhat) more useful than just greeting people! Let's suppose your 5-year-old son was interested in drawing a circle using some crayons as a compass. Since he has crayons of various lengths, you need to ensure the anticipated circles will fit on the sheet of paper.

We'll follow the three Computational Thinking steps we learned in Section 3.2 as we develop a computational solution for this very important problem:

1. **Problem Specification**: Compute the area of a circle based on the radius input by the user

2. **Algorithmic Expression**: Get the input from the user as a `float` value and use that to compute area using our mathematical model as the algorithm: $A = \pi r^2$

3. **Solution Implementation & Evaluation**: Implement this algorithm in Python and test with the following input values and results:

Input (Radius)	Output (Area)
1	3.14
2	6.28
2.3	16.62

Okay, now we're ready to do Step 3, the actual Python implementation, by running the code shown in Listing 4.3. We can type this in at the interactive shell, as shown there, or we could create a program, also known as a script, by using the Python IDLE's Text Editor as we saw in Section 3.4.

```
1  >>> radius = input("What is the length of your crayon? ") # Get user input
2  What is the length of your crayon? 2.3
3  >>> r = float(radius)       # Typecast string value to float value
4  >>> a = 3.1415 * r ** 2     # Actual Algorithm Here
5  >>> print("The area of a circle drawn with a crayon of length", radius, "is", a)
6  The area of a circle drawn with a crayon of length 2.3 is 16.618534999999998
```

Listing 4.3: Compute area of circle for crayon of given length

We could, if we wanted, get fancy and take advantage of **function composition**. Just like you can use function composition in mathematics to combine two functions, you can do the exact same thing in most programming languages. For example, suppose I had a function, $f(x)$, and a function, $g(y)$. I could use function composition to create the *composite* function, $g(f(x))$, by passing the *output* of one function, $f(x)$, as *input* to the other function, $g(y)$.

Similarly, in Python, we can take the output of one function, input(), and pass it as the input to another function, float(), to create a composite function, float(input()). This would let us combine the first two statements in Listing 4.3 into a single line as:

```
>>> r = float( input("What is the length of your crayon? ") )
```

Strings: a sequence of characters (numbers, letters, or whitespace) that is enclosed in quotation marks

Integers: a sequence of number characters that represents an integer numeric value

Floats: a sequence of number characters with a decimal point that represents a real numeric value; their numeric values "float" around the decimal point and there is no set number of digits before or after the decimal point

Boolean: a special data type that can only have the literal value True or False

List: A data structure made up of a changeable, ordered sequence of elements; each element or value in a list is called an item

Tuples: Same as lists except that tuples cannot be changed and they use parentheses instead of the brackets used in lists

Python built-in data types.

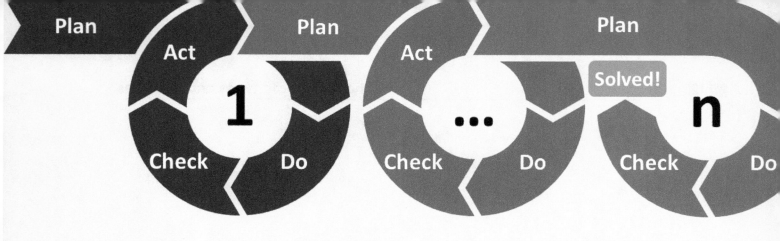

5. Control Structures

> *Of all men's miseries, the bitterest is this: to know so much and have control over nothing.*
> – Herodotus, *The Histories*, Book 9, Ch. 16.

5.1 Algorithms and Control Structures

In Section 3.3, we saw that it was possible to construct a minimal instruction set at the lower-level of the CPU and this minimal instruction set was sufficient to express *every* possible program or computational solution. Similarly, for higher-level, more abstract programming languages, Böhm and Jacopini [17] established the Structured Program Theorem which showed that all programs could be written in terms of only three control structures (along with some potential storage for variables): the sequence structure, the selection structure and the repetition structure.[1] These control structures determine the order in which a program's statements are executed. Let's explore each of the fundamental control structures next.

5.2 Sequence

So far, in Sections 4.2 and 4.3.1, we have seen that we can combine three of the fundamental elements of Python (functions, variables, and values/literals) into expressions. These expressions evaluate to some value. Those values, in turn, can be used in statements to have the Python interpreter carry out an instruction. Sets of such instructions form the algorithms, or computational solutions to our computational problems.

Each of these instructions is carried out by the CPU via the fetch-execute-cycle we saw in Section 3.1. By default, the CPU will carry out, or execute, the set of instructions that constitute the algorithm

---

[1]The Böhm-Jacopini Theorem demonstrates that any computable function can be computed by combining various subprograms using only three Control Flow Graphs (CFGs): sequence, selection, and repetition.

one at a time: i.e., in **sequence**. We can think of each instruction, or group of instructions, that the compiler or interpreter performs in sequential order as an **action** as it usually consists of an *imperative*.[2]

Some examples of common actions, or statements carried out in sequence, are things like calculating an arithmetic sum, assigning the value at some storage location to a variable name, computing the average, etc. All the programs we've seen in Python so far, like Listing 4.3, consist of actions, or statements carried out in sequence, one after the next.

The **order** of the sequence of instructions makes quite a bit of difference; e.g., if you were giving directions to the gas station near your house, telling someone to go straight for one mile and then turn right takes you to a dramatically different place than telling them to turn right and then go straight for one mile.

Here is another example of a set of statements that asks the user for two numbers and then displays the result; all of these statements are executed in *sequence*, one after the next:

```
>>> n1 = int(input("Enter first integer: "))
Enter first integer: 3
>>> n2 = int(input("Enter first integer: "))
Enter first integer: 5
>>> total = n1 + n2
>>> print("Total of", n1, "and", n2,"is:", total)
Total of 3 and 5 is: 8
```

5.3 Selection

The **selection** control structure, also called **decision**, is best summed up by Robert Frost's poem, "The Road Not Taken":

> Two roads diverged in a yellow wood,
> And sorry I could not travel both
> And be one traveler, long I stood
> And looked down one as far as I could
> To where it bent in the undergrowth;
>
> Then took the other, as just as fair,
> And having perhaps the better claim,
> Because it was grassy and wanted wear;
> Though as for that the passing there
> Had worn them really about the same,
>
> And both that morning equally lay
> In leaves no step had trodden black.
> Oh, I kept the first for another day!

Robert Frost, "The Road Not Taken," Mountain Interval, 1916.

---

[2]We can also think of a decidedly tortured analogy to Newton's first law of motion where an object persists in linear, uniform motion unless acted upon by a net external force. In a similar way, the CPU plods along in a linear, sequential manner, executing statements one after the next, in order, until it meets one of the other two control structures. This strained analogy is further stretched when we remember that the Action is the fundamental characteristic of a system we compute in physics, often to use in a Lagrangian or Hamiltonian. But, of course, by now we've pulled the analogy far beyond any credulity to the point of forming a wormhole through which we thankfully escape this analogy itself.

Yet knowing how way leads on to way,
I doubted if I should ever come back.

I shall be telling this with a sigh
Somewhere ages and ages hence:
Two roads diverged in a wood, and I –
I took the one less traveled by,
And that has made all the difference.

Despite the widespread misinterpretation of this poem,[3] it serves its purpose well in illustrating the need to make a decision, a selection. When faced with two diverging roads, the traveller made a decision to choose one over the other.

This decision is based on some condition: perhaps, as is widely believed, the decision was based on whether the traveller felt adventurous enough to take the road less travelled. If you come upon a similar fork in the road, perhaps you, too, might pause and ask yourself, "Do I feel adventurous enough to take the road less travelled?"

Your answer to this question will be either Yes or No → True or False → Boolean values! An expression that evaluates to a Boolean value is called a **Boolean expression** and it's usually composed of Boolean operators. Python gives us the Boolean and relational operators that evaluate to Boolean values as shown in Table 5.1. These operators can be used to create more complex or compound Boolean expressions. The Boolean expressions can then be used as the **condition** that will control which selection, or decision, is made.

Python implements the *selection*, or *decision*, control structure using the `if-else` control structure which takes the following form:

---

[3] Just like Bruce Springsteen's anthem, "Born in the USA," this poem is often (mis-)quoted more than it is read. It is usually said to be about choosing the road that was less worn, less travelled, and that choosing the more adventurous road made all the difference in the traveller's life. Upon a closer read, however, you might find that both roads were *equally* well-trod and the traveller is musing that, in a future telling, it would be cast as if the road was actually less travelled.

Purpose	Operator
Relational Operators	
Equal to	==
Not equal to	!=
Less than or equal to	<=
Less than	<
Greater than or equal to	>=
Greater than	>
Boolean (Logical) Operators	
And	and
Not	not
Or	or

Table 5.1: Boolean and Relational Operators in Python

```
if BOOLEAN_EXPRESSION_IS_TRUE:
    EXECUTE_STATEMENTS
else:
    EXECUTE_OTHER_STATEMENTS
```

If we examine just the `if` part of the control structure, we can see that it's made of the `if` control statement in the **header** followed by some number of statements that are indented the same amount in the **body** of the selection control structure. All the statements indented the same amount are assumed to be part of the `if` control structure and are executed following the usual rules if the Boolean expression is true. If the Boolean condition is false, these statements are skipped. The syntax of the selection control structure is shown in Figure 5.1. The same header and body syntax applies to the `else` part of the selection control structure and, as we'll see in just a bit, to the other control structures and even function definitions!

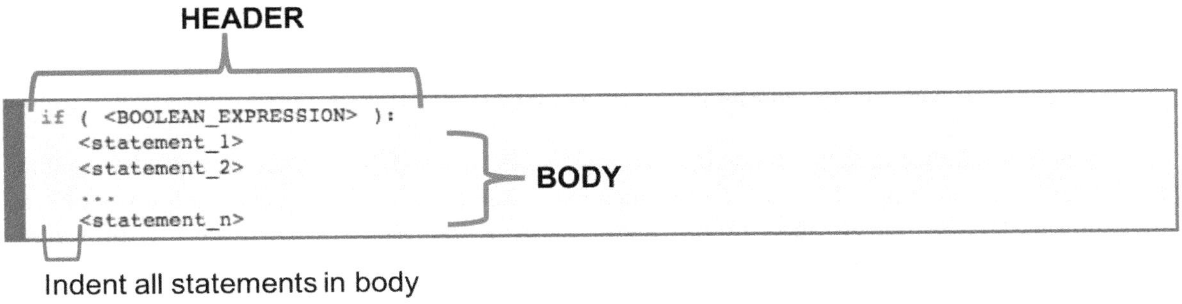

HEADER

```
if ( <BOOLEAN_EXPRESSION> ):
    <statement_1>
    <statement_2>
    ...
    <statement_n>
```

BODY

Indent all statements in body

Figure 5.1: Syntax of the selection control structure in Python. The **header** contains the `if` control statement and the **body** contains all the statements to execute if the Boolean expression evaluates to True.

So we might express the traveller's dilemma in English-like pseudocode, which we met in Section 1.7, as: If I'm feeling adventurous and the road is less travelled, take the road; otherwise, don't take the road. We can then translate it to Python as shown below:

```
>>> feeling_adventurous = True
>>> road_less_travelled = True
>>> if (feeling_adventurous and road_less_travelled):
...     print("Take the road!")
... else:
...     print("Just watch TV instead.")
...
Take the road!
```

5.3.1 Chained and Nested Conditionals

Sometimes, you might want to make more complex decisions or choices. For example, if you were trying to decide what to eat for dinner tonight, you might be trying to decide between the Chinese restaurant, the Burger Joint, or the local Taco Truck. Your choice might be dependent on the cost and, if you have more than $50, you'll go for the Chinese, if you have less than $50 but more than $10, you'll go for the Burger Joint, otherwise you'll hit the Taco Truck.

We can express this kind of **chained conditional** in Python using the if-elif[4] control structure which takes the following form:

```
if BOOLEAN_EXPRESSION_A_IS_TRUE:
    EXECUTE_STATEMENTS_A
elif BOOLEAN_EXPRESSION_B_IS_TRUE:
    EXECUTE_STATEMENTS_B
else:
    EXECUTE_STATEMENTS_C
```

For our hungry student problem, we can implement the various choices in Python as a chained conditional:

```
if (money > 50):
  print("Order some lo mein!")
elif (money > 10 and money < 50):
  print("Hit the BK!")
else:
  print("!Dos tacos de asada, por favor!")
```

As you might notice in the listing above, I typed this in Python IDLE's Text Editor rather than the interactive shell. Sometimes this makes for cleaner code, especially if it's long and complex, and if we don't immediately need to see the output, I'll go for this option. But, don't despair, I'll still use the interactive shell when I think it's more illuminative.

You can also, if you want, nest conditionals within other conditionals to get three-way branching like in the following **nested conditional** control structure in Python which tries to figure if two values are the same or not:

```
if x == y:
    print("x and y are equal!")
else:
    if x > y:
        print("x is greater than y!")
    else:
        print("y is greater than x!")
```

Since these nested conditionals can get pretty heinous with more than three branches, it's generally considered a good idea to avoid them by using an appropriate combination of the logical operators. In fact, other languages, like Java, provide control structures like the switch to handle multi-way selections.

5.4 Repetition

The great mathematician Carl Friedrich Gauss was about eight years old in 1785 when his schoolteacher, eager to have a quiet afternoon, assigned the students a task:[5] add all the numbers from 1 to 100. Gauss's teacher likely expected students to start by listing all the numbers and then adding each one. Let's follow that example but, rather than all 100 numbers, let's start by only adding the first 10 numbers:

---

[4]Nota bene: elif is an abbreviation for else if.

[5]I'm afraid I must report that this oft-repeated story may or may not actually be true (https://www.jstor.org/stable/27858762) but let's go with it anyway.

```
[1, 2, 3, 4, 5, 6, 7, 8, 9, 10]
```

Then, as the teacher likely thought, students would find the total by going through each number in the list, one at a time: they'd start with the total set to 0. Then they'd add the first number, 1, and cross it off the list. Then they'd add the second number, 2, to the total and cross that off the list, and continue repeating the process until they got to the highest number in the list, in this case, 10.

So the teacher came up with this pseudocode algorithm of how the students were expected to do the addition:

```
total = 0
for each number in [1, 2, 3, 4, 5, 6, 7, 8, 9, 10]
    total_new = total_old + current number
```

The `for`-part above is an example of **repetition**, or **iteration** or **looping**. Python gives you a way to *repeat*, or *loop*, some set of statements using the `for` or `while` looping control structures. The `for` loop control structure takes the following form in Python:

```
for EACH_ITEM in SEQUENCE_OF_ITEMS:
    EXECUTE_STATEMENTS
```

We can now translate this algorithm from pseudocode to Python as shown below:

```
>>> total = 0
>>> for eachNumber in [1, 2, 3, 4, 5, 6, 7, 8, 9, 10]:
...        total = total + eachNumber
...
>>> print(total)
55
```

The Python code is almost identical to the pseudocode algorithm the teacher came up with above! The only difference is the implicit time component we mentioned in Section 4.3 for the update of the `total` variable. Although carrying out this algorithm didn't take the computer much time, it would likely keep the students occupied for quite a while if they were to add the numbers up to 100 using this approach!

Gauss, however, took a different tack: he also wrote out the list of numbers but then he noticed that when you add the first and last number (1 and 10), you get 11. When you add the next two numbers (2 and 9), you also get 11. In fact, if you continue that way, all the subsequent number combinations also sum to 11, as shown in Figure 5.2.

How many such 11's do you get? Well, since you're adding two numbers at a time, you'll get half of 10, or 5 pairs that add to 11 (you can just count the number of lines in Figure 5.2, as well). So the total must be $5 \times 11 = 55$. He generalized this to any number, n, where the first and last number sum to

$n+1$ and there are $\frac{n}{2}$ such pairs that add to $n+1$ (you can check this by setting $n = 10$ to match our example so far). This means the total sum must be:

$$\text{SUM} = \frac{n}{2}(n+1) \quad \Rightarrow \quad \frac{n(n+1)}{2} \tag{5.1}$$

We can also implement this algorithm, expressed mathematically rather than as pseudocode in Equation 5.1, as a Python program. This version of our computational solution, however, avoids loops entirely and does everything in a sequence. The students in Gauss's class can now replace doing all of the steps of the loop using pen and paper to just that one step. When we later look at computational complexity, we'll see why it might be advantageous, in terms of the temporal or spatial resources of any computing system, to avoid loops if at all possible:

```
>>> n = 10
>>> sum = (n/2)*(n+1)
>>> print(sum)
55.0
```

The good news is both versions match! We could even have combined it all into one line, of course, but the 3-line version is a lot easier to read and, as we'll see when we get to the software engineering chapter, much easier to maintain.

There is an alternative approach to using `for` loops when you don't want to explicitly list all the numbers as [1, 2, 3, 4, 5, 6, 7, 8, 9, 10]. We can use the `range()` function to generate a list of numbers for us and adapt the `for` loop as follows:

```
>>> sum = 0
>>> for eachNumber in range(1, 11):
...     sum = sum + eachNumber
...
>>> print(sum)
55
```

This makes it easy to adapt our `for` loop algorithm for any number, as shown in Listing 5.1, where I entered 100 for the high number.

If you ever want to end a loop earlier, you can use the `break` command and, if you just want to skip a certain iteration of the loop, you can use the `continue` command. These are going to be especially handy when we examine the `while` loop construct for repetition/iteration.

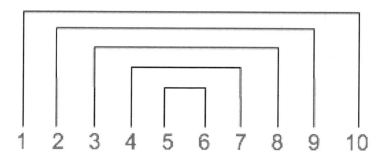

Figure 5.2: Gauss's Summation Trick

```
1  >>> n = int(input("What number do you want to sum up to?   "))
2  What number do you want to sum up to?   100
3  >>> sum = 0
4  >>> for eachNumber in range(1, n+1):
5  ...        sum = sum + eachNumber
6  ...
7  >>> print(sum)
8  5050
```

Listing 5.1: Final algorithm for normal students' approach to summing numbers

5.4.1 While Away the Time

Python also provides an alternative to the `for` loop called the `while` loop. The `while` loop control structure takes the following form in Python:

```
while BOOLEAN_EXPRESSION_IS_TRUE:
    EXECUTE_STATEMENTS
```

The only catch with the `while` loop is that the Boolean condition is checked each time the `while` construct loops so it's important that the basis of the Boolean condition gets updated within the loop body, which is the `EXECUTE_STATEMENTS` part of the `while` loop. For example, here is a sample Python implementation of the `while` loop that simply counts up to 10 rather than summing up to 10:

```
>>> n = 1
>>> while (n <= 10):
...        print(n)
...        n = n + 1
...
1
2
3
4
5
6
7
8
9
10
>>>
```

In this listing, our `while` control structure had more than a single statement and, instead, contained two statements over two lines. The 2nd line, `n = n + 1`, is called the *update* statement as it updates `n`, the variable that controls the loop. When you have more than one statement that should be repeated, Python requires you to indent all statements that belong within some control structure with the same **degree of indentation**. So if we didn't indent the update statement, `n = n + 1`, it wouldn't be repeated as it would be considered to be outside the `while` loop.

Problem 5.1 What would happen if you didn't include the `n = n + 1` update within the loop?

When to use what?

Figuring out when to use a `while` loop or a `for` loop might be a little tricky as each can replicate the other's functionality with minimal tweaks. In general, though, a good heuristic is to use the `for` loop for **definite iteration**, when you know how many iterations you'll need before your start looping. When you're not sure how many iterations you'll need and will have to keep looping until some condition is met, you can use a `while` loop for that **indefinite iteration**.

We could actually rewrite our `for` loop version of the summation algorithm in Listing 5.1 as a `while` loop version but it's more cumbersome and complex for the given data representation. As we've seen before, the *choice of the data representation* helps direct, or sometimes even dictate, the choice of the algorithm: some algorithms are better suited for certain data structures and end up being much simpler for that data structure.

Problem 5.2 Can you implement the `while` loop version of Listing 5.1?

5.5 An Example Using Computational Thinking

Just as with nested conditionals, we can also create nested repetitions. Let's look at an example of a nested iteration by trying to draw the following example of ASCII art, which uses printable ASCII characters to make pictures. In this case, we want to draw a backslash using asterisks as shown below:

```
*
 *
  *
   *
    *
     *
      *
```

We'll once again take the Computational Thinking approach from Section 3.2 that is made up of the following three steps:

1. **Problem Specification**: Create an ASCII art picture of a backslash made up of asterisks that has a total of seven rows with one asterisk per row.

2. **Algorithmic Expression**: Our approach will be to divide the printed out area into rows and columns. So our model of the asterisks is in a 7x7 table as follows:

We will therefore model the problem as a drawing area having seven rows and seven columns. We'll go through each row and, for each row, go through each of the seven columns. When the

	1	2	3	4	5	6	7
1	*						
2		*					
3			*				
4				*			
5					*		
6						*	
7							*

Table 5.2: ASCII Art for a backslash made out of asterisks

row number and column number match, we'll draw an asterisk there. If they don't match, we'll draw a blank space. Finally, at the end of the row, we'll add a newline. Our algorithm can then be expressed in pseudocode as:

Algorithm 5.1: Algorithm for printing an ASCII art picture of a backslash

---

```
1  Set NUMBER_ROWS_COLUMNS = 7
2  foreach ROW in the NUMBER_ROWS_COLUMNS do
3      foreach COLUMN in the NUMBER_ROWS_COLUMNS do
4          if ROW equals COLUMN then
5              Print Out an '*'
6          else
7              Print Out a blank space
8          end
9      end
10     Print out a new line to go to the next row
11 end
```

---

3. **Solution Implementation & Evaluation**: Implement this algorithm in Python and see if it reproduces the ASCII image of a backslash as above.

Let's write this as a script/program by choosing `File > New File` and entering the program given in Listing 5.2 (please note, the line numbers should not be entered). Once you've entered the program

```python
number_rows_cols = 7

for row in range(number_rows_cols):
  for col in range(number_rows_cols):
    if (row == col):
      print("*", end='')
    else:
      print(" ", end='')
  print("\n")
```

Listing 5.2: Print an ASCII art picture of a backslash made out of asterisks in the new file, you can choose Run > Run Module in order to execute your program (please note that you'll likely be prompted to save the file first if you haven't already done so).

As you can see, this is almost identical to the pseudocode we worked out in Algorithm 5.1. We did modify the invocation of the print() function slightly from our previous uses by adding an argument (end='') that is needed to prevent the addition of a newline after the print() calls within the inner for loop. We also used the range() function to generate a list of numbers from 0 to 6 (one less than number_rows_cols) over which the for loop will iterate.

6. Data Structures

> *Between the idea*
> *And the reality*
> *Between the motion*
> *And the act*
> *Falls the Shadow*
> – T.S. Eliot, "The Hollow Man"[1]

6.1 Abstract Data Types

Before we start talking about data structures, though, let's step back to see what we already know about data types. In Section 0.1.1, we initially talked about data[2] as being the structured raw facts, or values, observed from the physical world before giving a relatively precise definition of values in Section 4.2. Not only could we find a suitable representation of data by giving values some context (in this case, some structured representation) but we also saw, in Section 1.9.5, how further organizing data in some context (e.g., probability-based or logic-based) can give us a sense of information.

This, in turn, led us in Section 4.1 to the idea that data, the structured values, also has various operations defined on it, depending on the kinds, or **types**, of values it was structured to represent. Finally, in Section 1.9, we saw how **abstraction**, the idea of *ignoring* or **hiding** certain details about some system we're studying, can help us model or represent systems in a more structured manner. Let's formalize some of this for different data representations and structures now!

---

[1] Quoted in "VMS Internals and Data Structures", V4.4, when referring to system service dispatching.

[2] I'm going to follow somewhat sloppy form here and ignore the fact that the singular of data is datum and just use data as both singular and plural. As Walt Whitman once said, "*Do I contradict myself? Very well then, I contradict myself. I am large. I contain multitudes.*"

Type	Characteristics	Operations
Phillips Screw	X-Slotted Head	Screw in with a Phillips Screwdriver
Box Nail	Thin, Flat Head	Hammer in with a Claw Hammer

Table 6.1: Two Kinds of Fasteners: Two Fastener Structures

6.2 A Non-Technical Abstract Type

The idea that different types of data will hold different kinds of values and so have different kinds of operations associated with it isn't quite as foreign as you might think. If you've ever used a Phillips screwdriver or a hammer and nail, you're already well familiar with this idea. We might, if we want, replace the word data with fasteners and say the world has different types of fasteners; in this case, let's constrain the universe of fasteners to only two kinds:[3] Phillips screws and box nails.

We can distinguish between the two types of fasteners based on their **characteristics** (e.g., the *value* of the kind of head they have) and their **operations** (the kinds of things you can do to or with them). We might define a table like Table 6.1 for the two different kinds of Fasteners.

So every kind of Fastener has associated with it some *Characteristics* (the values) and some *Operations*. The Phillips Screw Fastener has the value of "X-Slotted" for its "Head" characteristic and has the "Screw in" operation it can do "with a Phillips Screwdriver".

If we start to think of all the various kinds of fasteners, and even all the various kinds of screws and nails, we might be able to *abstract* out the essential elements of all Fasteners: the fact that they have a certain *value* for the Head characteristic (is it flat or slotted, for example) and they have certain common operations (they can both be inserted using some driving implement like a screwdriver or hammer, for example). We can then specify the **Abstract Fastener Type** which applies to any kind of Fastener as shown in Figure 6.1.

The **Abstract** Fastener Type shown there is like a blueprint or an outline; it doesn't have any details for any specific kind of Fastener but describes those elements that *all* Fasteners must have. For example, it says that every kind of fastener has to have a value for the Head characteristic (like flat-head or Phillips head) and will have the ability to be driven in using some kind of driving implement (like with a hammer or screwdriver).

But the Abstract Fastener Type in Figure 6.1 doesn't actually specify what are those characteristics or driving implements. We can, instead, use the Abstract Fastener Type as the basis for each individual fastener and create an actual Fastener Structure for each kind of Fastener which specifies all the details

---

[3] Just in case you thought I was being facetious, please see all the scintillating details about the universe of fasteners here: https://en.wikipedia.org/wiki/Fastener.

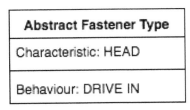

Figure 6.1: Abstract Fastener Type: every kind of fastener has to have a value for the Head characteristic and will have the ability to be driven in using some kind of driving implement like a hammer or screwdriver.

Type	Characteristics	Operations
float	Stores a real number value	Can only return a decimal number using the + operator
int	Stores an integer value	Can only return a whole number using the + operator

Table 6.2: Two Python Numeric Data Structures

as shown in Table 6.1.

If we now replace the word Fastener above with Data for any kind of generic element, we end up with the **Abstract Data Type (ADT)** which can be used to delineate the characteristics and operations for many different kinds of data. An Abstract Data Type simply denotes the kinds of characteristics a certain data structure can have and the kinds of operations it can do or have done on it.

We can re-create the previous table and figure for the floating point and integer data structures rather than the Phillips screw and box nail Fastener Types. Thus, in Table 6.2, we can see that the two Python data types, float and int, both store a value as their Characteristic (either a real number value or an integer value, respectively) and they both can be added using the + operator. Finally, Figure 6.2 shows the Abstract Data Type for these primitive data types which shows *what* they do but **not** the details of *how* they do it.

6.3 Advantages of ADTs

An ADT specifies the kinds of values some data type will hold and also what kinds of operations make sense for it. It says *what* they can do but doesn't give any **implementation** details of *how* any of those procedures will be carried out, though, since it is abstract. For this reason, ADTs are sometimes called the *specification* or the **interface** for the data type.

So what's the big advantage of ADTs if they don't actually do something? Abstract Data Types (ADTs):

1. Make our computational solutions **simpler** and easier to understand or modify by omitting details of how the operations will be implemented and carried out (e.g., all fasteners have the drive in operation but the Abstract Fastener Type doesn't specify that they should all use only hammers).

2. Give us the **flexibility** to structure the data in memory in the way that's optimal for a specific data type without forcing all data types to follow the same approach (e.g., all fasteners have a HEAD value but the Abstract Fastener Type doesn't dictate the same HEAD value for all fasteners).

3. Support **reuse** and **organization** by providing the ability to **generalize** the use of similar data types and the ability to group tasks (e.g., we can specify we'll use a fastener for two tasks in some solution and the two tasks can use different types of fasteners but we know both tasks are

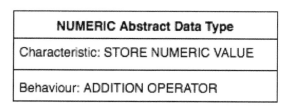

Figure 6.2: Numeric Abstract Data Type: every kind of primitive numeric data type has to have a value for the STORE_NUMERIC_VALUE characteristic and will have the ability to be added using the + operator which will do something different for each type.

"fastener tasks").

Nota Bene: We have been somewhat sloppily mixing up the phrase Data Type with Abstract Data Type. So, for example, *Integer* might be properly called a Data Type which describes the type (the kinds of values) and the operations that are allowed for that kind of *mathematical* data. We further specify an `Integer` ADT in Python which is implemented as the `int` variable type or data structure in Python. We can use this variable type `int` to create variables in Python.

In other languages, the `Integer` ADT might be implemented in different ways, for example as `integer` in Pascal or `long` in C/C++. We attempt to clarify this terminology below and also in Section 8.5:

1. A **Data Type** is the **logical** expression, independent of any language, of a **type**, the collection of **values**, and the **operations** that are permitted on that type

2. An **Abstract Data Type (ADT)** is the logical specification of a Data Type in some particular language but without any implementation details

3. A **Data Structure** is the implementation of that ADT in that particular language

6.4 Data Structures

Since the ADT is just the **interface** without any *implementation* details, it is a theoretical concept that is a representation of a Data Type; this representation only gives the possible values that are valid for that kind of data and the operations that are allowed for that data type. It doesn't give any information about what will be the actual stored value or how the operations will actually be carried out. So in this sense, an Abstract Data Type is a **logical** description while the Data Structure itself is a **concrete** implementation, as we see in Section 8.5.

A particular **data structure** gives you the concrete implementations for both the characteristics and the operations.[4] For example, we might imagine a Numeric ADT in Python as shown in Figure 6.2, where it specifies that a Numeric Data Type must store a Numeric Value and also allow for the Addition Operation. We could then use the Abstract Data Type to create a Variable Type or Data Structure, like `int`. The `int` Data Structure would allocate enough internal memory to store an integer value only (so it could not store a floating point value, for example) and, when it does addition, it would only allow for the sum to have integer values and no fractional values. The `float` Data Structure, on the other hand, would allocate more internal memory as it would need to keep track of a fractional part of the decimal, as well, and, when it does addition, it will always add a fractional part, even if it's 0. Both data structures, `int` and `float`, belong to the same Numeric ADT but differ greatly in their specific implementations.

Similarly, there is a more advanced ADT called `list`, which describes what kinds of values `lists` can hold and the operations they can have, like insert a new element, locate an existing element, delete an existing element, etc. Then, we can create specific implementations, or Data Structures, like `ArrayList`, `LinkedList`, etc. which implement that required behaviour in very different ways, depending on the kinds of problems those data structures will help tackle.

Logical Interface vs Physical Implementation

This idea of only examining *what* a system does is a form of abstraction, hence the word *abstract* in Abstract Data Type. Abstraction also allows us to differentiate between a **logical** view and a **physical** view of the system or problem. The logical perspective of the system is sometimes called the **interface** or *logical interface*.

For example, when you turn on your television, you use a remote control and don't need to know anything about how the TV works, how the image is produced, or what the circuits look like. The circuits and other machinery of the television are the **physical implementation** and the remote control would constitute the **logical interface**, which only references *what* the TV does and not the details of *how* it does it.

6.5 Strings

We have already seen a few data structures like strings and integers. It turns out that the `str` variable type is actually an example of a Sequential Data Type in Python. Some other (very useful) Sequence Data Structures that Python gives us are `list` and `tuple`. Let's explore some of these and, later on, we'll throw in the incredibly useful dictionary key:value pair-based Map Data Structure called `dict`, as well!

We haven't done much with strings so far, other than use string variables to store input from the user using the `input()` function and to print out both raw strings and string variables using the `print()` function. A string, as we've seen, is simply some **ordered collection** of characters, or valid symbols, in Python. This ordered collection is called a **sequence**. Since a string is composed of multiple characters, or objects, it is also sometimes called a **compound data type** as opposed to something like the `int` data type, which is a simple data type since it only holds a single value. It turns out that we can access individual components of a string as each character, or **element**, is assigned a unique **index** in the string.

---

[4]When we get to the Object-Oriented Paradigm in Section 8.5, we'll find that bundling the attributes and behaviours (the characteristics and the operations) together as we did for a Data Type is called **encapsulation**, a language feature. An ADT, in which we give the *interface* but not the *implementation*, is an example of **information hiding**, a design choice. There, we'll also see that the implementation of the ADT in a particular language is called a **class**.

For example, the string `mango` might be stored like this in Python:

M	A	N	G	O
[0]	[1]	[2]	[3]	[4]

As can be seen above, we can access each individual character via the index, which is a number indicating the position of a particular character, or element, in the string, the sequence of characters. The index starts at 0 as arrays and sequences are zero-indexed in both Python and Java. This often leads to the infamous off-by-one error, in which the programmer forgets that indexing begins at zero and mistakenly starts indexing from 1. This error is quite common in both beginning programmers and some highly experienced programmers who happen to write books on essential computational thinking.

We can use the **subscript operator**, which is indicated by [], to access any element at a specific index, or range of indices. We can see this below where we first initialized the variable `foo` to "mango" and then used the subscript operator to access the first character at index 0, for example:

```
>>> foo = "mango"
>>> letter = foo[0]
>>> print(letter)
m
>>> letters = foo[0:3]
>>> print(letters)
man
```

As you can see, we can access any subsequence of characters in a string value or variable using the subscript operator. We can indicate individual elements with a single numeric index or a subsequence using a numeric range with the : character. This is called **slicing** a string and it ranges from the lower index (including the element at the lower index itself) to the upper index (excluding the element at the upper index). We can also leave off either the lower or upper index to indicate the lowest or highest value, respectively, as seen below:

```
>>> print(foo[:3])
man
>>> print(foo[3:])
go
```

One other quick oddity about Python: strings are immutable (and, as we'll see later, this is true for all objects and values). So unlike other languages like Java, we can't use the subscript operator to assign values to strings. We can also use the subscript operator on a string to *access* (not modify) individual elements or a range of elements or also access any subset of elements via a `for` loop, as seen below:

```
>>> count = 0
>>> for eachLetter in foo:
...     if eachLetter == 'a':
...         count = count + 1
...
>>> print(count)
1
```

6.5.1 A First Look at Objects

Strings are actually **objects** which you can think of as being derived from an ADT, in a way; we'll be exploring objects and the classes which create them in quite some depth when we get to Object-Oriented Programming. For now, we just need to know that in Python, just about everything is an object. Objects have access to both their data, like the string value stored in a string variable, and **methods**, or *operations* that you can perform on their data, like string operations if the data is strings. We can use any string method using the string object's name (the name of the *variable* that represents that object) followed by the **dot operator**, just as we saw in Section 3.9.

Some of the methods available to string objects do a lot of neat things like convert them to upper case, lower case, etc. A method is a function and, just like some of the functions we've seen already like `print()` and `input()`, some methods return a value (like `input()`) while other methods don't (like `print()`). In addition, some methods take some input, also called **arguments** or **actual parameters**, which are listed within the parentheses, `()`. These methods, like `.upper()` and `.lower()` are *called* or *invoked* using the dot operator:

```
>>> bar = foo.upper()
>>> print(bar)
MANGO
>>> bar = foo.lower()
>>> print(bar)
mango
```

6.6 Lists and Tuples

Just like a string is a sequence of characters, a **list** is a sequence of values of any type at all, including other lists (or tuples). We've actually seen lists before when we looked at Gauss's classroom experience in Section 5.4. There are a few ways to construct new lists, as seen below:

```
>>> numbers = [1,2,3,4,5,6,7,8,9,10]
>>> emptyList = list()
>>> anotherEmptyList = []
>>> copiedList = list(numbers)
>>> populatedList = list(range(1,11))
>>> print(emptyList)
[]
>>> print(copiedList)
[1, 2, 3, 4, 5, 6, 7, 8, 9, 10]
>>> print(populatedList)
[1, 2, 3, 4, 5, 6, 7, 8, 9, 10]
```

Just like with strings, we can use the subscript operator to access elements or sub-sequences of lists. Unlike strings, though, lists are mutable. Thus, you *can* use the subscript operator to set or change elements of a list. And, of course, we can still use loops to traverse, or access all the elements of, the list:

```
>>> for eachNumber in populatedList:
...     print(eachNumber)
...
1
2
```

```
3
4
5
6
7
8
9
10
```

You can also use built-in methods of Python like `len()` to find the length of any sequence like strings, lists, or tuples:

```
>>> for i in range(len(populatedList)):
...     populatedList[i] = populatedList[i] * 2
...
>>> print(populatedList)
[2, 4, 6, 8, 10, 12, 14, 16, 18, 20]
```

Finally, you can do things like use the + operator to concatenate lists, the * operator to repeat a list for the number of times in the right operand, and do the same kind of slicing as you did for strings. There are also tons of methods available to list objects that allow you to do things like `append()` new elements to the lists, `extend()` the list with another list, and `sort()` the elements of the list.

6.6.1 Tuples

A tuple is just like a list but it's declared using parentheses, ''()'', rather than brackets, ''[]'', and it's not mutable once you've created it. Tuples are also objects that are **comparable**, which means that we can sort lists of tuples, and they're also **hashable**, although this won't mean much until we get to the `dict` data type.

Otherwise, it's essentially identical to a list:

```
>>> numbersTuple = (1,2,3,4,5,6,7,8,9,10)
>>> emptyTuple = tuple()
>>> anotherEmptyTuple = ()
>>> copiedTuple = tuple(numbersTuple)
>>> populatedTuple = tuple(range(1,11))
>>> print(nubersTuple)
>>> print(numbersTuple)
(1, 2, 3, 4, 5, 6, 7, 8, 9, 10)
>>> print(emptyTuple)
()
>>> print(copiedTuple)
(1, 2, 3, 4, 5, 6, 7, 8, 9, 10)
>>> print(populatedTuple)
(1, 2, 3, 4, 5, 6, 7, 8, 9, 10)
```

Yup, that's about it.

6.7 An Example Using Computational Thinking

Being fascinated with the Chinese zodiac, suppose you decide to write a little program that would give the corresponding Chinese zodiac sign for a given year of birth up to the year 1900. Let's once again

```
1  chinese_zodiac = [
2      (1900, "Rat"), (1901, "Ox"), (1902, "Tiger"),
3      (1903, "Rabbit"), (1904, "Dragon"), (1905, "Snake"),
4      (1906, "Horse"), (1907, "Sheep"), (1908, "Monkey"),
5      (1909, "Rooster"), (1910, "Dog"), (1911, "Pig")
6  ]
7
8
9  year = int( input("Please enter a Year of Birth: ") )
10 zodiac_index = (year - chinese_zodiac[0][0]) % 12
11 animal = chinese_zodiac[zodiac_index][1]
12
13 print("You were born in the year of the", animal)
```

Listing 6.1: Compute Chinese zodiac sign for a given year

use the three Computational Thinking steps from Section 3.2 to develop a computational solution for this very important problem:

1. **Problem Specification**: Compute the corresponding animal for a given birth year. The Chinese zodiac consists of 12 animals, 1 for each year, which repeats every 12 years. We will limit the search to just the years starting from 1900 to any future year.

2. **Algorithmic Expression**: We can maintain a list of year-name correspondences by using a list of tuples with each tuple is of the form YEAR-ANIMAL, where YEAR is an int and ANIMAL is a str as in (1900, ''Rat''). Our algorithm can then be expressed in pseudocode as:

Algorithm 6.1: Algorithm for computing the Chinese zodiac animal for a particular year

---

1 Set ZODIAC_LIST_OF_TUPLES = [(1900, "Rat"), (1901, "Ox"), (1902, "Tiger"), ...]
2 Get YEAR from User
3 INDEX_OF_YEAR = (YEAR - 1900) % 12
4 ANIMAL = ZODIAC_LIST_OF_TUPLES[INDEX_OF_YEAR][1]
5 Print "You were born in the year of the" + ANIMAL

Here, we use the modulus operator, %, to find the remainder of dividing the years since 1900 by 12 in order to get the index into our ZODIAC_LIST_OF_TUPLES. We then use that index to get the correct tuple from the ZODIAC_LIST_OF_TUPLES. Next, we return the 2nd element of that tuple by using the subscript operator with 1 to indicate the 2nd element, [1]. We save the returned string into the ANIMAL variable and print that out in the next line.

3. **Solution Implementation & Evaluation**: Let's finally implement this algorithm in Python and test with the following input values and results:

Input (Year)	Output (Animal)
1903	"Rabbit"
1950	"Tiger"
1985	"Ox"

Okay, now we're ready to do Step 3, the Python implementation, by translating Algorithm 6.1 into a Python program. We can again use IDLE's Text Editor by choosing `File > New File` and entering the program given in Listing 6.1. Then, you can choose `Run > Run Module` in order to execute your program.

This is, once again, very close to the pseudocode in Algorithm 6.1. The only note is that we use a double subscript (the `[0][0]`) on line 10 in order to get 1900, which is the first element of the first tuple of the `chinese_zodiac` list. We use this same double subscript trick to get the appropriate animal name in the next line, where `zodiac_index` contains a number between 0 and 11, corresponding to one of the 12 tuples in the `chinese_zodiac` list.

---

[5] Some might distinguish between an **ADT Specification**, which is more mathematical and language-*independent*, and is similar to a data type definition without any implementation details; an **ADT Interface**, which is language-*dependent* but still does not contain any implementation details and might be represented by a class or an abstract class in C++ or an interface class in Java; or a **Concrete Data Type**, which is language-*dependent* and includes the actual implementation of the ADT in that particular language, as we'll see in Section 8.5.

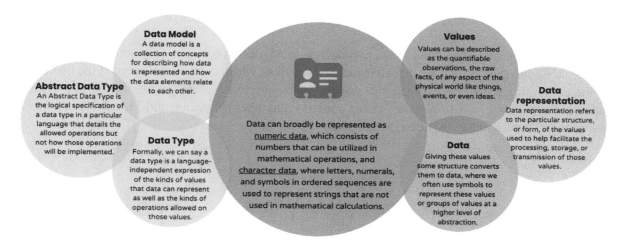

Figure 6.3: Data Types and Representations: **Values** can be described as the quantifiable observations, the raw facts, of any aspect of the physical world like things, events, or even ideas. Giving these values some structure converts them to **data**, where we often use symbols to represent these values or groups of values at a higher level of abstraction. **Data representation** refers to the particular structure, or form, of the values used to help facilitate the processing, storage, or transmission of those values.

Data can broadly be represented as *numeric data*, which consists of numbers that can be utilized in mathematical operations, and *character data*, where letters, numerals, and symbols in ordered sequences are used to represent strings that are not used in mathematical calculations. The kind of data, or its category as Aristotle might have said, is its **type**. Different types of data have different characteristics.

A **data model** is a collection of concepts for describing data that tells us how data is organized and represented. More formally, it is an *abstract model* that organizes how data is represented and how the data elements relate to each other. A **type** is the collection of *values* and a **data type** consists of the type along with the operations permitted to manipulate that type. A *data type* can also be thought of as a logical, language-independent expression of a data model and the associated operations that are valid on those data values, independent of any particular language.

The *data type* thus tells us both the kinds of values that data can represent as well as the kinds of operations allowed on those values. An **abstract data type** (ADT) is a data type that does not specify the details of how data will be organized in memory or which specific algorithms will be used for carrying out the operations on those data values. ADTs specify what operations can be performed on the data values but not how those operations will actually be implemented. While an ADT is the logical specification of a data type in some particular language but without the implementation details, a **data structure** is the actual implementation of that ADT in that particular language.[5]

A **variable** is the name for a stored value that represents some fundamental characteristic of the system or function. More abstractly, a variable is any symbol used to represent an unspecified element chosen from some set of elements. These values and variables can be combined in **expressions** and those expressions combined further into **statements**, the instructions which make up an **algorithm**.

7. Procedural Programming

> *Man is the best computer we can put aboard a spacecraft and the only one that can be mass produced with unskilled labor.*
> – Wernher von Braun, rocket engineer (1912-1977)

7.1 Functions Redux

Imagine you have a set routine every morning: you wake up, curse the alarm clock, and stumble out of bed, directly en route to the kitchen. You grab the nearest can of coffee grounds, boil some water, add the coffee grounds, and guzzle the resulting caffeine-induced nectar before finally waking up enough to realize it's Sunday and you didn't need to be awake at this ungodly hour anyway. We can illustrate this daily routine in Figure 7.1.

We can also represent the coffee making process as pseudocode in Algorithm 7.1.

Figure 7.1: Coffee making daily routine.

Algorithm 7.1: Algorithm for making coffee

---

1 Stumble Down
2 Take FOLGERS_COFFEE_GROUNDS
3 Add WATER
4 Boil WATER
5 Brew FOLGERS_COFFEE_GROUNDS and WATER for 5 minutes
6 Get Coffee
7 Drink Coffee

Wouldn't it be nice if this daily routine could somehow be automated? In fact, there is a modern marvel that does just this: the automated coffee maker! You can buy a coffee maker, set an alarm on it, and when you stumble down half-awake, that hot, refreshing beverage is already waiting for you. Your coffee maker took care of all the steps in Algorithm 7.1: from boiling the water, to adding the coffee grounds, to brewing the final concoction. We can think of the single coffee maker as replacing and automatically carrying out the different coffee making steps from your routine as shown in Figure 7.2.

A single entity that encapsulates a number of steps is referred to as a **subroutine** or **procedure** or **function** in computer science. In this context, you can think of a function as just a *name* for a particular sequence of instructions. For example, we might refer to the sequence of steps in our daily routine in Algorithm 7.1 as CoffeeMaker. This is a kind of *abstraction* and, once you've defined a CoffeeMaker function, you can just use the name CoffeeMaker everywhere you'd normally utilize that entire sequence of instructions just as you do when making some coffee in your morning routine.

A function in computer science is slightly different from a function as defined in mathematics. We've seen before, in Section 0.5, that a mathematical function can be thought of as some process that takes an input and maps it to an output.

Figure 7.2: Coffee maker metaphor.

What is the difference between a sub-routine, a procedure, and a function? In imperative languages:

1. A **sub-routine** is a (usually named) sequence of instructions to perform some task that is encapsulated as a single unit.
2. A **procedure** is a sub-routine that can possibly take some input, can have a side-effect, but does not return a value as output. A **side-effect** in computer science means anything that changes something, like changing a variable's value, writing to a file, reading from a file, sending data to a display, etc.
3. A **function** is a procedure that returns a value, where the output value returned can be different on different calls to that function. There are subtle distinctions that can sometimes be drawn: e.g., you might have a *pure* function which always returns the same value on all calls for some specific input and does not produce any side-effects.[1]

This is analogous to what our `CoffeeMaker` function does, as well, as seen in Figure 7.3. In the case of our `CoffeeMaker` function, it takes some coffee grounds as *input* and *processes* them to *output* a cup of coffee.

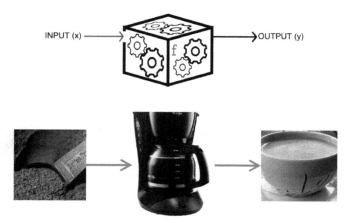

Figure 7.3: Coffee maker as a function.

We can also express the `CoffeeMaker` function in **pseudocode**, which we met in Section 1.7, as shown in Algorithm 7.2.

---

[1] These kinds of interpretations bring a function in computer science even closer to the definition of a function in mathematics by requiring it to further not affect anything outside itself and relying only on its direct inputs; this is also closer to the idea of a function in *functional programming* paradigms.

Algorithm 7.2: Algorithm for the morning coffee routine using Functions

---

INITIALIZE: Define the Helper Function and then wait for the Alarm Clock to go off

:

:

DEFINE: First, Define the CoffeeMaker Helper Function

1 **Function** CoffeeMaker(*COFFEE_GROUNDS*):
2 | Take *COFFEE_GROUNDS*
3 | Add WATER
4 | Boil WATER
5 | Brew *COFFEE_GROUNDS* and WATER for 5 minutes
6 | **return** *COFFEE*
7 **end**

:

:

START: Then, Start the *main* program here
   // The Alarm Clock starts everything and wakes you up
   // As you stumble on down, it also calls the CoffeeMaker Helper Function
8 CoffeeMaker(FOLGERS_COFFEE_GROUNDS)
9 Get Coffee
10 Drink Coffee

Notice we start off by first **defining** the function and then, when the program itself starts, we can **call**, or **invoke**, the function as many times as we want. We also follow the *functional notation* we first met in Section 0.5.3 and use parentheses after its name (CoffeeMaker()) to denote a function or procedure, with the input listed within the parentheses: CoffeeMaker(COFFEE_GROUNDS).

The input is referred to as the function's **parameter**; later on, we'll draw a distinction between the parameters in the function's definition (called *formal parameters*) vs the parameters that are passed to the function when it's called or invoked (these parameters are called the *actual parameters* or the **arguments**). In Algorithm 7.2, *COFFEE_GROUNDS* is the formal parameter and *FOLGERS_COFFEE_GROUNDS* is the actual parameter or argument.

7.2 Functions in Python

In Python, things work the same way. For example, suppose we had the following code, which just prints out the lyrics to Lead Belly's iconic "Good Night Irene":[2]

```
# Start the main program here:
print("Irene, good night")
print("Irene, good night")
print("Good night, Irene")
print("Good night, Irene")
print("I'll get you in my dreams")
print("Last Saturday night I got married")
```

---

[2]Huddie William Ledbetter, aka Lead Belly, likely heard a version of this song that was written in 1886 by Gussie Lord Davis, although some versions of it can be traced back to even earlier: https://www.ft.com/content/ba35fd76-6928-11e5-97d0-1456a776a4f5. You can hear the Smithsonian's recording of Lead Belly singing it here: https://folkways.si.edu/leadbelly

```
print("Me and my wife settled down")
print("Now me and my wife have parted")
print("I'm gonna take a little stroll downtown")
print("Irene, good night")
print("Irene, good night")
print("Good night, Irene")
print("Good night, Irene")
print("I'll get you in my dreams")
print("Some times I live in the country")
print("Some times I live in town")
print("Some times I take a great notion")
print("To jump in the river and drown")
print("Irene, good night")
print("Irene, good night")
print("Good night, Irene")
print("Good night, Irene")
print("I'll get you in my dreams")
print("Quit your ramblin', quit your gamblin'")
print("Stop staying out late at night")
print("Go home with your wife and family")
print("Stay there by the fireside bright")
# End of program
```

We might notice that the chorus is repeated in the song so we can parcel out those repeated statements into their own function or procedure, print_the_chorus(), as follows:

```
# First, define the helper procedure/function
def print_the_chorus():
  print("Irene, good night")
  print("Irene, good night")
  print("Good night, Irene")
  print("Good night, Irene")
  print("I'll get you in my dreams")


# Start the main program here:
print_the_chorus()

print("Last Saturday night I got married")
print("Me and my wife settled down")
print("Now me and my wife have parted")
print("I'm gonna take a little stroll downtown")

print_the_chorus()

print("Some times I live in the country")
print("Some times I live in town")
print("Some times I take a great notion")
print("To jump in the river and drown")

print_the_chorus()
```

```
print("Quit your ramblin', quit your gamblin'")
print("Stop staying out late at night")
print("Go home with your wife and family")
print("Stay there by the fireside bright")
# End of program
```

As you can see above, we did almost exactly the same thing as our pseudocode example about making coffee: we first **defined** the procedure or function, using the Python keyword def, and then **called**, or **invoked**, the procedure as many times as we wanted using *functional notation*, by using parentheses after the name of the procedure: print_the_chorus().

If our procedure needed some input, we could add that within the parentheses. One of the key points is that we needed to define the procedure *before* we could actually use it so the Python interpreter would know what the heck we meant when we instructed it to print_the_chorus()!

The general syntax for defining a new function in Python is thus:

```
def FUNCTION_NAME ( OPTIONAL_LIST_OF_PARAMETERS ):
    EXECUTE_STATEMENTS
```

One of the statements that are executed by the function must include the return keyword as a function is required to return a value of some sort. A procedure is defined the same way as a function since Python just considers a procedure to be a function that doesn't return a value. A procedure in Python, then, is simply a function that doesn't include a return statement.

In general, we can think of a sub-routine definition as having the following components, depending on whether it's a function or a procedure:

1. Name: Each sub-routine has to have a valid name, or **identifier**, that follows the rules of the language and is hopefully descriptive about its functionality.
2. Statements: a sub-routine packages, or **encapsulates**, the statements you want to execute together as a bundle; the sub-routine should therefore contain the code you want to run when it is called, or invoked. These statements might do things like print something to the screen, do a calculation, or even call other functions.
3. Inputs: Optional: A procedure or function might have optional inputs to help accomplish what it needs to do.
4. Outputs: A function returns a value so it should have an appropriate return statement as one of its bundled statements.
5. Comments: Optional: ideally, all sub-routines should also have header and in-line comments. **Header comments** describe what the procedure or function does while **in-line comments** delineate why certain coding choices were made by the programmer. There are more rules for programming style and we'll discuss them in just a bit.

Procedural vs Modular Programming

Breaking up a programmatic solution into procedural units like functions or procedures is called **procedural programming**. If the entire program can be decomposed using functions or procedures that are also independent and interchangeable, this approach is then called **modular programming**. As we'll see when we learn about *object-oriented programming*, taking a procedural approach isn't the only way to create modular programs.

7.3 Sub-Routines with Parameters and Values

Procedures and functions can both accept input. That input is represented by a formal parameter in the definition of the function or procedure and, when that sub-routine is invoked, the actual value to be manipulated is sent in either as a literal value or as a variable. Let's see some examples of these next.

7.3.1 Procedures with Parameters

A procedure can take some input in the form of a parameter, or more than one parameters. For example, we could first define print_the_chorus(name) and then call it from the shell, as seen below. Since this sub-routine does not return a value, we refer to it as a procedure. This procedure happens to take an input, which is represented by the formal parameter name.

```
##### Example of defining a procedure: notice no return value
def print_the_chorus(name):
    print(name +", good night")
    print(name +", good night")
    print("Good night, "+ name)
    print("Good night, "+ name)
    print("I'll get you in my dreams")
```

When we call the function below, we pass it the actual parameter, or argument, ''Jane''. The procedure then faithfully prints the chorus for Jane even though it doesn't quite have the same ring to it as Irene.

```
> ##### Calling, or invoking, the procedure
> print_the_chorus("Jane")
>
Jane, good night
Jane, good night
Good night, Jane
Good night, Jane
I'll get you in my dreams
```

7.3.2 Functions with Parameters

A function, like a procedure, can also take some input in the form of a parameter, or more than one parameters. For example, we could define get_value_squared(x) and then call it from the shell, as seen below where we invoke this function three times. Since this sub-routine *does* return a value, we refer to it as a function. This function happens to take some input, which is represented by the formal parameter x.

```
##### Example of defining a function: note that there IS a return value
def get_value_squared(x):
  return ( x*x )
```

When we call it below, we pass it the actual parameter, or argument, 3 in the call to the function: get_value_squared(3). Then, we invoke the function two more times and pass it the arguments 5 (in get_value_squared(5)) and 10 (in get_value_squared(10)).

A function is different from a procedure in that it returns a value. When a function does return a value, the call to the function is replaced with that value so you could then do further processing on that returned value, things like storing the returned value in a variable or using it as part of an expression or a call to some other function.

The three examples are:

1. Calling the function and not using the returned value (kinda useless in this particular case)[3]
2. Using the return value in an expression
3. Storing the return value in a variable and printing out the value of that variable

```
> ##### 1. Calling/invoking the function and discarding the return value
> get_value_squared(3)
>
=> 9


> ##### 2. Calling/invoking the function and using the return value in an expression
> 3 + get_value_squared(5)
>
=> 28


> ##### 3. Calling/invoking the function and storing the return value in a variable
> foo = get_value_squared(10)
> print(foo)
100
```

If, on the other hand, a function does not return a value, it should be used as an entire statement itself.

7.3.3 Input Values and Variables

We saw above that a function, or a procedure, can accept some input. This input can be a direct value or a variable that evaluates to some value. For example, instead of invoking our print chorus procedure with the literal value, "Jane", we could instead use a variable to store the name and then just pass that variable to the procedure when we call it, as seen below:

---

[3]In case 1 below, the interpreter echoes the result of the function call so we see the 9 displayed by the interpreter. If you used that same function call, get_value_squared(3), in a program or a script in the same way, it would not echo any value and so would not display anything, thus making it "kinda useless in this particular case."

```
> ##### Calling, or invoking, the procedure
> myName = "Jane"
> print_the_chorus(myName)
>
Jane, good night
Jane, good night
Good night, Jane
Good night, Jane
I'll get you in my dreams
```

We could do the same with the function for getting the squared value: instead of passing it the literal value, 3, we could store 3 in a variable and then pass it that variable, instead.

```
> ##### 1. Calling/invoking the function and discarding the return value
> foo = 3
> get_value_squared(foo)
>
=> 9
```

When the interpreter parses an instruction like `get_value_squared( foo )`, it first converts all variables (like `foo`) to their assigned values (in this case, 3) and then uses that value in the computation. So the end result is that the function, or procedure, always operates on some literal value but it just depends on whether you've *hardcoded* that value into your program (passing it the literal integer 3) or allowed it to be represented by a variable whose value could change, like `foo`.[4]

7.4 Namespaces and Variable Scope

Variables, like people, have a certain *lifetime* where you can access and interact with them. A variable comes into its electronic existence when we first define the variable and it is returned to its primordial electronic ether when it goes out of scope. The **scope** of a variable refers to the part of a program where a variable is valid and accessible.

In python, if a variable is declared[5] in the main body of a program file, and outside of any module like a sub-routine or class, it is called a **global variable**. Global variables are visible to every module throughout the file as well as within any file that imports the main file, as seen in this example:

```
# This function uses the global variable global_string defined below
def test_function():
    print(global_string)

# Define global_string: this has global scope
#     since it is defined outside any module
global_string = "I am GLOBAL!"
```

---

[4] On a bit of a historical side-note, you'll often find programs littered with variables called `foo` or `bar` or `foobar`. These variable names trace back to both MIT and DEC but also to the military use of the term FUBAR (*?$!ed Up Beyond All Recognition), which is similar to the origin of SNAFU in the military. The word `foo` also showed up in the 1930s Smokey Stover comic as an abbreviation for foolish, which led to it being referenced in the 415th Night Fighter Squadron's observation of UFOs as "foo fighters," a term that was later adopted by Dave Grohl when he wanted to release his post-Nirvana recordings.

[5] Things are actually a little funny in Python. Normally, declaring a variable is really the process of binding a name, or identifier, to a certain datatype. In Python, however, a variable is actually created during the assignment when its datatype is defined to be the same as the datatype of the value being assigned to it.

```
test_function()


### OUTPUT:
>
I am GLOBAL!
>
```

Variables that are defined *inside* of a module like a class or sub-routine are called **local variables**. Local variables are only accessible from the point where they are defined in the sub-routine (or module) to the end of that sub-routine (or module). That means you cannot access or use a local variable outside of the module within which it was defined; the scope of a local variable is restricted to the beginning and end of the module only. Here, we see an example of a local variable that is defined (created) within the function and, when we try to access it outside the function, we get an error:

```
1  # This function uses the LOCAL variable local_string
2  #      which was defined within test_function()
3  def test_function():
4    local_string = "I am LOCAL!"
5    print(local_string)
6
7  # First, test the function:
8  test_function()
9  # Now, try to print local_string, whose scope is limited to test_function(),
10 #      from a global scope
11 print(local_string)
12
13
14 ### OUTPUT:
15 >
16 I am LOCAL!
17 Traceback (most recent call last):
18   File "python", line 11, in <module>
19 NameError: name 'local_string' is not defined
20 >
```

In addition, local variables only exist in memory while the sub-routine is executing; when the sub-routine ends, local variables are deleted and their memory is freed. **Formal parameters** that are used in procedures or functions are also *local* variables.

Although global variables are also *visible* within functions, if you want to *change* the value of a global variable *within* the function, perhaps by assigning a new value to it, you have to use the global keyword in Python, as shown below:

```
# This function uses the global variable global_string defined below
def test_function():
    global global_string
    print(global_string)
    # Change global_string WITHIN the function:
    global_string = "I am a MODIFIED GLOBAL!"
    print(global_string)
```

```
# Define global_string: this has global scope
#      since it is defined outside any module
global_string = "I am GLOBAL!"
test_function()
print(global_string)


### OUTPUT:
>
I am GLOBAL!
I am a MODIFIED GLOBAL!
I am a MODIFIED GLOBAL!
>
```

Thus, you can modify the **state** of a program, which is determined by the values of its variables, by changing a global variable within any function in that same program. Although useful, global variables can have unintended consequences and lead to spaghetti code.

A Harmful Flow

When the computer scientist Edsger W. Dijkstra wrote a paper called, "Go To Statement Considered Harmful," it led to the acceptance of structured programming as we saw in Section 3.7. Even though goto statements have been mainly sidelined from programming for the most part, a call to a procedure or function is similar to the goto command in that the **flow of execution** of the program is interrupted when the interpreter comes upon a function call.

As soon as it hits the function call, the execution flow jumps to the first line of the invoked function and the interpreter starts executing all the statements packaged into that function. But raw goto statements are still considered evil for the most part.

Computer scientists followed up on this harmful trend and realized that global variables are actually quite similar to goto statements: they can also lead to inefficient spaghetti code. This led to the development of strong procedural or functional languages and, eventually, also to the object-oriented paradigm which avoids these kinds of issues with global variables and shared states, as we will see later.[6]

Most languages track all these local and global variables by forming various **namespaces**, which are just collections of the names, or identifiers, of the objects that are available in a particular context.

---

[6]I should add the caveat that a field within a Singleton design pattern object can essentially be considered to be a global variable in disguise.

Since *everything* in Python, from literals to lists to functions to classes, is an object, this kind of mapping of the name or identifier to the underlying object allows programmers to access an object by the name that was assigned to it.

Python provides three levels of namespaces: the built-in namespace (where it keeps track of the python keywords and built-in variables), the module namespace (where it keeps track of global variables), and a function namespace (where it keeps track of local variables). We can think of the built-in namespace as a kind of super-namespace.

In this approach, the scope of a variable just corresponds to the namespace that contains the mapping of that variable name to the underlying object. The order in which Python searches these namespaces to map the variable to the correct object is to first look in the Local scope, within the function or functions where the variable was defined and lives; then to look in the Global scope, which is the uppermost level of the program that contains that variable; and, finally, within the Built-In scope, which contains the special reserved keywords.

7.5 Exception Handling

As we saw in Section 3.5, errors are very common during the execution of programs. We met the three major kinds of errors there, as well, which we categorized as either Syntax, Semantic, or Logic errors. These three kinds of errors can be caught either at **compile-time** or at **runtime**. For example, we saw that most syntax and some semantic errors (the static semantic errors) are usually caught by the translator at compile time but the main way to catch logic errors is by testing at runtime. Dynamic semantic errors are also caught at runtime and often fall into a category of error called **runtime exceptions**.

These errors represent the occurrence of some exceptional circumstance during program execution that cause the program to terminate prematurely. Events like this which disrupt a program's normal flow of execution are referred to as **exceptions**. Most languages use exceptions for both compile-time and run-time errors. In languages like Java, exceptions that occur at compile-time are called **checked** exceptions whereas all run-time exceptions are called **unchecked** exceptions. In languages like Python, C++, and C#, the compiler does not force the programmer to deal with exceptions so all exceptions are unchecked.

Dealing with such errors is referred to as **exception handling** and is part of a larger strategy of **defensive programming** to make programs more robust. Whenever an exceptional situation of some sort occurs, an exception is *raised*. In Python, the exception is represented by an object which encapsulates the specific type of error that occurred when that exception was raised. The exception object contains information about what went wrong in a message string: whether it was due to a programming error, a user error, or an unexpected condition like an inaccessible file. Whenever a program encounters an exception, it must either handle the exception right away or terminate the program execution. We can handle an exception by **catching** the raised exception.

7.5.1 Handling Exceptions in Python

For example, let's say we wanted to ask the user to input a number in order to perform a division. If the user enters a string instead of a number and we try to divide a number by the given input, the program will output a `ValueError`. If we don't properly handle this kind of an error, the program will immediately terminate execution of any more instructions and show us the error message associated with the exception, as seen below where the user enters the string `three` instead of the integer 3:

```
x = int(input("Please enter an integer: "))
print("Let's divide 10 by", x, "to get :", 10/x)

### OUTPUT:
>
Please enter an integer:  three
Traceback (most recent call last):
  File "python", line 1, in <module>
ValueError: invalid literal for int() with base 10: 'three'
>
```

Suspicious code, like the one trying to divide by some undetermined user input above, can be handled by using adding a try statement block. The main idea of **exception handling** is to enclose the code which might raise an exception inside the try block as seen in the exception handling syntax for Python:

```
try:
    EXECUTE_STATEMENTS_THAT_MIGHT_THROW_AN_EXCEPTION
except <KIND_OF_EXCEPTIONS>:
    EXECUTE_STATEMENTS_IN_CASE_EXCEPTION_OCCURS
else:
    EXECUTE_STATEMENTS_IN_CASE_EXCEPTION_DOES_NOT_OCCUR
finally:
    EXECUTE_STATEMENTS_REGARDLESS_OF_EXCEPTION_OCCURRENCE
```

The try block is followed by an except block, which includes statements to help compensate for the exception occurring. A try block can have more than one except blocks following it, where each handles specific kinds of exceptions. If an except block doesn't specify a particular kind of exception, it will respond to any kind of exception that is raised by the try block. If it does specify a particular kind of exception, or a list of different exceptions, that except block will respond if any of those kinds of exceptions are raised.

If an exception is raised by some statement in the try block, control immediately shifts to the except block that contains the matching exception handler and the rest of the statements in the try clause are skipped. If there is no except handler with a matching exception, the program stops with that exception.

If no exception is raised in the try block, the except block is skipped entirely. The except block can also be followed by an else block, which is executed if the exception doesn't occur. The else block, in turn, can also be followed by an optional finally block, which is executed regardless of whether the exception occurs or not. We can also explicitly **throw** an exception using the raise statement within the try block; this will cause the program to immediately stop execution and also cause an exception to occur if it is not already handled in a corresponding except block.

So we can take the above error and handle any potential exceptions arising from incorrect user input as:

```
try:
  x = int(input("Please enter an integer: "))
  print("Let's divide 10 by", x, "to get :", 10/x)
```

```
  print("We made it without any exceptions!")
except:
  print("Whoops, the user messed up and did not enter an integer, I think!")
```

```
### OUTPUT:
>
Please enter an integer:  three
Whoops, the user messed up and did not enter an integer, I think!
>
```

```
### OUTPUT:
>
Please enter an integer:  3
Let's divide 10 by 3 to get : 3.3333333333333335
We made it without any exceptions!
>
```

That's much nicer! We can make it even better, and more useful, by including the exception handler within a loop and adding in all the bells and whistles, as follows:

```
keep_asking = True
while keep_asking:
  try:
    x = int(input("Please enter an integer: "))
    print("Let's divide 10 by", x, "to get :", 10/x)
    print("We made it without any exceptions!")
  except ValueError:
    print("The input was definitely not an integer! Please try again!")
  else:
    keep_asking = False
  finally:
    print("Value of keep_asking is:", keep_asking)
```

```
### OUTPUT:
>
Please enter an integer:  three
The input was definitely not an integer! Please try again!
Value of keep_asking is: True
Please enter an integer:  3
Let's divide 10 by 3 to get : 3.3333333333333335
We made it without any exceptions!
Value of keep_asking is: False
>
```

If everything is handled correctly in the above exception handler, the code continues after the exception handler clause as normal.

The one caveat is that if you do leave out the name of the exception entirely after the except keyword, the exception handler will then catch *all* exceptions and handle them all the same way! As you might guess, this is not optimal as you will then handle a `TypeError` exception the same way as you would have handled a `ZeroDivisionError` exception. In general, it is a good to be as specific as possible and only catch those exceptions that your code can handle.

As you can see in the example above, the `else` block contains code that has to be executed if the `try` block didn't raise any exceptions. This can also be a useful place to place code to ensure you don't add any code to the `try` block whose exceptions you don't catch. For example, in the code above, we could move the line that prints the result of our division inside the `else` block. Finally, the `else` block should go after all the `except` blocks but before the `finally` block (bad pun intended), which can also release any resources used by the code inside the `try` block since it is always executed. As our programs get more sophisticated, we can even raise our own custom exceptions to ensure it runs smoothly.

Problem 7.1 In the above code where we ask the user for a number and then divide by that number (i.e., we use the number input by the user as the divisor), what if the user enters a 0? Can you extend the exception handling code to account for these illegal division by 0 runtime errors, as well?

7.6   File I/O

A running program might get data from the user and do some calculations to reach some incredibly important conclusions but, as soon as the computer is turned off, all of those earth-shattering insights will be gone since all data in a running program is kept in the volatile RAM, as we saw in Section 3.1.3. If you want to make data **persistent**, i.e., to have it outlive the program run that created it, you have to store the data in some more permanent form, perhaps as a file on some secondary storage device like a hard drive or a solid state drive.

This is such a common task that it probably won't surprise you to learn that Python provides an easy way to both read and write data to files. But how exactly does a program connect to a secondary storage device and write data to it or read data from it? Before the advent of Unix, most programs had to form explicit connections to each secondary storage device. That means you had to figure out how things worked for each brand of hard drive, keyboard, monitor, etc. As you might imagine, this would be rather tedious after a while.

Rather than force the program to deal with each individual hardware component, Unix developed a *standardized* approach in which the idea of input and output was *abstracted* out and input/output was then represented by a *stream metaphor*. Instead of writing data to a physical hard drive, the program could deal with an *abstract* output device, modeled as an output stream or output file; rather than deal with a physical keyboard, the program could deal with an *abstract* input device, modeled as an input stream or input file. In these Unix-like systems, the programs no longer needed to know the details of the underlying physical device as the operating system took care of those messy details for you.

Since C was the language of choice on Unix systems, it provided support for these abstract *standard streams* on Unix-like operating systems; streams like standard input (STDIN), standard output (STDOUT), and standard error (STDERR). Consequently, most languages derived from C, like Python and Java, also provide support for such streams regardless of the underlying operating system.

If you don't like the stream metaphor, you can instead think of a stream as an automatically created local file that is transmitted by the operating system to your program and automatically destroyed after it's used. Using this metaphor, when your program opens up a connection to the keyboard, you can think of whatever the user types as being saved into this automatically created local file and then transmitted to the program by the operating system. When your program sends something to the output stream, you can think of it as being written to an automatically created local file and then transmitted by the operating system to the underlying physical disk drive. Depending on the underlying operating system, this might be closer to what it's actually doing, as well.

Regardless of your metaphor of choice, let's delve into the details of how Python actually uses these streams to let you access files for Input and Output (I/O).

Standards in the stream...

The computer scientist Dennis M. Ritchie talked about the ideas of standard streams in his 1984 paper entitled, "A Stream Input-Output System." These streams would then replace the "traditional rigid connection between processes and terminals" so that they would allow modules to "be inserted dynamically into the stream that connects a user's program to a device."

This idea of streams dated back to the early days of Unix and Multics where it was developed further by the likes of Ken Thompson, Dennis Ritchie, Rudd Canaday, Doug McIlroy, et al., when they dealt with data streams and also added the ability to *pipe* different streams in 1972. For more information about this, you can read Dennis Ritchie's, "The Evolution of the Unix Time-sharing System."

Reading from a file in Python

Python makes the task of dealing with files relatively simple and straightforward. For example, you can open an existing file you want to read like this:

```
myfile = open('filename', 'r')
```

The open() function lets you open a file for either reading or writing and takes two arguments: a string representing the filename you want to open and a string representing the kinds of operations you want to do on the file (read, write, etc.). The second argument above, 'r', indicates that we want to *read* from the file. The open() function returns an abstract file object and connects it to the variable called myfile (you can, of course, call it whatever you want). This file object then gives you access to many methods that allow you to interact with the underlying file.

For example, you can loop through all the lines in the file using a for loop:

```
for each_line in myfile:
  print(each_line)
```

Alternatively, you could read in all the lines in one go and store them in a Python list using the readlines() method as follows:

```
all_lines = myfile.readlines()
```

You could even read in the entire file as a single String using the read() method:

```
single_string = myfile.read()
```

Which approach you take usually depends on the constraints of the problem and resources you have available (or perhaps just your preference). For example, if you try to use `read()` or `readlines()` to process a very large file, your script may run out of memory and eventually crash. But, after you've opened a file, you can only read it once using this particular approach. Under this approach, if you want to read it again, you'd have to close it and open it again. In order to close a file, you can call the `close()` method on the file object as follows:

```
myfile.close()
```

When you're done working with a file, it is a very good idea, in general, to properly close the file as it would free up the resources that were tied with the file. Python also has a **garbage collector** that goes around and cleans up any un-referenced objects and removes them from memory. But the garbage collector isn't reliable in its expeditiousness. That is why you should always use the `close()` method to close the file explicitly after you finish any operations you like on the file.

The only problem is that this method isn't entirely safe. If an exception occurs when you're performing some operation with the file, the program will exit without closing the file. When such an exceptional situation occurs, the safest approach is to use exception handling and enclose the code in a `try...finally` block, as follows:

```
try:
  myfile = open('test_file.txt', encoding = 'utf-8')
  # Perform all desired file operations
finally:
  myfile.close()
```

By using proper exception handling, we can rest assured the file will be properly closed even if an exception is raised that causes the program flow to stop. There are lots of python-specific tricks you can use like using the `with` keyword, which ensures the file is closed internally, thus avoiding the need to explicitly call the `close()` method. Pythonistas are adept at such tricks of the trade and you can refer to a python-specific text for the skills and insights needed to qualify as such.

Writing to a file in Python

Writing to a file is very similar to reading a file. When you want to write some data to a file, you can open the file using very similar syntax:

```
myfile = open('filename', 'w')
```

The second argument above, `'w'`, specifies that the file should be opened for writing. We can then write something to the file use the `write()` method as shown below:

```
myfile.write("I as just written to the file on the disk!\n")
```

As you can see above, we added in the newline character at the end of the line as we have to explicitly add in newlines. It's not mandatory but, when desired, the \n escape sequence can be used to automatically add in the newline that is appropriate for the underlying operating system (e.g., carriage return (some Macs), line feed (Linux and Macs), or carriage return and line feed (DOS/Windows)). And, of course, just as with reading the file, it's a great idea to close the file once you're done with it and to also use exception handling just as we did then.

Finally, Python can also easily handle non-text files like images, videos, executable programs, zip files, etc. These kinds of non-text files are called **binary files** and usually must be opened with specialized text editors as they're not organized as lines of text.[7] You can open these binary files in Python by specifying `'rb'` or `'wb'` as the second argument in the `open()` method and then using the `read()` method to read the data. The only caveat is that the `read()` method will return bytes rather text strings.

Using the `print()` method instead

Sometimes, it can be easier to use a familiar function like `print()` to also write data to a file. Python allows you to do just this by re-directing print statements to the file, so the result of the print is sent to the file instead of the display terminal. In order to do so, you have to add in a second argument to the `print()` method that indicates the output filename as follows:

```
print("Print this to the file instead of the terminal!", file=myfile)
```

The second argument, the `file=` part, normally points to the STDOUT stream and is set by default to `sys.stdout` as `file=sys.stdout`. The one caveat to using the `print()` method is that it automatically adds a newline so we don't have to explicitly put a newline at the end of the string in this case. As always, once we're done writing all the data to the file, we should close it with the `close()` method, `myfile.close()`. And, as usual, we should also use exception handling with any file operations.

7.7 An Example Using Computational Thinking

We've already used functions that were written by others. For example, we used the built-in python subroutines such as `input()`, which takes a string argument that serves as the prompt for the user to enter some value. We've also used the library subroutine `math.factorial()`, part of the math library, which takes as its parameter the number for which you want to compute the factorial.

In this chapter, we learned how to create our own sub-routines, both procedures and functions. Let's build upon that and write our own handy mathematical functions. Suppose we want to start by creating a function that would calculate the distance between two points on the Cartesian plane. We can, as usual, employ the three Computational Thinking steps from Section 3.2 to develop a computational solution for this function:

1. **Problem Specification**: Given two points on the Cartesian plane, (x_1, y_1) and (x_2, y_2), compute the distance between them. We will constrain our problem to only dealing with integer values for the x and y components of the two points for now.

2. **Algorithmic Expression**: We can use the normal equation for determining the distance, d, between two points, (x_1, y_1) and (x_2, y_2), on the Cartesian plane:

$$d = \sqrt{(x_2 - x_1)^2 + (y_2 - y_1)^2} \tag{7.1}$$

We will also put the actual calculation within a function so our algorithm can then be expressed in pseudocode as:

---

[7] If you're in the market for a general-purpose text editor that has everything *including* the metaphorical kitchen sink and a built-in psychoanalyst, I highly recommend `emacs`, which is available for every operating system and is free and open source. An alternative is is `vim`, also known as the Editor-Which-Must-Not-Be-Named.

Algorithm 7.3: Algorithm for computing distance between two Cartesian points

INITIALIZE: Import any libraries, Define the Helper Function, and then Start the main program

$\vdots$

$\vdots$

DEFINE: First, Define the `Cartesian_Distance()` Helper Function

1 **Function** `Cartesian_Distance(` x_1,y_1,x_2,y_2 `):`

2 $\quad$ x_squared_distance = $(x_2 - x_1)^2$

3 $\quad$ y_squared_distance = $(y_2 - y_1)^2$

4 $\quad$ d = $\sqrt{\text{x\_squared\_distance} + \text{y\_squared\_distance}}$

5 $\quad$ **return** d

6 **end**

$\vdots$

$\vdots$

START: Then, Start the *main* program here

7 Print "Distance between (0,0) and (1,1) is: " $+$ `Cartesian_Distance(0,0,1,1)`

Here, we followed the same approach for functions as we did previously in this chapter by defining the helper method first and then using it in the main part of the program.

3. **Solution Implementation & Evaluation**: Let's finally implement this algorithm in Python and test with the following input values and results:

Input $((x_1,y_1)$ and $(x_2,y_2))$	Output (d)
$(0,0)$ and $(1,1)$	1.414
$(1,3)$ and $(3,5)$	2.828
$(8,10)$ and $(1,7)$	7.616

Okay, now we're ready to do Step 3, the Python implementation, by translating Algorithm 7.3 into a Python program. We can again use IDLE's Text Editor by choosing `File > New File` and entering the program given in Listing 7.1. Then, you can choose `Run > Run Module` in order to execute your program. Once again, the pseudocode in Algorithm 7.3 is close to the final solution but we had to translate some of the mathematical notation into Python's acceptable notation and also import the `math` library in order to access its `sqrt()` method.

```
1   # INITIALIZE: Import pre-processor directive
2   import math
3
4   # DEFINE: Define helper function
5   def cartesian_distance(x1, y1, x2, y2):
6     x_squared_distance = (x2-x1)**2
7     y_squared_distance = (y2-y1)**2
8     d = math.sqrt( x_squared_distance + y_squared_distance )
9     return ( d )
10
11
12  # START: Main program below:
13  print ("The distance between (0,0) and (1,1) is " \
```

```
14    + str( cartesian_distance(0,0,1,1) ) + ".")
15  print ("The distance between (1,3) and (3,5) is " \
16    + str( cartesian_distance(1,3,3,5) ) + ".")
17  print ("The distance between (8,10) and (1,7) is " \
18    + str( cartesian_distance(8,10,1,7) ) + ".")
```

Listing 7.1: Compute Cartesian Distance

Problem 7.2 Let's further explore the function cartesian_distance(x1,y1,x2,y2) in Listing 7.1 which **encapsulates** the statements that calculate the distance between two points on the Cartesian plane. What are the formal parameters for the cartesian_distance() function in Listing 7.1? How are those parameters used? Where in the code are the results of calling cartesian_distance() specified?

Exception Handling

Syntax, Semantic, and Logical errors can occur either at **compile-time** (syntax and static semantic) or at **run-time** (dynamic semantic and logical). Semantic and logical errors are also sometimes referred to as **exceptions** and we can use **exception handling** to take care of such exceptional situations.

Most languages use exceptions for both compile-time and run-time errors. In languages like Java, exceptions that occur at compile-time are called **checked** exceptions whereas run-time exceptions are called **unchecked** exceptions. In languages like Python, C++, and C#, the compiler does not force the programmer to deal with exceptions so all exceptions are unchecked.

Figure 7.4: Exception handling is used to handle most semantic and logical errors.

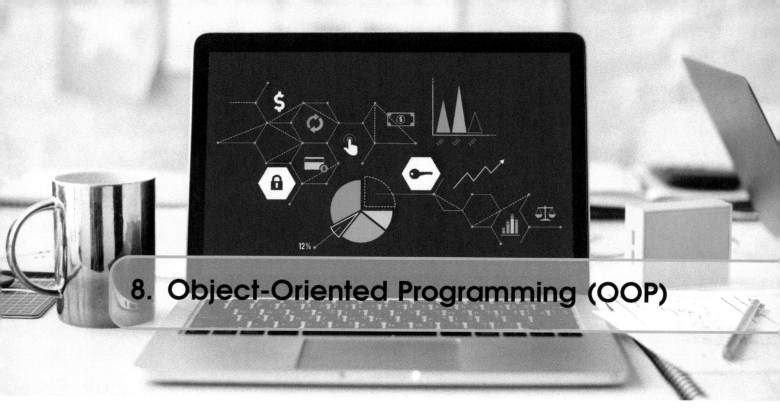

8. Object-Oriented Programming (OOP)

> *I have always wished that my computer would be as easy to use as my telephone. My wish has come true. I no longer know how to use my telephone.*
> – Bjarne Stroustrup

8.1 Zen and the Art of Object-Oriented Programming

As digital computers started to become more ubiquitous in the 20th century, scientists were intrigued with the idea of using these machines to solve complex, real-world problems. They started to simulate real-world problems like planetary systems and manufacturing systems using computationally intensive approaches like Monte Carlo methods and discrete event simulations.[1]

In 1962, computer scientists Kristin Nygaard and Ole-Johan Dahl developed a new language, SIMULA (SIMUlation LAnguage), and used it on the UNIVAC 1107 to model such events and systems. Their goal was to create a language that allowed researchers to concentrate on the problem and not the underlying computer. To achieve this greater degree of **abstraction**, they decided to model these kind of discrete event simulations as a bunch of interacting processes. The processes, in turn, modeled both the system **properties** and the system **behaviours**, or actions.

For example, they could apply this approach to looking at the problem of a toll booth where a car or a truck or a bus comes up to the booth and pays the attendant a toll. The discrete events, in this case, might be things like the car coming to the toll booth and paying the toll. Each of these events was modeled in SIMULA as a process so the whole simulation consisted of a collection of these **interacting**

---

[1] Systems can be studied by experimenting with the actual system or a model of the actual system. These models can be physical models or mathematical models, which could be analytical or simulations. Discrete event simulations model a system as a series of discrete events that evolve over time and contain some variables that are random, or stochastic, like the bottleneck in a production line. Monte Carlo simulations are similar and model systems that consist of events that are driven by a stochastic distribution where the temporal evolution is not important, like the estimation of risk.

processes. These processes were all, in fact, considered to be individual *objects* in the simulation.[2]

When computer scientist Alan Kay first saw SIMULA, he was struck by the idea that you could replace things like bindings and assignments with goals carried out by these objects. Working at Xerox's Palo Alto Research Center (PARC) in 1971, Kay led a group that developed a language called Smalltalk, a fully **Object-Oriented Programming (OOP)** language inspired by SIMULA. His goal was to make a programming language that was simple enough for children to use and, typical of how scientists at PARC like Alan Kay and Douglas Engelbart approached the things they were doing, one that might have the incidental side-effect of bringing a new way of thinking to human civilization![3]

Smalltalk took the ideas of SIMULA one step further by creating a general-purpose language that wasn't constrained to only simulations. In Smalltalk, all computation was done by passing **messages** between **objects**. For example, if you wanted to do the toll booth simulation, you might have a car object and a booth object. Then, the car object would pass the payment message to the booth object and complete the transaction. These objects, in turn, were created by templates called **classes**. For example, the specific car object would be made by the vehicle class template.

In 1974, Kay's group went on to develop Smalltalk GUI, which was a full Graphical User Interface (GUI) using the desktop metaphor. Smalltalk GUI was implemented on Xerox's Alto personal computer and included things like windows, icons, and menus. This GUI inspired the development of Apple's Macintosh OS and Microsoft's Windows OS.[4]

Smalltalk was so influential that it went on to inspire almost all modern Object-Oriented (OO) languages like Java and C++. All of these OO languages incorporate the fundamental ideas of OOP, like classes, objects, and messages. These fundamental entities also include ideas of encapsulation, composition, inheritance, data abstraction, and polymorphism which we'll explore in detail in just a bit. For now, let's start to get hands-on by first installing Java, the OO language we'll be using in this chapter!

8.1.1 Installing Java

The strategy for developing and running Java programs is very similar, in theory, to the approach we used in Python program development: i.e., we write our programs in a text editor and then have a translator run the program. The translator, and its associated tools, are usually distributed in a Software Development Kit (SDK). In the case of Java, this development kit is called the Java Development Kit (JDK) and includes both a compiler (usually called `javac.exe`) and a virtual machine to run the compiled program (usually called `java.exe`).

We can start using the JDK by either installing an Integrated Development Environment (IDE) or by installing the compiler and associated tools separately. There are many different IDEs we can use and, for the most part, they offer very similar functionality that includes an editor, a compiler, a debugger, and a console to see the output. One IDE that's popularly used with Java is NetBeans.[5]

---

[2] As they developed their approach further, they realized that these processes, or objects, often shared some common properties. For example, the cars or trucks or buses could all be considered vehicles and that allowed for a simplification of the simulation rather than considering each kind of vehicle separately.

[3] There is Zen in this: "The place to improve the world is first in one's own heart and head and hands." – Robert Pirsig

[4] This was really by way of Apple's Lisa, the brainchild of businessman Steve Jobs that resulted after his tour of Xerox PARC which included a demo of Smalltalk GUI by Dan Ingalls and Adele Goldberg. Businessman Bill Gates has also credited Xerox PARC with the inspiration for the development of Windows.

[5] Before the flame wars start, I should add the disclaimer that I'd highly recommend exploring the plethora of wonderful IDEs, like Eclipse, IntelliJ, etc., to see which one resonates best with you. Although I still favour `emacs`, there are even some excellent online IDEs for various languages, including Python and Java, as you can see here `http://www.sethi.org/tutorials/references_java.shtml#online-compilers`

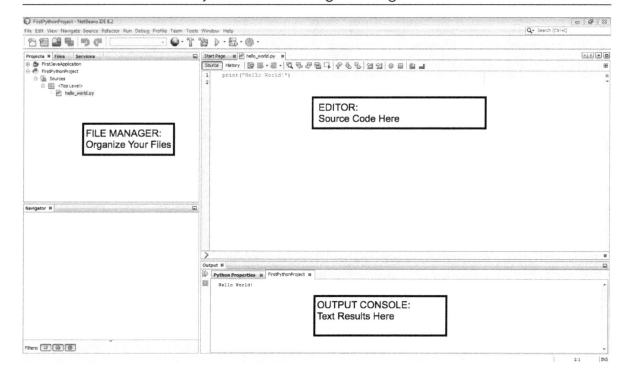

Figure 8.1: The NetBeans Integrated Development Environment (IDE), consisting of an Editor and Output Console. It usually also has a Debugger (not pictured above) and can work with multiple languages, like Python, Java, etc.

You can download and install NetBeans and the JDK by following the guide here: http:// research.sethi.org/ricky/book/netbeans.html. You can either install a NetBeans + JDK bundle or install the JDK first and then install NetBeans. As a side note, this same NetBeans installation can be used to develop programs in Java, C++, Python, etc., as well.

Once you have the NetBeans + JDK bundle fully installed, the IDE should look somewhat similar to Figure 8.1 when you first start it up. Just as with Python, we have an editor, where you can write your code, and an output console, where you can see the result of the compilation. The file manager, on the left hand side, is a view of all your project files.

Let's dive right in and make our canonical Hello World program in Java now! The process might be slightly different depending on which version of the IDE you have but, in general, you should start a new Project, in this case for a new Java Application.

You can choose all the default options for now and, when the editor comes up after you click OK on all the remaining dialogs, you will see the default code scaffolding provided for you by NetBeans. You

```
public class HelloWorld {
    public static void main(String[] args) {
        System.out.println("Hello World!");
    }
}
```

Listing 8.1: "Hello World!" program in Java for NetBeans

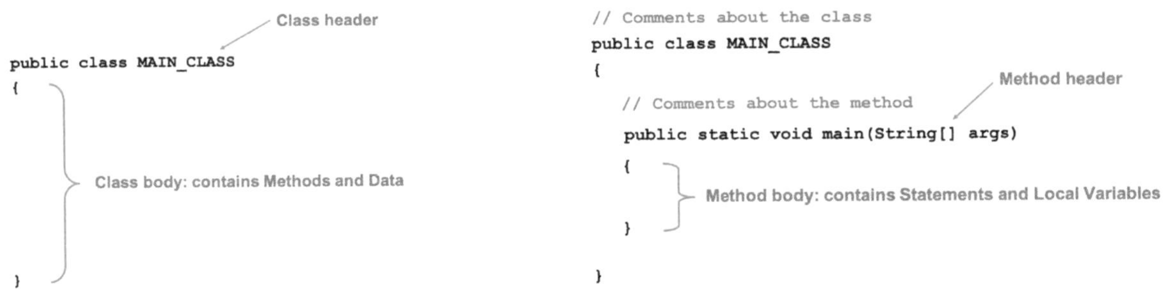

```
                        ⌐ Class header
public class MAIN_CLASS
{

                    ⌐ Class body: contains Methods and Data


}
```

(a) Java class outline

```
// Comments about the class
public class MAIN_CLASS
{                                                    ⌐ Method header
    // Comments about the method
    public static void main(String[] args)
    {
                ⌐ Method body: contains Statements and Local Variables
    }

}
```

(b) Java method outline

Figure 8.2: A Java application always contains a method called `main()`. If a Java program does *not* contain a `main()` method, then it's a program and not an application.

can replace the line that says `// TODO code application logic here` with Line 3 from Listing 8.1: `System.out.println(''Hello World!'');`. If everything has gone well so far, you can click the play button in the menu bar or choose Run Project from the Run menu.

If you then see the "Hello World!" message displayed in the console, please feel free to do your happy dance as you've just successfully run your first Java program. If it didn't work, you can still do the happy dance as you celebrate the debugging we *all* have to do every day and start the process of searching your favourite search engine like Google for what might have gone wrong with the syntax.

The general syntax for defining a new Java application usually takes this form:

```
public class CLASS_NAME {
    public static void main(String[] args) {
        EXECUTE_STATEMENTS
    }
}
```

Not all Java programs are applications; if you intend to actually run a program, it must include the `main()` method in order to become an application and have a point of entry for the statements it needs to execute. Without a `main()` function, or method in Java-speak, the Java program can still be useful but cannot run on its own and cannot initiate execution of its statements.

In addition, Java requires that all executable statements should be placed inside a function, like `main()` above. All statements, like the one on line 3 in Listing 8.1, must also include a trailing semi-colon (`;`) to indicate the end of the statement.

Unlike Python, Java relies upon explicit delimiters to indicate where a statement ends as well as to indicate the beginning and end of components, like function definitions and class definitions. As seen above, the opening and closing curly braces (`{` and `}`, respectively) indicate the beginning and ending of the `main()` method (lines 2 and 4) and the class definition (lines 1 and 5). There are also many rules for naming files and where they're placed but all of those details are handled for you by the IDE. If you download and use the JDK without an IDE, you'll have to ensure you follow those rules manually.

Although this code might seem confusing at first, we'll dig into the different components of a Java program, including some of the keywords like `public`, `static`, etc., in just a bit. There is necessarily some complexity to designing Object-Oriented (OO) solutions and we see some of it here as Java is object-oriented from the ground up and nearly everything in a Java program is an object.

8.2 **The Road to OOP**

So what exactly are software objects and object-oriented programming anyway? Let's build up our understanding of the Object-Oriented (OO) approach by starting with the fundamentals of programming we've learned so far. We saw that a program essentially consists of some data structures and executable statements. These executable statements were commands, or *imperatives*, and, in this kind of **imperative programming**, statements change a program's state, as represented by its data.

Before delving into Java, let's look at an example of a simple program in pseudocode, as shown below. **Pseudocode** is an English-like, high-level, informal, language-independent representation of a computational solution, or program, intended for humans as it is not executable by a machine.

```
MAIN Program Here:
   data_structure: x := 5
   imperative_1: x := 7
   imperative_2: print x        // Print the current value of x to the console
   imperative_3: x := x + 3     // Set current value of x to old value of x + 3
   etc.
```

Here, the // indicate a comment, the same way # indicated a comment in Python. In the above code, our data structure consists of a simple variable x which holds integer values and the imperative statements can *access or change* its value, as seen here.

 Nota Bene: in this section's code listings, the imperatives, like `imperative_1`, can be either an expression (e.g., 2*2) or a statement (e.g., x=5) as both constructs **can** cause *side effects*. Most of these imperatives will be statements but they could be expressions, as we'll see when we get to function calls in just a bit.

These *data structures* are derived from data types, which are a set of values and a set of operations defined on those values. As we saw in Section 3.7, data types can be used in different programming paradigms to create variables. One such programming paradigm, *non-structured programming*, also called un-structured programming, allowed the flow of execution to jump to any part of the program, often by using `goto` statements. This kind of programming paradigm sometimes leads to complex, unreadable, and difficult-to-maintain code that is pejoratively called "spaghetti code".

In *structured programming*, control structures are used along with various data types in order to solve computational problems. Control structures, like sequence, selection, and repetition, allowed finer granularity of program flow execution by confining program flow to a single entry and exit point.

A structured program might then look something like this:

```
MAIN Program Here:
   data_structure: x := 5
   imperative_1
   imperative_2
   selection-control-structure
      imperative_3
   loop-control-structure
      imperative_4
   imperative_5
   etc.
```

As algorithms were developed to solve increasingly complex problems, such programs soon grew to be thousands of lines long and became increasingly harder to maintain and understand. **Procedural programming**, another subset of imperative programming, allowed such long programs to be broken up into manageable sub-components called *procedures*. As we saw in Section 7.1, procedures, and their cousins sub-routines and *functions*, were essentially little blocks of code that could be called, or invoked, from anywhere in the program. Since they could also be called over and over again, as many times as desired, they not only made for more sensible program organization but also saved code duplication. So our structured pseudocode program above could now look something like this in the procedural programming paradigm:

```
DEFINE PROCEDURE Foo():
  loop-control-structure
    imperative_1

MAIN Program Here:
  data_structure: x := 5
  imperative_1
  imperative_2
  selection-control-structure
    imperative_3
  call Foo()   // Call, or invoke, the Foo procedure
  imperative_5
  etc.
```

Here, we call, or invoke, the Foo() procedure once but we could invoke it as many times as desired. Because these procedures, or functions, are expressions in most imperative languages, functions can be used as part of other expressions or statements, as well. Although this kind of modularization was helpful, as programs got still more complex, even this kind of procedural program could get unmanageable. The abstraction of the functionality into procedures was thus further codified into **modules**, which are often bundles of functions and the (optional) data structures the functions utilize. So a more *modular* program might look something like this:

```
DEFINE MODULE FooBar:
  data_structure: x := 5

  FUNCTION Proc_1():
    imperative_1

  FUNCTION Proc_2():
    loop-control-structure
      imperative_1

MAIN Program Here:
  imperative_1
  imperative_2
  call FooBar.Proc_1()   // Call, or invoke, Proc_1() method from FooBar module
  selection-control-structure
    imperative_4
  call FooBar.Proc_2()   // Call, or invoke, Proc_2() method from FooBar module
  imperative_6
  imperative_7
  etc.
```

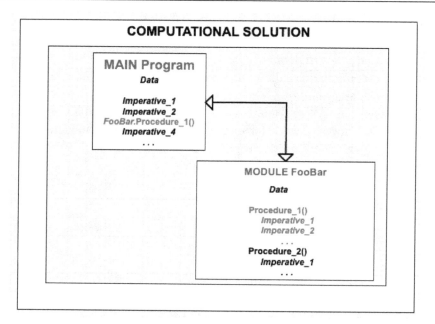

Figure 8.3: Modular Programming Representation: in general, a program can contain multiple modules, each with varying numbers of procedures, not just one module with two procedures as pictured above. Finally, depending on the particular programming paradigm, a module may or may not contain data.

In the pseudocode listing above, we define a **module** FooBar and then utilize the FooBar module within the MAIN program, just as we did with the math module, or library, in Python previously. In Python, we invoked the factorial() method of the math library by issuing the command math.factorial(). This invocation uses the **dot operator**, represented as a period (.) in most programming languages, in order to access a sub-element of any module or library.

Similarly, we issue a command like FooBar.Proc_1() in order to call, or invoke, the Proc_1() function that's defined in the FooBar module. If we further wanted to invoke the Proc_2() function, we would issue the command FooBar.Proc_2().

We are thus able to *abstract* our code into modules where we can think of the FooBar module as a single unit that can be managed separately, as seen in Figure 8.3. In fact, as we saw in Python, modules like the math module gave the language some of its great power, like the ability to calculate factorials or the ability to calculate combinations. These modules were even broken out into different files so they could also be maintained independently.

Modules will, therefore, ideally exhibit *high* **cohesion** but *low* **coupling**; i.e., the functions in a module like math all go together to work fully and exclusively with their concomitant data structures (high cohesion) and don't depend on any other modules or functions to carry out their purpose (low coupling). With the introduction of Object-Oriented Programming, this sort of abstraction was taken to yet another level!

8.2.1 Designing the Objects

Object-Oriented Programming (OOP) extended the idea of modules by using them as templates, as well; rather than just creating and using a single module, like the math module, you can instead use modules as a blueprint for creating many entities, or **objects**, of the same kind. Rather than having one

CLASS BLUEPRINT FOR HUMAN OBJECTS

Attributes [Properties]	Behaviours [Actions]
Eye colour	Walk()
Hair length	Eat()
Number of limbs	Talk()

Table 8.1: The attributes and behaviours, also referred to as the properties and actions respectively, associated with Human objects are defined in a **class**, which serves as a blueprint for building many objects of that type. Here, this class blueprint can be used to build many Human objects, like Joe and Hannah in Figure 8.4.

module for a car and another module for a truck, where both have the ability to drive, we can create a single vehicle module that has the ability to drive and use it as a blueprint, or **class**[6], to create many separate car objects or truck objects that will also have the ability to drive in a software program.

What exactly are these software objects? As we noted above, software objects represent objects in real-life but can actually model abstract ideas, as well. In the real world, objects are usually a person, place, animal, or thing; software objects can model all of these kinds of real-world objects but they can also model abstract ideas like bank accounts or dates or other non-physical concepts. A general heuristic, or rule of thumb, is that an object in software is anything you can reference using "the": examples of objects are thus things like the person, the building, or the fox but also abstract ideas like the bank account, the date, etc.

How do we represent these objects in software then? Let's first step back and see how we can characterize an object in real life. A real-life object is usually a *thing* that has some **attributes**, or *properties*, and can carry out some **behaviours**, or *actions*. For example, humans are objects and they have some properties (like a certain colour for their eyes, a certain length of hair, etc.) and some abilities or actions (like being able to walk, talk, etc.).

The particular attributes and behaviours we choose to model depend on the problem context: e.g., characteristics like hair colour and abilities like being able to walk are great for an application to figure out if someone can come to your hair salon; they're less helpful if you're trying to write an application to do payroll, where hair colour doesn't usually affect your final paycheck.

In the end, we can **abstract** out whichever characteristics and abilities we consider to be the *core elements* of those objects for a particular problem context. This lets us create a software **model** of the real-life objects. This model only retains what we deem to be its essential characteristics for that particular problem context while ignoring all other details.

The *conceptual model* of human objects that we might brainstorm consists of characteristics that uniquely identify them and the things they can do. We can organize these properties and actions in a table like Table 8.1. These core elements that we will isolate in the software model represent the *class* blueprint we can use to create many human objects.

We can then use this class blueprint to create a human object named Joe and another human object named Hannah. All human objects can carry out the same **actions** like Walk(), Eat(), and Talk(). I.e., both Joe and Hannah, and any other human objects we might create in the future, can also Walk(), Eat(), and Talk(). However, each human object has their own values for the various **properties**; e.g., Joe happens to have blue eyes and long hair while Hannah has green eyes and short hair.

---

[6]The term class is analogous to the idea of Aristotlean Categories as discussed in Section 1.4.2.

The values of the properties for an individual object determine the **state** of that object. Just like the variables of a system determine the state of a system, as we saw in Section 1.5.1, the values for the *data variables* of an object determine its state. Then, the *actions* available to the class can use and change the state of individual objects by using and changing these variables, or properties.

We can take this model of *conceptual objects* and implement them in software programs to create software versions of the human objects. In order to create these *software objects*, we need to *implement* their properties and actions in some programming language. The *actions* are implemented using normal imperative programming statements within **functions** and the *properties* are set via data **variables**. Some of the different terms that are used to describe objects at the physical, conceptual, and software levels are shown in Table 8.2.

As you start to identify and translate physical objects (objects in the real world) to software objects (objects in your program), there are some heuristics you can use in carrying out this **Object-Oriented Design**. One such heuristic, or rule of thumb, to model objects in the real world is to write out a description of your problem and then circle all the nouns and underline all the verbs. Most of the **nouns** will map to a software *object* or a *data variable* (a property) while the **verbs** will map to some kind of *function* (an action) in the class blueprint for those objects.

The class blueprint we eventually create in software has three essential components:

1. A **Name** for the class blueprint
2. Some **Properties** that are customized for *each* object created with the class blueprint
3. Some **Actions** that are available to <u>all</u> objects created using the class blueprint

For example, the class blueprint for Human objects, and two of the Human objects created from it, are shown in Figure 8.4. As seen there, we can then use the Human class blueprint to create a Human

Attributes	+	Behaviours	=	Physical Objects
Properties	+	Actions	=	Conceptual Objects
Variables	+	Functions	=	Software Objects

Table 8.2: Characterizing objects at the physical, conceptual, and software level: the different terms that are sometimes employed when representing objects in the real world (physical objects), at some degree of further abstraction (conceptual objects), and in a software program (software objects). Properties and Actions are sometimes also called **Characteristics** and **Operations**.

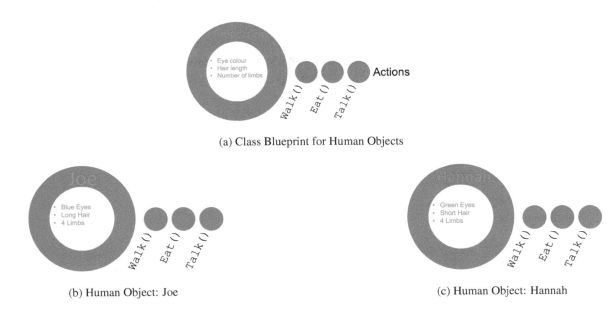

(a) Class Blueprint for Human Objects

(b) Human Object: Joe   (c) Human Object: Hannah

Figure 8.4: The **class** blueprint is used to build any number of Human **objects**, like the two human objects, Joe and Hannah, shown above. All Human objects, including Joe and Hannah, can carry out the indicated **Actions** like Walk(), Eat(), etc. But the **state** of each object, as determined by the values of its **properties**, is unique to that object: e.g., Joe has long hair and blue eyes while Hannah has short hair and green eyes. Actions, in turn, affect the state of the objects.

object named Joe, who happens to have blue eyes and long hair, and another Human object named Hannah, who has green eyes and short hair. That same Human class blueprint can be used to build any number of additional Human objects. All such Human objects, including Joe and Hannah, can carry out the indicated **actions** like Walk(), Eat(), etc. But the **state** of each object is unique to that object: e.g., Joe has long hair and blue eyes while Hannah has short hair and green eyes.

8.3 Solving Problems with Software Objects

What can we do with these software objects? In other words, how do we use classes and objects to actually solve computational problems? The process of creating computational solutions in an Object-Oriented paradigm involves a three-step process:

1. Define the class
2. Use the class to create one or more objects
3. Have the objects send messages to each other and do stuff!

We've already seen how we might create a class blueprint and use that class to create objects. We can then use those objects to send messages, either to other objects or even to itself. Sending a message, in the OOP way of thinking, means calling, or invoking, some action that's defined for that module or class.

In the object-oriented paradigm, the salient aspect of objects is that they have properties, represented programmatically by some data variables, and these properties determine the state of a specific object. Since the actions are represented programmatically by functions, invoking an object's action is equivalent to calling, or invoking, some function that's defined inside the module or class.

When a message is sent to an object, that message, or function, often utilizes or changes some data variable the object contains. This is how the state of an object can change. These actions can thus use the state of the object and can also change the state of objects. Eventually, changing the state of objects leads to the solution of the computational problem!

Let's make all this more concrete by extending our previous *modular programming* pseudocode from Section 8.2 and putting it in an OO context. So our evolving pseudocode program now becomes:

```
DEFINE CLASS FooBar:
  HIDDEN data_structure: x := 5

  PUBLIC METHOD Proc_1():
    imperative_1

  PUBLIC METHOD Proc_2():
    loop-control-structure
      imperative_1

MAIN Program Here:
  imperative_1
  myObject := new FooBar()       // Create a new object of class FooBar
  myObject.Proc_1()              // Send message Proc_1() to myObject
  selection-control-structure
    imperative_3
  myObject.Proc_2()              // Send message Proc_2() to myObject
  imperative_5
  etc.
```

In the OOP paradigm, our evolving program first defines a **class** FooBar, just like we defined the **module** FooBar in Section 8.2. We then utilize the FooBar class within the MAIN program to create a new FooBar object called myObject. We can then send the message Proc_1() to myObject by issuing the myObject.Proc_1() command.

The OOP approach of using these "modules on steroids" proved effective and soon became a dominant programming paradigm due to its ability to manage the size and complexity of computational solutions, especially in regards to modifying and maintaining software systems. This ability of OOP comes from its shift in focus from writing separate functions or procedures to creating and using software *objects*, entities which bundle together both the data and the functions into a single unit. These entities are built using *classes*, an extension of the modular programming approach we saw above where those modules are now used as a blueprint or template to create multiple objects of the same kind.

In general, as we saw earlier with modules, we send messages to objects by also using the **dot operator**, represented as a period (.) in both Java and Python. These messages are the actions defined for the objects and the actions can change the state of the objects as represented by their data variables. This ability to change their state is also why objects in the real-world are interesting to model: they do things and can affect changes, both to themselves and to others. So the whole OO approach boils down to having a program that creates a bunch of objects, having these objects interact via messages, which results in changing the state of some objects and eventually leads to a solution for the problem we're modeling.

8.3.1 A Detailed Example in Java

How exactly does this kind of **message passing** eventually lead to a solution? Let's examine a detailed example of setting up and using a bank account to see what all this actually looks like in Java.

Suppose our local bank learned about our brilliant performance in our CS0 course and decided to pay us an obscene amount of money to come up with a program that allows a user to open an account and simply deposit money into that account.[7] We quickly cobble together the solution shown in Listing 8.2; let's take a quick tour of our awesome program to see what it does and how Java works.

Designing the class

There are a lot of structural issues that come with Java and we'll put some of them on hold for now. The main goal of our program, after discussing it in detail with the bank manager, is captured in the program **requirements**, which state that the program should allow the bank to:

> Create new bank accounts, allow deposits of money into the accounts, and display the new balance.

Following good object-oriented design practices, we go through the above description and **bold** the relevant nouns and underline the verbs. We know the nouns will likely become either objects themselves or properties (data variables) of those objects in our new program and the verbs will likely become the actions, or functions, in our class blueprint.

> Create new **bank accounts**, allow deposits of money into the accounts, and display the new **balance**.

The first bold'ed noun is *bank account*; since we'll be creating many bank accounts for different people, we'll likely need to create bank account objects. So we'll have to create a class blueprint for the bank account objects and the functions will be defined inside that class blueprint, as well; in Java-speak, any function that's defined inside the class blueprint is called a **method**.

Since we're building bank account objects, we can use a self-documenting approach and call the relevant class something meaningful like BankAccount. We could have called it FooBar, as we've been doing so far, but FooBar doesn't give us much insight into what the class does; this isn't a big deal right now but imagine a program made of hundreds of classes all called some variant of Foo and Bar; this would, very quickly, become a nightmare to fix, or maintain. So when we assign classes, variables, and functions identifiers that are descriptive, we create **self-documenting code**, code that uses descriptive names in order to make it easy to understand from just reading the code directly rather than adding additional documentation comments.

---

[7]In case the sarcasm didn't already drip all over your shoes, this example, like most introductory examples in most applied math disciplines, is terribly convoluted and unrealistic. The bank would never pay you an obscene amount of money for such a simple application... unless you dropped out of graduate school and started your own software company, of course.

```java
1  // DEFINE CLASS BankAccount:
2  class BankAccount {
3    // Hidden Data Structure
4    private double balance;
5
6    // PUBLIC Method
7    public void printBalance() {
8      System.out.println("Balance is: $"+ balance);
9    }
10
11   // PUBLIC Method
12   public void makeDeposit(double depositAmount) {
13     System.out.println("  --> Depositing $"+ depositAmount);
14     balance = balance + depositAmount;
15   }
16 }
17
18 // MAIN Program Here:
19 public class Main {
20   public static void main(String[] args) {
21     // Create a new BankAccount object called joeAccount
22     BankAccount joeAccount = new BankAccount();
23
24     // Check the balance in Joe's Account and make some deposits
25     joeAccount.printBalance();
26     joeAccount.makeDeposit(30);
27     joeAccount.printBalance();
28     joeAccount.makeDeposit(100);
29     joeAccount.printBalance();
30   }
31 }
```

Listing 8.2: Java application to create a BankAccount for Joe and make some deposits.

Defining the class

Now that we have a name for the class, we need to actually define the class blueprint. In Java, you can define a class by preceding its name with the keyword class, and that's exactly what we do on line 2 when we define the BankAccount class since we had bold'ed Bank Account in the description.

The other item that was bold'ed in our description was the balance and since each BankAccount object will have to maintain its own balance, it makes sense to designate balance as a property of the BankAccount objects. We implement properties in Java as *data variables* so we add the balance into the class definition on line 4.

This data variable is the only kind of data structure our class likely needs, at least as determined by the simple description of the program requirements above. The data structures contained, or encapsulated, in a class blueprint will correspond to the data variables that determine the state of each object. Since the state of our object, in this case the balance in that account, is of paramount importance and we don't want bad actors maliciously or accidentally changing the balance, we'll make it private so it stays hidden from the outside world. We do this on line 4 by using the keyword private to indicate that nothing outside the object should be able to access the `balance` data variable directly.

In general, Java has four **access modifiers**: `private`, `public`, `protected`, and `package` (the default). If you don't specify an explicit access modifier for a particular class or its component, Java assumes it should assign it `package` access, like the `BankAccount` class on line 2. These different modifiers determine whether an element is accessible from outside the class; we'll learn more about them when we discuss inheritance.

Unlike Python, Java is a **strongly-typed** language; as such, it requires the programmer to declare exactly what kinds of values a particular variable will hold. Since the `balance` will contain numeric, real values, we tell Java, on line 4, the data type of the `balance` variable should be a `double`.

On line 7, we define the `printBalance()` method, which is just a function that's defined inside a class. Java also follows a naming convention called *camel case*, where the first letter of an identifier is lower case but the first letter of every other word in the identifier is upper case. Classes, on the other hand, are written with the first letter in every word, including the first word, capitalized. It's important to note that this convention is a *design decision* and not a *language requirement*.

When we met functions in Python, we saw two kinds of functions: those that returned a value, which we called functions, and those that did not return a value, which we also called procedures. Other than the nomenclature, though, there really wasn't any difference between the syntax for the two. In Java, things are different: a method, which is just a function defined inside a class, has to declare what kind of value, if any, it returns in the function definition itself.

Since neither of our two methods, `printBalance()` starting on line 7 or `makeDeposit()` starting on line 12, return any values, the return type of both of those methods is set to `void`. If they did return a value, for example by ending their method definition with a `return` statement, then the keyword `void` in the method definition would have to be replaced by the data type of the value that was returned. E.g., if we had a method called `getBalance()` that ended with the statement `return balance;`, its method definition would then be `public double getBalance() {}` since `balance` is a data variable of type `double`.

Finally, on line 12, we also define `makeDeposit()` to take a *formal parameter*, namely the amount of money we want to add to that bank account object. When we used formal parameters in Python, we only had to specify the name, or identifier, of the formal parameter as Python is a dynamically typed language. In Java, however, we have to also specify the data type of all the formal parameters. This is exactly what we do on line 12 when we define `makeDeposit()` to require a `double` argument when that method is called, or invoked. The final **function signature** of a method like `makeDeposit(double depositAmount)` consists of both the identifier, or name, of the function as well as the data type, but *not* the identifier, of the formal parameters; the function signature is how the compiler keeps track of different functions, especially in the context of function **overloading** as we'll see later on.

Creating objects and passing messages using the driver class

Now that we have our `BankAccount` class blueprint all set, we need to start creating `BankAccount` objects. In order to do so, we need to create a class that contains a `main()` method; as mentioned earlier, a `main()` method is what transforms a Java program into a Java application that can actually run and do stuff. This **driver class** is exactly what we define on line 19.

The driver class only consists of a single method, the `main()` and doesn't contain any data structures. Within `main()`, we first create a `BankAccount` object called `joeAccount` on line 22. The left side of the assignment operation is just like a normal variable assignment. In Java, creating a variable is a two-step process: a *declaration* and an *instantiation*; e.g., if we wanted to create an integer variable called `x`, we would issue a command like `int x = 5;`.

The declaration is the left-hand-side of the assignment operation, int x. Since Java is a strongly-typed language, the data type of the variable has to be specified, or declared, before it can be created. In Python, which utilized dynamic typing and relied upon the interpreter to figure out the type of the value itself, a variable declaration was something akin to, x = 5. Variable declarations in Java are similar except they're preceded by the data type and they end with a semi-colon (;). Once a variable is declared to be of a certain type, that's the only kind of value that variable can hold. It is, of course, still possible to change the kind of values it holds by **typecasting** it to a different type, just as in Python.

The instantiation is the right-hand-side of the assignment operation, 5;. This is a lot simpler in the case of a simple variable, also called a primitive data variable as it is not an object.

> Java consists of both **primitive variables**, like x, as well as **object variables**, like joeAccount. Object variables are like "*variables on steroids*" in that they can both hold values and you can also pass messages to them, which you can't do with simple, primitive variables as they can only hold values. Instead of a single item (the value) used to instantiate a primitive variable, instantiating an object variable requires three items:
>
> 1. The new operator to start the process of building a new object
> 2. The name of the class blueprint used to build the object
> 3. Optional value(s) to initialize the object

On line 22, we use the new operator on the right side to actually *construct* our new BankAccount object. Later on, we'll learn about special constructor methods that are defined, either implicitly (as here) or explicitly, to carry out the task of actually creating new objects of the class type. For now, all we need to remember is that using the name of the class with parentheses, as in BankAccount(), invokes the constructor method and carries out the actual construction of the object.

One of the main tasks of the construction task is to assign default values to any of the data variables that represent the properties of the new object. If any of the properties need to be initialized to non-default values, we can provide those optional values to the constructor as arguments. In this case, our call on line 22 uses the constructor with default values, called the default constructor, and doesn't specify any special values.

As we saw earlier, the values of the properties determine the state of the object. So one of the first things we do after constructing our new joeAccount object is check its state by passing it the Print Balance message by invoking that method using the dot operator on line 25: joeAccount.printBalance(); This prints out the initial balance which is initially 0. So passing messages to objects, like invoking the Print Balance message, allows us to *access the state* of an object.

Then, on line 26, we pass the Make Deposit message to the joeAccount object by using the dot operator again: joeAccount.makeDeposit(30); Since the makeDeposit() method is defined to accept a formal parameter, we pass it an argument, 30, representing the amount we want to deposit into Joe's bank account. This is how passing messages, like invoking the Make Deposit message, can change the values of the data variables, or properties, associated with a particular object. Since the properties of an object determine its state, passing these messages can also *change the state* of an object.

8.3.2 Solving Computational Problems Using Objects

Joe's bank account, represented by the joeAccount object, initially had a state of $0 for its account balance property, represented by the balance data variable. Then, after we passed it the Make

Deposit message using the dot operator, as `joeAccount.makeDeposit(30)`, its state changed as the `account balance` increased by $30.

This is the essence of the object-oriented approach to solving computational problems: a program creates an object, like Joe's bank account object, `joeAccount`. This object's properties, represented by the object's data variables, determine its state. We can then pass messages to that object using the dot operator; e.g., we pass Joe's bank account object the Make Deposit action, represented by the `makeDeposit()` method, by issuing the `joeAccount.makeDeposit(30)` command. This changes the value stored in the `balance` data variable and therefore changes the state of Joe's bank account.

So if the goal of the computational solution would be to ensure Joe's bank account had $130 in it, we can accomplish that by creating Joe's bank account object (on line 22), then passing it the `Make Deposit` message twice, once on line 26 to add $30 and then again on line 28 to add $100. Once Joe's bank account object is in the desired goal state (i.e., it has $130 in it), the computational problem is considered solved and the program ends.

Object (Reference) Variables in Java

We've been using a bit of a shorthand so far by calling things like `joeAccount` an object. In Java, they're actually object reference variables since Java doesn't explicitly support pointers or pointer arithmetic. We should therefore refer to these as object references rather than objects.

In a way, you can think of an object (reference) variable like a variable on steroids. For example, you might declare a regular variable as:

```
int x = 5;
```

This variable is a regular variable or a Primitive Variable. It's created from a Primitive Data Type, in this case, `int`. It has a Primitive Variable Name or identifier, in this case x. And we use the assignment operator to assign a Primitive Value to the Primitive Variable Name. Thus, x is a primitive integer variable that stores the value 5.

You can then use x to do things like print out the value it holds:

```
System.out.println( x );
```

Here, the variable x is converted back to its value, 5, which is then sent to the `PrintStream`. Similarly, you can also use x in expressions as in:

```
System.out.println( x + 3 );
```

which prints out 8 since the x is again evaluated to its value, 5, and then added to 3 before being printed out to the `PrintStream`. And that's all that a Primitive Variable can do because it's a primitive, or simple, variable and can only let you access its value and that's it.

But you can also create an Object (Reference) Variable using a Class Data Type as when we create a new `String` object below:

```
String y = new String("Hello World!");
```

In this case, the Object (Reference) Variable, y, is like a variable on steroids! That's because, unlike a Primitive Variable, it can do things that a regular Primitive Variable can't do.

Like a Primitive Variable, an Object (Reference) Variable can also give us the value it holds. In addition, the Object (Reference) Variable can do different things related to its value by invoking methods defined in its corresponding Class Data Type; like giving us the length of the string value or changing the string value to all uppercase: `y.length()` and `y.toUpperCase()`.

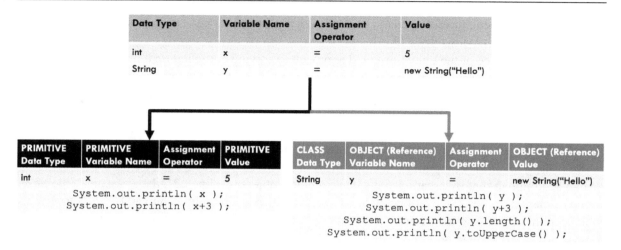

Data Type	Variable Name	Assignment Operator	Value
int	x	=	5
String	y	=	new String("Hello")

PRIMITIVE Data Type	PRIMITIVE Variable Name	Assignment Operator	PRIMITIVE Value
int	x	=	5

```
System.out.println( x );
System.out.println( x+3 );
```

CLASS Data Type	OBJECT (Reference) Variable Name	Assignment Operator	OBJECT (Reference) Value
String	y	=	new String("Hello")

```
System.out.println( y );
System.out.println( y+3 );
System.out.println( y.length() );
System.out.println( y.toUpperCase() );
```

Figure 8.5: Object Reference Variable vs Primitive Variable: an Object (Reference) Variable is like a variable on steroids when compared to a Primitive Variable since it can do things to the value it holds by invoking the methods defined in that Class Data Type.

We can picture the difference between a Primitive Variable and an Object (Reference) Variable in Figure 8.5. Although this notation is more precise, it's also a little clunky so we'll take some liberties and just call it an object for now.

8.3.3 OOP Fundamentals

In the OOP paradigm, we can further model our programmatic solutions as a collection of interacting **objects**. Just like with a module, an object **encapsulates**, or bundles together, the data and the set of functions[8] into a single entity.

However, unlike a module, an object also adds some crucial advantages:

- An object hides the data *encapsulated* within the object so nothing outside the object can see or access it. This is called **information hiding** and the data that is hidden is a design decision the programmer makes when they design an object. The data an object contains also determines the object's **state** and that data can be **composed** of any data type, including other objects. In fact, a module with information hiding is also similar to an abstract data type, as we saw in Section 6.1.
- An object is designed, or defined, using a template called a **class**. The class completely defines all aspects of an object and is often thought of as a cookie cutter or a blueprint. The class is used to create as many objects of that type as needed. Creating an object is also called object **instantiation** and is very similar to the idea of declaring a variable. Once an object is created, you can call, or invoke, any functions defined in the class, just as you could with modules.
- Unlike a module, a class is also much more cohesive and is a more concrete **abstraction** in that it often represents something in the real world directly.
- In addition, classes can **inherit** both data and functions from other classes. These classes can add additional data and functions that weren't present in their "parent" classes.
- Finally, all these objects created from their templates, or classes, interact with each other by sending **messages** to each other. You can ask an object to do something by sending it a message,

---

[8]I should add that a function, in the OOP paradigm, is usually called a **method**; i.e., a method is simply a function that is defined inside a class, as we'll see in a bit. In addition, the data variables associated with objects are called **fields**.

which invokes one of its functions without knowing anything about its internal state whatsoever! In addition, since an object inherits some functions, or **behaviours**, from its parent classes, it can exhibit **polymorphism**, which means that when you send it a message, it might respond by calling one of its own functions or calling a function from its parent object instead.

8.4 What Is Java?

Java is often considered to be three things:

- The Java Programming Language
- The Java Virtual Machine (JVM)
- The Java Class Library (JCL)
    - This includes several helpful packages in the API like the GUI Java Foundation Classes (JFC), etc.

Java started life at Sun Microsystems, Inc., as a language called Oak. Sun was working on a new generation of hand-held devices and these kinds of embedded systems had very limited resources. The current crop of programming languages, usually some variation of the popular C++ language, had certain shortcomings that made them cumbersome in these smaller domains. Sun's solution was to form a guerilla team, called the Green Project, that was led by James Gosling and Mike Sheridan, to make the new device, which was designed to run on different platforms.

Around 1990, Bill Joy proposed designing a full object-oriented environment based on the principles embodied in C++; the Green Project team responded by creating a new OS and a new language that followed the principle of Write-Once, Run-Anywhere (WORA) so that developers didn't need to recompile their programs for use on different platforms. This required the use of a virtual machine architecture, the **Java Virtual Machine**, which operated much like the model shown in Figure 3.4. They designed it to be object-oriented from the ground up and included things like garbage collectors to simplify management of resources. They called the operating system Green OS and the language Oak, after an Oak tree that was outside Gosling's office.

Before they could release their new Oak language, the legal team at Sun realized there was already a language named Oak. So, after a brainstorming session, one of the names chosen was Java, which didn't have any trademark limitations. Around 1995, the Sun team re-targeted their new WORA language for the Web and released the **Java Programming Language** to great success. Over the years, the popularity of Java waxed and waned and, more recently, with the advent of mobile technology and Big Data challenges, and concomitant Machine Learning methods to make sense of them as we'll see later, Java came to the ascendancy once again.

As Java became more popular, many developers started to create additional libraries that proved helpful for many applications. Over the years, these libraries were vetted more and more thoroughly and their functionality, and usability, improved. This powerful set of libraries was packaged into the **Java Class Library** and is one of the great strengths of Java.

8.4.1 Class Structure

As seen in Figure 8.6, in the Java programming language:

1. a **program** is made up of one or more *classes*
2. a **class** contains one or more *methods* and *data variables*
3. a **method** contains executable *statements* and *local variables*

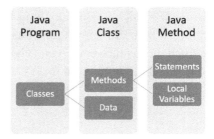

Figure 8.6: In Java, a **program** is made up of one or more *classes*, a **class** contains one or more *methods* and *data variables*, and a **method** contains executable *statements* and *local variables*.

All Java programs are composed of classes. A Java application, however, always contains a method called `main()` method. If a Java program does *not* contain a `main()` method, then it's a program and not an application.

Each Java class contains *data* and *methods*. The data represents the *properties* of a class and are implemented via *data variables*. Although almost all classes will contain both, some rare classes might contain only data variables while others might contain only methods. The data variables contained by a class are called **fields** in Java.

The data variables in Java come in two flavours: **instance variables** and **class variables**. The instance variables are associated with individual objects and each object, or *instance*, maintains its own values for those variables. Class variables, on the other hand, are associated with the class itself, rather than individual objects. Methods, in turn, can only define **local variables**, which are available only to the method itself and no other component of the class or object can access them.

When we create an object in Java, we refer to it through an **object reference variable**. An object reference variable is just like a normal variable in that it has a name, or identifier, and a value. But it's also like a "variable on steroids" because it can access all the actions, or methods, of the underlying class and so can send or receive messages in the object-oriented paradigm.

We can use a **class** definition to create **object reference variables** and the **objects** themselves. Each object is a specific **instance** of the class blueprint. The *object reference variable* is linked to the new object using the *assignment operator*, =, the equals sign.

The new object is created, or initialized, using a **constructor** method from the class definition via the `new` operator. The assignment operator, =, then links the memory address for the object to the object reference variable. You can then use the object reference variable to invoke, or call or use, any of the public methods defined for the underlying object. These methods are invoked, or accessed or used, using the dot operator, ., which is the period or full stop.

Just like there are instance and class variables, there are also **instance methods** and **class methods**. In languages like Python, there is a third category of method called **static methods**. In Java, class methods and static methods mean the same thing. In addition, classes can contain an optional method for doing setup tasks when an object is first created; these kinds of methods are called **constructors** and they take care of things like initializing the instance variables so the object is created in a sensible state and doing any other supplementary setup to ensure the object's state is stable and correct.

All instance and class variables are immediately accessible to every instance method. However, no instance variables can be accessed by a class, or static, method. An instance variable, as its name implies, requires an instance of the class, an object, in order to be set to a valid state. Let's look at an example to clear this up somewhat.

Let's start, as computer scientists often do, by creating a new superhero group. Nothing too extravagant like the Justice League or the Avengers but something a little more intimate and a lot more nerdy. Our superheroes are simple creatures and we model them them with the following **requirements statement**:

> **Superheroes** have a **secret identity name** and a **super-power**. They also have a **super-hero name** and have a certain **height** and **weight**. Superheroes can <u>join</u> our **group** or <u>leave</u> our group and they can also <u>fight</u> super-villains by <u>using</u> their super-powers.

As usual, we bold'ed the elements that would become either a *class* itself or a data variable and underlined the elements that will likely become the actions, or methods. Some of the data variables will be associated with each instance, or object, of the class; these will be our *instance variables*. And some data variables will be associated not with a specific object, or instance, but the entire class, and these will be our *class variables*.

Since we're dealing with super-heroes (the first bold'ed term in our requirements), we will obviously need a SuperHero class. Let's start by creating a SuperHero class blueprint. Once that's fully drafted, we'll also need to create a driver class that contains a main() method in which we'll create instances, or objects, of the SuperHero class. We might define our SuperHero class blueprint with the following instance variables from the bold'ed terms in our requirements statement above:

> **Instance Variables**: superHeroName, secretIdentityName, superPower, height, weight

We've accounted for all the bold'ed terms except for the **group** term; there are many options in how we might incorporate that, everything from creating another class to making it an instance variable or making it a class variable, specified with the static keyword.

For purposes of illustration, we'll make this our sole class variable; we'll assume that super-heroes can only join or leave one group. As such, we won't track any details about the group as none were specified in the requirements statement; instead, since super-heroes can join or leave our group, we'll only keep track of the number of super-heroes currently in our super-hero group, as seen below:

> **Class/Static Variables**: numberOfGroupMembers

If we were to represent our burgeoning super-hero group, we might start with creating a few objects, or instances, of our new SuperHero class. Let's list three such superheroes along with their properties:

- supermanObject: instance of the SuperHero class definition with following properties:
  1. superHeroName: Superman
  2. secretIdentityName: Clark Kent
  3. superPower: Super Strength, Flight, Invulnerability
  4. height: 6'3"
  5. weight: 225 lbs.
- hulkObject: instance of the SuperHero class definition with following properties:
  1. superHeroName: The Incredible Hulk
  2. secretIdentityName: Bruce Banner
  3. superPower: Super Strength, Healing
  4. height: 7'8"
  5. weight: 1,400 lbs.
- spidermanObject: instance of the SuperHero class definition with following properties:
  1. superHeroName: Spiderman

2. `secretIdentityName`: Peter Parker
3. `superPower`: Super Strength, Stickiness, Spidey Sense
4. `height`: 5'7"
5. `weight`: 153 lbs.

As we can see above, each superhero has their own copies of the instance variables. However, there's only one copy of a class/static variable that is shared by any instances of that class. As such, if all three superheroes joined our superhero group, our class/static variable would be:

- `numberOfGroupMembers`: 3

With our instance and class/static data variables decided, we can turn our attention to the Instance, Class, and Static methods. Python uses all three of these categories but languages like Java tend to blur the line between Class and Static methods. The main difference between Class and Static methods in Java would be in the context of *inheritance*, as we'll see later; as such, in Java, we only need to consider Instance Methods and Class Methods, which ironically are declared using the `static` keyword:

Instance Methods: useSuperpower(), fightSupervillain(), joinGroup(), leaveGroup()

These **instance** methods can affect both instance and class variables. Thus, they can affect both the object **state** and class state. For example, the `fightSupervillain()` instance method would use the `superPower` instance data variable. In addition, the `joinGroup()` instance method would change the `numberOfGroupMembers` class data variable. Instance methods can only be called through an object.

Class/Static Methods: listNumberOfSuperheroesInGroup()

The `listNumberOfSuperheroesInGroup()` class/static method, on the other hand, can only utilize the `numberOfGroupMembers` class/static variable. Class/static methods can be called either through an object or by using the class name itself in Java.

Finally, there's another category of methods called **constructors**. Constructors cannot be called directly by non-constructors; instead, constructors are called *implicitly* by the `new` operator. Constructors must have the same name as the class itself but cannot have any return type, not even `void`. Also, in Java, constructors can call other constructors, especially constructors of their parent class (using `super()`), or of the same class itself (using `this()`); we'll talk more about the `super()` method when we get to *inheritance* in Java.

Let's see what these methods might look like by writing out their method headers and adding only minimal code in their method bodies for now:

```java
public SuperHero(String hero, String secret, String p, String h, int w) {
  superHeroName = hero;
  secretIdentityName = secret;
  superPower = p;
  height = h;
  weight = w;
}

private boolean useSuperpower() {
  System.out.println("Attacked with " + superpower);
  return true;
}
```

```java
public boolean fightSupervillain() {
  return useSuperpower();
}

public int joinGroup() {
  numberOfGroupMembers += 1;
  System.out.println("Joined the group!");
  return numberOfGroupMembers;
}

public int leaveGroup() {
  numberOfGroupMembers -= 1;
  System.out.println("Left the group... :(");
  return numberOfGroupMembers;
}

public static int listNumberOfSuperheroesInGroup() {
  System.out.println("Our group has "+ numberOfGroupMembers + " superheroes!");
  return numberOfGroupMembers;
}
```

As you can see above, we decided to make useSuperpower() a private method. That means only other components within our class can utilize that method and no other element *outside* our class even knows of its existence. We then utilize useSuperpower() when we invoke the fightSupervillain() method.

The rest of the methods use the public access modifier so their method headers *are* visible to components outside the class (their method headers are visible to them but not their method bodies!). These public class members constitute the class's **public interface** or **Application Programming Interface (API)**.

Problem 8.1 Use the method headers and pseudocode above to write the full definition of the SuperHero class. Then, please add a driver class to create the three superheroes above and have each of them join the group. Finally, please print out the number of superheroes in our group (and, if you've kept up with the math so far, the answer should be 3 since, as we all know from Schoolhouse Rock and Blind Melon, that's a magic number).

8.4.2   Object-Oriented Concepts and Computational Thinking Principles

Now that we have the basics of OOP under our belt, let's explore some of the fundamental aspects of OOP and how they're related to Computational Thinking:

- Abstraction, Encapsulation, and Information Hiding
  - Computational Thinking Principles: Abstraction
- Inheritance and Polymorphism
  - Computational Thinking Principles: Generalization and Pattern Recognition
- Composition and Association
  - Computational Thinking Principles: Decomposition

Let's explore each of these in more detail next.

Abstraction, Encapsulation, and Information Hiding

We previously met the idea of **abstraction**, one of the central computational thinking principles, as the idea of ignoring details we deem to be irrelevant for the problem at hand. When we apply this computational thinking approach to the object-oriented programming paradigm, we look at the elements of objects at a high level and ignore low-level details. We can apply this approach to both the data and function elements that constitute objects. This gives us two kinds of abstraction in the OO paradigm: data abstraction and procedural abstraction.

Data abstraction is the idea of representing complex data types as a single, high-level entity rather than at the level of the low-level details of the data representation. This allows us to concentrate on *logical* properties of the data instead. In the OO paradigm, this is what we did when we created a SuperHero object with various properties and could then just deal with a supermanObject instead of the individual aspects of a secret identity name, a height, a weight, etc. In addition, we only chose to model certain data components and ignored others, like the job the super-heroes secret identity might have, as being irrelevant to our problem context.

Procedural abstraction can be thought of as the idea of focusing on *what* something does rather than *how* it's done. Instead, we only define the high-level actions for that sub-routine. This allows us to once again concentrate on the *logical* properties of an action only. In the object-oriented paradigm, this idea of procedural abstraction is what we use when we define the **public interface**, or **API**, of our object, as represented by the messages our SuperHero objects could be passed, without worrying about how they're actually implemented. For example, when we pass the supermanObject the fightSupervillain() message, we do so without knowing any details about how exactly Superman would fight the super-villain. This kind of abstraction is familiar to us; e.g., you might drive a car or use a microwave without knowing anything about the details of the internal combustion engine or waveguides and wave propagation.

Another idea that's employed in the object-oriented approach is the idea of **encapsulation**, where we bundle together both the data and the methods into a single entity. Hand in hand with encapsulation comes the idea of **information hiding**. In most OO paradigms, the bundling together of data and methods via encapsulation is a *language feature* and enforced by the language to some extent. Information hiding, on the other hand, is a *design decision* made by the developer and not enforced by the language itself. So, Java, for example, provides the language feature of being able to bundle the data and methods together into a single entity called a class. Although Java provides access modifiers to make data, and other elements, private, it doesn't force the developer to declare anything as private. However, making all the data variables private is an important design decision as it helps protect the integrity of the data values, which determine the state of each object.

Inheritance and Polymorphism

Just like Human children can inherit certain characteristics and abilities from their parents, the software objects we create in the OO paradigm, like the Human Objects, can also incorporate these same ideas of **inheritance**. We can take a class like the Human class and, from it, derive a sub-class like Employee or maybe Firefighter using the keyword extends. In this way, a child *sub-class* can reuse some of the properties and actions of its parent *super-class*. The access modifiers we already met control which elements are heritable for software objects as only those fields, methods, and nested classes that are not private are the ones that can be inherited in Java. Sub-classes can also add functionality that's not available in the parent super-class by adding in additional fields, methods, and nested classes.

In addition, a sub-class can change the behaviour of of some inherited methods, as well. **Polymorphism** usually refers to the idea of using a reference to a parent super-class to access child sub-class methods. It can also refer to the idea of a single class inheriting from two different kinds of classes. This makes sense as the word polymorphism is derived from the root words *poly*, meaning many, and *morph*, meaning shape. Hence, we might imagine a new class called HumanSuperHero, which inherits from the Human class. Inheritance is therefore sometimes also called an **IS-A** relationship, and is a class-level relationship, as in a HumanSuperHero IS-A Human. One restriction in Java is that it only allows direct inheritance from a single parent super-class to avoid problems like the diamond problem in languages that allow multiple inheritance.[9]

Another aspect of polymorphism is the idea of **method overriding**, in which a base super-class's method is implemented differently in a child sub-class so that both the parent super-class and the child sub-class contain a method with the same signature. Suppose we had the SuperHero class and, from it, derived two other classes, FlyingSuperHero and SwimmingSuperHero. If the *base* SuperHero class had a method called move(), the two sub-classes might implement move() differently: e.g., the FlyingSuperHero objects would fly when they were passed the move() message whereas the SwimmingSuperHero objects would start swimming upon receiving the same message. This is possible because we can refer to a child sub-class using an object reference variable of the parent super-class's type. Let's see a quick example to make this clearer:

```
// Base Class
class SuperHero {
    void move() {
        System.out.println("PARENT is just moving on move!");
    }
}


// Inherited class
class FlyingSuperHero extends SuperHero {
    // This method overrides move() of Parent SuperHero class
    void move() {
        System.out.println("CHILD is FLYING on move!");
    }
}


// Driver class
class Main {
    public static void main(String[] args) {
        // SuperHero object reference variable that points to SuperHero object
        SuperHero obj1 = new SuperHero();
        obj1.move();

        // SuperHero object reference variable that points to FLYINGSuperHero object
        SuperHero obj2 = new FlyingSuperHero();
        obj2.move();
    }
}
```

which results in this output:

```
PARENT is just moving on move!
CHILD is FLYING on move!
```

---

[9]To allow the benefits of multiple inheritance, however, Java does allow classes to implement multiple Interface Classes, as we'll see later.

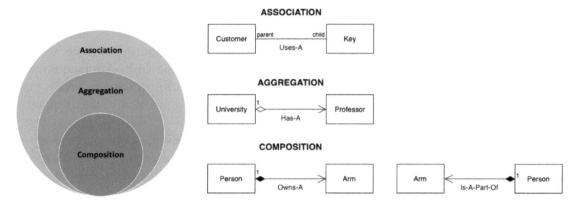

Figure 8.7: Association, Aggregation, and Composition and their associated UML diagram representations. **Association Examples**: a Customer USES-A Key or a Student USES-A Instructor; **Aggregation Examples**: a University HAS-A Professor or Car HAS-A Passenger; **Composition Examples**: an Arm IS-A-PART-OF Person or a Human OWNS-A Heart.

This idea of having the sub-classes respond differently when passed the method defined in the base super-class is the core of method overriding. Method overriding has a dynamic binding since which class's method is called is decided at run-time.

The final form of polymorphism is **method overloading**, where a single method name may have many method signature variations. Sticking with the `SuperHero` class example, suppose we wanted to model the idea that superheroes sometimes change clothes in their human identity and sometimes in their superhero identity. So we might define a `changeClothes()` method where the superhero changes from a civilian identity to their superhero identity. We might create another method with the same name but an additional argument indicating changing clothes for a specific task, like changing into pajamas for bedtime, as `changeClothes(forSpecificTask)`. This is the essence of method overloading where both methods have the same name but different signatures due to the different arguments. Method overloading has a static binding as it occurs at compile-time.

Inheritance and polymorphism therefore not only allow sub-classes to reuse code and behave differently in different programmatic contexts but also to generalize functionality. This ability to generalize functionality from one domain to another is also a centerpiece of computational thinking. In addition, being able to find heritable relationships between different kinds of classes also requires the ability to recognize patterns, another central aspect of computational thinking.

Composition and Association

Although inheritance is one way to reuse code, another way to do so is through the idea of composition, and its cousins association and aggregation. In particular, inheritance, also called **generalization**, is a relationship between the *classes* themselves; association, aggregation, and composition, on the other hand, are relationships between *instances*, or objects, of different classes.

For this reason, composition is often considered a better choice for re-using code as inheritance introduces some additional complexities that can lead to unintended consequences. Inheritance is best-suited for those use-cases where the re-use also represents a specialization; in other words, when a child sub-class represents a specialization of the parent super-class.

The idea of **composition** though is just having a class use other objects as its instance variables. By doing so, the using class doesn't need to re-implement any of the functionality of those included objects that it uses. Composition is an instance-level relationship and is called an **IS-A-PART-OF** or **OWNS-A** relationship. An example might be a Person object also having an Arm object; therefore, an Arm IS-A-PART-OF a Person and a Person OWNS-A Arm, ignoring the grammatical mis-match of the article, of course. In these cases, the contained object (an Arm) can't be shared by other Person objects and the lifetime of the Arm object depends entirely on the Person object.

A slightly weaker relationship than composition is the **aggregation** relationship, which is a **HAS-A** relationship. In these relationships, one object *contains* another. For example, a University object HAS-A Professor object. In an OO paradigm, an aggregation relationship is established whenever some method creates and uses the aggregated object; e.g., the University class definition might have a method which creates a Professor object. In these cases, contained objects, like the Professor object, *can* be shared by other containing objects, like other University objects. In addition, when the containing object is destroyed, the contained object's class definition can still persist and does not have to be re-defined, thus helping with code reusability. This is a happy circumstance as Professor objects can then just get other jobs if their University object gets destroyed.

Finally, the weakest kind of relationship is an **association** relationship, in which one object **USES-A** different object. An example of this would be a Customer object that USES-A gas station bathroom Key object. The object that's used, the Key object in this case, can be utilized by many Customer objects and the Customer object doesn't have any ownership over the Key object, which is a good thing regardless of the circumstances which forced someone to use a gas station restroom. In an OO paradigm, an association can be implemented by passing a variable to a method or returning it from the method.

These kinds of relationships utilize the computational thinking principle of decomposition. Decomposition helps identify which elements should be contained within a class and whether those elements, those objects, should be included as an instance variable (composition), or used within a method (aggregation), or passed as an argument (association). We could also express all these relationships using **Unified Modeling Language (UML)** diagrams, as seen in Figure 8.7.

8.4.3   OOP Advantages and Motivations

Limiting interactions to sending and receiving messages to other objects is a different way of solving computational problems but it ends up having some significant advantages over procedural approaches. When objects interact with each other, there's a certain amount of *coupling* between them.

In general, the objects we create are **loosely coupled** but **highly cohesive**. Loose coupling means these objects don't know much about the other objects with which they interact; they know just enough about the object to know what it can do but not any of the details of *how* it does what it does.

Cohesion, for an object or class, means that it only does a few things and it does them in a self-contained way. That is, all the instructions and data to accomplish some task are bundled together inside that single class instead of being spread out over many classes. Coupling refers to the relationships between objects and loosely coupled objects are relatively independent of each other. In this sense, coupling refers to interactions *between* classes while cohesion refers to the elements *within* the class itself.

A well-designed class, then, does just a few things, contains all the data and operations to do those things within itself, and, when it needs to interact with other objects to do more tasks, doesn't keep track of any details of how the other objects do their tasks. These kind of well-designed classes and objects have several advantages that make OOP desirable because they:

- Reduce maintenance costs by improving troubleshooting and modifications

- Reduce development time via code reuse and extensive APIs, or code libraries in which the objects often model the real world
- Improve reliability and standardization of the development process

The motivation for these OOP approaches were influenced by several different perspectives that helped shape the development of the Java language and led to its widespread adoption. These perspectives included economic, technological, and scientific concerns. Let's look at some of these perspectives below:

- Economic Perspective: As software started to become ubiquitous and useful in industry and government, a whole economy formed around software development, which was soon becoming a very expensive enterprise. There was a need to make it more cost-efficient; to help ameliorate these costs, scientists applied engineering ideas to software development to help defray costs, especially maintenance costs which account for the majority of the costs of any reasonably sized software project. These design principles are incorporated into the OO design and development approach, as captured by the technological and scientific perspectives.
- Technological Perspective: In order to cut costs and make software development more economically feasible, engineering principles were utilized to make software easier to maintain, modular, and self-contained. This had distinct advantages in terms of reusing components, avoiding duplication of code, and breaking a problem up into modules or sub-components.
- Scientific and Modeling Perspective: The problems people most wanted to solve in the real world were tough and required quantitative solutions. People started working on such tough problems in the real world, those that were beyond simple calculations and could not be modeled analytically and realized these were the majority of problems. Scientists started to model the parts of the world they wanted to predict and realized the world consisted of things, or objects. So by modeling the real world, by abstracting it out as software objects in simulations and beyond, the object-oriented approach facilitated usability and the solving of very hard computational problems thus increasing the popularity of this approach even more.

In Java, all these different perspectives, combined with features like its extensive API, came together to propel its popularity. But it still had some disadvantages: Java introduces a lot of overhead which can be overkill for a small problem. In addition, Java might not be the most effective in some low resource environments. Sometimes, speed is also an issue with interpreted languages like Java, despite the use of just-in-time compilers. Java tries to tackle some of this by becoming a bit of a compromise language.

For example, although it was designed to be object-oriented from the ground up, it's not a completely object-oriented language. Java has primitive types and does not support the fact that all operations must be performed by sending messages to objects (e.g., it has static methods you can call without an object and operator overloading for string concatenation uses StringBuilder). But the advantages of Java, having a single language for different microprocessors, works well in a world where small computers are everywhere especially since it helps manage the associated data structures and data types, as well.

8.5 Data Structures and I/O in Java

Before we delve into the data structures that are available in Java, let's start by looking again at data types: a data type is a set of values and a set of operations defined on those values. The primitive data types that we have used so far are supplemented in Java by extensive libraries of classes that are tailored for a large variety of applications, as we've already seen with the String class.

Java has the usual assortment of primitive data types, like int, double, boolean, etc. but it also provides wrapper classes for these primitive data types which have names like Integer, Double, etc. Since Java is object-oriented from the ground up, it often requires the use of objects, rather than primitives, as arguments or parameters and so having these wrapper classes is quite useful.

In addition to these pre-defined classes, or abstract data types, like String, Integer, etc., the power of an OO approach is that users can define their own data types and then create data structures from those user-defined data types to use in their computational solution. Since a data structure is also the physical implementation of an Abstract Data Type (ADT), quite a few standard data structures are implemented from ADTs in Java. These include such fundamental data structures like the Array, Linked List, Stack, Queue, Tree, ArrayList, HashMap, TreeMap, TreeSet, etc.

Abstractions and Implementations

- A <u>data model</u> is a **conceptual**, abstract model that organizes how data is represented and how the data elements relate to each other
- A data type is a **logical**, *language-<u>independent</u>* expression of a data model and the associated operations that are valid on those data values
    - An Abstract Data Type (ADT) is a *logical, language-<u>dependent</u>* model of the data type, the data and its operations, but *without* implementation details
        * A <u>class</u> is the *logical representation* of an Abstract Data Type *implemented* in a particular OOP paradigm[10]
- A <u>data structure</u> is the **physical** implementation of the data type in a particular language
    - The physical implementation of an abstract data type is also called a data structure since it helps organize a value that consists of multiple parts
        * An <u>object</u> is the actual physical implementation of a class in a specific OO language

---

[10]I should add the caveat that some might differ in the full extent of these meanings and often consider objects to be distinct from data structures. For example, you can implement an abstract data type as a data structure in a non-OO language like C using a pointer to a structure, struct. Some also endorse the perspective that an object only shows its functions (with data implied) while data structures only show the data (with the operations implied). However, what is hidden in an object, or its corresponding class, is usually a design decision by the programmer rather than a feature imposed by the language design. This is apparent in most languages like Java as they can have all their data elements publicly visible if they so choose and other classes can be data stores with no defined operations.

8.5.1 **Arrays and ArrayLists**

For now, we'll concentrate on two of the most useful data structures: `Array` and `ArrayList`. Similar to the `list` in Python, an `Array` in Java is an ordered, sequential collection of elements stored in contiguous memory locations where each element can be accessed by its position index. Unlike Python `lists`, an `Array` is a homogenous, fixed-size collection. This means that it can only hold a single kind of element rather than the hodge-podge of any kind of element in a heterogenous collection like the Python `list`. The `Array` is a ubiquitous data structure in Java.

Arrays, in general, are available in many languages but since `Array` is a class in Java, any `Array` object reference variables are, like all object reference variables, "variables on steroids." Not only do they store the values but they also have additional properties and actions. They keep track of things like how many elements they contain and can do actions like `get()`, `set()`, etc., in addition to using the subscript operator (`[ ]`) to access elements of that array. In addition, Java offers an enhanced for-loop to make using arrays a little more intuitive. Let's look at an example of arrays in action:

```java
class Main {
  public static void main(String[] args) {
    // Declare an integer array object reference variable
    int[] arr;

    // Create a new Array object to hold 5 integers:
    arr = new int[5];

    // Initialize the array using a traditional for loop:
    for (int i = 0; i < arr.length; i++) {
      arr[i] = i*i;
    }

    // Print the array using the enhanced for-each loop:
    for(int i : arr) {
      System.out.println(i);
    }
  }
}
```

There are several variations of both creating and using `Arrays` in Java, as well as caveats in terms of passing arrays by value vs reference, but, in the interest of brevity, let's move on to its more useful cousin, the `ArrayList`. The `ArrayList` data type is much easier to use and more similar to how the `list` worked in Python. One of the main advantages is that an `ArrayList` is not fixed-size and provides us with dynamic arrays for storing elements. It implements the Java List Interface Class.[11]

Just as with an `Array`, an `ArrayList` lets you access the elements using the index along with functions like `get()` and `set()`; however, Java does not allow the use of the subscript operator (`[]`) with an `ArrayList`. Despite this limitation, the various methods of the `ArrayList` class make it very

---

[11] In Java, the word interface can have three meanings: the public interface of a class, or API; the user interface of a Graphical User Interface (GUI) which determines how a user can interact with a GUI program; and interface classes, which are Java's implementation of abstract classes with pure virtual functions. In general, Java also provides the ability to create an `abstract` class, which can contain functionality that a sub-class can implement or override. But Java also gives us the ability to make interface classes, which only give the possible functionality without *any* implementation details. As such, a Java class can inherit from a single abstract class only but can `implement` multiple interface classes.

helpful in terms of data retrieval and manipulation and a popular choice for doing basic list processing. Let's look at the same example as before but converted to using an `ArrayList` now:

```java
import java.util.ArrayList;

class Main {
  public static void main(String[] args) {
    // Declare an ArrayList to hold Integer values
    ArrayList<Integer> arrayList = new ArrayList<Integer>();
    int numEntries = 5;

    // Initialize the ArrayList using a traditional for loop:
    for (int i = 0; i < numEntries; i++) {
      arrayList.add(i*i);
    }

    // Print the ArrayList using the enhanced for-each loop:
    for(int i : arrayList) {
      System.out.println( i );
    }
  }
}
```

As you can tell, one of the main differences is that we needed to add an `import` directive in order to import the `ArrayList` class from the Java Class Library (JCL). In addition, we had to specify the types of values our `ArrayList` would hold; since an `ArrayList` can only hold objects, we had to specify the `Integer` wrapper class as the data type for our `ArrayList` elements.

8.5.2 Exception Handling in Java

We previously saw that the modern way to deal with errors and exceptional situations is to use exception handling. Java is no different and also utilizes exception handling extensively, even moreso than Python.

The three kinds of errors, *syntax*, *semantic*, and *logical*, occur at either *compile-time* (syntax and static semantic) or *run-time* (dynamic semantic and logical). Semantic and logical errors are also sometimes referred to as exceptions and we can use exception handling to take care of such exceptional situations. Most languages use exceptions for both compile-time and run-time errors. In languages like Java, exceptions that occur at compile-time are called **checked exceptions** whereas run-time exceptions are called **unchecked exceptions**. In languages like Python, C++, and C#, the compiler does not force the programmer to deal with exceptions so all exceptions are unchecked. Java also has a third type of exception, called an **error**, when the situation is irrecoverable, like running out of memory, for example.

In Java, all exceptions are instances of a class. For example, all *checked exceptions* inherit from a class called `Exception` which, in turn, inherits from a class called `Throwable`. In fact, *error exceptions* also inherit from the `Throwable` class directly while *unchecked exceptions* inherit from the `RuntimeException` class, which is itself a sub-class of `Throwable`.

Despite this somewhat convoluted hierarchy, the syntax for exception handling is very similar to Python, where the main idea again is to enclose the code which might raise an exception inside the `try` block, as seen in the exception handling syntax for Java below:

```
try {
    // block of code that can throw exceptions
    EXECUTE_STATEMENTS_THAT_MIGHT_THROW_AN_EXCEPTION
} catch (EXCEPTION_TYPE_1 e) {
    // exception handler for EXCEPTION_TYPE_1
    EXECUTE_STATEMENTS_IN_CASE_EXCEPTION_OCCURS
} catch (EXCEPTION_TYPE_2 e) {
    // Exception handler for EXCEPTION_TYPE_2
    EXECUTE_STATEMENTS_IN_CASE_EXCEPTION_OCCURS
} finally {
    // finally block always executes
    EXECUTE_STATEMENTS_REGARDLESS_OF_EXCEPTION_OCCURRENCE
}
```

The `try` block is followed by a `catch` block, which includes statements to help compensate for the exception occurring. A `try` block can have more than one `catch` blocks following it, where each handles specific kinds of exceptions. A `catch` block can also catch a generic Exception object to respond to any *checked exception* or *unchecked exception*.

If a block of code **throws** an exception, the appropriate block will respond to that kind of exception. If an exception is thrown by some statement in the `try` block, control immediately shifts to the `catch` block that contains the matching exception handler and the rest of the statements in the `try` clause are skipped. If there is no `catch` handler with a matching exception, the program stops when that exception is thrown.

Let's see an example by having a simple block of code try to divide by 0, hence causing that operation to `throw` an `ArithmeticException` which we'll catch in the corresponding `catch` block:

```
class Main {
  public static void main(String[] args) {
    try{
        int x = 0;
        int y = 10;
        int fraction = y/x;
    } catch(ArithmeticException e) {
      System.out.println("CATCH_BLOCK: caught Exception = "+e);
    } finally {
      System.out.println("FINALLY_BLOCK: not doing anything here.");
    }
    System.out.println("Outside the try-catch-finally blocks now.");
  }
}
```

The above code produces the following output:

```
CATCH_BLOCK: caught Exception = java.lang.ArithmeticException: / by zero
FINALLY_BLOCK: not doing anything here.
Outside the try-catch-finally blocks now.
```

Just like in Python, you can also `throw` any kind of exception. In addition, if you know some code might produce an exception but you're not interested in catching those exceptions, your can include the `throws` keyword in the method definition to indicate your method will just throw those exceptions back to the calling code without trying to catch them. The syntax for throwing the exception via the method definition is as follows:

```
public static void myMethod() throws Exception1, Exception2, ... {
    // Method's statements here
    EXECUTE_STATEMENTS
}
```

It's important to draw a distinction between the keyword `throw`, which can be used to throw an exception, and the keyword `throws`, which is used to indicate that a method will pass an exception on and send it on to the calling code instead, as above.

8.5.3 I/O in Java

Almost all the classes for Input/Output (I/O) in Java are contained in the `java.io` or `java.util` packages. Just like most POSIX compatible systems, Java also provides access to the three standard streams: `stdin`, `stdout`, and `stderr`, as we saw in Section 4.4.

The standard input stream is connected to the `System.in` object and the standard output stream is connected to the `System.out` object, as we've already seen. Each of these objects has several methods to facilitate the processing of data. In addition, Java uses the stream model for Input/Output operations; streams in Java are sequences of data that can utilize byte data directly in a **byte stream** or use character data in a **character stream**.

Once we know how to handle exceptional situations, we can start to read or write files as the process of File I/O, which requires your program to interact with the underlying operating system and the user, can often lead to things going awry. We can get a handle on File I/O by starting with standard I/O where we prompt the user for some input and then process it. Let's start with an example program to read input from the user and print it out again:

```java
// Import the Scanner class for I/O
import java.util.Scanner;

class Main {
  public static void main(String[] args) {
    // Declare scanner object and connect it to stdin stream
    Scanner scan = new Scanner(System.in);

    // Read some string input from the user
    System.out.println("Please enter your name: ");
    String name = scan.nextLine();

    // Read some integer data from the user
    System.out.println("Please enter your age: ");
    int age = scan.nextInt();
    System.out.println("Please enter your weight: ");
    double weight = scan.nextDouble();

    // Print it out to stdout:
    System.out.println("Name: "+ name);
    System.out.println("Age: "+ age);
```

```
    System.out.println("Weight: "+ weight);
  }
}
```

Here, we created a `Scanner` object called `scan` and used that to read input from the user; first a `String` value, then an `int` value, and finally a `double` value before we echo these three values back to the user. This code thus produces the following output:

```
Please enter your name:
Foo Bar
Please enter your age:
21
Please enter your weight:
153.5
Name: Foo Bar
Age: 21
Weight: 153.5
```

In the same way, we can read from a file, as well. We start by creating a new `File` object called `myFile` and attach it to the `foo.txt` file. We then use a `Scanner` object called `myReader` and, instead of attaching it to `System.in`, we attach it to the `File` object, `myFile`. Since we're dealing with files and they may or may not exist on the underlying operating system, we add in some exception handling to handle those situations gracefully.

```
// Import the File class, Exception class, and Scanner class
import java.io.File;
import java.io.FileNotFoundException;
import java.util.Scanner;

public class Main {
  public static void main(String[] args) {
    try {
      // Create a File object in order to read data from foo.txt
      File myFile = new File("foo.txt");
      Scanner myReader = new Scanner(myFile);
      while (myReader.hasNextLine()) {
        String myData = myReader.nextLine();
        System.out.println(myData);
      }
      myReader.close();
    } catch (FileNotFoundException e) {
      System.out.println("Whoops, I'm sorry I didn't find the file!");
      e.printStackTrace();
    }
  }
}
```

Finally, we can also write data to a file programmatically. The overall approach is to use the `FileWriter` class from `java.io` to create the `myWriter` object and use that object to write some data to a file called `foo.txt`. In case something goes wrong with any of the writing commands, we catch and respond gracefully to any `IOExceptions`, as well.

```java
// Import the FileWriter class and the IOException class to handle errors
import java.io.FileWriter;
import java.io.IOException;

public class Main {
  public static void main(String[] args) {
    try {
      FileWriter myWriter = new FileWriter("foo.txt");
      // Write to foo.txt
      myWriter.write("Hello Written World!");

      // Close the FileWriter object and allow the resources to be re-allocated
      myWriter.close();
      System.out.println("Finished writing to the file!");
    } catch (IOException e) {
        System.out.println("Oops, we had an issue writing to the file!");
        e.printStackTrace();
    }
  }
}
```

9. Databases and MDM

There's a metaphor that's only been available to us in the past 30 or 40 years, and that's the desktop interface. Suppose there's a blue rectangular icon on the lower right corner of your computer's desktop - does that mean that the file itself is blue and rectangular and lives in the lower right corner of your computer? Of course not. But those are the only things that can be asserted about anything on the desktop - it has color, position, and shape. Those are the only categories available to you, and yet none of them are true about the file itself or anything in the computer. They couldn't possibly be true. That's an interesting thing. You could not form a true description of the innards of the computer if your entire view of reality was confined to the desktop. And yet the desktop is useful. That blue rectangular icon guides my behavior, and it hides a complex reality that I don't need to know. That's the key idea.
– Donald Hoffman[1]

9.1 Mind Your Data

Imagine you start a home business to supply pre-packaged magic tricks to young magicians in the neighbourhood. Kids, and aspiring magicians of all ages, drop by and business starts to boom. Soon, doing the billing starts to get out of hand, and, looking at the mess of notes lying around your home, you can't figure out if the Bob who owes you $2,178.28 is Bob Wood or Robert Seger! You decide it's time to get a handle on your burgeoning business and ensure your invoices don't go unpaid.

Having taken CS0 and learned about the transformation of Data → Information → Knowledge, you realize the data needs to be organized so it can be utilized effectively. That means you'll need to organize all the multiple copies of calls and bills and notes you've just been throwing into a single,

---

[1] In *The Case Against Reality*, which is available here: https://www.theatlantic.com/science/archive/2016/04/the-illusion-of-reality/479559/

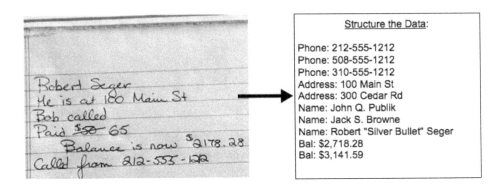

Figure 9.1: The raw notes for our burgeoning home business transformed into **structured data**: all the written notes are converted into labelled, structured data. The image on the left is just a snippet of the handwritten notes but the table on the right has all the data from the entire handwritten note sheet.

bulging folder up to now. So you start to gather all the disparate notes that you've been keeping on your customers, as seen in Figure 9.1.

9.1.1   Data Abstraction

This is reminiscent of what we did in Section 0.1.1, where we realized all the gathered facts, or individual observations, eventually have to be structured into Data. Once we have the Data, we can transform it into Information and, subsequently, into the actionable Knowledge all enterprises depend upon to optimize their mission-critical metrics.

This familiar process of converting Data → Information → Knowledge is shown again in Figure 9.2. The knowledge we gain, in the context of our current business enterprise of selling magic tricks, will be used to take action and make a decision about which overdue customers to bill first. So how should we go about solving our business problem?[2]

In this case, we know we have to start by first getting the raw facts. We can do so by using the idea of **abstraction**. We've previously referred to abstraction as ignoring any details we deem to be non-essential to our computational solution. We can use abstraction to create a **model** of our problem. That model can be mathematical, computational, graphical, etc., as we saw in Section 2.1.1. In the case of our magic tricks business, we can use abstraction to ignore unessential details and extract the important raw facts from our random notes. But how do we actually do this kind of abstraction?

We can get a more intuitive sense of abstraction in the context of a map of campus, as shown in Figure 9.3. Suppose a classmate asks you for help in getting from the Science building to the IT building. You might draw them a map at a high level of abstraction with only the relevant **entities**,

---

[2]When we refer to a business problem or business rule, we really mean the problem or rule for any organization, not just a commercial enterprise.

Figure 9.2: The Data → Information → Knowledge data processing workflow

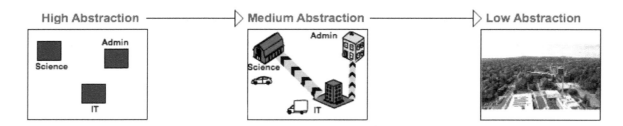

Figure 9.3: The idea of abstraction in the context of a map. At the *highest* level of abstraction, you represent the relevant building entities as squares with no other detail. At the *medium* level of abstraction, you add more details like connecting roads, parking lots, and colours of buildings. The actual campus itself is the *lowest* level of abstraction and contains the most details, including things like trees, grass, people, etc.

the buildings represented as squares, since you assume they're familiar with campus. This map is our model of just the essential concepts at a high level or our **conceptual model**.

Now suppose your grandmother wants to get from the IT building to the Science building when she comes to visit you on campus. You might make a different campus model for her by drawing a map of campus at a medium level of abstraction with a few more details, or semantics, as she's likely unfamiliar with campus. For example, you might give the entities, the buildings, more details like colour and height and also show how they're connected by roads. This model which contains more semantics would be an example of a **logical model**.[3]

If, on the other hand, you have to give a tour of campus, then you'd do it at the level of the physical campus itself; this would be considered our **physical model** of campus. The physical campus itself is the lowest level of abstraction and contains the most details, including things like trees, grass, people, etc.

Similarly, we can look at the *data* from our magic tricks business at three different levels of abstraction, where each level corresponds to a different model. The lowest level is looking at the physical data itself, the actual values, like the numbers 212-555-1212. This is the physical model of our data, or our **physical data model**.

We can also go to a high level of abstraction and refer to those numbers as what they represent: a phone number. This idea of the numbers relating to some underlying concept would be our **conceptual data model**. At an intermediate level of abstraction, we can add some semantic meaning, or logical meaning, to this concept by relating it to other concepts, like the name of a person, the address of a person, etc., and refer to that whole as the *contact information* of a person. This contact information structure would represent the **logical data model** for our collection of data.

We can use this kind of abstraction to structure the raw facts into Data as seen in Figure 9.1 and Figure 9.4, where this **structured data** starts to associate the core elements of the raw facts (e.g., the number 212-555-1212) with a label (i.e., Phone). We end up with the kinds of data with which we deal in our particular enterprise; things like phone numbers, names, addresses, etc., that comprise our transactions.

---

[3]**Logical**, in this sense, means the rules or relationships that govern how elements are related to each other, and to the whole, in order to convey some meaning.

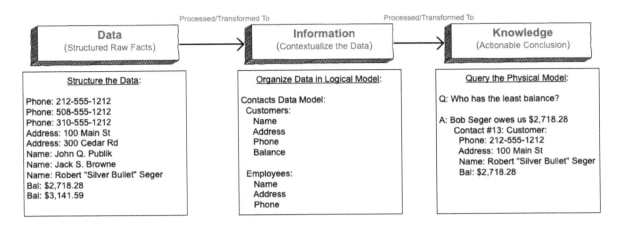

Figure 9.4: The Data → Information → Knowledge data processing workflow for the Contacts "database"

9.1.2 Data Models and Master Data Management

After extracting the facts from our notes and structuring them into Data, you notice that there are multiple copies of seemingly the same data but with different values. For example, Jack S. Browne's address is listed as both 300 Cedar Rd. and as 100 Main St. Which one is the correct one? You have no idea!

One way to fix this would be to have a single copy of the data that serves as the master reference. This *single master copy* of the data would be unique and accurate to prevent just this kind of disastrous result. That single authoritative version of the data is called **master data** and managing your data to ensure the accuracy of the master data is called **master data management**.

A useful way to manage the data is to organize it and collect it so you can manage it as a single unit. You can create a collection of related data items that are organized in a structured format called a **database** to do exactly this. You could, for example, take the disparate notes and sheets of paper you have and organize them as a collection of data stored in spreadsheets contained in a single file or folder; that could be considered a database of sorts.

We can start to organize this data even more. We can continue to use the idea of abstraction to get a better handle on our data's underlying potential organization in order to manage our master data. This higher level of abstraction, and organization, can be represented as a data model for our data.[4]

A **data model**, as we saw in Figure 6.3 in Section 6.7, is a collection of concepts for describing data that tells us how it is organized and represented. A data model is an abstraction of complex, real-world data structures which, as for databases, can be diagrams, like we'll see in-depth when we examine entity-relationship diagrams. It provides a logical structure that shows how data are inter-connected and how they're stored and processed.

We can see an example of these data models in Figure 9.4, where we took the structured data and organized it further into an abstract data model called the **Logical Model** or the **Logical Data Model**. In this case, we realized that the collection of data we had, like the Phone, Address, Name, etc., represented *contact* information for people.

---

[4]In a sense, we can think of this as decreasing the **entropy** of the system with each higher level of abstraction, or organization, as seen in Section 10.6.4. As the data gets more organized, its distribution of probability shifts and spikes, and the entropy of the system decreases and the **information gained** from the system thus increases, just as we'd expect.

ABSTRACTION	MAP EXAMPLE	BUSINESS EXAMPLE
High (10,000 ft level)	Objects like Buildings, Cars, etc.	Entities like Customers, Products, etc.
Medium (100 ft level)	Objects with Attributes Buildings - Doors - Height - Colors Cars - Windows - Wheels - Doors	Entities with Attributes Products - Name - Description - Cost Customers - Name - Address - Phone - Balance

Low (1 ft level)		Contact 1:
		  Phone: 212-555-1212
		  Address: 100 Main St
		  Name: Robert "Silver Bullet" Seger
		  Bal: $2,718.28
		Contact 2:
		  Phone: 310-555-1212
		  Address: 300 Cedar Rd
		  Name: Jack S. Browne
		  Bal: $3,141.59

Table 9.1: Different levels of abstraction: the lowest level of abstraction is the actual geographical area for the map example while it is the actual contacts' data for the business example. At the highest level of abstraction, you ignore all non-essential details and all you note in the map example is that you have some buildings and all you note in the business example is you have some people whom you've contacted.

So rather than deal with each person's Phone separately and each person's Address separately, we bundle it together into the *Contacts Logical Model*. Then, we can just refer to the Contact information for each person as a single unit rather than needing to gather and process each individual element separately. As we can see in Table 9.1, the actual list of all the contacts is the lowest level of abstraction, called the **Physical Data Model**, and is the actual structured data represented in a particular data model (in this case, the Logical Data Model).

The three levels of abstraction are summarized in Table 9.1 for two different **use cases**: the map you might draw for your grandma or your colleague and the contacts information you might collect for your magic tricks business.

At the highest level of abstraction, you ignore all non-essential details. So, in the map example, at the highest level of abstraction, all you note down is that you have some building entities with an associated name, like the Science building. Similarly, at the highest level of abstraction in the business example, all you note down is that you have some **entities**, the people whom you've contacted, and each person has an associated name, like "Bob Seger". This is our **Conceptual Data Model**.

At the intermediate level of abstraction, we create the **Logical Data Model** for both the map and the contacts. For the map, it has more parts of the structure, like the building details and connecting roads but no people or objects inside the buildings. For the contacts, it has the full contact information structure but no values; it's like a *template* that shows what the structure of all contact records are but the actual values are not populated.

The lowest level of abstraction is the actual geographical area for the map example while it is the actual contacts' data for the business example; for the contacts, it's all the actual values in the structured data record for *all* your contacts, the **Physical Data Model**.

9.1.3 Three LEVELS of Data Model Abstractions

We can thus have three levels of data abstraction as represented in the following Data Models for our magic tricks business and seen in Table 9.2:

1. **Conceptual Data Model**: Highest Level of Abstraction: at this level, we identify just the **entities** involved in our business like a Customer and a Product and establish a **relationship** between the two: a Customer can buy a Product. At this level of abstraction, we only list the *kinds* of entities, not any details about them.

2. **Logical Data Model**: Medium Level of Abstraction: at this level, we expand our entities to also include their attributes. For example, we realize that a Customer entity consists of: Name, Phone, Address, and Money Owed. We have thus organized our data and represented it as a single unit in this data model although, at this point, we still don't add any values. The Customer Logical Data Model, represented as a schema, is just a template that we'll use to create actual Customers, in the same way a class was a template in the OOP paradigm.

3. **Physical Data Model**: Lowest Level of Abstraction: at this level, we structure all our values into the appropriate Logical Data Model. The actual records are the values for *all* of the different contacts in our rolodex.[5]

The set of integers, $\mathbb{Z}$, can also be modeled at these same three levels of abstraction, as also seen in Table 9.2. For example, at a high level of abstraction, you'd say that $\mathbb{Z}$ just consisted of numbers. At the medium level of abstraction, you might say that $\mathbb{Z}$ is the set of numbers that includes 0, the set of positive natural numbers, and the set of negative whole numbers. At the lowest level of abstraction, you might say that $\mathbb{Z} = \{\ldots, -3, -2, -1, 0, 1, 2, 3, \ldots\}$.

9.2 Database Management

A database models data items at various level of abstraction to **organize** related data items into a **single unit**. In order to optimize these data items for information management, they're stored in a more **abstract** form than the simple spreadsheet based "database" we alluded to earlier.

This abstract form is usually represented as a **table** as we'll see in a bit but, more generally, can be any **named data structure** that is stored in the database; these named data structures are the *database objects* that need to be managed to ensure a properly functioning database. At a very simple level, we can think of each table as being analogous to a spreadsheet and the database then would be a collection of multiple tables of this sort.

A **DataBase Management System (DBMS)** is software that allows users to manage their databases, including enabling the creation, access, and modification of databases. It provides basic services like moving data to and from the database's underlying physical files, allowing users to

---

[5] A rolodex is an ancient, contact organizational tool used in the dark ages of the 20th century.

ABSTRACTION	DATA MODEL	MATH EXAMPLE	MAP EXAMPLE	BUSINESS EXAMPLE
High	Conceptual	Set of Integers consists of Numbers	Objects	Entities and Relationships
Medium	Logical	$\mathbb{Z}$ is the set of numbers that includes 0, the set of positive natural numbers, and the set of negative whole numbers	Objects & Attributes Buildings - Doors - Height - Colors Cars - Windows - Wheels - Doors	Entities & Attributes Products - Name - Description - Cost Customers - Name - Address - Phone - Balance

Low	Physical	$\mathbb{Z} = \{\ldots, -2, -1, 0, 1, 2, \ldots\}$		Contact 1:
				  Phone: 212-555-1212
				  Address: 100 Main St
				  Name: Robert "Silver Bullet" Seger
				  Bal: $2,718.28
				Contact 2:
				  Phone: 310-555-1212
				  Address: 300 Cedar Rd
				  Name: Jack S. Browne
				  Bal: $3,141.59

Table 9.2: Different levels of abstraction in the Conceptual, Logical, and Physical Data Models: the Physical Data Model is the actual geographical area for the map example while it is the actual contacts' data for the business example

concurrently access the database, providing security mechanisms, and providing support for a **query language**.

A **query** is a command or procedure for retrieving and manipulating data; you can run queries against a database using a query language designed specifically to facilitate retrieval and modification of the values contained in the database. An **instance** of the database is a snapshot of the database in the database management software at one particular time and is made up of all the tables and all the values contained in all the records at that time.

A database model is a collection of concepts for describing data that also adds in integrity rules, as shown in Section 9.3. There are many such database models, including flat, network, relational, etc. As we'll see, the relational database model and its variants are the most popular nowadays, although the flat model is making a bit of a comeback with document-oriented databases.

A **schema** is a mathematical description of a particular collection of data, a database, using the given database model. In the relational model, the schema is basically an abstract description of the columns, or **fields**, in a table. In essence, a schema for the Customer table in our database might look like this: `Customer(cust_id:string, cust_name:string, cust_address:string, cust_phone:integer, cust_balance:real)`

In addition to the actual tables, you can define **virtual tables**, also called *sub-schema* or database **views**, that are used by the technical end user. We'll explore these views in more detail in Section 9.2.2.

A **database** is a structured collection of related data that is optimized to support management of data and transformation of data to information. A **DataBase Management System (DBMS)** is a software application that supports the creation, access, and modification of such databases.

9.2.1 DataBase Life Cycle (DBLC) PHASES

Now that we know what a database is and how to manage it using a DBMS, we could, if we wanted, just start hacking out our database in some DBMS. That might work well for small projects but, for any significant project, this can be an issue if the database is critical for the organization. There are four kinds of critical systems: business critical, security critical, mission critical, and safety critical.

You might be okay with hacking a small database that's business critical for a lemonade stand but would you be as confident to hand over a database you hacked together in the last 30 minutes for a safety critical application like sending astronauts to the moon where failure could cost lives?

For this reason, engineering principles have been applied to database design just as they've been applied to software design. The goal of the database design phase is to:

- Decide how the database is going to be used
- Try to avoid data redundancy and
- Ensure data integrity so that data is accurate and verifiable

This helps not only reduce errors but also helps support good decision-making based on the data, as we'll see in Chapter 10.

Databases, like software, have a life cycle that takes it from the stage of being a glint in some developer's eye to the sunsetting of a mature database that served its stakeholders well. The DataBase Life Cycle (DBLC) tracks all the events in the lifetime of a database and is usually divided into stages, where each stage is associated with some finite set of deliverables, as shown in Figure 9.5 for both system development and software development, as well.

The DataBase Life Cycle builds upon the traditional System Development Life Cycle used in information systems. The **System Development Life Cycle (SDLC)** is broken down into the following five **phases**:

1. Planning Phase – in this first phase, we initiate project planning, ensure feasibility of the project, plan the schedule, obtain approval for the project from stakeholders, etc.
2. Analysis Phase – next, we have to understand and delineate the business needs and processing requirements
3. Design Phase – here, we define the solution system based on the requirements and analysis decisions from the previous phases
4. Implementation Phase – finally, we construct the actual solution, test it, train users, and install the new system as needed

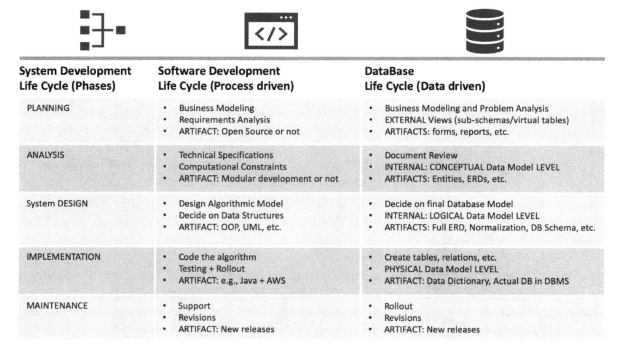

System Development Life Cycle (Phases)	Software Development Life Cycle (Process driven)	DataBase Life Cycle (Data driven)
PLANNING	• Business Modeling • Requirements Analysis • ARTIFACT: Open Source or not	• Business Modeling and Problem Analysis • EXTERNAL Views (sub-schemas/virtual tables) • ARTIFACTS: forms, reports, etc.
ANALYSIS	• Technical Specifications • Computational Constraints • ARTIFACT: Modular development or not	• Document Review • INTERNAL: CONCEPTUAL Data Model LEVEL • ARTIFACTS: Entities, ERDs, etc.
System DESIGN	• Design Algorithmic Model • Decide on Data Structures • ARTIFACT: OOP, UML, etc.	• Decide on final Database Model • INTERNAL: LOGICAL Data Model LEVEL • ARTIFACTS: Full ERD, Normalization, DB Schema, etc.
IMPLEMENTATION	• Code the algorithm • Testing + Rollout • ARTIFACT: e.g., Java + AWS	• Create tables, relations, etc. • PHYSICAL Data Model LEVEL • ARTIFACT: Data Dictionary, Actual DB in DBMS
MAINTENANCE	• Support • Revisions • ARTIFACT: New releases	• Rollout • Revisions • ARTIFACT: New releases

Figure 9.5: The DataBase Life Cycle (DBLC) and its relationship to the System Development Life Cycle (SDLC) and the Software Development Life Cycle (SDLC).

5. Maintenance Phase – lastly, we undertake the tasks necessary to keep the system running and improve it, as needed

There are many variations on the exact delineation of these life cycles but most methodologies will inevitably contain the same basic components, perhaps organized into different tasks or sub-tasks. Systems development is used for decision-making in the data → information → knowledge architecture. In fact, traditional development of computational solutions also follows a similar life cycle, called the Software Development Life Cycle (SDLC), but here the focus is more on the processes that do the transformations in the data → information → knowledge architecture. The processes are the applications in this context. Figure 9.5 shows the Life Cycles for System Development, Software Development, and DataBases, where they all use the same five phases.

Let's examine the five **phases** in more depth for the **DataBase Development Life Cycle**:

1. Planning Phase – Assess the organization's data goals and identify stakeholder needs and requirements for the database
2. Analysis Phase – Design of the database's *Conceptual Data Model*
3. Design Phase – Design of the database's *Logical Data Model* and detailed system specification
4. Implementation Phase – Actual creation of the database's *Physical Data Model*, including the database itself and the queries
5. Maintenance Phase – Troubleshoot and update the database as needed

The **Planning Phase** is also where we establish and document the **business rules** of an organization; these are the precise, unambiguous, and often brief descriptions of business operations. The business rules are based on the business' policies, procedures, and principles and help standardize the organization's view of their data. They can help create and enforce actions by the organization's personnel and are usually established by conducting interviews, examining the organization's written documentation, and by observation of the organization's operations, although that's subject to the Hawthorne Effect, where people behave differently when observed.

The *Conceptual Data Model*, in the **Analysis Phase**, is represented by the entities in our enterprise; we usually model these entities as diagrams called **Entity Relationship Diagrams (ERDs)** and create initial ERD representations of the entities in this phase. This model of the data is independent of all physical considerations and is based on the system's requirements and specifications.

The *Logical Data Model*, in the **Design Phase**, is based on a specific database model but is independent of any specific DBMS. This phase often contains fully developed ERDs, normalization, database schema, etc., as we'll see in detail later.

Finally, the *Physical Data Model*, which is developed in the **Implementation Phase**, is where the implementation of the database on secondary storage is actually created. Additional constraints, relations, security, etc., are also defined, usually using **Structured Query Language (SQL)**.

What are Entity Relationship Diagrams (ERDs)?

An **entity** is anything about which we collect and store data. It's usually the *noun* in a specification statement, just as we saw in Object-Oriented Design in Section 8.2.1. Also as with objects, entities have certain **attributes** which represent the characteristics of that entity. So an Entity might be a Customer and the attributes might be Phone, Address, etc.

An **Entity Relationship Diagram (ERD)** is a graphical representation of an entity and its attributes. In addition to attributes for entities, different entities can be *related* to each other and this association is usually quantified by the **cardinality** of the relationship. The entities can also specify the **constraints** on the data as derived from the *business rules*.

For example, for a university database, our entities might be things like students and courses. Then, we can define relationships like students can take courses (e.g., Jane Doe is taking CSC 3011). The cardinality would be the constraints on that relationship; in this case, it might be something along the lines of: one student can only register in one section of a course so that the same student isn't put into multiple sections of the same course.

We can see an example of an ERD for our customers in Figure 9.6, where we see the ERD diagram for the Customer entity and its relationship to the Product entity. The cardinality of their relationship is many-to-many which, as we'll find out, cannot be implemented as is in a relational database. The particular relationship in Figure 9.6 indicates that zero or more Customers can buy zero or more Products.

The main advantages of these different Data Models is increased *abstraction* and *independence* between the layers. With abstraction, you don't have to worry about any of the implementation

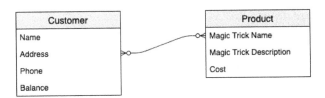

Figure 9.6: An ERD diagram for Customer entity and its relationship to a Product entity. The cardinality of their relationship is many-to-many which, as we'll find out, cannot be implemented as is in a relational database.

details. With independence between layers, you can make changes at one level without affecting the previous layers. For example, you can change the hard disk drives, indexes, etc., at the physical level without affecting the Logical Data Model; this is an example of **Physical Data Independence**. Similarly, end-user views, as utilized in application programs or external schemas in the Planning Phase, aren't affected by changes in the Logical Data Model made by changing the entities, attributes, or relationships; this is an example of **Logical Data Independence**.

This layered independence also helps the project meet its goals in terms of balancing costs, quality, and delivery time. Together, these three characteristics epitomize the **Project Triangle** in project management which tries to balance these three qualities by trading off between any two at a time:

1. Quality
2. Delivery Time
3. Cost

This is also reflected in the following quote:

> "Everyone who comes in here wants three things:
> They want it quick.
> They want it good.
> They want it cheap.
> I tell 'em to pick two and call me back."
> – A sign on the back wall of a small printing company

9.2.2 LAYERS of Database Abstraction

In early database systems, manipulating the data depended on the physical file structure and thus required a lot of effort to maintain. In addition, end users couldn't just make up a query on the fly, a so-called **ad-hoc query**, and run in it on the database; instead, they had to depend upon database programmers to implement these in the database system directly. The **relational database model** developed by computer scientist E.F. Codd separated the idea of the *physical representation* of the database at the machine level from the *logical representation* at the user level. This helped propel relational databases, and its many variations, to become the dominant database model today.

In this delineation, we often describe a database itself as having three different **layers** of abstraction that are relatively independent of each other; these **Layers of Database Abstraction** are:

1. **External Layer of Database Abstraction**: This layer determines how the end user interacts with the database. The end-user, in this case, is a Technical user, which is usually a person or an application. This layer presents the data in as virtual tables, which are created from the actual underlying physical tables, using database views or sub-schema. This layer is usually determined in the *Planning Phase of the DBLC*.
   - The external layer of database abstraction provides different "views" of the data for different technical users, which can be either people or software programs. For example, the finance department might be interested in a "view" of people being modeled only as a userID and an amountOwed but HR might be interested in a "view" of people being modeled as a userID, an address, and an annualSalary. These "views" can also be utilized in other database objects like forms, reports, etc.
2. **Internal Layer of Database Abstraction**: This layer is sometimes described as being made up of two layers, a Conceptual and Logical Layer, and other times as just the Logical Layer. This is

where the Conceptual and Logical Data Model Schema are constructed, as well. It deals with things like the final Database Schema, ERDs, etc. The details of this layer are determined in the *Analysis Phase* and *Design Phase of the DBLC*.

- One of the most important aspects of the internal layer of database abstraction is to identify all the entities, their attributes, and their relationships.

3. **Physical Layer of Database Abstraction**: This layer consists of the actual DBMS implementation in hardware and software, as captured in the Physical Data Model. It describes the files and indexes used, b-trees, linear hashing, hash tables, XML, optimizing indices, relaxing constraints, etc. This layer is addressed in the *Implementation Phase of the DBLC*.

- The physical layer of database abstraction consists of the actual data files that hold the data values. In a relational database model, these are stored as tables, of course, but it also addresses other aspects, like hardware, indices, constraints, etc.

9.2.3 Client-Server Database Application TIERS

Software programs, or applications, that rely on databases nowadays usually follow a **three-tiered** Client-Server Database **Application** Architecture which consists of the:

1. Presentation **Tier**: This is also called the Client Tier and is the front-end or user interface of the application that the Business End User sees. The Business End User is the person using the application.
2. Business Logic **Tier**: This is the middle-layer and is also called the Business Tier or the Application Tier. It consists of the actual software application that implements the functional business logic running on an application server.
3. Data **Tier**: This is the back-end and is sometimes called the Storage Tier, as well. This is where the database lives and the DBMS usually runs on an Enterprise server. The Business Logic Tier interacts with the database through its database views or sub-schema which are exposed in this Data Tier.

   (a) The database views, or sub-schema, are exposed via the External Layer of Database Abstraction, as we saw in Section 9.2.2, where we examined the Layers of Database Abstraction.

The relationship between Data Models, Phases, Layers, and Tiers is shown in Figure 9.7.[6]

9.3 Relational Database Model

As we've seen so far, a database can be thought of as a *collection of related data*. That data is usually stored in files so the files will be somehow related to each other. Exactly how they're related depends on the **database model** used; a database model is a *particular collection of data* built upon a given data model with integrity rules added. Early databases were essentially collections of plain text files, or **flat files**. Over time, as more *semantic structure* was added to the data models used to *characterize the*

---

[6] More generally, a **two-tier** application architecture essentially consists of two **logical** layers: a **client** tier and a **server** tier which communicate directly without any middleware. The advantage of a two-tier client-server architecture is that it runs faster but it's disadvantage is that it's more tightly coupled and less secure.

A **three-tier** application architecture, on the other hand, consists of three logical layers: a client tier, an **application** tier, and a server tier with communication between the client and server being mediated by a **middleware** application tier. The advantage of a three-tier client-server architecture is that it's loosely coupled and provides greater security but the disadvantage is it might run slower.

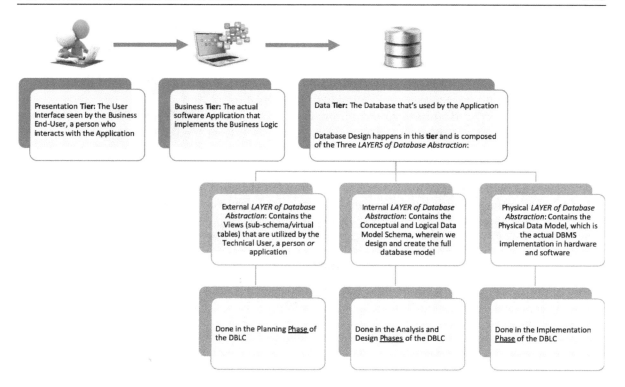

Figure 9.7: This is the Three-**tiered** client-server database **Application** Architecture. It shows the Application Development **Tiers** and their relationship to the **Layers** of Database Abstraction, as well as the DataBase Life Cycle (DBLC) **Phases**.

data and its relationships, several database models were developed, like the **hierarchical model**, the **network model**, etc.

The **relational database model** represented data as tables, with rows and columns; a relational database is a collection of such tables where tables represent entities in the problem space and are related to each other. This relationship between two tables is established via having a common field in both tables. This common field is called the **primary key** in the first table and the **foreign key** in the second table. This approach not only makes the model very flexible but also gives it several advantages over previous database models and flat files.

9.3.1 Data Models and Database Models

A **data model** describes how data is represented and how the data elements relate to each other. It thus consists of the **structure** of the data as well as the **actions** or operations allowed on that data. A **database model** extends the underlying data model by adding in **constraints**, which are the *integrity rules* on the relationships between the data. Thus, a database model consists of three aspects: structure, actions, and constraints.

In Table 9.3, we can see these three aspects of database models for three different database models: flat-file, relational, and multi-dimensional. One form of flat-file databases popular today are document-oriented databases that also use a key-value store as in some NoSQL databases.

But a significant advantage of the relational database approach is that it's much faster than flat file

Database Model	Structure	Actions	Constraints
Flat File	Data is structured as defined by each application	Ability to read, write, lock, etc.	Constraints are defined by each application
Relational	Data is structured as relations (tables) with attributes (columns)	Structured Query Language (SQL) commands	Primary key, foreign key, etc.
Multi-Dimensional	Data is structured as a multi-dimensional cube	Tuple-based addressing, filtering, set operations, etc.	Members belong to single dimension, etc.

Table 9.3: Database models extend data models by adding in constraints, or integrity rules, on the relationships between the data. A database model thus consists of a structure for the data, actions allowed on that data, and constraints on how the data is related. These three aspects are shown for three different database models: flat-file, relational, and multi-dimensional database models.

processing used in traditional software programming when running complex queries on large amounts of data with complex structures. A DBMS also allows multiple users to do synchronous access and editing of the database and is able to manage any conflicts that might arise due to this access.

In addition, relational DBMSs like MySQL, PostgreSQL, Oracle, etc., offer flexible tools for security and for querying data using aggregations and joins, while also accounting for constraints as captured by the business rules.

This is because when Codd proposed the relational model, one of the major innovations was to remove the use of pointers and instead use **tables** to represent data at the Physical Data Model level. These tables, in their Logical Data Model representation, were called *n*-ary **relations**, which is the basis of the name, *relational* database. A relation, in this sense, is a set of tuples, which are sequences of *n* elements.

We know that a table represents, or models, some **entity** in the problem space. An entity is a group, or template, and the individual **instances** are specific examples of that group. For example, a `Customer` entity describes the group of customers. An individual customer, like "Robert Seger," would be an instance of the `Customer` entity.

Each row of the table contains data about each instance of that entity. For example, the `Customer` entity would be modeled by a `Customer` table whose rows contain information about all the different customers, or different instances of the `Customer` entity.

The columns contain the **features** or **attributes**. We can also assign a **data type** to each column, or attribute. These data types vary by DBMS but are usually along the lines of `strings`, `integers`, `floats`, etc., just as we saw earlier. Most DBMSs also add in more complex and helpful datatypes to store non-standard values like `blobs`, `date`, `time`, etc.

A table thus stores information about all instances of an entity. Each row in the table is unique and is identified by a distinct identifier or key for that instance. That unique identifier is the **primary key**, which is **indexed** to optimize lookups, but other columns can also be indexed in order to expedite lookups.

Let's look at an example of how the `Customer` entity from Figure 9.6 might appear in our database. A snapshot of the `Customer` relation, or table, and its corresponding data for different `Customer` instances, is shown in Table 9.4. You'll notice that we've added in a new column, the `customerID`, which serves as the primary key for our table.

We can now see how the primary key from the `Customer` table becomes a foreign key in another

customerID	name	address	phone	balance
1	"Robert Seger"	"100 Main St"	2125551212	2718.28
2	"Jack S. Browne"	"300 Cedar Rd"	3105551212	3141.59
⋮	⋮	⋮	⋮	⋮

Table 9.4: Customer table in the DBMS. Each row of the table contains information about a different instance of the Customer entity.

table by looking at the Orders table, which shows the magic tricks purchased by each customer. A snapshot of the Orders table, and its corresponding data for which instance of Customer ordered which magic trick, is shown in Table 9.5.

There, we can see that the Customer with CustomerID of 1 ordered the magic trick "Bunny in Hat". We can match the CustomerID of 1 from the Orders table with the customerID in Table 9.4 to find that Customer's name is "Robert Seger". The only caveat I'd add is that this is a very artificial example and that real tables will reflect more self-contained entities, as we'll see when we get to the idea of *normalization* in Section 9.5.

The benefits of the Relational Database Model are plentiful. For example, it can support very fast retrieval in most cases. The data structures can also be easily changed and users don't need to know the details of how the data is stored at the physical level. Once you've implemented the database, complex queries can be easily created and deployed, including **ad-hoc queries** that are built on the fly and not re-used. The DBMSs organizational approach also results in more accurate data.

The table *header*, combined with the table *name* and the *datatypes* for each column, is captured in the **schema** for that table. The schema for the Customer table in our database might then look like this:

```
Customer(customerID:integer, name:string, address:string, phone:integer,
balance:float)
```

Although we've been somewhat cavalier in our terminology, in Table 9.6, we can see a mapping between the terminology used to describe the elements of a table (the *physical representation* in a relational database) and the elements of a relation (the *logical representation* of a relational database) as well as the elements of a file system (which is how things used to be stored before relational databases). Of course, the relational database model does have some major competitors, including the object-oriented relational database model and the NoSQL (ostensibly, "Not Only SQL") model, along with their hybrid variations, as they're all dependent on the efficiency of querying based on the resources and the problem domain, as we'll see next.

orderID	productName	customerID
30	"Spoon Bending"	2
31	"Bunny in Hat"	1
⋮	⋮	⋮

Table 9.5: Orders table in the DBMS.

Logical Relational Term	Physical Relational Term	File System Term
Relation	Table	File
Tuple	Row	Record
Attribute	Column	Field

Table 9.6: Comparison of Terminology between Logical Relational Term and Physical Relational Term in Relational Databases. We compare them to the analogous terms in a normal file system, as well.

9.4 Database Modeling and Querying

A **database** is a collection of related data items that are managed as a single unit organized in a structured format. How these data items and their relationships are represented is captured in the database model. A **database model** extends the *structure* and *actions* encapsulated in a data model by also adding in *constraints*, or integrity rules, on the relationships between the data. A **data model** is a collection of concepts for describing how each data element is organized and represented and is an *abstraction* of complex real-world data structures.

The **relational database model** is the most widely used database model today. The main concept of the relational database model is the idea of a **relation**, basically a table with rows and columns. Every relation has a schema, which describes the columns, or fields. A **schema** is a description of a particular database model for a particular collection of data.[7]

A **relational database** models the problem by organizing the data into several *tables*, with each table representing a different **entity**. These entities, or tables, might have a certain **relationship** with each other that is captured in the relational database model. The database itself is managed by a software program called the DataBase Management System (DBMS). A **DBMS catalog** stores the object definitions, like the table definitions, and keeps track of where the objects are physically stored, as well.

The central purpose of a database is to be able to efficiently, reliably, and correctly **query** and *manipulate* data. The main advantage of the relational approach is that it facilitates the transformation of data to information by revealing its meaning in some context via the ability to query the database in complex and varied ways. As the underlying data gets ever more complex and substantial, these basic relational database concepts are often extended into more complex database structures like data warehouses and data lakes, as well.

9.4.1 Databases, Data Warehouses, and Data Lakes

A **database** stores data, compiled into a single unit following the specified data model, related to specific projects or data pools. A database generally helps **data processing** by guaranteeing the correctness of transactions and the validity of data using **ACID** (Atomicity, Consistency, Isolation, Durability), a set of properties to ensure database reliability. Database-oriented applications are transaction-based and fall under the rubric of **OnLine Transaction Processing (OLTP)** to guarantee data validity under a large volume of short on-line transactions. This gives us the ability to track and manipulate data in support of an organization's **decision-making** process.

A **data warehouse** provides further infrastructure for **data analysis** by storing and disseminating databases from multiple sources. These data warehouses are capable of executing more complex

---

[7] ERDs are the conceptual representation and Tables and DB Schema are the logical representation of the underlying data. Relations are the mathematical abstraction of tables, the primary unit for storage of data in a relational database where the data itself is stored physically on disk differently, depending on the particular DBMS.

queries than a database and help with mining the data to drive business decisions. This **data mining** of the historical or archival data involves a small volume of transactions and is classified as **OnLine Analytical Processing (OLAP)**, which can utilize complex queries that often involve aggregations of large amounts of data.

Extract, Transform, and Load (ETL) processes are used to fetch and model data that can then populate data warehouses, which contain data relevant to the whole enterprise. When data is needed for a specific subset of the organization, like a certain department or functional organizational unit, ETL processes are then used to create a **data mart** that contains a subset of the data in order to reduce response time, provide easy access to frequently needed data, and minimize costs.

A **data lake** stores a variety of data, whether structured, semi-structured, or unstructured, from multiple sources in its native format directly and does not impose any data model or structure on it until the data is actually referenced as opposed to a data warehouse which stores structured data that already follows a specific data model.

9.4.2 Structured Query Language (SQL)

Querying the database allows us to manipulate and access information reliably and efficiently. In fact, the whole reason for doing the whole database design process, including normalization, etc., is to run these queries reliably. This is the real magic that a DBMS provides and is the last part that we actually do after all the design work we've learned so far.

In order to make this querying process efficient, a fourth generation reporting language like Structured Query Language (SQL) is often used in relational databases to build and query tables. It grew out of QUEL, which was IBM's original relational query language. Because it's a reporting language, it's not Turing complete as it's not computationally complete with branching and looping constructs. Instead, like some fourth generation languages, it just specifies *what* to do but not the details of *how* to do it. Some database vendors do add in the other control structures to make it Turing complete but the ANSI standard implementation does not define those constructs for SQL.

SQL is a very limited language and only has a small set of commands defined in the ANSI standard. These SQL commands are divided into five main categories:

1. Data Query Language (DQL): These are statements that query the data but don't change anything. DQL is implemented with the `SELECT` statement.
2. Data Manipulation Language (DML): These statements modify data values but do not modify any of the underlying data structures, like tables, views, etc. DML is implemented with the `INSERT`, `UPDATE`, `DELETE` statements.
3. Data Definition Language (DDL): These statements can add, change, or delete database objects but do not affect the data within them; it affects the containers but not the contents. DDL is implemented with the `CREATE`, `ALTER`, `DROP` statements.
4. Data Control Language (DCL): These statements help manage users' access privileges in connection with various database objects. DCL is implemented with the `GRANT` and `REVOKE` statements.
5. Transaction Control Language (TCL): These commands are used to manage **transactions** and changes made to the data by individual or grouped DML statements. TCL is implemented with the `COMMIT`, `ROLLBACK`, `SAVEPOINT`, `SET TRANSACTION` statements.

We can see even try out some example statements in a SQL session that we can try out in an online SQL IDE like `https://paiza.io/en/projects/new?language=mysql`. Let's see some example code where we `create` a `Customer` table, `insert` some data into it, and then `select` the information for a particular `Customer`:

```
1  create table Customer(id integer, name varchar(100), address varchar(100),
2    phone integer, balance float);
3  insert into Customer(id, name, address) values(1, "Bob Seger", "100 Main St");
4  select * from Customer where name = "Bob Seger";
```
Listing 9.1: Example of SQL statements

When Codd first proposed his relational model, he used a **relational algebra** as the basis for his query language. Thus, the bread and butter of SQL is the **join**, which represents compositons of relations, and also things like *projections* (Π), where you pick certain columns, and *selections* (σ), where you pick certain rows, as we'll explore later on.

9.4.3 Embedded SQL

It's possible to put SQL statements directly in a programming language like Java. We take a **Call Level Interface (CLI)** approach, as opposed to a **Statement Level Interface (SLI)** approach, and create an application made up of Java statements where SQL statements are passed as arguments to functions. This allows us to combine the data manipulation ability of SQL with a programmatic approach using a programming language like Java.

This is helpful because a third-generation programming language like Java is Turing Complete but ANSI SQL, a fourth-generation reporting language, is not. Listing 9.2 shows the Java code from an online compiler that includes embedded SQL at `https://www.tutorialspoint.com/compile_jdbc_online.php`.

As we can see there, on Line 1 we import the requisite Java SQL package and then utilize the `Class.forName()` method on Line 9 to load the MySQL driver from the Java DataBase Connectivity (JDBC) API. We also setup `DB_URL` to access our default MySQL database, called `CODINGGROUND`, on Line 3 and include that `DB_URL` in the connection object, `conn`, we create on Line 10. We then use `conn` to create a statement object, `stmt`, on Line 11. Finally, we execute our SQL query on Line 12 by using `stmt`'s `executeQuery()` method on Line 13.

The result is a table containing all the matching rows; this is modelled in Java as a `ResultSet` object and is used on Line 13 to store all the matching rows that were returned. Once we have the rows in the `ResultSet`, we loop through the `ResultSet` starting on Line 14 and, for each row, get the `id`, `phone`, and `name`. Once we're done processing all the returned rows, we close our various objects on Line 22 to release the resources and we're done and can resume normal operations!

9.5 Normalization

Around 1970, President Richard Milhous Nixon was starting to normalize relations with China. At about the same time, computer scientist E.F. Codd was preparing his paper, "A Relational Model for Large Shared Databanks," in which, as the story goes, inspired by the normalization of relations with China, Codd introduced the idea of database normalization.[8]

Normalization is an essential concept in relational database management that is captured in a quote used in most introductory database courses: "The Key, the whole Key, and nothing but the Key, so help me Codd." Keeping this simple mnemonic in mind will easily take us to a very respectable 3rd Normal Form, which is usually sufficient for most database applications.

---

[8]This story might be more apocryphal than history as the term normalization is also used in various contexts in mathematics and the paper addressed it from a very mathematical perspective in 1970, two years before Nixon's visit to China.

```java
import java.sql.*;
public class JDBCExample {
    static final String DB_URL = "jdbc:mysql://localhost/CODINGGROUND";

    public static void main(String[] args) {
        Connection conn = null; Statement stmt = null;

        try{
          Class.forName("com.mysql.jdbc.Driver");
          conn = DriverManager.getConnection(DB_URL,"username","password");
          stmt = conn.createStatement();
          String sql = "select * from users";
          ResultSet rs = stmt.executeQuery(sql);
          while( rs.next() ){
              int id   = rs.getInt("id");
              int phone = rs.getInt("phone");
              String name = rs.getString("name");

              System.out.print("ID: " + id + ", Name: " + name);
              System.out.println(", Phone: " + phone);
          }
            rs.close(); stmt.close(); conn.close();
        } catch(Exception e) {
            e.printStackTrace();
        }//end try
    }
}
```

Listing 9.2: Example of Embedded SQL in Java

Normalization is a process of adjusting the table structures in order to reduce data anomalies and improve data integrity. It does so by reducing data redundancy and optimizing data structures.

In a relational database model, we manipulate data using SQL in three major ways:

1. inserting new data
2. deleteing unwanted data
3. updateing existing data

OrderID	CustID	OrderDate	Items	CustName	CustAddress
1	1	Jan 15	Nt Nuts q=5, Bo Bolts q=10	John Doe	100 Main St
2	1	Jan 17	Sc Screws q=12	John Doe	100 Main St
3	2	Jan 18	Nt Nuts q=15, Sc Screws q=5	Jane Doe	5 Water St
4	3	Jan 18	Bo Bolts q=5	Jack Doe	160 Pearl St

Table 9.7: Table showing the three anomalies

In an un-normalized relational database, there are usually three problems or *anomalies* that can occur when we work with the data using the above mechanisms. These three anomalies are discussed below, set in the context of Table 9.7 which contains all our customer and order data in a single table:

1. `insert` anomaly: This refers to the situation when it is not possible to insert certain types of data into the database; e.g., we might not be able to *add a customer without an order* which means we couldn't have customers who haven't ordered yet.

2. `delete` anomaly: The deletion of data leads to unintended loss of additional data, data that we had wished to preserve; e.g., if *order 3 is deleted, the data for customer 2 is lost*.

3. `update` anomaly: This refers to the situation where updating the value of a column leads to database inconsistencies; e.g., *if item Bo is renamed*, how could we update all the values everywhere in the table easily and efficiently?

Normalization addresses all three of these anomalies. As we go through the normalization process, we **increase the number of tables** in the database and decrease the amount of data stored in each table. There are several different levels of database normalization, as we see in Figure 9.8:

- 1st Normal Form (1NF)
- 2nd Normal Form (2NF)
- 3rd Normal Form (3NF)
- Boyce-Codd Normal Form (BCNF)
- 4th Normal Form (4NF), 5th Normal Form (5NF), 6th Normal Form (6NF)

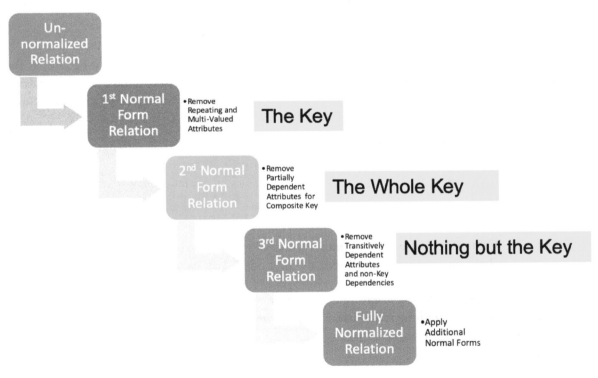

Figure 9.8: Database Normalization: At each step, we create more tables/entities. We also see the guiding maxim of database normalization, "The key, the whole key, and nothing but the key" for getting to the 3rd Normal Form.

1NF: No repeating attributes or multi-value attributes.

2NF: No partial dependencies with a composite key *or* no composite key at all.

3NF: No transitive dependencies on non-key attributes.

All of these normal forms rely upon the idea of a primary key and a foreign key; these keys can be **natural** keys but, in general, creating an **artificial** key, or a *surrogate* or *synthetic* key, is a better idea. For example, you might be tempted to uniquely identify customers by using their social security number as their primary key since it's derived from the application data. However, sometimes people accidentally (or perhaps not so accidentally) give the same social security number despite not being the same person. As such, it's usually better to just create a synthetic key that's automatically generated and maintained by the DBMS. Normalization requires that we choose a unique primary key for each table.

9.5.1   1st Normal Form (1NF)

1st Normal Form (1NF) ensures that all non-key attributes, or columns, are uniquely determined by the table's primary key alone. This can be an issue when you end up having either **repeating groups** or **multi-valued attributes**. For example, suppose students at a school could have more than one email address. Some might have a single email address while others have 10 or more email addresses. How would we capture that in a table? We could just add a new column, or attribute, for each email address; e.g., if John Lennon had two email addresses, this might look like Table 9.8.

StudentID	Name	Email1	Email2
101	Lennon	jlennon@gmail.com	johnlennon@fitchburgstate.edu

Table 9.8: Emails Repeating Group

But how do we know how many Email Address *groups* we should add? Should it be two, as for John Lennon? Or 10, as for Paul McCartney? If you use just the primary key on the Student tables, how will you know how many email address *groups* you'll get? So maybe instead you can just dump all the email addresses into a single column, or attribute, as in Table 9.9.

StudentID	Name	Email
101	Lennon	jlennon@gmail.com, johnlennon@fitchburgstate.edu

Table 9.9: Multi-Valued Attribute in Email column

In this case, if you were to use the Student's primary key to try to look up the email address, you wouldn't know which one should be returned: the first one? The second one? What if there is no second one?

These problems are solved by **creating a new table** with the StudentID as the *foreign key*, say in a column labelled SID, and the email itself as the *primary key* if each email address can only be associated with one student, as in Table 9.10.

Email	SID
jlennon@gmail.com	101
johnlennon@fitchburgstate.edu	101

Table 9.10: New Email-Student Table

This is also related to why relational databases **cannot directly implement** many-to-many relationships. For example, if many Students can take many Classes, that would mean a Student can have many Classes and a Class can have many Students. But we can't simply add the primary key of one table to the other (or both) as these would only implement a single relationship and we need to model multiple relationships. We wouldn't be able to do this as it would also create multi-valued attributes, where a single column would store multiple values which increases the difficulty for maintenance and querying. Similarly, we couldn't add multiple columns for the ClassID values as that would create repeating groups with their concomitant problems, as well!

The way to address such many-to-many relationships and maintain 1st Normal Form is to thus create a new table, variously called an **Association Table** or **Intersection Table** or **Bridge Table**, with a 1-to-many relationship on the left side and a Many-to-1 relationship on the right side. Thus, we might create a new intersection table called Students-Classes, where we'd have a 1-to-many relationship from Student to Students-Classes and then a many-to-1 relationship from the Students-Classes intersection table to the Class table.

9.5.2　2NF and 3NF

In order to address 2nd and 3rd Normal Forms, we need to define the idea of functional dependencies. We say that a column B is **functionally dependent** on a column A if, for every value of A, there is exactly one value of B; this is written as $A \rightarrow B$. Mathematically, we say that A *determines* B; physically, we might say that A is a unique identifier for B.

This can become an issue when more than one column is needed to uniquely identify a row; if more than one column is used as a primary key, that key is called a **composite** primary key. For example, suppose we had a table where two columns, the EmployeeID and CompanyID columns, together were the primary key for a table, as in Table 9.11.

EmployeeID	CompanyID	FName	LName	DeptID	DeptName
111	ATT	John	Doe	1	Acct
122	IBM	Jane	Doe	2	Mktg

Table 9.11: 2NF and 3NF Issues: a table showing both partial dependency and transitive dependency.

In this case, if one of the non-key columns, like FName, is dependent on only a sub-component of the key, like EmployeeID, and not the **whole** composite primary key, then this is an example of a **partial dependency**. In order to remove a partial dependency and reach 2nd Normal Form, you have to either decompose the tables or just add in a surrogate, or artificial, primary key.

Finally, you can also have **transitive dependencies**, where a non-key column uniquely determines the value of another non-key value. An example of this is shown in Table 9.11, as well, where we see that $DeptID \rightarrow DeptName$. 3rd Normal Form removes such transitive dependencies by parcelling the dependency off into another table and using its primary key as a foreign key in the original table.

In general, at every stage of normalization, we increase the number of tables that we have in our relational database model. However, we usually only normalize up to 3rd Normal Form as the anomalies that are resolved by higher level normalizations are exceedingly rare.

9.5.3　Denormalization

In fact, sometimes, we might even reverse normalization and go back to a less normalized form. The opposite of normalization is called **denormalization**, where we might want to combine multiple tables together into a larger table. This is helpful in some situations like when designing the fact table in a data warehouse, for example.

Some other disadvantages of normalization are that it can potentially slow performance since normalization increases the number of tables and thus more joins are required with increasing normalization. Although the normalized data is logically simpler, some people view having more and more tables as being more complicated. As there are some disadvantages to normalization, in practice, people usually only normalize to the 3rd Normal Form and do de-normalization as needed, depending upon the particular use-case.

Problem 9.1 Suppose, following accepted guidelines, you normalized your magic tricks database to 3rd Normal Form. Under what circumstances might you want to de-normalize it back to lower than 3NF? Can you think of some situations where you might want to normalize to higher than 3NF?

10. Machine Learning and Data Science

Man is the best computer we can put aboard a spacecraft and the only one that can be mass produced with unskilled labor.
– Wernher von Braun, rocket engineer (1912-1977)

10.1 Computational Thinking and Artificial Intelligence

Computational thinking can be thought of as an extension of thinking critically or reasoning with evidence. In a way, it systematizes critical thinking and evidence-based reasoning. This often involves logical thinking and argumentation, where we mean the classical, formal sense of argumentation as opposed to bickering. We could say, as we saw in Section 1.2, that this kind of logical thinking builds upon three fundamental ways to approach a problem: ad hoc thinking, deductive thinking, or inductive thinking.

Thinking, then, seems to be at the very core of being human and being intelligent enough to solve problems in the world. As such, people began to wonder if we could model thinking and intelligence. In the 17th century, as we saw in Section 2.5.1, Leibniz postulated the *Characteristica Universalis*, a new language to represent human thought where each letter represented some concept and these could then be combined and manipulated according to a set of logical rules via the *Calculus Ratiocinator* to compute all mathematical and scientific knowledge. Somewhat more recently, Turing started to think about machines, hypothetical ones which came to be called Turing Machines as we saw in Section 0.7.1, that could solve any computable function, and which seemed to lay some of the foundation for an eventual *Calculus Ratiocinator* of sorts.

It was at this point that neurophysiologist Warren S. McCulloch and logician Walter H. Pitts entered the scene. McCulloch, known for drinking whiskey and eating ice cream till 4am every day[1], was

---

[1] See http://nautil.us/issue/21/information/the-man-who-tried-to-redeem-the-world-with-logic

interested in modeling a theoretical foundation for the human brain in the style of Leibniz's logical calculus, and using this simple, logical foundation to build complex neural activity in the same way that Russell and Whitehead's *Principia Mathematica* showed all of mathematics could be built from a simple logical foundation.

So when he read Turing's 1936 paper entitled, "On Computable Numbers, With an Application to the Entscheidungsproblem," McCulloch made the connection that the brain could act like a Turing Machine. He further reasoned that chains of neurons could be linked together by rules of logic to create thoughts just as Russell and Whitehead had built all of mathematics by chaining together simple propositions. McCulloch and Pitts built this computational theory of the brain, using Turing's mathematical definition of computation combined with logic, in their seminal 1943 paper, "A Logical Calculus of the Ideas Immanent in Nervous Activity."

At the time, neurons were known to be the building blocks of human thought and intelligence in the brain and people had been studying them for a while. Neurons themselves were thought to be relatively simple cells that did some processing on multiple inputs and produced a single output spike, the action potential. McCulloch and Pitts had showed that these spikes could be combined to do logical and arithmetical operations.

Meanwhile, several biologists had been studying the squid's giant neuron in the early 20th century, and biophysicists Alan Hodgkin and Andrew Huxley soon created a circuit model of neurons as a set of nonlinear differential equations to calculate how conductances in cell membranes varied with time and voltage. People like the mathematician Norbert Wiener started to see the connection between biological systems like neurons and neural networks and control systems. Wiener, who was at MIT, had taken Pitts under his wing. Soon, Pitts also met von Neumann, who had separately been having conversations with Shannon and Turing about intelligence and machines that could also simulate the kind of thinking encoded in neural networks.[2]

In fact, Turing gave a talk to the London Mathematical Society in 1947 in which he said, quite presciently as we'll see in just a bit: "What we want is a machine that can learn from experience." He went on to say,

> "It would be like a pupil who had learnt much from his master, but had added much more by his own work. When this happens I feel that one is obliged to regard the machine as showing intelligence."

Turing even went on to propose a test, now called the Turing Test, to gauge if a machine could be considered as intelligent as a human. This test was based on a Victorian parlour game called the Imitation Game[3] and posited that machines should be considered as intelligent as humans when objective observers couldn't distinguish between a human and machine participant.

The idea of intelligent machines soon garnered quite a bit of interest. In 1955, computer scientist John McCarthy coined the term "Artificial Intelligence" for it and organized the famous Dartmouth conference in 1956, which was attended by such luminaries as Claude Shannon, Marvin Minsky, Allen Newell, and Herbert A. Simon and marked the birth of the field of **Artificial Intelligence (AI)**.

Artificial intelligence, in the computational sense, is often described in textbooks like Russell & Norvig in terms of a rational agent or intelligent agent, which is any entity, virtual or physical, that can

---

[2] As an interesting side-note, when von Neumann published his historic paper, "First Draft of a Report on the EDVAC," in 1945, it described the first proposed modern computer as a stored-program binary computing machine. In the paper, he modelled the proposed machine after McCulloch and Pitts' neural networks but replaced the neurons with vacuum tubes as logic gates. The published paper only had one citation: McCulloch and Pitts' 1943 paper.

[3] See https://hsm.stackexchange.com/questions/5890/did-turing-invent-the-imitation-game-did-he-name-it

take sensory input from its environment and interpret it, put it into context with its existing knowledge, and then take actions which would maximize its chances of achieving its goals.

The real problem is that, like for life itself,[4] there is no good generalizable definition of intelligence. Although we've made quite a few advances in neurobiology, we still don't have any exact idea of what humans do when they do things that we deem to be intelligent. All we know is that humans do things which we cannot yet automate with computational systems.

Over the years, the popularity of AI waxed and waned and, with it, the definition of what constituted intelligence. The original goal of mimicking human intelligence soon came to be known as **General AI** (also known as Strong AI or Hard AI). The more modest, and achievable, goal of simply having "machines that learn," as Turing himself had initially suggested, in a specialized context or in niche applications was then given the corresponding term of **Narrow AI** (also known as Weak AI or Soft AI). Over time, this Narrow AI, where you simply have a "machine that learns," has also come to be called **Machine Learning**.

10.1.1 What Is Machine Learning?

One of its earliest definitions was proposed by the computer scientist Arthur Samuel, who coined the term in 1959 and defined it as a "field of study that gives computers the ability to learn without being explicitly programmed." In some sense, every useful program learns something. For example, an implementation of Newton's method learns the roots of a polynomial.

As we saw in Section 0.2, we tend to learn new things by **memorization** and **generalization**. We use memorization to accumulate individual facts and generalization to deduce new facts from old facts. The most widely used definition of **machine learning** uses these ideas and follows Turing's intuition as elaborated by computer scientist Tom Mitchell:

> A computer program is said to learn from experience "E", with respect to some class of tasks "T" and performance measure "P", if its performance at tasks in "T" as measured by "P" improves with experience "E"

We can visualize this in Figure 10.1 where we add in the idea that once its performance is deemed to be sufficient, it outputs a final prediction, the result of its learning.

10.2 Getting Started with Machine Learning

Machine learning is thus the process of using past experiences to improve future performance on a particular task. Algorithms accomplish this by automatically learning to make useful inferences from implicit patterns in data. For example, linear regression learns a curve that is a model of a collection of examples. This model that's created can then be used to make predictions on new data points.

■ **Example 10.1 The Grumpy Cat:** Suppose you have a jumbled up collection of pictures, where each picture is of a dog or a cat. Perhaps you gathered the photos from your grandparents' Facebook feed which seems to be dominated by such photos and now they want them sorted. Your task, in this case, would involve separating the pictures into two categories: one pile of dog photos and one pile of cat photos. A program could learn to perform this task for you by modeling pictures that have already been sorted.

---

[4] You could argue that biology is the only science that cannot define the object of its study. I once read something like that in an introductory Biochemistry textbook but a more precise perspective is given by Carol E. Cleland and Christopher F. Chyba in their paper, "Defining 'Life'," where they conclude there is no broadly accepted definition of life.

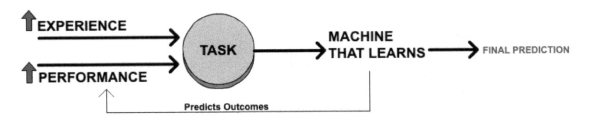

Figure 10.1: Following the ideas of Turing and Mitchell, one definition of Machine Learning can be: a Machine, or a computer program, is said to Learn if its Performance at a Task improves with Experience. The Experience is the input Data and the Performance is quantified by a Performance Measure. Once its performance is sufficient, it outputs a final prediction, the result of its learning.

As such, you might sort through the first hundred or so pictures and provide these sorted photos to the program so it could learn about dog and cat photos. Once it learns how to separate the photos, you can then then evaluate its performance by calculating the percentage of correctly classified pictures and, if that performance is satisfactory, set it loose on the rest of the unsorted photos. This is the machine learning task in a nutshell.   ■

So why machine learning? The reason is that it is often too difficult to design a set of rules "by hand". Machine learning is about **automatically** extracting relevant information from data and applying it to analyze new data. For these machine learning algorithms, the experience is captured in the data that's used as input for the algorithm. Performance of the algorithm improves with experience as the algorithm learns. Learning, in this case, is guided by a quantitative assessment that's often called an **objective function** or a **loss function** and is associated with a notion of some loss that should be minimized or, alternatively, a gain that should be maximized.[5]

Machine learning is thus the study of algorithms that:

- improve their performance, P
- at some task, T
- with experience, E

The business problem[6] determines the tasks, T; so once a business problem is defined, we can figure out the kinds of tasks involved and classify algorithms by the kinds of tasks they can solve. Once you know the kinds of tasks and the associated algorithms, you pick the most appropriate algorithm based on its learning style, which will be dictated by the kinds of data and resources (labelled, unlabelled, etc.) that are available to help solve the task.

---

[5] As a side note, most **optimization** problems seek to minimize a loss function, which is analogous to optimizing the objective function by either minimizing the loss or maximizing the gain. In regards to terminology, a loss function **is a part of** a cost function **which is a type of** an objective function. One of the most popular optimization algorithms is **Gradient Descent (GD)**, and its cousin **Stochastic Gradient Descent (SGD)**, which minimizes the cost function. GD finds a global minimum only for convex loss functions whereas SGD, which is similar to **Simulated Annealing**, is much more likely to find a global optimum in general.

[6] As usual, when we use the term business here we mean a generic organization of any sort, not just a corporation or commercial enterprise.

Supervised Learning in a Nutshell...

The main purpose of this kind of machine learning algorithm for supervised learning is to figure out what **boundaries** to draw around groups of data so that it can assign a **label** to new, unknown **samples**. For instance, if we're trying to separate cat pictures from dog pictures, as in Example 10.1, we need to use some characteristics, or **features**, of cats and dogs to differentiate between them. Perhaps we decide that we'll distinguish between cats and dogs by looking at their ears and whiskers: big ears and big whiskers means dogs and small ears and small whiskers means cats.

Suppose we measure these features for every animal in our known dataset, in which we already know whether each sample, or each animal, is a cat or a dog. We can then plot each animal *instance* on a graph of ear size vs whisker size, as shown in Figure 10.2. As you examine that figure, where would *you* draw the **boundary** to separate the cat group from the dog group?

The sole objective of a *machine learning algorithm* is to figure out the optimal boundary for these groups. It finds this optimal boundary by **optimizing** some **objective function**, which you can think of as optimizing some score that it assigns to each potential boundary. Different machine learning algorithms take different approaches to figuring out where to best position the boundary, how to determine the best shape for the boundary (a straight line? angled lines (decision trees)? a squiggly line (neural networks)?), etc.

Once the algorithm has tweaked its parameters and found an optimal boundary to separate the two groups, we call this final version of the algorithm our **model**. This model is now capable of **deciding**, or **predicting**, to which group a new sample belongs. For example, if we find a new animal with big floppy ears and short whiskers, we feed the values of these features to our model and the model will then spit out a label for the new animal, which will be either a cat or a dog, depending on which side of the boundary it falls when you plot it on the graph in Figure 10.2.

10.2.1 Movie Night with the Family

An example might help illustrate the overall process. Let's start with the task of choosing a show to watch for the next family movie night.[7] But before we actually embark on figuring out that complex task, as a first approximation, let's start with something simpler, take my wife, for example.[8]

---

[7] Our movie nights never last long and, coupled with our ~~laziness~~ adherence to tradition, we've resorted to just keeping the name and watching TV shows instead.

[8] There are, of course, a plethora of jokes that could be made here but, as the saying goes, it takes a smart husband to have the last word and not use it. Besides which, I am of the same mind as Winston Churchill in knowing for a fact that, "My most brilliant achievement was my ability to persuade my wife to marry me."

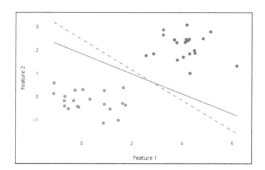

Figure 10.2: Plot of Cats (red) and Dogs (blue) by Feature 1 (ear size) and Feature 2 (whisker size).

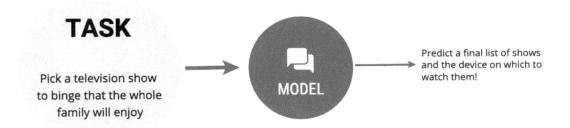

Figure 10.3: Machine Learning Model for the initial task of recommending shows.

Having known my wife for a number of years, I have a pretty good sense of the kinds of shows and movies she likes or dislikes. For example, I know she likes *Outlander* based on all the times she forced me to watch it, only to have me actually become a fan of the show.[9] Of course, she wasn't quite as enthusiastic when we watched *Man From Earth* and *TinTin* but I know she was happy for me.

After all these shows and movies that we've seen together, I've formulated a model in my head of my wife's thought processes in regards to whether she'll like a certain show or not. In addition to the shows themselves, I know whether she likes watching them on Hulu on TiVo or on Netflix on the FireTV box. All of these factors contribute to my overall mental model of my wife.

Following the machine learning model in Figure 10.1, picking a show my wife enjoys would be the *task* and my mental **model** would be the *machine that learns*; the **data** I've gathered over the years about shows my wife enjoys would be the *experience*; realizing she didn't like *Man From Earth* but did enjoy *Supergirl* when I suggested it helps me gauge the **accuracy** of my suggestions, which would be the *performance measure*. After fine tuning my mental model over the years, I should then be able to use that model to reliably predict if she would like a potential new show.

In the next approximation, I might create a similar mental model for the whole family and use this more generalized model to predict whether the family, as a whole, would like a certain show on a certain device, as shown in Figure 10.3.

10.2.2 Building the Generalized Movie Night Model

So our general task, as seen in Figure 10.3, is to pick a TV show the whole family will enjoy. Now that we know the task at hand, we need to work on the *experience* (the **data**), the *machine* that learns (the **model**), and the *performance measure* (the **accuracy**).[10] Instead of relying upon my own mental model, let's take a more structured approach and use a *machine learning model* instead.

There are many parts to finding the full machine learning solution but the first part of our Machine Learning Life Cycle involves:

- Figuring out the task specifications
- Finding the available data and resources
- Deciding on the appropriate algorithm

We've already figured out the task so let's start to find the data and resources. To keep things simple, assume we have two kids, two parents, and two grandparents. If your particular family structure

---

[9]Who knew a show about time travel that never discussed the physics of time travel could turn out to be actually good?

[10]In general, we have many options for both the model and the performance measure but accuracy is generally an intuitive measure so we'll use that as a stand-in for some of the more informative measures we'll meet in places like Section 10.5.7.

User	Show	UserRating	UserAge	Genre	Year	AgeRating	Runtime
Son	Octonauts	ThumbsUp	5	Kids	2017	E	30
Mom	Outlander	ThumbsUp	35	Fantasy	2015	A	60
GrandParent	Outlander	ThumbsDown	65	Fantasy	2015	A	60
⋮	⋮	⋮	⋮	⋮	⋮	⋮	⋮

Table 10.1: Past show preferences for the entire family.

is lacking in any of these member numbers, please feel free to substitute your hamster, cat, dog, or other favourite pet for the missing role. Similarly, if you have a surfeit of family members beyond the requisite two in each category, please feel free to delegate the extra family members to the role of pets (this can be a fun, if somewhat emotionally devastating, family activity in its own right, of course).

We can then survey each family member about all the shows anyone in the family has seen and record each family member's ratings for each show. We can gather all of this data for the whole family in Table 10.1.

In general, the *rows* of our dataset are called **samples** or **instances** or **observations** and the *columns* of our dataset are called **features** or **variables**. We'll use these features to learn about the problem and one of these columns, or features, will be designated to be the **label** or **target variable**. The target variable is our **dependent variable** and our features are the **independent variables**.

This kind of task, in which we have a column with a label indicating to which category, or *class*, the sample belongs, is called **classification** and it falls under the rubric of **supervised learning** because we have example data with the label of the class already determined in the dataset we previously gathered. This is the same kind of task we dealt with above in Example 10.1 about the Grumpy Cat where we had to *classify* whether a picture was a dog picture or a cat picture.

Classification depends on having one column, or feature, that indicates to which class the sample belongs, this is the *target variable*. That *label*, or target variable, in our case is the UserRating column, which can have one of two values: either a ThumbsUp or a ThumbsDown, to indicate whether that person liked or disliked that show.

Our model will use some combination of the other features, or columns, to make its **predictions**; the columns it uses to **learn** *what prediction to make* are called **predictor variables** and, for us, they'll be things like the Genre, Runtime, etc.

We'll also want to make sure our dataset is in good shape; according to the well-tested aphorism, "*Garbage in, garbage out,*" if our data is junky our machine will learn junk. So **pre-processing** the dataset is very important and this kind of **data cleaning** or **data munging** usually involves things like:

- Finding missing or incorrect values; e.g., did everyone fill in all the columns for each show?
- Transforming categorical data, like text or boolean, into numeric data as some algorithms don't work well with non-numeric data; e.g., we'll probably want to change the ThumbsUp and ThumbsDown ratings to 1's and 0's since most algorithms probably don't understand the concept of a thumb, let alone whether its state is up or down.
- If an algorithm compares values of different features directly, you have to take care of differences in scale between different features or columns; e.g., the Year's numeric value is much higher than just about any UserAge (for most humans in this century, at least) so we should probably do things like normalize the values in both columns otherwise the value of a Year will always dominate in any simple sum of values of Year and UserAge.

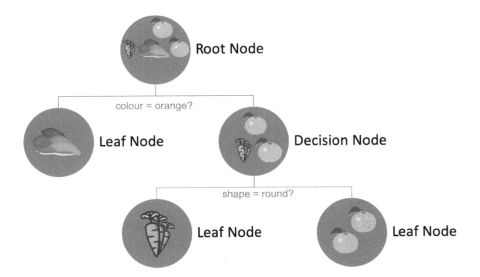

Figure 10.4: Decision Tree Classification Example. This tree deals with our healthy movie snacks of fruits and vegetables and is concerned with classifying each fruit or vegetable as either lettuce, carrots, or oranges. The root node has 4 fruits or vegetables, while the first decision node only has 3 fruits or vegetables. All leaf nodes have only one kind, or **class**, of fruit or vegetable.

In addition, if we have a lot of columns or features, we might need to reduce the **dimensionality** of our dataset. We might do **feature engineering** by combining different columns or adding in new ones or do **feature selection** and remove the least informative ones. It's not a terribly big problem here but imagine Netflix or Amazon and the crazy number of features they might track in trying to figure out if someone enjoys a certain show or movie. We'll likely have to do some feature selection when we decide on a particular algorithm so let's turn our attention to selecting an appropriate algorithm next.

10.2.3 Selecting a Movie Night Algorithm

One of our goals is to increase stakeholder buy-in and, since the kids are also pretty smart, we want them to understand how we arrived at our final prediction rather than just giving them an answer without any justification.[11] One of the easiest algorithms to visualize and understand is the **Decision Tree**.

A decision tree example is shown in Figure 10.4. As you can see, this particular decision tree deals with our regular movie snacks: a bunch of fruits and vegetables.[12] Anticipating picky eaters, we'll use the decision tree to **classify** each snack as either lettuce, carrots, or oranges. The goal of a decision tree is to take *heterogenous* collections of items and separate them so that, at the end, they're all in *homogenous* subsets; in other words, take a jumbled up collection of cat and dog photos and, in the end, have two subsets made up entirely of only cat or only dog photos.

Some of the terminology associated with a decision tree is root node, decision node, and leaf node. The **root node** is at the very top and contains the full jumbled mess of stuff in it. The **decision nodes** start to separate one kind of thing from other kinds of things. Finally, the **leaf nodes** only have one kind, or class, of entities; in the case of the tree in Figure 10.4, each leaf node has only one class of

---

[11] Getting buy-in from the kids, as all parents know, is the secret to a calm, restful night.

[12] This is, of course, pure fiction; regular movie night snacks in our house consist of candies and popcorn like any other sane household. But, my father is a dentist and since this will be in print, let's together pretend to have healthy inclinations.

show	cartoon	year	runtime	label
Octonauts	1	2015	30	1
Men of a Certain Age	0	2016	60	0
HeMan	1	1983	30	0
BrainChild	0	2018	60	1
90 Day Fiance	0	2017	60	0
Outlander	0	2017	60	0
Daniel Tiger	1	2015	60	1
Brain Games	0	2017	60	1
Lost in Space	0	2018	60	0
Password Plus	0	1980	30	1

Table 10.2: Decision tree dataset for the family movie night. In the above dataset, 1 stands for True and 0 stands for False in the Cartoon column. In the Label column, the 1 indicates Watch and 0 indicates Don't Watch, corresponding to ThumbsUp and ThumbsDown in Table 10.1.

fruit or vegetable.

A decision tree typically uses a binary tree to model the data using selection conditions at each decision node. It looks like an upside down tree as it normally takes the form of a series of cascading questions. Each of these questions is cast as a selection that tests if a certain feature satisfies a certain condition; e.g., in the sample tree, one of our decision nodes asks, "Is the shape of the fruit or vegetable round?" For our dataset, a selection question might well be along the lines of, "Is the Genre or Format of the show a cartoon?"

Therefore, in order to create a decision tree, we'll need to make a table of the data: each row, or instance, should be a show we've asked the family about. Each column, or feature, should represent some characteristic of the show like Format or Runtime. The values of those features should be amenable to being used for asking a yes or no question so we'll have to transform our initial dataset in Table 10.1 to meet this format requirement. We'll also take this opportunity to do some feature selection and keep only the columns we think will be most helpful, or, as we'll see in Section 10.7, most informative in the sense of Shannon Information, in making our final predictions. The cleaned and munged version of our original dataset is now shown in Table 10.2, where we also add a final column for the **label**, or target variable, to indicate whether we should or should not watch that show, analogous to the UserRating column in our original dataset.

10.2.4 Implementing the Movie Night Decision Trees

Decision trees are easy to understand, interpret, and visualize. They have many advantages like the ability to automatically do feature selection or the ability to handle categorical and numerical data with little data preparation. They're unaffected by non-linear relationships but they are susceptible to overfitting with overly-complex trees. They can also be unstable and have high variance where small variations in data can cause very different trees to be generated. However, this can be mitigated by using bagging or boosting ensemble approaches as we'll see in Section 10.2.5. Random Forests, which utilize a bagging approach, can also help with finding a more global solution as greedy methods alone are unable to guarantee global optimization. But they might create biased trees so a balanced dataset is very important in such cases.

We'll see some of these more technical details about decision trees in Section 10.7 but let's summarize some of those details here, as well. We won't spend too long on these details for now, as it'll be more helpful to first see the actual code to implement the full decision tree algorithm. In brief, though, decision trees try to create homogenous subsets that have low impurity or low entropy. There are many ways to grow these trees. Things like the criteria to use for splitting nodes, the number of splits per node, when to stop splitting, how to prune the trees, etc. The different values we use for these parameters will result in different possible structures of the trees, as we'll see in gruesome detail for our fruit and vegetable tree in Section 10.7.

For now, let's implement our initial decision tree model! We will use Python to implement all our initial models in this chapter; not only is Python very popular in machine learning and data science but the vast array of specialized libraries make the analytic task almost trivial, almost as much as some *Business Intelligence* tools like Qlik, PowerBI, etc.

One of the most popular libraries is `scikit-learn`, which allows us to create a wide variety of models with very little code. There are some vocabulary differences in `scikit-learn`'s implementation: machine learning algorithms are called *estimators* and the library itself is often referred to as `sklearn`. We'll use `sklearn` to train, test, and evaluate our models all while only using the default parameters and hyperparameters.

Let's start by loading the required libraries in Python. Any libraries that are not already installed on your system can be installed by using `pip` or `pip3`. The only exception is `graphviz`, which also needs its binaries installed on your system separately.

```
### Load Required Libraries
from sklearn.tree import DecisionTreeClassifier # Decision Tree Classifier
from sklearn.model_selection import train_test_split # train_test_split function
from sklearn import metrics                  # scikit-learn metrics for accuracy
from sklearn.tree import export_graphviz  # Generates graphviz of DT model
from sklearn.metrics import confusion_matrix  # Get Confusion Matrix
from sklearn.metrics import accuracy_score    # Get Accuracy
from sklearn.metrics import classification_report # Get Classification Report
from sklearn.metrics import average_precision_score # Get Avg Precision
from IPython.display import Image  # Alternate to matplotlib
import pandas as pd   # DataFrames
import numpy as np    # Numeric Python Library
import graphviz       # Graphs in DOT language
import pydotplus      # Python interface to DOT language
```

Once we've gotten a bunch of those libraries out of the way, we can start loading the dataset, printing summary statistics, and extracting our three feature columns (`cartoon`, `year`, and `runtime`) and the target class column (`label`). We will first have to separately save the movie night dataset from Table 10.2 into a file called `ml-dataset.csv` so that we can then load it and process it with a decision tree classifier in our program; you can call that file something different but please do change the code below to reflect that change, as well:

```
### Load the dataset and print summary statistics
df = pd.read_csv("ml-dataset.csv")
print("Summary Statistics:")
print(df.describe())

### Split dataset into feature columns (data) and target variable (label)
feature_cols = ['cartoon', 'year', 'runtime']
```

```
X = df[feature_cols]     # The Features; Predictor Variables
y = df.label             # The Labels;   Target Variable
```

This creates a numpy dataframe object called X which contains all the *instances* in our dataset. It also creates a dataframe object called y which contains the *class labels* for each instance. We'll use both of these in Listing 10.1 where we'll create and use our main decision tree classifier method for the movie night dataset from Table 10.2:

```
1   ### Split dataset into training set (70%) and test set (30%)
2   indices = range(X.shape[0])
3   (X_train, X_test, y_train, y_test, indices_train, indices_test) = \
4     train_test_split(X, y, indices, test_size=0.3, random_state=1)
5
6   ### Create the Decision Tree classifier default model
7   clf = DecisionTreeClassifier()
8
9   # Train the model then Predict with it:
10  trained_model = clf.fit(X_train,y_train) # Train Decision Tree Classifer
11  y_pred = trained_model.predict(X_test)   # Predict the response for test dataset
12
13  # Model Accuracy determines how often the classifier is correct
14  print(metrics.accuracy_score(y_test, y_pred))
15  print(metrics.average_precision_score(y_test, y_pred))
16
17  ### Get actual/predicted shows and statistics:
18  shows=df['show']
19  [print(shows[i]) for i in indices_test]
20
21  actual = np.array(y_test)
22  predicted = np.array(y_pred)
23  print('Confusion Matrix:', confusion_matrix(actual, predicted))
24  print('Accuracy Score :', accuracy_score(actual, predicted))
25  print('Report: ', classification_report(actual, predicted))
```

Listing 10.1: Decision Tree Classifier for the movie night dataset.

We start by splitting the dataset into **training** and **testing** datasets on Lines 1 - 4. Next, we create the decision tree classification algorithm object, clf. We then **train** the algorithm on the training data using its fit() function on Line 10 to create our tentative model, trained_model. We learn by **training on the data** and checking the **performance** so a **trained model** is also often called the model we learned and this process is also called **learning the model** and the model is called the **learned model**. We can then use the trained model on Line 11 to **predict** the class label for each sample, each show, as either Watch (0) or Don't Watch (1). That's it, *our main classification task is done!*

Next, we start to **assess** how well our trained model did. On Lines 13 - 15, we calculate and print the accuracy and precision scores to help evaluate our algorithm's **performance**. On Lines 18 - 19, we get the list of shows that were labelled as Watch (1) and then, in Lines 21 - 25, we calculate a few more evaluation metrics to get a sense of how well our decision tree algorithm did.

Here are some of the results for our classifier:

```
Accuracy: 0.6666666666666666
Average PrecisionScore: 0.6666666666666666

Shows to watch:
HeMan
Password Plus
Daniel Tiger
```

We can also visualize the decision tree itself by using the `graphviz` binaries and `graphviz` python interface as shown below; the resulting image is shown in Figure 10.5.

```
### Visualize the result with graphviz library and binary:
from sklearn.externals.six import StringIO  # Get StringIO functions
dot_data = StringIO()
export_graphviz(trained_model, out_file=dot_data, filled=True, rounded=True,
  special_characters=True, feature_names = feature_cols,
  class_names=["Watch","DON'T Watch"])
graph = pydotplus.graph_from_dot_data(dot_data.getvalue())
graph.write_png('ml-results.png')
Image(graph.create_png())
```

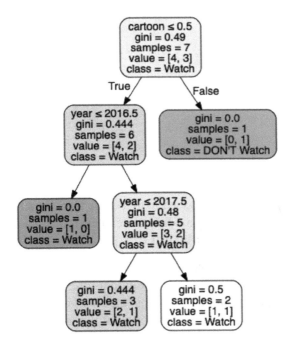

Figure 10.5: Decision tree built from the movie night example python code showing the nodes and splitting on the `cartoon` and `year` features.

We could do some additional processing like creating a ROC curve and computing the AUC, as well; we'll see what the ROC, AUC, and some of these more funky measures are in Section 10.5.7:

```
### Make ROC Curve
from sklearn.metrics import roc_auc_score # Get ROC and AUC score
```

```
from sklearn.metrics import roc_curve       # Get ROC data

#y_score = trained_model.fit(X_train, y_train).predict_proba(X_test)
y_score = trained_model.predict_proba(X_test)[:,1]

print("ROC AUC Score:")
print(roc_auc_score(actual,y_score))

(fpr,tpr,thre) = roc_curve(actual,y_score)
print("False Positive Rate, True Positive Rate, and Threshold:")
print(fpr,tpr,thre)

# Create ROC Curve
import matplotlib.pyplot as plt              # Matplotlib's Plotter
plt.plot(fpr, tpr, label='ROC curve')
plt.plot([0, 1], [0, 1], 'k--', label='Random guess')
_ = plt.xlabel('False Positive Rate')
_ = plt.ylabel('True Positive Rate')
_ = plt.title('ROC Curve')
_ = plt.xlim([-0.02, 1])
_ = plt.ylim([0, 1.02])
_ = plt.legend(loc="lower right")

# Save ROC Curve
plt.savefig('ml-roc_curve.png', dpi=200)
```

We can even use automated machine learning (autoML) tools like tPot and auto-sklearn to automate the following tasks:

- Feature Selection
- Feature Processing
- Feature Construction
- Model Selection
- Parameter and Hyperparameter Optimization

These tools are very powerful, as can be seen in this quote from the tPot documentation where we see it evaluates multiple machine learning models and can even do data cleaning and dimensionality reduction (which we'll learn about in just a bit) all with just a handful of lines of code!

> "AutoML algorithms aren't as simple as fitting one model on the dataset; they are considering multiple machine learning algorithms (random forests, linear models, SVMs, etc.) in a pipeline with multiple preprocessing steps (missing value imputation, scaling, PCA, feature selection, etc.), the hyperparameters for all of the models and preprocessing steps, as well as multiple ways to ensemble or stack the algorithms within the pipeline."

Although our decision tree did pretty well, we can expand our analysis to be more accurate by using not just one decision tree but lots of trees in what's termed a **random forest**, one of a powerful class of machine learning algorithms called ensemble methods which combine multiple models.

10.2.5 Ensemble Methods

In general, combining models tends to be surprisingly effective. There are three main approaches to creating these **ensemble methods**: stacking, bagging, and boosting.

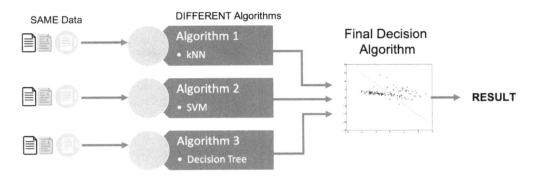

Figure 10.6: Ensemble Method: Stacking.

Stacking, as seen in Figure 10.6, feeds the **same** original data to several **different** algorithms and the output of each of those intermediate algorithms is passed to a final algorithm which makes the final decision.

Bootstrap AGGregatING (**Bagging**) uses the **same** algorithm on several **different** *subsets* of the original data that are produced by **bootstrapping**, random sampling with replacement from the original data. The result of each component is then averaged in the end, as seen in Figure 10.7. The random forests we saw before used Bagging on Decision Trees.

Boosting uses several **different** algorithms in a linear, sequential way rather than in a parallel way as in Bagging. Similar to Bagging, though, each subsequent algorithm is fed a subset of the original data that is produced by random sampling with replacement from the original data but, different from Bagging, the **mis-classified** data in the previous step is weighted more heavily in a subsequent step. As a result, the different algorithms are trained sequentially with each subsequent algorithm concentrating on data points that were mis-classified by the previous algorithm, as seen in Figure 10.8.[13]

10.2.6 Miss the Random Forests for the Decision Trees

Although decision trees themselves are pretty good, as you can tell, there are many different divisions you can get depending on the particular hyperparameter choices you might make. Since ensemble

---

[13]These ensemble methods, in general, increase the accuracy and, for bagging, reduce the variance as they combine several estimates from different models; for boosting and stacking, they will reduce the bias compared to the components, even if the variance can also be reduced.

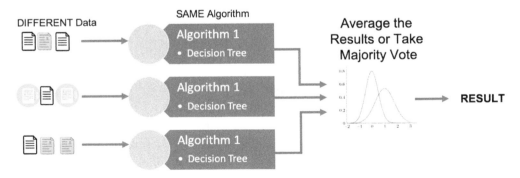

Figure 10.7: Ensemble Method: Bagging.

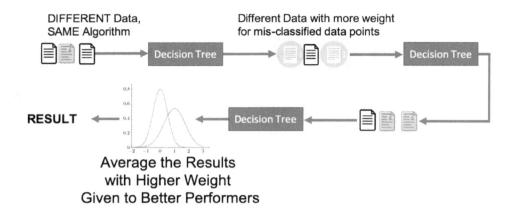

Figure 10.8: Ensemble Method: Boosting.

methods tend to be very accurate, one strategy we can employ is to combine multiple single decision trees where each individual decision tree is based on a random sample of the training data. This kind of **random forest** of individual decision trees is usually more accurate than any one decision tree itself.

The random forest approach is very fast and works well with un-balanced and sparse data and does both classification and regression. Random forests are, however, prone to overfitting and the number of trees hyperparameter often needs to be tuned separately in order to control it to some extent. In addition, for regression problems, they are limited to predicting values in the range of the training data only. We'll learn more about classification, regression, etc., in Section 10.3.

One reason a random forest tends to be more effective is that it doesn't do any pruning as in a single decision tree and the fully grown tree gives us a higher resolution feature space that is split into more regions that are also smaller and more granular. In addition, since each individual decision tree in a random forest is learned from a random sample of the dataset and, at each node, a random set of features are used for splitting, the diversity amongst the trees is increased substantially. Random forests are more capable of handling noise, outliers, and overfitting because of its randomness in picking observations and variables for the model and its voting approach.

10.2.7 Generalized Classification Task

Our final process for the movie night algorithm involved all the parts outlined in Figure 10.9 and is what we use for most approaches to machine learning. Some machine learning approaches (like the **supervised learning** with decision trees we saw in Section 10.2.4) might utilize all these steps while others (like the **unsupervised learning** via the **k-Means** clustering algorithm in Section 10.2.8) might skip some steps like the training, etc.

In large measure, though, most machine learning approaches follow a similar stratagem. Let's go through the process we will usually follow in making our predictions by seeing how it applies to determining what to watch on Family Movie Night:

1. Our **task** of selecting a show to watch for the next Family Movie Night started by identifying our most important stakeholders. This choice of stakeholders, along with the *kind* of task we're addressing, dictated the *choice* of algorithm. In this case, we chose a *decision tree* **classification** algorithm to make the decision-making process understandable. Our intention is to use this *supervised learning* **algorithm** as our **model** to make the final prediction of a show to watch.

2. Next, we need to know what kinds of shows each group likes: parents, kids, and grandparents.

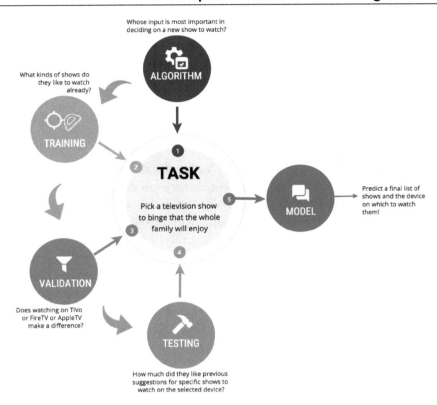

Figure 10.9: Machine Learning Model details for the initial task of recommending shows:
  1. Pick an algorithm relevant for both the stakeholders' needs and the task
  2. Train the algorithm based on the kinds of shows they liked in the past
  3. Did that group care about the setting, the particular device, or the app?
  4. Did that group like the last suggestion for that setting?
  5. Now we can finally predict a show for tomorrow night!

The different groups might like different kinds of shows; maybe they like a show based on the genre (e.g., cartoon) or runtime (e.g., 50mins), etc. We gather all the data about those shows into our initial **dataset**, with each show as a row and all the details of the different characteristics of the shows, like genre, runtime, etc., as columns. We then split the dataset into both a **training dataset** and a **testing dataset**, as well as an optional **validation** dataset.

   • The columns are the **features**, or attributes, for our model and will be used to tune the **parameters**, the internal configuration variables of our model that will be estimated from our training data. The features are the **input** to our model and the number of features determine the **dimensionality** of our model. We'll use the training dataset to set these parameters for our model, and then evaluate our model's performance using the appropriate **performance measures** or statistical **metrics** on the results.

  3. Then, we need to see if tomorrow will be a school night and also determine which device we'll use to watch the show.

   • On school nights, we tend to favour what the kids want; on holidays, we don't mind seeing what the grandparents might want; on weekends, the wife wins.
   • We will also check if people like one kind of device or app over another: e.g., everyone

hates the ads on Hulu and would rather watch it on FireTV or TiVo but TiVo has a more limited selection.

- These are our **hyperparameters**: they have nothing to do with the show itself but are part of our **model** (who gets more weight depends on the night) or **architecture** (the device and app we'll use to watch the show).
- We can use the things we watched on similar nights over the last couple of months on all the devices to figure out who was watching what to get the preferences for those nights and those devices/apps.
- We would adjust these hyperparameters with our **validation** dataset.

4. Next, we need to use another part of the recent History (on the device we finally selected) to see which genre won on which night (did cartoons win on weekday nights?). We'll use this from our **testing** dataset and we'll evaluate the results with our **performance measures** or statistical **metrics** to decide on our **final model**.

5. Finally, we can get a list of the new shows that are available tomorrow night (this is our **unseen dataset**) and then apply our *final model* to make the final selection based on the parameters (day of week, holiday or not, who's at the house, etc.) that we determined earlier → This will be our **final prediction** for the show and setting for tomorrow night's family movie night.

This generalized approach for any supervised learning task is shown in Figure 10.10.

10.2.8 Unsupervised Learning via k-Means

Besides the *supervised* learning approach we've seen with our *classification* model so far, one of the most frequently used techniques when exploring a new dataset is to use **clustering**, a form of **unsupervised learning**. Unsupervised learning techniques don't need any labelled data and skip the training phase entirely!

Clustering is a simple technique that tries to put sets of objects that are similar into the same group; these groups are the clusters. The approach used for **k-Means** clustering is to minimize the sum of squared distances from each point of the cluster to the center point, the mean, of the cluster. It iterates between first assigning each data point to its nearest centroid by minimizing some distance measure and then re-calculating the center of the cluster by taking the mean of all data points (the *mean* in k-Means) assigned to that cluster.

We can utilize this unsupervised learning approach on our Family Movie Night problem and dataset by adding this code to the bottom of our current program so far:

```
### Do the Clustering (unsupervised so no training)
from sklearn.cluster import KMeans # kMeans classifier from scikit-learn

clf = KMeans(n_clusters=2) # Declare model with 2 clusters (via prior knowledge)
model = clf.fit(X)          # Fit the model (no training)
print("\nCluster Centers:\n", model.cluster_centers_) # View cluster centers

### Prediction: All Observations and New Observation
y_pred =  model.predict(X)     # Predict all observation labels
print("\nPredict labels for all shows:\n", y_pred)
```

Those 8 lines are the entirety of the code we need in order to implement the k-Means algorithm, run it on our dataset, and compute the performance measure results for the Family Movie Night! In the above code, we import the KMeans object and use it to fit() the data, X. Note we fit it on the

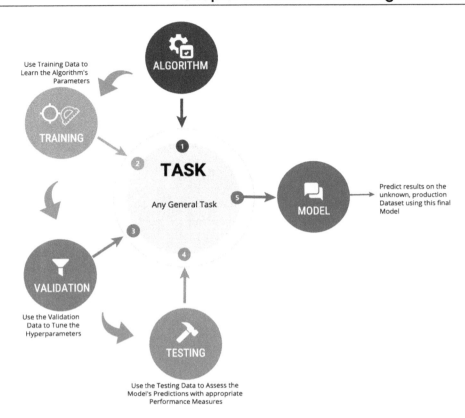

Figure 10.10: Supervised learning approach for a general **predictive model**:
1. Start by picking a **learning algorithm** that's appropriate for the task at hand
2. Use the **Training Dataset** to learn the algorithm's **parameter** values
3. Use the **Validation Dataset** to tune the algorithm's **hyperparameters** and **architecture**
   The resulting algorithm is the tentative **model**
4. Use the **Testing Dataset** to gauge the tentative model's **performance**
   If no changes are needed, this is the final model
5. Now you can apply the final model to **unseen data** to make your final **prediction** for that task

entire dataset without breaking it up into the training/testing datasets using `train_test_split()` as we did in our decision tree code above. We can view the clusters the k-Means model creates via `model.cluster_centers_`, which will result in the following output:

```
Cluster Centers:
 [[5.00000000e-01 1.98295455e+03 3.44545455e+01]
 [4.82142857e-01 1.98237500e+03 9.08392857e+01]]

Predict ALL labels:
 [0 0 0 1 1 1 0 1 1 1 0 0 1 0 1 0 1 1 1 0 1 0 0 0 0 1 0 1 0 0 1 1 0 1 1 0 1
 1 1 1 0 0 0 0 1 1 1 0 0 1 1 1 0 0 1 0 0 0 0 1 1 0 0 1 1 0 1 0 1 0 1 1 1 1 0
 0 1 1 0 1 1 1 0 0 0 0 1 1 1 1 1 1 0 1 1 0 1 1 1 1 0]
```

Here, we see that there are two clusters (two rows) with the center-point of each cluster, its **centroid**, being determined by three values, one for each of our **predictor variables**: the `cartoon`, `year`, and

```
1  ### Load libraries
2  from sklearn import datasets        # Various datasets in scikit-learn
3  from sklearn.cluster import KMeans   # kMeans classifier from scikit-learn
4  import matplotlib.pyplot as plt      # Plotting library for graphs
5  import pandas as pd                  # Data processing library
6
7  ### Get Iris Data
8  iris = datasets.load_iris()  # Load the dataset
9  X = iris.data                # Features
10 y = iris.target              # Labels/Targets
11
12 ### Iris Exploratory Data Analysis (EDA)
13 iris_df = pd.DataFrame(iris.data, columns = iris.feature_names)
14 print("\nSummary:\n", iris_df.describe())      # Summary Statistics
15 print("\nFeatures:\n", iris.feature_names)      # Feature Names
16 print("\nLabel Names:\n", iris.target_names)    # Target Names
17 print("\nActual Labels:\n", y)                  # Print the class labels
18 # Slice the Dataset and Plot it as a scatter plot
19 x_axis = iris.data[:, 0]  # Sepal Length
20 y_axis = iris.data[:, 2]  # Petal Length
21 plt.scatter(x_axis, y_axis, c=iris.target)
22 plt.show()    # Display the scatterplot
23
24 ### Do the Clustering (unsupervised so no training)
25 clf = KMeans(n_clusters=3)    # Declare the model (make 3 clusters using prior k
26 model = clf.fit(X)            # Fit the model (no training)
27 print("\nCluster Centers:\n", model.cluster_centers_) # View cluster centers
28
29 ### Prediction: All Observations and New Observation
30 y_pred =  model.predict(iris.data)     # Predict all observation labels
31 new_pred = model.predict([[3.1, 1.3, 5.7, 7.5]]) # Predict new observation label
32 print("\nPredict ALL labels:\n", y_pred)
33 print("\nPredict New label:\n", new_pred)
```

Listing 10.2: k-Means clustering on the Iris Dataset.

runtime features. Not bad for about 8 lines of code!

k-Means on the Iris Dataset

But let's get a better handle on the details of how easy it is to use clustering on a new dataset by doing some **Exploratory Data Analysis (EDA)** on the well-known Iris dataset and clustering the samples.[14] EDA usually involves doing both statistical analysis and visualization of the dataset in order to characterize the dataset and get a more intuitive sense of it before we formally model it.

The Iris dataset consists of 150 **samples**, where each sample is an Iris flower. Four measurements are taken for each flower and these measurements will be our **features**: sepal length, sepal width, petal length, and petal width. There are three kinds of Iris flowers and so these are our **class labels**: setosa, versicolor, and virginica.

We start by loading the dataset from the scikit-learn package on Line 8 of Listing 10.2 and then

---

[14]Please see https://en.wikipedia.org/wiki/Iris_flower_data_set

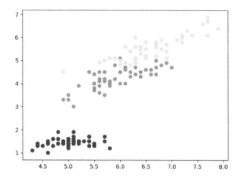

Figure 10.11: Scatterplot graph of the Iris dataset showing three different classes: setosa, versicolor, and virginica.

separating out the Features and Labels on Lines 9 - 10. Then, in Lines 12 - 22, we do some EDA; in this case, we load the `numpy` data matrix (`iris.data`) into a `pandas` `dataframe` object and then use the `dataframe`'s `describe()` method to display the statistical summary as shown below.

We also print out the feature names (these are the flower measurements we used as our features or columns) as well as the label names for the three classes. Then, on line 17, we print out the actual labels for all 150 samples; each of the 150 flowers has a label of 0, 1, or 2 depending on whether it's a setosa, versicolor, or virginica. After that, we use the `matplotlib` library's `pyplot` object to continue our EDA and create a scatterplot of the sepal length vs petal length, as shown in Figure 10.11.

We then get back to the analysis and do the actual clustering, creating the `clf` classifier object. We `fit()` the data to the classifier to create our final `model`. We then view the clusters formed by the model on Line 27. The clusters are shown as a 3 x 4 dimensional matrix. This is because we selected 3 clusters (the 3 rows) and each row is made up of 4 dimensions, 1 column for each of the 4 features (sepal length, sepal width, petal length, and petal width).

Finally, in Lines 29 - 33, we predict the labels for each of the samples as per the k-Means algorithm (on Line 30) and for a new, fake flower observation that would form the 151st sample (on line 31). We finally print these values and the entirety of the results from running the code in Listing 10.2 is below:

```
Summary:
          sepal length   sepal width   petal length   petal width
count     150.000000     150.000000    150.000000     150.000000
mean        5.843333       3.057333      3.758000       1.199333
std         0.828066       0.435866      1.765298       0.762238
min         4.300000       2.000000      1.000000       0.100000
25%         5.100000       2.800000      1.600000       0.300000
50%         5.800000       3.000000      4.350000       1.300000
75%         6.400000       3.300000      5.100000       1.800000
max         7.900000       4.400000      6.900000       2.500000

Features:
  ['sepal length', 'sepal width', 'petal length', 'petal width']

Label Names:
  ['setosa' 'versicolor' 'virginica']
```

```
Actual Labels:
[0 0 0 0 0 0 0 0 0 0 0 0 0 0 0 0 0 0 0 0 0 0 0 0 0 0 0 0 0 0 0 0 0 0 0 0 0
 0 0 0 0 0 0 0 0 0 0 0 0 0 1 1 1 1 1 1 1 1 1 1 1 1 1 1 1 1 1 1 1 1 1 1 1 1 1
 1 1 1 1 1 1 1 1 1 1 1 1 1 1 1 1 1 1 1 1 1 1 1 1 1 1 1 1 1 1 2 2 2 2 2 2 2 2 2
 2 2 2 2 2 2 2 2 2 2 2 2 2 2 2 2 2 2 2 2 2 2 2 2 2 2 2 2 2 2 2 2 2 2 2 2 2 2 2
 2 2]

Cluster Centers:
[[5.006       3.428       1.462       0.246      ]
 [5.9016129   2.7483871   4.39354839  1.43387097]
 [6.85        3.07368421  5.74210526  2.07105263]]

Predict ALL labels:
[0 0 0 0 0 0 0 0 0 0 0 0 0 0 0 0 0 0 0 0 0 0 0 0 0 0 0 0 0 0 0 0 0 0 0 0 0
 0 0 0 0 0 0 0 0 0 0 0 0 0 1 1 2 1 1 1 1 1 1 1 1 1 1 1 1 1 1 1 1 1 1 1 1 1 1
 1 1 1 2 1 1 1 1 1 1 1 1 1 1 1 1 1 1 1 1 1 1 1 1 1 1 1 2 1 2 2 2 2 1 2 2 2 2
 2 2 1 1 2 2 2 2 1 2 1 2 1 2 2 1 1 2 2 2 2 2 1 2 2 2 2 1 2 2 2 1 2 2 2 2 1 2
 2 1]

Predict New label:
[2]
Accuracy:
0.8933333333333333
```

Report:	precision	recall	f1-score	support
0	1.00	1.00	1.00	50
1	0.77	0.96	0.86	50
2	0.95	0.72	0.82	50
accuracy			0.89	150
macro avg	0.91	0.89	0.89	150
weighted avg	0.91	0.89	0.89	150

It will produce different clusters each time you run it so you might see different results per run. We can also tune various hyperparameters of the k-Means algorithm, like the number of clusters, initialization, maximum iterations, random state, etc., in order to optimize our results.

10.3 Elements of Machine Learning

The rise of machine learning is connected to the increase in the amount of digital data that the human species has started producing of late. Man has been around for about 2 million years; Homo Sapiens for probably close to 300,000 years; behavioural modernity was achieved about 50,000 years ago and written history has been around for about 5,500 years. According to some estimates, in the year 2009 CE alone, human beings have generated more data than in all these previous years combined. In fact, in each subsequent year since then, the amount of data we've generated has only increased!

The amount of data we collect from social, scientific, and other organizational systems seems to be increasing exponentially. Data from the various sub-fields of physics and computation is huge but even biological data collection is quite daunting: for example, the human brain consists of around 100 billion neurons and about 100 trillion synapses. Human beings, on average, consist of about 30

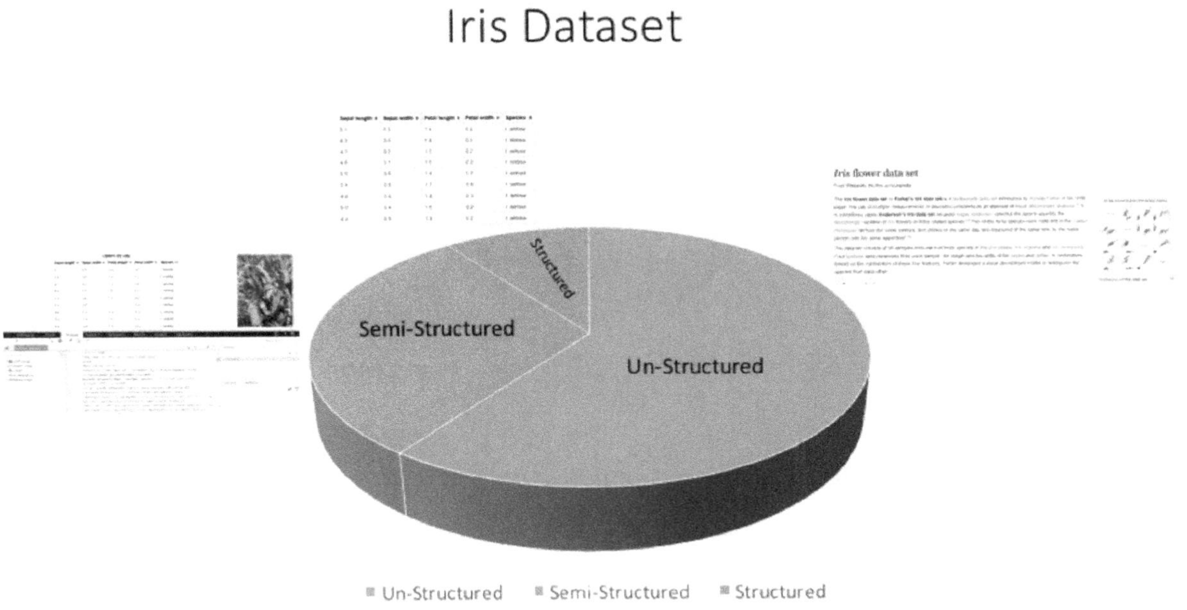

Iris Dataset

Figure 10.12: Structured, Un-Structured, and Semi-Structured Data for the Iris Dataset.

trillion cells with about 35 trillion more cells that are made up of microbial hangers-on. Analyzing these connectomes and biological systems generates an enormous amount of data.

This growth in data is popularly referred to as **big data**. Although the *volume*, or size, of data is one aspect of big data, other characteristics like the *velocity* of data (how fast it's increasing) and the *variety* of data (the different formats and media of the data) are also cause for concern.

This kind of data comes in many forms: it can be highly **structured**, like typical database tables or Excel spreadsheets; it can be **un-structured**, like emails, documents, images, etc. – anything that doesn't neatly fit into a database; or it can be **semi-structured**, living somewhere between the two, like XML or JSON files. It's important to note that un-structured data, in this sense, does not mean the data itself doesn't have some internal organization; instead, data is called un-structured in the sense that normal data mining tools cannot easily parse it. Most data generated today is either semi-structured or un-structured, as shown in Figure 10.12.

This is relevant for us as the type of data we have will determine the kinds of analyses and visualizations we can make. Whenever we deal with different kinds of data, we need to consider:

- What kinds of questions can we ask using this kind of data?
- What types of analytics can be carried out on this data?
- What data sources are available?
- What types of data will we have (structured, semi-structured, un-structured)?
- Who uses or consumes this type of data?

As you might imagine, analyzing this amount of data is quite challenging and studying these kinds of data-intensive problems is almost prohibitive using traditional tools. In these cases, statistical machine learning techniques have proved especially effective in tackling such big data problems.

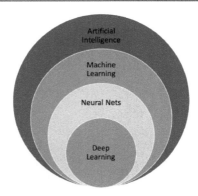

Figure 10.13: How Artificial Intelligence (AI) and Machine Learning (ML) are related.

10.3.1 Machine Learning Writ Large

Machine learning is thus used in contexts that involve large-scale complex systems, multi-dimensional datasets, or computational solutions that are simply too complex to be written manually. Complex systems like the billions of nodes that make up the internet, sensor networks from multi-modal sensors, genomics, proteomics, connectomics, etc., have significant analytical complications.

For such problems, having machines (or, more accurately, programs and algorithms) that can learn is invaluable. Thus, we don't use machine learning when we need to calculate the payroll for a company but we do use it when we're dealing with situations where:

- Big Data challenges loom large (as outlined above)
- The requisite human expertise isn't readily available (e.g., exploring new planets)
- We cannot explain the mechanism behind existing human expertise (e.g., motion recognition)
- The actual solution changes in time (e.g., how routing occurs over a computer network)
- The final solution must be adapted for particular cases (e.g., in user biometrics)

In these kinds of situations, machine learning is indispensable. For example, it is easier to write a program that learns to play chess by self-play instead of fully characterizing the expertise of chess masters as a rule-based program. Indeed, machine learning is used successfully in a wide spectrum of applications, including natural language processing, search engines, medical diagnosis, detecting credit card fraud, stock market analysis, bio-informatics, classifying DNA sequences, speech and handwriting recognition, object recognition in computer vision, playing games, robot locomotion, etc.

As we saw earlier, machine learning started off as an off-shoot of artificial intelligence, which not only gave birth to machine learning but is still concerned with designing approaches to support learning and perhaps replicate human intelligence in the future. This relationship is shown in Figure 10.13, where it also shows some of the more powerful sub-fields of machine learning, including **deep learning**, a variant of artificial neural networks (ANNs) which does hierarchical feature learning, or representation learning, using neural networks with considerably more layers than is typical for simpler neural networks. We'll learn more about this especially effective approach to tackle large, unstructured datasets in just a bit.

Machine learning is also intimately related to and borrows from several fields, including: **statistics**, which is usually concerned with inference from a sample; **data mining**, which develops techniques for searching through large volumes of data; and, in general, **computer science**, which, in broad terms, deals with developing efficient algorithms and complex models.

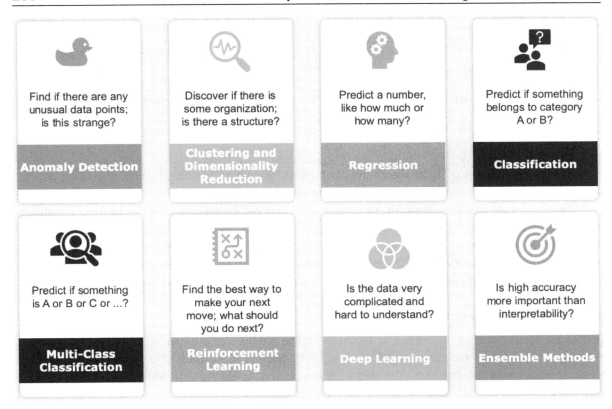

Figure 10.14: Eight Common Machine Learning Approaches: pragmatically speaking, there are usually eight kinds of questions we answer in most data analytic applications. Each of these eight questions is usually addressed using a different machine learning algorithm. These eight common questions and their corresponding approaches are shown above.

10.3.2 ML Definition: Tasks

Pragmatically speaking, there are usually eight kinds of questions a machine learning algorithm can answer or tasks that it can do. Each of these eight questions is usually addressed using a different machine learning algorithm. These eight common questions and their corresponding approaches are shown below and in Figure 10.14:

1. Find if there are any unusual data points: is this weird? → Anomaly Detection
2. Discover how this is organized or structured? → Clustering and Dimensionality Reduction
3. Predict a number, like how much or how many? → Regression
4. Predict if something is A or B? → Classification
5. Predict if this is A or B or C or ...? → Multi-Class Classification
6. Find the best way to make your next move; what should you do next? → Reinforcement Learning
7. Is the data super-complicated and hard to understand? → Deep Learning
8. Is accuracy quality really important? → Ensemble Methods

There are also additional questions that are often asked like "Is this the best?", which can be answered using optimization or some such approach. In fact, most machine learning is about optimization: either an explicit reward as in reinforcement learning or a score or loss function used in estimating parameters (e.g., the weights in a neural network) or learning structures (e.g., the directed tree structure

(a) Traditional Computer Science Paradigm   (b) Machine Learning Paradigm

Figure 10.15: Traditional Computer Science vs Machine Learning paradigms

created in decision trees). These algorithms, or models, learn based on the data we give them and we can then measure how much they've learned using some performance metric.

There are many machine learning methods but they're differentiated from the previous computational solutions we have usually developed in computer science. In traditional computational solutions, the input data and the program for a specific task together determine the output; in the machine learning paradigm, this is usually turned on its head and instead the input data and the output help determine the structure of the computational model or program we develop for a task, as shown in Figure 10.15.

10.3.3 ML Definition: Models

A computer program, or algorithm, is based on some model. So we can group different machine learning algorithms by the category which characterizes those algorithms or the tasks those machine learning algorithms can perform. We also need to specify the metrics, or performance measures, to gauge the success of those algorithms, as we'll do in Section 10.3.4.

These main categories of machine learning are shown in Figure 10.16. We can further categorize these different machine learning algorithms in many ways. We can group them by learning style or by similarity in the form and function or by the model type. If we categorize them by learning style, we might end up with a listing like this, which sometimes also adds Reinforcement Learning, Representation Learning (Feature Learning), and Combined Models to the list:

- Supervised
- Un-supervised
- Semi-supervised

The two most ubiquitous learning styles are Supervised Learning and Unsupervised Learning; the

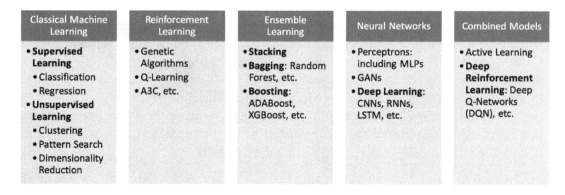

Figure 10.16: Major categories of machine learning. Sometimes, semi-supervised learning, which includes approaches like adversarial training, is also added to the Classical Machine Learning listing.

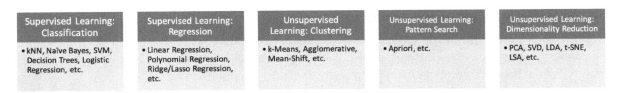

Figure 10.17: Elements of the classical machine learning components of supervised and unsupervised learning.

various kinds of supervised and unsupervised learning are shown in Figure 10.17. The third kind of learning style, Semi-Supervised Learning, lies somewhat intermediate to Supervised and Unsupervised Learning. Semi-supervised algorithms use a combination of labelled *and* un-labelled data for their training like in semi-supervised SVMs.

One of the easiest ways to categorize different models is to group them based on the input to or the output from that algorithm. For example, we can see what kinds of input we might have:

1. If the input data is labelled, the problem is one of supervised learning
2. If the input data is not labelled, we can find the structure in this kind of unsupervised learning problem
3. If the algorithm needs to concentrate less on the data and more on the environment, continuously getting input by interacting with the environment in order to optimize an objective function, this kind of problem would involve Reinforcement Learning (RL)[15]

We could also choose to categorize based on the kind of output we'll produce:

1. If our algorithm needs to output a number, the problem is called regression
2. If our algorithm needs to output the class to which something belongs, it's called classification
3. If our algorithm needs to find any outliers, it's called anomaly detection

The complexity of the input data can introduce additional complications, as well. For example, if the number of features in a dataset is huge, you might need to employ some method for reducing the number of dimensions in your dataset. Why do we need this kind of **dimensionality reduction**?

One reason is the **Curse of Dimensionality**, which is concerned with the issues that arise with high-dimensional problems and which aren't seen in lower-dimensional problems. The number of dimensions is related to the number of features, or columns, in our datasets. As the number of features increases, the number of samples needed to well-represent all combinations of feature values also increases commensurately. But if we increase the number of features, we also increase the complexity of the model. As the model becomes more complex, the chances of **overfitting** increases and when we apply it to new data, it will give poor results as it won't **generalize** well. Thus, dimensionality reduction helps reduce this risk of overfitting which accompanies the Curse of Dimensionality.

Dealing with complex models also makes it harder to understand how the machine actually learned what it did. For example, ensemble methods, which blend multiple models, and highly complex models with millions of parameters, like neural networks, are effective but are often hard to understand and so we just treat them as an opaque black box which ineffably churns out answers. If the answers and their accuracy are more important than understandability, then you might very well pick these algorithms for a certain problem.

---

[15] In RL, the machine keeps track of the **state** of the environment, represented by a feature vector. Like a Turing Machine, it associates different **actions** with different states, and each action can elicit a **reward** and move the machine to a different state. The machine then formulates a **policy** that outputs the optimal action, the one that maximizes the reward.

10.3.4 ML Definition: Performance Measures

In general, we determine an appropriate machine learning algorithm based on the desired performance measures and available resources with consideration for the data and computational complexity, including training time and model complexity. We would normally create a **test harness** for any complete machine learning solution that utilizes training data, testing data, and validation data along with the performance measures. We'll meet some of these performance measures in detail later but, for now, let's see just a brief overview of the kinds of measures we might utilize:

Figure 10.18: Splitting the full dataset for supervised learning.

1. We can use measures like a confusion matrix, heat map, lift charts, etc. to visualize and evaluate the results
2. We can evaluate the statistical significance of the proposed solution, like r-square, f statistic, p-value, etc., as we'll see in Section 10.5
3. We can employ standard statistical evaluation metrics like precision, recall, accuracy, F1, ROC curve, etc., as seen in Section 10.5.7; we often need precision, recall, and their various combinations as accuracy is insufficient for imbalanced classification problems[16]

Making Reliable Predictions

The process for making reliable predictions requires rigorous testing and validation of your learning model. You should only use it on unknown data to make your final prediction once you're confident in its reliability.

At a minimum, as you develop your model, you should:

- Test it on a toy dataset or a simulated dataset
- Validate it on a known dataset
- Only then use it for predictions on an unknown dataset

10.3.5 Model Building and Assessment

In order to properly assess our model, we need to construct two **hold-out** sets (that aren't used to assess the algorithm) called the **training** and **validation** datasets, as well as a **testing** dataset; all three should follow the *same probability distribution* as the underlying problem space. For small datasets, the split is usually 70/15/15 and, for large datasets, can be 90/5/5 or even 95% for training, if needed, since often more data helps. Sometimes, though, **model complexity** needs to be increased to manage the **bias-variance tradeoff** in classification tasks. This kind of N-fold Cross-Validation with Bias-Variance Tradeoff analysis in supervised learning can help set the algorithm's configuration to avoid overtraining.

The main idea of machine learning is to first select an algorithm or multiple candidate algorithms to address some problem. Each algorithm will learn certain **parameters** using the training dataset. Once the parameters are set for the learning algorithm, we will have determined our *tentative* **model**.

---

[16]In a 2-class problem, if the positive class greatly outnumbers the negative class, as with diseases, terrorists, etc., we encounter the **accuracy paradox** where accuracy is no longer an effective measure.

Parameters are the configuration variables that are internal to the algorithm and are usually estimated or learned from the data rather than set manually; once learned, they're often stored as part of the learned model. If a model has a fixed number of parameters, the model is called **parametric**; if the number of parameters in a model is not fixed, that model is called **non-parametric**. Parameters in a model are things like the weights and biases in a neural network, the support vectors in SVMs, the coefficients in linear regression, etc.

Then, the validation dataset is used to tune the **hyperparameters** and choose the best-performing validation dataset. A model's hyperparameters are external to the algorithm and cannot be estimated or learned from the data. The values of the hyperparameters can help estimate or learn the values of the model's parameters. They are often set manually but can also be set using heuristics or tuned via techniques like assessing validation curves, doing grid search, etc. Tuning the algorithm to come up with a good predictive model for a particular task involves tuning the hyperparameters in order to find the model parameters that give you the best predictive capability. We can see this process for a general machine learning task in Figure 10.19 where the Testing Metrics are the Performance Measures from Section 10.3.4.

Examples of hyperparameters are things like the number of trees in a random forest, the regularization parameter c in SVMs, which determines the tradeoff between testing and training error, the sigma smoothing parameter in the RBK of an SVM, various parameters (number of layers, size of each layer, number of connections in neural networks, the learning rate) in neural networks. Finding the best values for these hyperparameters can be cast as a search problem so typical approaches are search methods like grid search, random search, etc.

If the validation set is very small, we can use **cross-validation** to construct a simulated validation set. We can do 5-fold cross validation on the training set to create both a training and validation set in each fold. The test dataset is used to *assess* the final chosen model's performance to see how well it **generalizes** beyond the training/validation tuning. We can also do things like use *grid search*, as we saw in Section 10.2.4.

We often need to do **feature selection**, where we determine which variables don't add any new information or are correlated with others, and **feature engineering**, in which we develop new features (feature generation or feature extraction) or transform existing features (feature transformation and aggregation). This can be facilitated by gauging the information content of features using measures like information gain, entropy, gini impurity, chi-square, etc., as in Section 10.6.2 or automatically via representation learning or feature learning, as in neural networks.

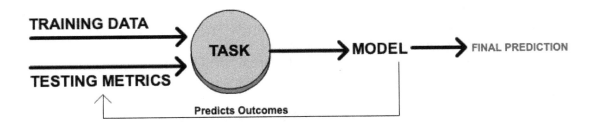

Figure 10.19: The machine learning paradigm visualized with data: training data helps train the model's parameters which are then tweaked depending on how it performs on the testing data. Hyperparameters are also tuned separately.

10.4 Data Science and Data Analytics

This kind of approach to making new predictions is helpful not only in a home application like the Movie Night example but also in applications to organizations, as well, especially for applications that are mission critical or safety critical.[17] No wonder then that there is an interplay between the different fields that create and utilize machine learning algorithms.

The three main areas that exhibit this interplay can be categorized as:

- **Computer Science** emphasizes theoretical and empirical approaches to manipulating data via computation or algorithmic processes.
- **Informatics** deals with a broader study of data and its manipulation in information processes and systems, including social and cognitive models.
- **Data Science** tackles structured and unstructured data and uses both computational methods and cognitive or social methods, especially when visualizing complicated data analytics.

All three of these approaches rely upon the usage and manipulation of data, especially in regards to making decisions. The central idea behind a **data-driven decision-making** approach is summarized by these three components:

1. Analyze historical trends
2. Forecast future outcomes
3. Assist decision making with actual quantitative predictions

These three components can be thought of as the result of three kinds of activities: Exploratory Data Analysis, Data Analytics, and Data Science. When these kinds of activities are applied to business problems, the field of **Business Intelligence/Business Analytics (BI/BA)** can map its components to these three activities as: Descriptive Analytics (maps to Exploratory Data Analysis), Predictive Analytics (maps to Data Analytics), and Prescriptive Analytics (maps to Data Science).

Let's examine each of these, along with their corresponding terms, next:

- **Exploratory Data Analysis (EDA)** mainly asks, "What happened in the past?" It thus analyzes historical data and, in the BI/BA paradigm, is called **Descriptive Analytics**.
  Descriptive analytics tells us what happened; this involves using data to understand past and current performance to make informed decisions. This is sometimes said to include **Planning Analytics**, where the plan for the forecasted goals is established, including planning and budgeting concerns.

- **Data Analysis** tries to answer, "What could happen in the future?" In the BI/BA paradigm, this is called **Predictive Analytics** and, sometimes, also called **Business Informatics** when it addresses organizational behaviour/science and systems, as well. Usually, this involves building a *machine learning model* to **predict** an outcome.
  Since predictive analytics deals with what could happen, it will involve using historical data to predict future outcomes. This sometimes also includes **Diagnostic Analytics**, which looks at why things happened in the past using data mining and data discovery to also establish correlations, causal relationships, and patterns in historical data. The focus is mainly on processing *existing* data sets and performing statistical analyses on them.
    - Data analysis involves using machine learning algorithms to derive insights and support decision-making. This also requires extracting, cleaning, and munging data in order to transform it into a useable format for modeling that data to support decision-making and

---

[17]There are 4 kinds of critical systems (mission, business, safety, and security), with machine learning essential for each.

confirming or informing conclusions. Cleaning and munging the data involves dealing with missing fields and improper values, as well as converting raw files to the correct format and structure.

- **Data Science** answers the question, "What should we do next?" It uses predictions and helps decide what to do next and how to make it happen. In the BI/BA paradigm, it is called **Prescriptive Analytics**.

  In essence, prescriptive analytics looks at what you can do about what's about to happen; this involves a consideration of what we can do about what's going to happen and how we can make it happen; prescriptive analytics sometimes concentrates on optimization and tries to identify the solution that optimizes a certain objective.

  – Data science requires the user to be able to innovate algorithms, find unique, additional data sources, and have deep domain knowledge. It uses ideas from computational science and information systems in order to gain *actionable insights* and make **predictions** from both structured and un-structured data about what to do or which **decisions** to make. This is why a data scientist should also have some *domain knowledge* in addition to the ability to create machine learning models and identifying ways to predict trends and connections by exploring novel, perhaps disconnected, data sources.

10.4.1 Business Intelligence/Business Analytics

Each of these three layers, EDA (Descriptive Analytics), Data Analysis (Predictive Analytics/Business Informatics), and Data Science (Prescriptive Analytics), builds upon or incorporates the previous layer. In addition, Prescriptive Analytics usually incorporates new data sources for supporting decision making while Descriptive and Predictive Analytics use previously available historical data sources.

These three different kinds of analytics usually fall under the rubric of **Business Intelligence (BI)**. Although these definitions aren't rigorous, in general, they encompass the idea of applying data analysis and data science to business data at the enterprise level.[18] In fact, Business Intelligence is often used interchangeably with the term **Business Analytics (BA)**. Sometimes, though, Business Intelligence is defined as covering only up to Descriptive Analytics while Business Analytics is then defined to cover Predictive Analytics and Prescriptive Analytics.

As such, in the BI/BA paradigm, while descriptive analytics looks at what has happened from a statistical perspective, predictive analytics looks at what could be and also makes relevant predictions based on that data. Prescriptive analytics not only foresees these identified trends and predictions but also focuses on complete solution strategies relevant to the organization, often using optimization to identify the best alternatives, identifying new data sources, and prescribing what actions need to be taken in order to meet these trends. Prescriptive Analytics thus adds a causal part, not just a correlation, somewhat akin to the difference between kinematics and dynamics in physics. This also focuses on suggesting a course of action and takes on the role of **data-driven decision support systems**, helping transform data into actionable insights to inform an organization's strategic and tactical decision making.

A somewhat surprising heuristic maps the BI/BA activities to the Army Physical Fitness Test (APFT): in this approach, you can make a quick decision by following three simple rules; those three rules can be mapped to our three Business Intelligence categories as follows:

---

[18]So far, there are no standardized definitions of these terms derived from first principles. There are some standardization efforts that are more popular than others but none that is universally accepted so far. So none of these terms should be taken as hard "definitions" as the terms themselves are somewhat ambiguous, overlap with each other, and are still being refined.

1. Understand the overall situation or mission intent: Descriptive Analytics
2. Enumerate the possible outcomes: Predictive Analytics
3. Create and execute the plan: Prescriptive Analytics

Some of the factors that affect a choice of specific machine learning algorithm have more to do with the business constraints than optimization and technical characteristics of the particular algorithm. As such, there is often an overlap of terminology between Data Science and Business Intelligence/Business Analytics.

We can contextualize all three aspects of business intelligence/business analytics with a financial example based around <u>balance sheets</u>. In terms of **Exploratory Data Analysis** (or *Descriptive Analytics*), we might identify areas of influence on the bottom line by examining the underlying data by drawing charts for budgets, sales, revenues, costs, etc. This allows us to get a rigorous picture of the balance sheet which provides plain fact information about an organization's finances for some period of time, thus giving you insight into the facts of what happened to the organization, by drilling down to see which exact resources are most profitable.

In terms of **Data Analysis** (or *Predictive Analytics*) of the balance sheet, we might combine the information from multiple balance sheets and compare that over a period of time to gain information about where the finances may trend, such as surges in revenue during certain periods or decline in market profits. Finally, **Data Science** (or *Prescriptive Analytics*) would use these identified trends, combined with analysis of new supporting datasets, to propose several options to achieve the desired outcome, usually along the lines of maximizing profit while minimizing costs.

10.4.2 The Jataka Analytics

Following the example of the Jataka Tales,[19] suppose a troop of monkeys in an Indian jungle go on their weekly foraging trip to find some yummy bananas. They contract a free-lancing parrot to gather data detailing all the places it discovered bananas last year as it flew around in the vicinity of their water hole. The parrot summarizes its findings in a report and this report would be an example of **Descriptive Analytics**. In practice, rather than the parrot, such historical patterns are accumulated and analyzed constantly by companies like Google, who gather all kinds of data on your web and social media activity and then sell it to data houses that accumulate these historical patterns.

Suppose, after analyzing the parrot's historical data, our troop of monkeys **predicts** that they would be able to find bananas on the east side of their regular water hole. This insight would be an example of **Predictive Analytics**. In practice, this process results in **hypotheses** about how an organization might maximize some element of their practice, usually the profit for a commercial enterprise. For example, suppose a company wanted to create a new product; they might consider questions like: does it align with what the markets want and need? Will it reach the right target market? Does the public want it but just don't know what it is yet? The answers to these questions would be the hypotheses that formulate our *predictions*.

Finally, our enterprising troop of monkeys uses this data, along with their hypotheses about the best places to forage bananas, to modify the routes they take for their weekly foraging trip. Their goal is to maximize the number of bananas they find and, as they adjust their routes, they also record data about all the banana trees along these new routes so that they can further optimize their routes to increase the number of bananas and also to collect them before other banana foragers. These plans and the new datasets they collected are the result of their **Prescriptive Analytics**. Companies, in fact, often utilize such prescriptive analytics to strategize about approaches to make their organizations more efficient and capitalize on the information created and discovered by the organization. This might help them do things like optimizing their supply chain, targeting new products to appropriate markets, etc.

Recap of Analytics

1. Descriptive analytics is what happened; this involves using data to understand past and current performance to make informed decisions
2. Predictive analytics is what could happen; this involves using historical data to predict future outcomes
3. Prescriptive analytics is looking at what you can do about what's about to happen; this involves a consideration of what can be done about what's going to happen

Thus, the goal of data science is to make predictions: precise, quantitative predictions that will be useful in any organization or organizational context for decision-making. **Decision analysis** uses ideas from computer science, psychology, economics, management science, and decision science to deal with uncertainty and complex, sometimes competing, objectives in order to evaluate possible actions.

---

[19]The Jataka Tales tell various parables, often humorous and insightful, about the former lives of Gautama Buddha, especially those that were in animal forms. Jataka is derived from the Sanskrit word, Jaatak ("birth"), and most of these stories were written between 300 BCE and 400 CE in Pali. Some of the most entertaining, and enlightening, stories center around a troop of monkeys, hence the simian example above. The ever-popular Amar Chitra Katha series of comics also devoted a special series to the Jataka Tales.

10.4.3 Is Data Science a Science?

Before we tackle the idea of whether Data Science is a science or not, something that doesn't seem to have a definitive answer, let's step back and look at the idea of proof. This is a word that is overused quite frequently as there are many different kinds of proof: for example, there are scientific proofs, legal proofs, and mathematical proofs.

In mathematics, a proof is an *inferential argument* that shows a statement is true as supported by axioms, definitions, theorems, and postulates. Mathematicians normally use *deductive reasoning* to show that the premises, also called statements, in a proof are true in a direct proof. A direct proof is one that shows a given statement is always true and the proof is usually written in a symbolic language. In an indirect proof, mathematicians usually employ proof by contradiction, where they assume the opposite statement is true and eventually reach a contradiction showing the assumption is false.

In law, legal proof is the process of establishing a fact by using evidence. In science, we might call this a validation of some theory as that usually also takes the form of an argument where you present a series of premises in support of some conclusion. Similarly to law, proof in science is usually limited to proof of facts in the sense of using data to establish the validity of facts. This is discussed at length by D.H. Kaye in [18] which shows that the use of quantitative observation-statements provide evidence to prove or, as we'd say in science, show the validity of, facts.

In science, an inherently *inductive* enterprise,[20] we cannot prove any hypothesis to be true as that would require an infinite number of observations so the best we can hope to do is use inductive reasoning as the basis of our generalization and hold it to be provisionally true. As noted by Lee Loevinger about Karl Popper, "In this view, which is fairly widely accepted, an hypothesis can be falsified, or disproved, but cannot be verified, or proved." Once it's *validated* extensively and consistently, and we deem it to be sufficiently substantiated, we then call it a theory. So we could, in some sense, say that legal arguments use evidence to show the validity of a theory whereas science uses data to falsify a theory.

For example, following [18], collecting quantifiable **data** of the intensity and polarization of radiation at various frequencies from a radio telescope pointed at the Crab Nebula is the **evidence** that shows (in law, proves) something in the direction of the Crab Nebula is a radio source, the **fact**. Such facts can be deduced or induced from statements of observations, the evidence. Thus, a fact is based on some repeatable observation or measurement that is generally agreed upon to recur with the same value or in the same way under the same kinds of circumstances.

These facts are then used to inductively reason about a hypothesis or model of the system being studied. The *predictions* made by that model are further *verified* and, when enough predictions are verified independently, the hypothesis, or set of hypotheses, is considered sufficiently validated to be called a theory.

This process, this scientific method, is exactly what we employ when we utilize our machine learning models, like Hypothesis Testing in Section 10.5.1 or Decision Trees in Section 10.7, within a Data Science framework and use *data* to iteratively test and improve our models. I might further argue, following Feynman's formulation, that as long as you're using a **systematic model** to make **predictions** and then **testing** those predictions with data and using those results to *validate or improve* your model **iteratively**, you're *doing science*.

Applying these scientific models to specific business problems[21] without iteratively changing or further developing those models results in engineering and technology principles. As such, I might be

---

[20]Inductive at least to the extent that thinkers like Richard Feynman and Karl Popper would find it to be so, Feynman in his exposition on the Key to Science and Popper in his formulation of conjecture and criticism.

[21]Where, once again, we mean any organization when we say business.

inclined to categorize Data Analysis as an engineering discipline and Exploratory Data Analysis as a technological application.

10.5 Bayesian Inference and Hypothesis Testing

Now that we have some of this mathematical machinery under our belt, let's build upon it by looking at an essential tool for validating scientific inquiries. We know that all of science is built upon the foundation of falsifying hypotheses so looking at how this is done is central to any scientific endeavour.

10.5.1 Null Hypothesis Significance Testing

Suppose someone takes a pregnancy test to check if they're pregnant. The test, which looks for hCG levels in urine, reports a negative result, indicating the hCG levels are below the test's threshold for establishing pregnancy. Since the result was negative, they feel safe going to the dentist to take some X-Rays. But what if the test was wrong and they were actually pregnant? As you might surmise, a **false negative** like this might be devastating!

These kinds of situations often arise in **Null Hypothesis Significance Testing** (NHST), also known as **Hypothesis Testing**. NHST is a way to draw a conclusion, or **infer**, whether some expression is true or not, usually by comparing two datasets or a sample from some dataset.

NHST depends upon a **Null Hypothesis**, H_0, the **falsifiable expression** that's assumed to be true unless there's evidence to the contrary. In this case, we might think of it as the fact that we're not pregnant unless there's evidence to the contrary.

As a side note, the hypothesis should usually be stated in terms of an **independent variable**, a **feature** of the experiment we don't directly control but that can help predict the value of a **dependent variable**, where the researcher gets to decide which variable is independent or dependent in a given experiment. The independent, or **predictor**, variable is usually plotted on the x-axis (abscissa) and is usually the input to some function where the output, or the y-axis (ordinate) value, is the dependent variable.

The **hypothesis statement** can then be written as an "if ... then" construction, as we saw in our discussion of formal logic, in terms of the independent and dependent variables as such, "If (we do something to the independent variable) then (we expect some result in the dependent variable)." Using the hypothesis statement, you'll formulate a *null hypothesis*, which should be a falsifiable expression of a result that follows from the hypothesis statement. Since the null hypothesis is falsifiable, you can end up with the opposite state of the null hypothesis for a result, as well. This opposite expression is termed the **Alternative Hypothesis**, H_1 or H_A.

In terms of the person taking the test, perhaps their hypothesis statement was, "If there is a full moon night, then they cannot get pregnant," where the full moon night is the independent variable and not becoming pregnant is the dependent variable.[22] To test this hypothesis statement, they might formulate the null hypothesis they're not pregnant since there was a full moon last night: $H_0 = \text{Not\_Pregnant}$. This will also give them the alternative hypothesis that they *are* pregnant, despite the full moon: $H_1 = H_A = \text{Pregnant}$.

In order to check their pregnancy state, they take a pregnancy test and the result is negative. The result of this pregnancy test is the data we use to assess whether our falsifiable H_0 is true or not. We can determine the probability, or **p-value**, of this assertion being true as:

$$\text{p-value} \equiv P(\text{ observing this data} \mid H_0 \text{ is true }) \tag{10.1}$$

---

[22]As with all examples in this book, the situations tend to either be convoluted, unlikely, or, as in this case, both.

Thus, the p-value is the **conditional probability**, or likelihood, of seeing the current data, or data that is *more* extreme than the current data, if the null hypothesis is true. As you can see in the definition above, the p-value assumes that H_0 is true; the p-value is **not** the probability of H_0, or H_1, being true but rather the likelihood of seeing the current evidence **if** H_0 is true.

The goal of NHST is to see if it's *reasonable* to reject H_0. The way that's normally determined is by deciding that a probability lower than a certain level, the **significance level** (α), indicates the results are too unlikely to be by random chance alone.[23]   You can use different levels for this significance level but a generally accepted rule of thumb is to reject the null hypothesis if the p-value is below $\alpha = 0.05 = 5\%$ or, for an even stricter standard, if the p-value is below $\alpha = 0.01 = 1\%$.

Null Hypothesis Significance Testing consists of three components:

1. The hypotheses: a Null Hypothesis, H_o, and one or more Alternative Hypotheses, H_A
2. The statistical test: often a z-test or t-test, for H_o
3. The significance evaluation: a probability, the p-value, is compared to a threshold, α

Hypothesis testing determines whether the data provides enough evidence to indicate if our initial guess, H_o, was wrong or if our initial guess was actually right and random chance alone generated the data we see. The significance level, α, is the percentage, or probability, of risk we are willing to take in accepting the null hypothesis even if it is actually wrong. The p-value is the probability of seeing the data and it is calculated for the sample statistics, not the population, by looking it up in a z-table or using statistical software.

If you find the p-value, the probability of seeing the data if H_0 were true, is below this significance level, α, then you have to reject the null hypothesis (that H_0 is true) as the relationship in the sample is then unlikely to be by chance alone and likely reflects a relationship in the underlying population. This

---

[23] Suppose you have to analyze some values, or **parameters**, like the average height, of a large population; because you can't examine the entire population, you might instead draw a random subset of the population, called a **sample**, and measure a **variable**, like the height, for that sample. You might then compute some descriptive statistics on the values of that variable, e.g., the *mean* of the heights, for that sample. These **sample statistics** on the values of the variables from the sample can help you draw some conclusions about the corresponding values, or parameters, of the underlying population.

The sample statistics can thus be used to **estimate** the population parameters. This idea of drawing conclusions about a population by computing statistics on small samples drawn from that population is called **inferential statistics**. However, these sample statistics cannot perfectly estimate the corresponding population parameters because of the **random variation** in computing any statistic for multiple samples. This random variation is inherent in the process of drawing samples and is called the **sampling error**, even though it's nobody's fault. When you draw different samples from a population, the values of those variables will usually exhibit some random variation by virtue of picking different subsets of the underlying population.

So we calculate statistics using samples and not the entire population; thus, every sample mean we calculate will be somewhat different since sampling causes variation. NHST checks the probability that a particular sample mean's variation is from random chance. All this means that if you notice some statistical relationship in a *sample*, it might be from random variation and that statistical relationship might not exist in the underlying *population* at all! NHST is thus a formal method to check if the statistical relationship in the sample occurred by chance and only reflects sampling error; the idea that the relationship in the sample occurred by chance and is not found in the underlying population is your null hypothesis, H_0.

Once you formulate the null hypothesis, H_0, which reflects a sample statistic relationship but no relationship between the parameters in the population, then you have to compute the probability of the sample statistic relationship, or how likely the sample statistic relationship would be if the null hypothesis were true. This probability is the p-value.

If the probability, or p-value, is lower than the significance level that means the sample's statistical relationship would be extremely unlikely, then we reject the null hypothesis and accept the alternative hypothesis, H_1 or H_A, which says that the statistical relationship in the sample reflects a similar statistical relationship in the underlying population, as well. NHST on the sample estimates can also be used to create a **confidence interval**, a range of values derived from the sample statistics that is likely to contain the actual value of the population parameter.

means that the likelihood of seeing the data you observed is so low that the alternative hypothesis, H_A, must be true.

In our running example, if the probability, or p-value, of the pregnancy test *showing positive* given that we're *not pregnant* is **lower** than the significance level, or $\alpha = 0.01 = 1\%$, we will **reject** the null hypothesis ($H_0 = $ Not_Pregnant) and start printing baby shower announcements instead. If that probability is higher than 0.01 (or 1%), though, then we will **not** reject H_0 and instead grab a drink and go to the dentist as planned. So how do we determine this probability?

We employ some kind of a statistical test like the Student's t-Test or Welch's t-Test, or, in the case where you know the actual population standard deviation, the one-sample z-Test. Suppose we decide on the one-sample z-Test; the next step is to compute the z-score associated with the significance level, α, we chose. In addition, we have to calculate the z-score for our problem. Then, if our problem z-score is *higher* than the z-score associated with α, we reject the null hypothesis, H_0.[24]

Alternatively, we can state this in terms of probabilities by looking up the p-value probability corresponding to the z-value in a table. If this problem probability, or p-value, is *lower* than the significance level probability, $\alpha = 0.01 = 1\%$, then we have to reject the null hypothesis, H_0.[25]

By the power of hypotheses... I have the power analysis!

Hypothesis testing basically asks the question: for a given *initial position*, does the evidence we've seen compel us to change our minds away from that initial position? Thus, we start by assuming the **null hypothesis** is true; this is our initial position. We then look at some evidence and calculate a **p-value**, the *probability* or likelihood of our initial position, the null hypothesis.

This p-value helps determine if we learned enough from the evidence to change our minds and reject our initial position, the null hypothesis. We do that only if the evidence is *surprising* or, as we might say in the information theory paradigm, increases the amount of **information gained**. If the p-value, the probability of our null hypothesis being true, is lower than some *significance level*, the amount of surprise, or the amount of information gained, is large and we should likely change our minds and reject the null hypothesis.

The **power** of an experiment is the probability of avoiding a false negative (β): i.e., the probability of rejecting the null hypothesis when it actually is false: $Pr(reject\ H_o | H_1)$. In essence, the power of a process measures whether we have collected enough evidence to justify changing our minds. Power is equal to $1 - \beta$ and is proportional to the sample size and inversely proportional to the significance level (α) and effect size, d, (using something like Pearson's Correlation Coefficient).

Power analysis helps identify how much power is associated with a given amount of data and usually determines the sample size for given values of alpha, beta, and the effect size, which are sometimes set to default values of $\alpha = 0.05, \beta = 0.8$, and $d = 0.8$, respectively.

10.5.2 Hypothesis Testing

Let's calculate some of these probabilities so we can quantify the test of our hypothesis. Suppose the pregnancy test claims it can successfully detect 98.5% of pregnancies. This usually refers to **True Positives (TP)**, where it tests positive (t+) when the person *is pregnant* (p+) with probability $P(t+|p+)$, as seen in Figure 10.20b. The test kit's insert also gives you the **True Negative (TN)** probability as 95%, i.e., the probability of testing negative (t-) when they're *not pregnant* (p-): $P(t-|p-)$.

---

[24]In the case of a two-tailed test, we would also compute the z-score for the left tail and would reject H_0 if the problem z-score was *lower* than that.

[25] In Bayesian Hypothesis Testing, we add a prior probability and then compute the posterior probability, which is the conditional probability after all the evidence is considered, as encapsulated in Bayes' Theorem shown in Section 10.5.3.

This means the p-value, the probability of testing positive if they're not pregnant, $P(t+|p-)$, is 5% for this pregnancy test kit, as seen in Figure 10.20a. That means the likelihood of the test coming back positive and your *not* being pregnant is only 5%. Since this p-value probability is **not lower** than our stricter significance level probability, $\alpha = 0.01 = 1\%$, you *cannot reject* the null hypothesis, $H_0 =$ Not_Pregnant, and decide to further confirm being not pregnant.

We can do so by using a z-score based approach towards checking our hypothesis. We might calculate the z-score corresponding to our p-value, the probability of testing positive if they are not pregnant, and then compare that to the value 2.58, the two-tailed z-score at $\alpha = 0.01$ as seen from a standard z-score table or by using the Python `scipy.stats` package: `scipy.stats.norm.ppf(1-(1-0.99)/2)`. For our pregnancy test kit, the z-score corresponding to our p-value of 5% is 1.96.[26] Since the test's z-score of 1.96 is **not higher** than the z-score of 2.58 for $\alpha = 0.01 = 1\%$, we again *cannot reject* the null hypothesis, $H_0 =$ Not_Pregnant. But can we be sure we're <u>really</u> not pregnant?

This points to one of the most common misconceptions about p-values: the p-value by itself isn't intended to be a final probabilistic threshold of truth; instead, it's usually intended to be a guide to help answer the question of interest when it's combined with some prior knowledge. For example, combining a low p-value with the prior probability of pregnancy in the population, along with the general viability of the person using the test, will help you gauge the likelihood of being pregnant.

Suppose the prior probability of someone using a pregnancy test kit actually being pregnant is 40%: $P(p+) = 40\%$. For our pregnancy test kit, when someone pregnant takes the pregnancy test, it will correctly indicate pregnancy 98.5% of the time, so that $P(t+|p+) = 98.5\%$. Someone who is not pregnant, on the other hand, would get a correct indication 95% of the time, so that $P(t-|p-) = 95\%$ (and thus, $P(t+|p-) = 5\%$, which is our p-value probability). Continuing our example, we can combine these probabilities with the prior probability to get the probability of someone being pregnant, given that the test gives a positive result, as:

$$P(p+|t+) = \frac{P(t+|p+)*P(p+)}{P(t+)} = \frac{0.394}{0.424} = 93\% \tag{10.2}$$

since the numerator is $P(t+|p+)*P(p+) = 0.985*0.4 = 0.394$ and the total probability for a test showing positive is $P(t+) = P(t+|p+)*P(p+) + P(t+|p-)*P(p-) = 0.985*0.4 + 0.05*0.6 = 0.424$.[27] This rather high probability might make us consider taking the test again, just to confirm!

10.5.3 Bayes Theorem

How should retaking the test inform or change our current understanding? It turns out that Equation (10.2), also known as Bayes Theorem or Bayes Rule, lets us do just that! It is usually written as:

$$P(p+|t+) = \frac{P(t+|p+)P(p+)}{P(t+)} \tag{10.3}$$

where the left hand side is the probability of the hypothesis being true, $P(p+|t+)$, called the **posterior**, or the probability we're interested in figuring out; in this case, the posterior is the probability of being pregnant given the test returns a positive. The right hand side is made up of three parts:

- The probability of the observed data/experimental outcome, $P(t+|p+)$, called the **likelihood**

---

[26] In a normal distribution, approximately 95.45% of the area under the curve lies between $(\mu - 2\sigma, \mu + 2\sigma)$.

[27] This is also the Precision, as we calculate in Section 10.5.7 and see in Figure 10.20.

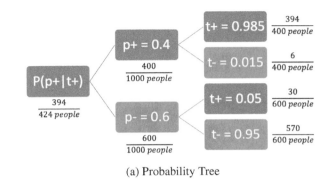

(a) Probability Tree

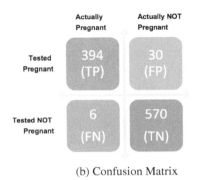

(b) Confusion Matrix

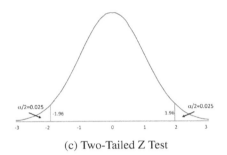

(c) Two-Tailed Z Test

Figure 10.20: Probability Tree, Confusion Matrix, and Two-Tailed Z Test:

(a) Probability Tree: Suppose in a population of 1,000 people, the prior probability of being pregnant, $P(p+)$, and not being pregnant, $P(p-)$, is 40% ($\frac{400}{1000}$) and 60% ($\frac{600}{1000}$), respectively.

(b) Confusion Matrix: shows number of people who tested pregnant versus those actually pregnant, along with False Positives (FP), False Negatives (FN), True Positives (TP), and True Negatives (TN).

(c) A Two-Tailed Z-Test showing the significance levels.

From the probability tree, we can see that $P(p+) = 40\%$, $P(p-) = 60\%$, $P(t+|p+) = 98.5\%$, $P(t-|p+) = 1.5\%$, $P(t+|p-) = 5\%$, $P(t-|p-) = 95\%$. So the probability of being pregnant, given that the test gives a positive result, is $P(p+|t+) = \frac{P(t+|p+)P(p+)}{P(t+)} = \frac{98.5\%*40\%}{98.5\%*40\%+5\%*60\%} = \frac{0.394}{0.424} = 93\%$.

- The a priori probability, $P(p+)$, called the **prior**
- The overall probability of the observed data, $P(t+)$, called the **evidence**

In a Bayesian approach, we'd combine the prior with the likelihood and then iteratively update the formula as per Bayes Theorem in Equation (10.3).[28] This is an alternative to the **frequentist** approach in NHST. In **Bayesian hypothesis testing**, evidence can be provided against the null hypothesis but also in favour of it. This is important as one of the biggest critiques against NHST, as explained by Zoltan Dienes in "Bayesian Versus Orthodox Statistics: Which Side Are You On?", is that the NHST approach gives us the probability of the data being observed if the theory is true, $P(Data|Theory = \text{"true"})$, whereas what we really want in experiments is the probability of the theory being true given that the

---

[28] For our running example, the evidence, $P(t+)$, is the probability for a positive result on the test, regardless of whether or not the underlying condition is true. That is, it includes probabilities for both the true positives AND the false positives. As such, we could even think of Bayes theorem as expressing the precision, $\frac{TP}{TP+FP}$, as seen in Section 10.5.7.

data is seen, $P(Theory|Data = \text{"observed"})$.

Thus, the only conclusion NHST can give us is whether or not to reject the null hypothesis, H_o, but this is often misunderstood and a significant p-value is incorrectly interpreted as evidence for the alternative hypothesis, H_A. There are also issues with the effect size and the size of the sample, as well.

Bayes rule, on the other hand, allow us to assess and adjust our confidence in the alternative hypothesis against the competing null hypothesis. But the Bayesian approach is not free from criticism, especially its reliance upon priors without a clear method for designing and setting priors.

10.5.4 Bayesian Hypothesis Testing

As we look at these pregnancy test examples, it's important to note, from a probabilistic perspective, that the *test* for pregnancy is different from the **event** of being pregnant. Tests themselves can be flawed: they might say you're pregnant when you're not (**false positive**) or say you're not pregnant when you actually are (**false negative**).

False positives can especially skew results: suppose some phenomenon, unlike pregnancy, were fleetingly rare in the population, like 1 in every million people is super-rich (there are something like 2,500 billionaires in the world so that would be closer to 1 in 3 million or so). In this case, if someone tests positive for being a billionaire, it's highly likely that the test is a false positive, given the rarity of billionaires in the wild. So if you see someone spending big money at a fancy restaurant, are they likely to be a billionaire? One way to make your guess, or prediction, better is to look for more data.

Problem 10.1 Besides eating an expensive meal at a fancy restaurant, what other evidence might make you more inclined to think a person was a billionaire? What kind of evidence would make you *less* inclined to think that?

As more data comes in, you might start to revise the probability of that person being a billionaire, either making it more likely or less likely. This idea of revising your beliefs (defined as the probability assigned to a certain event) based on new facts or evidence, is not only at the heart of science but also captured in Bayes' Rule or Bayes' Theorem, where the strength of evidence leads to revising our predicted probabilities.

This lets you do things like correct for measurement errors if you know the underlying probabilities as well as the false positive/negative rates and predict the actual probability from the measured test probability and known error rates. Let's see a quick example of how to use this **evidence-based reasoning** approach by going back to our pregnancy test example.

As we worked out in Equation (10.2), if the a priori probability of your being pregnant is given by the prior, $P(p+) = 0.4$, and the probability of the test showing positive if you're already pregnant is given by the likelihood, $P(t+|p+) = 0.985$, then the probability of the test showing positive, regardless of whether someone is pregnant or not, is given by the evidence, $P(t+) = P(t+|p+)*P(p+)+P(t+|p-)*P(p-) = 0.985*0.4+0.05*0.6 = 0.424$.

Then, the posterior probability of our alternative hypothesis, H_A ("you *are* pregnant"), is given by Equation (10.3) which gives us the odds of being pregnant if the test comes back positive as:
$P(p+|t+) = \frac{P(t+|p+)*P(p+)}{P(t+)} = \frac{0.394}{0.424} = 93\%$

In the Bayesian approach to Hypothesis Testing, we form a **Bayes Factor**, which is just the ratio of the posterior odds divided by the prior odds of the two competing hypotheses, H_o and H_A. In our case, the null hypothesis, H_o, was that "you're **not** pregnant" and the alternative hypothesis, H_A, was that "you *are* pregnant." The corresponding posteriors are $P_o(p-|t+) = \frac{P(t+|p-)*P(p-)}{P(t+)}$ and $P_A(p+|t+)$

and the corresponding priors are $P_o(p-)$ and $P_A(p+)$. Then, the Bayes factor is given by:

$$BF_{H_A H_o} = \frac{\text{posterior odds}}{\text{prior odds}} = \frac{\frac{P_A(p+|t+)}{P_o(p-|t+)}}{\frac{P_A(p+)}{P_o(p-)}} = \frac{\frac{.93}{.07}}{\frac{.4}{.6}} = \frac{13.28}{0.67} = 20.12 \qquad (10.4)$$

The Bayes factor uses the observed data to provide a measure of the evidence for H_A versus H_o. In this case, the probability to observe the data (positive test result) under the alternative hypothesis ("you *are* pregnant"), H_A, is about 20 times more likely than observing that same data (the positive test result) under the null hypothesis ("you're **not** pregnant!"), H_o.

Although thresholds are viewed skeptically in the Bayesian formulation, there are some suggested scales for interpreting the relative plausibility of the two models. In one popular approach, as elaborated by Alonso Ortega and Gorka Navarrete in "Bayesian Hypothesis Testing: An Alternative to Null Hypothesis Significance Testing (NHST) in Psychology and Social Sciences," a value of 1 is considered to be no evidence; a value above 100 is considered extreme evidence for H_A; and a value less than $\frac{1}{100}$ is considered extreme evidence for H_o. In our case, a value of 20 is strong evidence for H_A, that "you *are* pregnant." Should we cancel the dental appointment to have X-Rays then?

As a final confirmation, perhaps you decide to take the test again just to confirm everything and it comes back positive again. We can use the Bayesian approach iteratively to calculate the actual probability of being pregnant given this new data. In the Bayesian approach, we use the *previously calculated posterior* probability as our **new prior**.

We then do the calculation just as we did before: in this case, the new prior becomes $P(p+) = 0.93$, our previously calculated posterior probability. We then calculate the new likelihood as $P(t+|p+) * P(p+) = 0.985 * 0.93 = 0.916$ and the new evidence as $P(t+|p+) * P(p+) + P(t+|p-) * P(p-) = 0.985 * 0.93 + 0.05 * 0.07 = 0.9195$.

The final **new posterior** then becomes $P(p+|t+) = \frac{0.916}{0.9195} = 99.6\%$; that means our posterior probability, $P(p+|t+)$, of the alternative hypothesis, H_A, "you *are* pregnant," went from 93% after the first pregnancy test to 99.6% after the second pregnancy test and it confirms our expectation as we slowly throw all the alcohol out of our house.

10.5.5 Bayesian Inference and Statistics

Bayes theorem is a very good starting point to infer individual posterior probabilities and learn iteratively from new data, one observation at a time. But it can be extended to continue to iteratively learn statistically in Bayesian statistics by modeling each of the components (the prior, likelihood, posterior, and evidence) as probability distributions rather than individual probability values. **Bayesian inference** deals with the properties of probability distributions and deducing the properties of a population using some observed data and Bayes Theorem.

In this statistical approach, the end result is that rather than using single numbers for each of the terms in Bayes rule, we instead use **probability distribution functions (PDFs)**. Since we use PDFs for the likelihood, the prior, and the evidence, the posterior is also expressed as a PDF. These PDFs constitute the particular model for our data and the system and are represented with certain symbols. Instead of dealing with an event like $p+$, we now deal with probability distributions that are characterized by some set of parameters, Θ. For example, a Gaussian distribution is characterized by its mean and standard deviation so we'd represent those parameters as $\Theta = \{\mu, \sigma\}$.

The data we saw in the single number version of Bayes theorem was something like $t+$, which represented the test result and is used to calculate probability numbers like the evidence, $P(t+)$. In a statistical inference model, the data consists of some set of observations and is usually represented as $Y = \{y_1, y_2, \ldots, y_n\}$; instead of Y, you might see the letter D used for the observed data instead. In this formulation, the evidence $P(Y)$, the denominator in Equation (10.3), doesn't reference any of the model parameters (Θ) in which we're interested and, in fact, the evidence isn't even a distribution; it's just a number that's needed to ensure the final product is normalized between 0 and 1 like a good probability should be.

As it turns out, this normalizing constant which ensures that the integral (or the sum) of the PDF adds up to 1 is usually very difficult to compute so the evidence (the denominator in Equation (10.3)) is often just ignored and we instead change the equality in Equation (10.3) to a proportionality and carry on as if nothing else has changed as we're usually interested in only the peaks of the distribution not the actual value of the entire distribution itself. When we visualize these probability distributions, the narrower the curve (e.g., for the posterior), the more informative it is about the value of the parameters; so a wider curve is, in general, less informative about the parameter values.

Statistical inference problems are hard as these probability distributions can get quite messy. One trick that's widely used to make the math easier is to employ distributions that can serve as **conjugate distributions**: these are distributions that belong to the same family of distributions (like the Gaussian or multinomial) such that when you multiply them together, you end up with another distribution in the same family.

Suppose you have a likelihood PDF, as observed from data, that follows say a Gaussian distribution; if you then pick a prior probability distribution function that's also a Gaussian, your posterior probability distribution function will end up also being a Gaussian. In this case, a Gaussian is considered **self-conjugate** but you have other such pairings which are quite popular, like the Multinomial-Dirichlet conjugate prior pairing for *topic modeling* approaches such as **Latent Dirichlet Allocation (LDA)** or the Binomial-Beta conjugate prior pairing for simple question scenarios.

Topic models like the LDA are an approach for unsupervised classification of unlabelled data by clustering words, either text words or other symbolic representation "words", into natural groups that might correspond to an abstract semantic label, or topic. For example, documents on physics will mention entropy more often than documents on cake recipes. Topic models model both topic and word distributions as Dirichlet distributions so a document is made up of a mixture of topics and each topic is made up of words, all following such distributions.

If you can't pick your own priors to be nice like conjugate priors, you have to rely on other approaches like using **Markov chain Monte Carlo (MCMC)** methods and its many variants. MCMC is useful for *sampling* from a complex distribution, perhaps like the posterior distribution we want, when we can't easily *compute* that entire distribution. The MCMC variants will allow us to draw samples from such distributions and can also be used to do things like compute high-dimensional integrals which are common in machine learning and physics.

10.5.6 Supervised Learning with Naive Bayes

Bayes Theorem tests how much you can trust the evidence that's coming in, as we saw in the case of the pregnancy test, in which the second test confirmed even more strongly our initial suspicion. In the same way, we can utilize Bayes rule to help machines learn from data as the machine sees more and more of the data, or evidence.

The most popular application of Bayes theorem to machine learning is in classification and it makes a couple of seemingly strong assumptions: it assumes that feature sets for both of the two classes are identical and most importantly, and naively, that all features are independent of each other; that means for two features, *A* and *B*, their joint probability will be, $P(A, B) = P(A)P(B)$ since they're independent of each other. This naive assumption sometimes actually helps the classification as it counts the same evidence twice for the two different independent features; if the features weren't independent, that evidence would only be counted once.

The approach of using this naive assumption is called Naive Bayes and it often performs better than other models like Logistic Regression when classifying categorical variables. In these cases, it is fast and doesn't require a lot of training data. When dealing with numerical data, you can model it as a normal distribution, although that might be a strong assumption in some cases. With all these assumptions, Naive Bayes can be a bad estimator sometimes but it's usually good enough for some applications and an easy benchmark to implement and compare with more sophisticated approaches.

```
### Load Required Libraries
from sklearn.datasets import load_iris # Get Iris dataset
from sklearn.model_selection import train_test_split
from sklearn.naive_bayes import GaussianNB
from sklearn import metrics

# Load Iris Dataset and get the Features matrix and Label vector
iris = load_iris()
X = iris.data
y = iris.target

### Create the Training and Testing Datasets
(X_train, X_test, y_train, y_test) = \
    train_test_split(X, y, test_size=0.4, random_state=1)

### Create and train the model:
gnb = GaussianNB()
gnb.fit(X_train, y_train)
y_pred = gnb.predict(X_test) # Make the predictions on Test Dataset

### Get accuracy of ground truth (y_test) vs predicted labels (y_pred)
acc = metrics.accuracy_score(y_test, y_pred)*100
print("Our model's accuracy on the Iris dataset is:", acc)
```

Listing 10.3: Gaussian Naive Bayes classifier on the Iris Dataset.

We can see how easy it is to implement such a Naive Bayes classifier in Python, as seen in Listing 10.3, where we again use `scikit-learn`, just as we did earlier for the decision tree classifier in Listing 10.1. Just as we saw there, we first import the required libraries in Lines 1 - 5, load the default Iris dataset which has data like the sepal length for various Iris flowers, and then use the same `train_test_split()`, `fit()`, and `predict()` functions before we also use the same `metrics.accuracy_score()` metric to evaluate how well our classifier did which, in this case, gave a result of 95%; not too shabby for a default classifier cobbled together in about 20 lines of code![29]

---

[29] The only difference is that we used a Gaussian Naive Bayes classifier since we're dealing with continuous values; as such, each continuous value (like sepal length = 5.1 for Iris flower #1) is assumed to be distributed according to a Gaussian distribution and so the likelihood is converted to the result of a Gaussian, like 5.1 being converted to 1.094 as follows:

$$P(x_i|Y) = \frac{1}{\sigma_Y\sqrt{2\pi}}e^{-\frac{(x_i-\mu_Y)^2}{2\sigma_Y^2}} \rightarrow P(x_i = 5.1|Y = ''I.setosa'') = \frac{1}{\sigma_{Y=''I.setosa''}\sqrt{2\pi}}e^{-\frac{(x_i=5.1-\mu_{Y=''I.setosa''})^2}{2\sigma_{Y=''I.setosa''}^2}}$$

$$= \frac{1}{0.35\sqrt{2\pi}}e^{-\frac{(5.1-5)^2}{2(0.35^2)}} = 1.14e^{-0.041} = 1.094$$

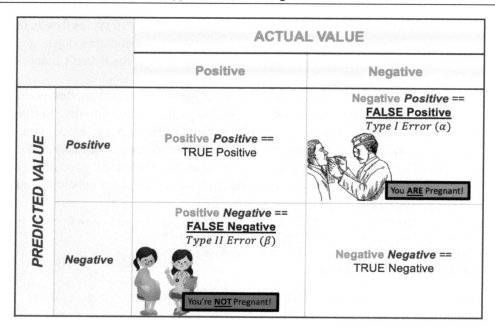

Figure 10.21: Confusion matrix with True Positive, True Negative, False Positive, and False Negative classifications. In a Hypothesis Testing framework, the null hypothesis, the statement we want to falsify, usually indicates there is no real effect. A **false positive** (α) is incorrectly rejecting the null hypothesis while a **false negative** (β) is incorrectly accepting the null hypothesis. Alpha, α, is the significance level used in Hypothesis Testing and Beta, β, is used to determine the statistical **power** of a study, which is the probability that it rejects a false negative, $1 - \beta$.

10.5.7 Common Statistical Metrics

We can figure out all the possible combinations of true positives, false positives, true negatives, and false negatives in a **confusion table**. We can then use this confusion matrix, as shown in Figure 10.21, to derive some associated metrics to help gauge the validity of our machine learning models:

1. **Accuracy**: The ratio of the correctly predicted observations to the total number of observations. Accuracy works well for symmetric datasets where the values of FP and FN are proportional or for datasets with an even, balanced distribution where the TN or TP are not dis-proportionately large; if the dataset is imbalanced, it leads to the **accuracy paradox**, which requires other measures like Precision, Recall, or F1 Score to fully assess a model. Overall, how often is it right?

$$\frac{\text{All Correct Picks}}{\text{All Possible Choices}} = \frac{TP+TN}{TP+TN+FP+FN}$$

2. **Error**: Also known as **Misclassification**: the complement of Accuracy is **Error** = (1 - Accuracy). Overall, how often is it wrong?

$$\frac{\text{All INcorrect Picks}}{\text{All Possible Choices}} = \frac{FP+FN}{TP+TN+FP+FN}$$

3. **Prior Probability**: P(Disease+) = (TP+FN) / (TP+FP+TN+FN) Also called the **Pre-Test Probability**, this is the estimated likelihood of disease before the test is conducted. If this is calculated

on the entire population, it will also be the **Prevalence** of the disease in the population at large.

$$\frac{\text{ACTUAL Positives}}{\text{All Possible Choices}} = \frac{TP+FN}{TP+TN+FP+FN}$$

4. The **Predictive Value of a Negative Test**: P(Disease- | Test-) = TN / (TN+FN) This is the proportion of patients who do not have the disease and test negative for the disease. The **Post-Test Probability** of the disease given the patient tests negative is 1 - Predictive Value of a Negative Test.

$$\frac{\text{TRUE Negatives}}{\text{Predicted Negatives}} = \frac{TN}{TN+FN}$$

5. **Precision**: P(Disease+ | Test+) = TP / (TP+FP) The **Predictive Value of a Positive Test** is the proportion of patients who actually have the disease and test positive for the disease. This is helpful when *False Positives are costly*. When it predicts positive, how often is it correct?

$$\frac{\text{TRUE Positives}}{\text{Predicted Positives}} = \frac{TP}{TP+FP}$$

6. **Recall**: P(Test+ | Disease+) = TP / (TP+FN) This is also known as **Sensitivity** and the **True Positive Rate**. This is helpful when *False Negatives are costly*. When it's actually positive, how often does it predict positive?

$$\frac{\text{TRUE Positives}}{\text{ACTUAL Positives}} = \frac{TP}{TP+FN}$$

7. **Specificity**: P(Test- | Disease-) = TN / (TN + FP) Also known as the **True Negative Rate**. When it's actually negative, how often does it predict negative?

$$\frac{\text{TRUE Negatives}}{\text{ACTUAL Negatives}} = \frac{TN}{TN+FP}$$

8. **False Positive Rate**: When it's actually negative, how often does it predict positive?

$$\frac{\text{False Positives}}{\text{ACTUAL Negatives}} = \frac{FP}{TN+FP}$$

There are also alternate measures that are effective like the **F1 Score**, the weighted arithmetic mean of Precision and Recall. This measure can be helpful if you need to strike a balance between Precision and Recall in a dataset with an un-even, skewed distribution where it has a large number of TN, for example.

$$F1 = 2 \times \left(\frac{\text{Precision} \times \text{Recall}}{\text{Precision} + \text{Recall}} \right)$$

Although this weighted average isn't as intuitive as accuracy, it's more useful for *uneven class distributions* as it accounts for both the False Positives and the False Negatives. E.g., if we want to catch terrorists and examine a billion people, we can label all of them as Not Terrorists. In this case, our accuracy is awesome but our TP is 0 so both Precision and Recall are 0 and so our F1 is also 0.

There are also additional measures that are widely used, like the Receiver Operating Characteristic (ROC) curve, Area Under the ROC Curve (AUC), etc., which are useful under certain circumstances, especially when you want to rank predictions about both the positive and negative classes and your dataset is relatively well-balanced. The ROC curve gives a measure of the performance of a classification model at all classification thresholds. When it is well-balanced, accuracy is also an informative metric. But it's likely always a good idea to show the confusion matrix and F1 score and, especially if your data is unbalanced or costly, to use the false positive and false negative via the precision and recall, respectively.

When to use which metrics?

Many classification algorithms like decision trees use all of these metrics as well as metrics used for general **predictive models** like the **cross-validation error**. In general, the following metrics are usually good fits with Supervised and Unsupervised learners as a rough heuristic:

- Supervised Learning: Classification: Precision-Recall, ROC, AUC, Accuracy, Log-Loss, etc.
- Supervised Learning: Regression: MSPE, MSAE, R-Squared, Adjusted R-Square, etc.
- Unsupervised Learning: Rand Index, Mutual Information, etc.

Problem 10.2 We know that, when evaluating a potential model, we can gauge it as:
- High Precision + High Recall: Great model
- High Precision + Low Recall: Misses positive cases but great at the ones it does catch
- Low Precision + High Recall: Gets most of the positives but has lots of false alarms
- High Specificity: Minimize false positives: let 10 guilty go free but don't convict an innocent
- Low Precision + Low Recall: Terrible model, better to just guess randomly

So the first model obviously performs the best and the last model obviously performs the worst but, of the remaining three evaluation metrics for three different models, which model would you use to detect diseases like cancer? How about for spotting terrorists? How about winning football teams?

10.6 The Entropy Strikes Back

The mathematical underpinnings of creating decision trees are important as they're applicable to many other algorithms, not just algorithms for classification. These underpinnings also bring together fundamental ideas from Part I, especially the idea of Shannon Information and Shannon Information Entropy as we saw in Section 1.9. Let's dive right in by looking at **random variables** in detail. *This section will be a bit concept heavy so please do feel free to skim it if it seems to plod along.*

Summary of Entropy

As we saw in Section 1.9, $h(p)$ is **Shannon's Information Function** and is a *measure of the decrease in uncertainty* at the receiver's end: $h(p) = log_2(\frac{1}{p})$. It's a *measure of unpredictability* or uncertainty. It is also the *amount of surprise*: the smaller the probability, the higher the surprise and the higher the information. The goal in machine learning is usually to reduce uncertainty.

Shannon's Information Entropy is $H(p)$ and is the average Shannon Information per symbol: the sum of Shannon Information for each symbol weighted by the probability of that symbol and is defined as $-\sum_i^N p_i log_x(p_i)$, as seen in Section 1.10. The higher the entropy, the higher the Shannon Information content of a system: this is how many bits of Shannon Information we need on average to describe its exact state. We can also think of it as the average of the surprise associated with all the possible observations. This is also the average uncertainty: the goal of most machine learning is **to lower** uncertainty and hence **to lower** Entropy!

Entropy is *maximized* when the states are *equiprobable* and all have the same likelihood. In order for the average Shannon Information to be high, the distribution of probabilities must allow for a large number of unlikely events. We can think of it as a measure of the spreading out of the probabilities. So the more spread out the probabilities (all states are equally likely), the higher the entropy.

10.6.1 Random Variables

In order to define a random variable, we'll need to establish a few other definitions related to the possible observations of some random phenomenon. A random phenomenon or a random experiment, ε, is one where we don't know exactly what the result will be ahead of time. A random action or a series of actions, perhaps the result of an experiment, is called a **trial**. A random, non-deterministic phenomenon or experiment can result in a certain **outcome**, ω. The outcome is the result of the trial.

The set of all possible outcomes is the **sample space**, Ω. The specific outcomes recorded for a particular experiment are a subset of the sample space and are called the **event**. The event is just a specific collection of outcomes and the size of an event is the number of outcomes in that event. The set of all possible events is the **event space**, Σ. An event space contains all the possible events for a particular experiment or phenomenon.

Although an individual random event is non-deterministic or unpredictable, random phenomena often follow a probability function overall so we can assign a probability or frequency to different outcomes over a number of events or trials. Randomness can also be considered a measure of the uncertainty of a particular outcome. A random process thus follows a probability distribution.

We can then define the **probability** of a particular event, E, as:[30]

$$P(E) = \frac{\text{Size of Event}}{\text{Size of Sample Space}} = \frac{\text{\# of Outcomes in the Event}}{\text{\# of Possible Outcomes in the Sample Space}}$$

For example, if you have a die, the sample space, Ω, might be all possible rolls: $\Omega = \{1, 2, 3, 4, 5, 6\}$. A particular outcome, ω, might be $\omega = 3$, where you roll a 3. An event, E, might be rolling a number greater than or equal to 3: $E_{\text{roll} \geq 3} = \{3, 4, 5, 6\}$. Then, the $P(E_{\text{roll} \geq 3})$ is:

---

[30]The most fundamental, and unrealizable, definition of probability is the frequentist one: $P(E) = \lim_{n \to \infty} \frac{n(E)}{n}$ where n is the number of trials of an experiment and $n(E)$ is the number of trials that result in E.

$$P(E_{\text{roll} \geq 3}) = \frac{\text{\# of Outcomes in the Event}}{\text{\# of Possible Outcomes in the Sample Space}} = \frac{4}{6} = \frac{2}{3}$$

A **probability distribution function (PDF)** defines the probability of every possible *event* in order to compute the **probability distribution**. It assigns a probability to *every* event possible such that the probability of Ω, the entire sample space, is equal to 1. A **probability space**, thus, is a sample space that has a probability function defined on it. We can then define a **random variable** as a **function** on that probability space that *maps outcomes* in the sample space (like ω) to the set of real numbers, $\mathbb{R}$.

Notational Information

To simplify notation, I differentiate between the probability of an event in Σ, described by a probability distribution function, and the intermediate functions used to calculate the probability of a random variable assuming a certain value. So I use $P(\cdot)$ to indicate the former (the probability value from the Probability Distribution Function) and $Pr(\cdot)$ to indicate the latter, the probability of a random variable having a specific value (discrete random variable) or being near a specific value (continuous random variable).

In addition, I abbreviate a general Probability Distribution Function as **PDF** and I abbreviate the particular functions used to calculate the probability of a random variable as either **pmf** (Probability Mass Function), if it has a specific value, or as **pdf** (Probability Density Function), if it's near a specific value, as we'll see shortly.[31]

Suppose we are interested in the event of a die roll being greater than or equal to 3 for a single die roll. Our event would be made up of four outcomes as, $E_{\text{roll} \geq 3} = \{3, 4, 5, 6\}$. We could create a random variable called X that has the values of 0 or 1, two real numbers. The random variable X *maps* those two real values to the outcomes as follows: it maps 0 to the outcomes of rolling a 1 or 2 and it maps 1 to the outcomes of rolling a $3, 4, 5$, or 6. We can say the first mapping corresponds to the event of rolling less than a 3: $E_{\text{roll} < 3} = \{1, 2\}$ and the second mapping corresponds to the event of rolling a 3 or higher: $E_{\text{roll} \geq 3} = \{3, 4, 5, 6\}$. The random variable X is then $X = \{0, 1\}$. We can calculate a probability for each of these values of the random variable, X:

---

[31] Another function that's related to the probability distributions of random variables is the **Cumulative Distribution Function (CDF)**. In general, a non-random, known, deterministic variable doesn't need a distribution to describe it, of course. But for a random variable, the CDF gives us the probability of a particular random variable having a value up to a certain quantity. For example, the probability distribution for rolling a die is given by a **pmf**. You could compute the probability for this discrete random variable assuming a value less than or equal to 3. The 3 outcomes which fulfill that condition each have a probability of $\frac{1}{6}$. The *cumulative* probability would be the *addition* of those three probabilities and so is $\frac{1}{2}$. The CDF of a discrete random variable is then $F(x) = Pr(X \leq x) = \sum_{x_i \leq x} Pr(X = x_i)$, with integrals replacing sums for **pdf**s.

$$Pr(X = 0) = \frac{\text{Number of Outcomes in } E_{\text{roll}<3}}{\text{Number of Outcomes in } \Omega} = \frac{2}{6} = \frac{1}{3}$$

$$Pr(X = 1) = \frac{\text{Number of Outcomes in } E_{\text{roll}\geq 3}}{\text{Number of Outcomes in } \Omega} = \frac{4}{6} = \frac{2}{3}$$

It's important to note that the random variable X is a **function**, regardless of what the name might imply. As such, the random variable X is a function that maps outcomes to real numbers. We could technically represent this as $X = 0 \implies \{\omega \in \Omega : X(\omega) = 0\}$ which says that $X = 0$ is a shorthand for referring to the **set** that consists of all the outcomes ω that are mapped to the real number 0. We forego this rather cumbersome technical expression and just look at $X = 0$ without any direct reference to Ω.

The random variable X has its own sample space and events so we can refer to the probability that X takes on a specific value, or a range of values, as the value of the probability function for X: $Pr(X = 1) = 4/6 = 2/3$. We can think of this as $Pr(X = \text{value}) = \textit{probability of that value}$ and this is read as "Probability that X is equal to 1 is 2/3".

Discrete vs Continuous Random Variable

A **Discrete Random Variable** is a random variable that can take any of a discrete set of values from the set of integers. In this case, the Probability Distribution Function (PDF) uses the probabilities calculated by a **Probability Mass Function (pmf)** which is defined, for any value x, as the probability that the random variable X equals the value x: $Pr(x) = Pr(X = x) = P_X(x)$. The pmf $Pr(x)$ has to be non-negative for each possible value x and must sum to 1; these conditions are expressed as $Pr(x) \geq 0$ and $\sum_x Pr(x) = 1$. For example, the pmf for a die is $Pr(x) = \begin{cases} \frac{1}{6} & \text{if } x \in 1,2,3,4,5,6 \\ 0 & \text{otherwise} \end{cases}$

A **Continuous Random Variable**, on the other hand, can take any real number on the interval $[0, 1]$ with equal probability. It can take any value from any continuum actually but it's easier to transform, or normalize, it to the $[0, 1]$ range. Since a continuum is uncountable, we can't sum over it directly and must integrate over that range instead. Thus, the Probability Distribution Function (PDF) for a continuous variable depends upon a **Probability Density Function (pdf)**, which is represented as $\rho(x)$ and which assigns a probability that X is *near* a value x rather than exactly equal to a value x. We use the pdf to get the probability distribution by calculating the probabilities as $Pr(X \in A) = \int A \rho(x) dx$.

Thus, the probability that X is in any set A (such that $X \in A$) is obtained by integrating $\rho(x)$ over the set A. This means the probability for a single point is 0 since the integral over a single point is 0 (i.e., the set A contains a single element above). In addition, the pmf must be positive and integrate to 1 since $\rho(x) \geq 0$ and $\int \rho(x) dx = 1$ (the integral is over all values of X).

A common pdf that's often found in nature is a Gaussian distribution which, for standard Gaussian Random Variables with mean $\mu = 0$ and standard deviation $\sigma = 1$, is:

$$\rho(x) = \frac{1}{\sqrt{2\pi}\sigma} e^{-\frac{(x-\mu)^2}{2\sigma^2}} \rightarrow \frac{1}{\sqrt{2\pi}} e^{-\frac{x^2}{2}} \text{ (Standard Gaussian)}$$

For a Gaussian Distribution the mean = mode = median, which is a very helpful property as you can then completely specify it with just the mean, μ, and standard deviation, σ. For the standard Gaussian random variable above, this is shown as $X \sim N(0, 1)$.

In addition, the **Central Limit Theorem** states that if you take sufficiently large random samples from some population, the mean of the *sampling distribution* will be the mean of the population for many systems. In fact, quite a few systems exhibit a Gaussian distribution naturally; systems like diffusion of particles, heights of people in a university, etc., since any natural process that preserves information about only the mean and the standard deviation can be characterized as a Gaussian.

Finally, as we saw in Section 10.5.5 when we discussed *conjugate priors*, unlike other distributions, a Gaussian tends to produce another Gaussian as the result of a transformation like product, sum, convolution, fourier tranform, etc.

Binomial Distribution

The binomial distribution is another popular distribution in which we deal with the likelihood of things like coin tosses, a pregnancy test, making a basketball shot, etc. In all these situations, each **outcome** has only **two possibilities** or states: success or failure. The **event space** is finite, which means we have a **finite** number of trials only.

Each event's outcome must be **mutually exclusive** (either success or failure but not both) and the event's likelihood should be **complementary**, in that the sum of the probabilities for each outcome must be 1. Finally, each sample or trial should be **independent** of the previous one such that the previous trials don't affect the current trial.

If an experiment meets these criteria, its distribution can then be described as:
$$P(X = k) = nC_k * p^k (1-p)^{n-k}$$
where nC_k is "n choose k" and is defined to be:
$$nC_k = \binom{N}{k} = \frac{n!}{k!(n-k)!}$$

10.6.2 Shannon Information, Shannon Information Entropy, and Information Gain

We can then define the entropy of a random variable in a couple of ways: either we can define it axiomatically as a certain measure with certain properties or we can motivate its definition by showing it can answer natural questions that arise in studying physical phenomena. Once we've defined entropy, perhaps as in Section 1.10, we can see that the larger the entropy of a specific distribution, the harder it will be to predict it (or compress it) and the more spread out (or less spiky) it will be.

Overall, **entropy** becomes a *measure of how much information* can be encoded in a message. The higher the entropy, the higher the information content that can be potentially resolved from it. Entropy can also be considered to be a *measure of the amount of uncertainty* in a message since information and uncertainty are equivalent concepts in this formulation. When looking at message encoding, entropy can even give the actual number of bits of information that are contained in a message source.

We can also look at entropy from a physical perspective, as we saw in Section 1.10.1. Since any given macrostate can be achieved by a large number of **microstates**, which particular microstate describes the current state of the system is missing and is captured by this idea of entropy. For example, if I roll three dice and say the sum was 11 (this is the macrostate of the three dice system), you don't know which particular configuration of the dice (which microstate) corresponds to that macrostate: was it two 5's and one 1? Was it two 4's and one 3? Was it two 3's and one 5? etc.

As we saw in Section 1.10.1, entropy is really a **bookkeeping tool** to keep track of all the degrees of freedom we abstracted out by not including them directly in our calculation. We can do a little bookkeeping and keep track of the possibilities by calculating a number to represent all the microstates; if all these *microstates* of a System P, Ω_P, are equally likely, the number we can use to make sure we can add the microstates and probabilities correctly (e.g., if we add more die to our dice system) uses the logarithm. And our bookkeeping quantity becomes the Entropy, $S = ln(\Omega_P)$, what we called $S = ln(N)$ earlier in Section 1.10.1. If there's only one possible microstate, then $S = ln(1) = 0$ and we know everything there is to know about the system. As we increase the number of microstates, the amount we don't know, the **missing information**, increases, as does the uncertainty about which state we'll discover when we measure or observe the system. Entropy is a way to keep track of our ignorance about the underlying physical system: it is not a property of the system itself but a property of what we know or measure about the system.

And this is what we keep track of when we observe a particular outcome of one random variable of the system and see how it reduces the overall uncertainty based on another random variable of the system; i.e., $\Delta H = H(X) - H(X|Y = y_i)$ and this **reduction in uncertainty** is our **increase in information** of the system. Shannon Information, which is defined as $h(x) = -log(p(x))$, reflects a *decrease in uncertainty* (or an *increase in the amount of surprise*) when that **event** x occurs: this is what we call the amount of information **contained** in a discrete event x that we can *potentially observe*. An *event* is a particular *outcome*, or a subset of the sample space, from an experiment or a physical system that is modelled by a random variable.

The idea is to gauge how surprising some **single event** is; if it has a low probability of occurrence (like winning the lottery), it's very surprising and reduces a larger uncertainty (high information); if it has a high probability of occurrence and will almost definitely happen (like the sunrise tomorrow), it's not very surprising and so doesn't really reduce the uncertainty as it was expected (low information).

We can generalize that *decrease in uncertainty* (or an increase in the amount of surprise) to a **random variable** itself: this lets us quantify the amount of information that we can potentially observe for a random variable X with a probability distribution P. We can do this by calculating the amount of information we can potentially observe for the probability distribution of **all the events** for that random variable. In terms of just the probability distribution of a random variable, we can think of it as the number of bits required to encode or represent or transmit an event that is drawn from the probability distribution for that random variable.

In terms of physical systems, this is the amount of **potential information** in that system. Entropy is sometimes also called the expected value of self-information: entropy is the average amount of information we could gain about a system when we sample the random variable. The more balanced the probability distribution, the more surprising drawing a single event will be, so the higher the entropy, and the higher the potential information in that system. Conversely, the more skewed a probability distribution is, with some events being exponentially more likely than others for example, the less surprising it is to draw one of those likely events, so the lower the entropy, and the lower the potential information in that system.

Information gain is the decrease in entropy when we transform a system or a dataset in some way. The decrease in entropy is the same as a decrease in uncertainty (or an increase in the amount of surprise) and so an increase in the **amount of information gained**: $I(X : Y) = H(X) - H(X|Y) = H(Y) -$

$H(Y|X)$ for the *random variables* X and Y and is derived from the **Joint Entropy**, $H(X,Y) = H(X) + H(Y|X) = H(Y) + H(X|Y)$. You can calculate it by comparing the entropy before the transformation to the entropy after the transformation (of the dataset or the physical system). Information Gain is also called **Mutual Information** when it's applied to variable selection and is used in decision trees and *feature selection*. In decision trees, it's weighted by the number of elements in each side, as we'll see.

10.6.3 Entropy and Information in Terms of Number of States of Physical Systems

Information, therefore, allows us to make predictions about a system that are better than by chance alone. In order to assess a physical system, we characterize it by first defining what we consider to be the system (using **abstraction**) and what we'll measure on that system. Different definitions of the same underlying mechanism can resolve to different models of the system.

As we've seen, entropy is the lack of information, or the amount of uncertainty, and is given in terms of the log of the number of unknown states so that joint entropies can be added instead of multiplied. For example, if System 1 has N_1 states and System 2 has N_2 states, their joint system would have $N_1 \times N_2$ states.

We then consider **information to be a difference of entropies**. Information, the difference between two entropy values, is the actual content whereas the entropy values themselves can vary depending on how the system is defined. In fact, as noted by physicist and biologist Christoph Adami, the entropy of any physical object is infinite and only has a finite realization due to the finite nature of the measuring devices chosen (the choice of which depends on how the system is defined). This, as Adami shows in [6], is analogous to renormalization in Quantum Field Theory.

A **Random Variable** defines which states some system can take and with what probability for each state. These states were the outcomes with which we associated real numbers previously; those real numbers were like the labels or identifiers for those outcomes. How do we get those probabilities? Perhaps by frequencies of observation as we saw in the footnote to the definition of probability above. A random variable assumes you know things about the underlying system such as: the number of possible states to expect, what those states are, and possibly even what the likelihood is of experiencing those states. The entropy formula depends on the random variable and thus on knowing the possible outcomes and the probability distribution, perhaps from some underlying theory or frequentist observation.

Conditional Probability is the likelihood of two events occurring simultaneously when the second event has already occurred. Simultaneity means conditional probability cannot be defined unambiguously in a relativistic physics framework. We know that entropy is the uncertainty defined for a random variable. In addition, physical systems can be modeled by random variables only when you create a model, abstracting out information as reflected in the measurement devices we can use on that system. Entropy is defined by this model (and the corresponding measuring device). Information Theory, then, is just the theory of the relative states of measurement devices!

Conditional Entropy

Specific Conditional Entropy, $H(X|Y = v)$, is the entropy of the **random variable** X among only those cases in which the random variable Y has the value v. The **overall conditional entropy** or general conditional entropy, $H(X|Y)$, is the *average* of all the specific conditional entropies; i.e., it is the average of the specific conditional entropy across *all* values of Y. Since this involves probabilities, we cannot simply take the mean of the values but can, instead, weight them with the probabilities themselves.

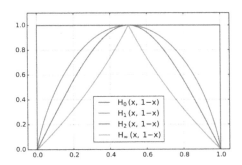

Figure 10.22: Rényi Entropy: generalizes the Hartley entropy, the Shannon entropy, the collision entropy, and the min-entropy: (H_0, H_1, H_2, and H_∞ respectively).

If the probabilities in $H(X)$ are not uniform (equiprobable), then they can be considered conditional probabilities by default (for any non-uniform distribution). The entropy of the equiprobable probability states is the **Unconditional Entropy** H_{max} and is the maximum value it can have. Information is then $H_{max} - H_{conditional}$, the unconditional entropy minus conditional entropy. Information can also be characterized as the *Shared Entropy*: $I(X:Y) = H(X) - H(X|Y) = H(Y) - H(Y|X)$. These are the *observed* entropies of X, $H(X)$, and the actual observed entropy of X given what we know about the state of Y, $H(X|Y)$. This means that we're not aware we got our information from source Y. This can be derived from the *joint entropy*, $H(X,Y) = H(X) + H(Y|X) = H(Y) + H(X|Y)$.

Entropy can also be thought of as "potential" information: how much we *could* know. Here, we say $I = H_{max} - H(X)$; in this case, H_{max} is what we don't know about X and $H(X)$ is what we observed about X (without regard to another system Y). This means that we're not aware of how we got the information.

10.6.4 Entropy for Classification

Entropy is very useful for classification algorithms, as well. Categorical features, like non-numeric features, are unordered. We can encode the classes as integers but the numeric order will still be meaningless for them. Because of this, for class variables, we can check the mode but not other averages like the mean.

Instead, we can use Entropy as a way to measure the "amount of mix" in class variables since entropy measures the extent of mixture of values in the variable(s). It's analogous to the "spread" in a numeric variable. As we saw earlier, entropy can also be thought of as the expected surprise from some observation. How surprising an event is depends on its probability. If it has a really low probability, we'll be really surprised to see it → That means, it has higher entropy!

Let's see an example by examining how to define entropy for a variable with only two possible values. Let's say we have a coin; in this case, $Pr(X = Heads) = 0$ means we never get heads while $Pr(X = Heads) = 1$ means that we always get heads. Those are extreme probability values; for intermediate probability values, we'll need a "mix" of the possible values.

Entropy is the function that allows mixing of the two possible values to intermediate values. Entropy measures the uncertainty in the state of a system and is a measurement function that is maximum at maximum **impurity**, where we would say that the values 0 and 1 would be **pure** values. Maximum uncertainty is when it's "mixed" or "impure". Entropy is thus used in machine learning for feature selection or deciding on splits in decision trees.

In general, entropy is at a maximum when all outcomes have equal probability. Any movement away from that, in either direction, reduces the entropy value regardless of whether it's towards heads or tails, as seen in Figure 10.22; in other words, the order or the class doesn't matter. For more than two values, or classes, evenly spaced or evenly spread probability distributions have higher entropy than distributions with concentrations of probability values in a subset of possible values.

We can then use joint entropy, $H(X,Y) = H(X) + H(Y|X) = H(Y) + H(X|Y)$, to derive the information as, $I(X : Y) = H(X) - H(X|Y) = H(Y) - H(Y|X)$. Here, we use the conditional entropy, $H(X|Y)$, which measures the entropy remaining in a system or variable after it has been conditioned by another variable. The main goal of machine learning is to lower the entropy or uncertainty, which is the weighted average of the entropies of the various possible conditions or variables. The total entropy can be thought of as the remaining entropy or uncertainty: the lower the conditional entropy, the lower the remaining entropy!

As we saw in Section 1.9, there are many different types of entropies. Rényi Entropy generalizes these various entropies, including the Hartley entropy, the Shannon entropy, the collision entropy and the min-entropy: H_0, H_1, H_2, and H_∞ respectively (but it does not include the von Neumann or other quantum entropies). In general, entropy is at a maximum when the system is *impure* or *maximally mixed* or where all the *outcomes have equal probability*, as seen in Figure 10.22.

Problem 10.3 Suppose you've been busy with this CS0 course and your room has descended into chaos and become a complete mess. You come in and clean it up so it's neater than it's ever been. Has the entropy of your room system gone up or down after you cleaned it up? Was information gained or not?

10.6.5 Entropy for Decision Trees

We know that entropy is related to the number of microstates: that's why it's often said to be a measure of disorder. Data might be similarly disordered or unorganized or impure; this means that entropy is like a measure of the **variance** or the **impurity** of the data. The goal of a lot of machine learning, like decision trees, is to **reduce entropy** which will **decrease uncertainty** and so **increase information**.

This means that information **gain** is equal to a **decrease** in entropy. This is also the amount of uncertainty an observation resolves. This then implies that *the greater the Shannon Entropy, the greater the Information we could gain after observing the outcome of a probabilistic event*. This is a way to quantify the potential reduction in uncertainty, the amount of information that's lacking before observing the outcome of a probabilistic process. Since entropy can measure how *impure* or *mixed* some system is, we can use entropy in cases where we need to separate out parts of it, just as we do in decision trees, as we'll see next.

10.7 Learning in Decision Trees

Now that we have all the mathematical and theoretical underpinnings, let's revisit our original decision tree model from Section 10.2.3. Our first algorithm needed to be simple and intuitive and to allow us to clearly see the logic that leads to solution, as opposed to some esoteric algorithm that worked like a black box. The decision tree algorithm fit these criteria by creating a graph structure that looks like an upside down tree, as seen in Figure 10.4.[32] This directed tree structure consists of a top, root node which branches to other, internal nodes via edges or links; the final, terminal level of nodes are called the leaves of the tree.

---

[32] A decision tree, in general, is a non-linear classifier that is locally linear, piecewise linear in a neighbourhood, and can deal with both categorical (classification tree, binary or multi-class) and numerical values (regression tree). In fact, decision

Each of the nodes represents a different feature or attribute we deem to be informative; the branches represent the questions or decisions or rules associated with each feature; and the leaves represent the final outcome, which is usually a categorical answer to the question or the result of the decision/rule (it could also be a continuous value like a probability in the general case). Our overall goal is to use our dataset to end up with a single classification outcome.[33]

Our approach will be to find characteristics, or features, in our data. We'll map each feature to a node that will test that feature. Each outgoing branch from the node will correspond to a feature value and, at the end, each leaf node will assign a classification, or a probability distribution over the classifications. The decision tree will thus be a *function* that maps training examples from our dataset to one of the possible classes or categories. The path from the root node to leaf node contains all the training samples that will be used for the final outcome's calculation where each branch is considered an AND operation.

The **learning** in this algorithm will consist of deciding how to build the tree, including the ordering of the features, represented as nodes, as well as the number of splits or branches that go out from each node. The algorithm thus learns the structure of the tree (e.g., the number of splits per node), the threshold values at each node, and the final values output by the leaves. These are the parameters.[34]

Entropy itself for a random variable X is defined as:

$$H(X) = -\sum_{i=1}^{N} p(X = x_i) log_2(p(X = x_i)) \tag{10.5}$$

So the total entropy of the Root Node is:

$$\begin{aligned} H(X_{root-node}) &= -p(X = "lettuce")log_2(p(X = "lettuce")) - p(X = "carrots")log_2(p(X = "carrots")) \\ &\quad - p(X = "oranges")log_2(p(X = "oranges")) \\ &= -\frac{1}{4}log_2(\frac{1}{4}) - \frac{1}{4}log_2(\frac{1}{4}) - \frac{2}{4}log_2(\frac{2}{4}) \\ &= .25 * 2 + .25 * 2 + .5 * 1 \\ &= 1.5 \end{aligned}$$

For our first potential split, we ask the question, "Is it orange coloured?" To answer this question, we need to work out the class probabilities for Orange vs Not-Orange elements. We use upper case $P(\cdot)$ for the class probabilities in this calculation:

---

trees would be inefficient for linear relationships where a linear classifier, like the generative Naive Bayes or discriminative Logistic Regression, or regression for linear problems, like Linear Regression or Support Vector Regression, might be better suited.

[33] We could also think in terms of minimizing the training error or maximizing the training accuracy instead of the single classification outcome. Each leaf node can predict its final outcome based on the average outcome of the training data in the nodes in that path. More precisely, each unique path from the Root node to a Leaf node defines a specific region, R; the outcome is either set to the most common value for the training examples in R (for a classification tree) or their mean (for a regression tree).

[34] The hyperparameters of the decision tree would be pruning parameters, either pre- or post-pruning, of a tree, like the maximum depth, maximum number of terminal nodes, and minimum samples for a node split. We can even create ensembles of multiple trees, either using boosting or bagging as in random forests. Each hypothesis in this approach, h, is a decision tree and all the hypotheses constitute the set of function hypotheses, $H = \{h | h : X \rightarrow Y\}$ where the output of the learning algorithm is the $h \in H$ that best approximates the unknown target function, f, based on the training examples from the dataset, by either minimizing the training error or maximizing training accuracy.

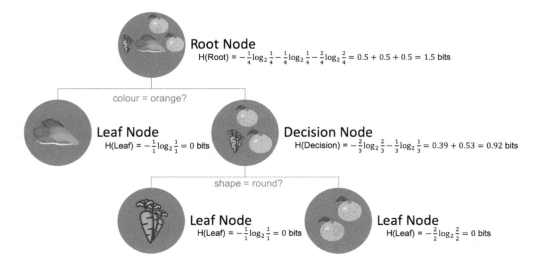

Figure 10.23: Decision Tree Example with Entropies for each node. The root node has 4 fruits and vegetables, while the decision node only has 3. The leaf nodes all have only one kind of fruit or vegetable. In each node, we calculate the entropy using the fraction of the total fruits and vegetables each kind of fruit or vegetable has in that particular node. E.g., in the Root Node, there are 4 fruits and vegetables with 2 oranges, 1 romaine lettuce, and 1 set of carrots. Hence, the fraction of carrots is $\frac{1}{4}$, the fraction of oranges is $\frac{2}{4}$, and the fraction of romaine lettuce is $\frac{1}{4}$. The entropy is measured in units of *bits*; the information gained would be the difference between the entropies between two nodes.

$$P(Y = "orange") = \frac{2}{5} = 0.4$$

$$P(Y = "not-orange") = \frac{3}{5} = 0.6$$

Then, let's compute the specific conditional entropy of the root node if we pick an Orange fruit or vegetable. This is the entropy of the remaining elements in the node after we've taken out the Orange elements; this is the same as the entropy of the first Decision Node in Figure 10.23. We can also compute the entropy of the "not-orange" part of the split and this would be the first leaf node on the left in Figure 10.23.

$$H(X|Y = "orange") = -p(X = "oranges")log_2(p(X = "oranges")) - p(X = "carrots")log_2(p(X = "carrots"))$$

$$= -\frac{2}{3}log_2(\frac{2}{3}) - \frac{1}{3}log_2(\frac{1}{3})$$

$$= .67 * .585 + .33 * 1.585 = 0.392 + 0.523$$

$$= 0.915 \approx 0.92$$

$$H(X|Y = "not-orange") = -p(X = "lettuce")log_2(p(X = "lettuce"))$$

$$= -\frac{1}{1}log_2(\frac{1}{1})$$

$$= 0$$

Finally, we can compute the *overall* or general conditional entropy, which is composed of all the specific conditional entropies weighted by their respective probabilities, as:

$$
\begin{aligned}
H(X|Y) &= \sum_{i=1}^{N} P(Y = v_i) H(X|Y = v_i) \\
&= P(Y = "orange") H(X|Y = "orange") + P(Y = "not - orange") H(X|Y = "not - orange") \\
&= 0.4 * 0.92 + 0.6 * 0 \\
&= 0.368
\end{aligned}
$$

10.7.1 Sources of Error in Machine Learning

In supervised learning algorithms like decision trees, we can measure how well our machine learning model is performing by measuring the error in our model, which can also be thought of as how well it fits the problem and can be gauged using the signal to noise ratio. The **signal** of a dataset can be thought of as the underlying pattern we're trying to discern while **noise** might be considered to be the randomness or irrelevant parts of the dataset. **Generalization** is the idea of how well a model can predict the signal on new data after being trained on known data.

Overfitting is when a model learns too much from the known, training data and is so customized to the known data that it performs poorly when faced with new, unseen data. An overfit model is usually too complex, with too many parameters or features, and starts capturing the noise and outliers in the training data. As such, an overfit model will perform well on training data but poorly on testing data. This often occurs with nonparametric and nonlinear models, like neural networks, SVMs, and decision trees, which usually contain parameters or techniques to limit how much detail the model learns.

Underfitting occurs when a model is too simple and doesn't learn enough from the known, training data and so cannot generalize well on new data, either. An underfit model usually hasn't seen enough data and might be too simple; in fact, it cannot even model the training data well and performs poorly in training. As such, it is easy to detect by using an appropriate performance metric and can be mitigated by increasing complexity or trying multiple machine learning algorithms. Simple models that cannot capture complex patterns in the data, like linear regression and logistic regression, often exhibit underfitting.

Although both underfitting and overfitting can be mitigated by trying multiple models, using *cross-validation*, or incorporating *early stopping* for algorithms with multiple iterations, overfitting is usually a more common problem in machine learning. We can help reduce the effects of overfitting by using **regularization**, which helps reduce the complexity of the model, and **ensemble learning**, which combines multiple algorithms. Underfitting and overfitting also exhibit a **bias-variance tradeoff**, where an increase in one results in a decrease in the other so a lot of machine learning ends up tweaking the model to get a reasonable balance between underfitting and overfitting.

Variance error is how sensitive the model is to small fluctuations in the dataset. This is the error due to how much a predicted value varies for a given data point. High variance is usually due to an overly-complex model that fits the training data too closely. **Bias error** usually occurs when not all the features are taken into account and measures how far off the predicted values are from the actual values. Bias error is thus the error that arises from incorrect assumptions in the algorithm, usually from a model with overly simplistic or faulty assumptions that cause it to miss important trends in the dataset's features. *Bias* error can also be thought of as not being able to capture all of the *signal* in a dataset while *variance* error can be thought of as capturing too much of the *noise* in a dataset.

Models that **overfit** usually have *high variance and low bias* whereas **underfitting** models exhibit *low variance and high bias*. There is also an **irreducible error**, which is the noise that might be present regardless of which particular algorithm is used since it depends on things like missing variables, measurement imperfections, unknown forces, etc. Sometimes, data cleaning can help reduce this somewhat but usually there's some effect from such noise that cannot be completely eliminated. The total error can thus be expressed as:

$$\text{Total Error} = \text{Bias Error}^2 + \text{Variance Error} + \text{Irreducible Error}$$

10.8 Machine Learning, Data Science, and Computational Thinking

Let's bring it all together in the end by going back to the beginning. As shown below, the same guiding principle of Data $\rightarrow$ Information $\rightarrow$ Knowledge that has led us from the very beginning of our adventure also provides a framework for the various fields that we've considered on our computational voyage so far. It culminates with the computational thinking principles like abstraction, pattern recognition, generalization, etc., being explicitly reflected in the final Machine Learning case.

In that final component, we also relate it to the sub-fields of Machine Learning (Exploratory Data Analysis, Data Analysis, and Data Science) and Business Intelligence/Business Analytics (Descriptive Analytics, Predictive Analytics, and Prescriptive Analytics). It's been quite a journey but the lands that lie over the horizon as you delve into these areas in depth and discover new frontiers are even more exciting. With this framework in your toolbox, you're ready to embark on these exciting new adventures... to quote another adventurer, "Excelsior!"

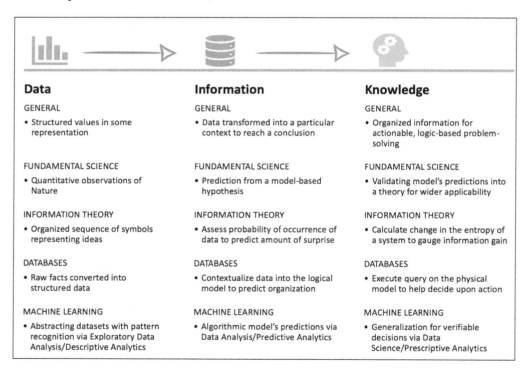

Data	**Information**	**Knowledge**
GENERAL	GENERAL	GENERAL
• Structured values in some representation	• Data transformed into a particular context to reach a conclusion	• Organized information for actionable, logic-based problem-solving
FUNDAMENTAL SCIENCE	FUNDAMENTAL SCIENCE	FUNDAMENTAL SCIENCE
• Quantitative observations of Nature	• Prediction from a model-based hypothesis	• Validating model's predictions into a theory for wider applicability
INFORMATION THEORY	INFORMATION THEORY	INFORMATION THEORY
• Organized sequence of symbols representing ideas	• Assess probability of occurrence of data to predict amount of surprise	• Calculate change in the entropy of a system to gauge information gain
DATABASES	DATABASES	DATABASES
• Raw facts converted into structured data	• Contextualize data into the logical model to predict organization	• Execute query on the physical model to help decide upon action
MACHINE LEARNING	MACHINE LEARNING	MACHINE LEARNING
• Abstracting datasets with pattern recognition via Exploratory Data Analysis/Descriptive Analytics	• Algorithmic model's predictions via Data Analysis/Predictive Analytics	• Generalization for verifiable decisions via Data Science/Prescriptive Analytics

Data $\rightarrow$ Information $\rightarrow$ Knowledge: The final Data $\rightarrow$ Information $\rightarrow$ Knowledge paradigm details for the General, Fundamental Science, Information Theory, Database, and Machine Learning cases.

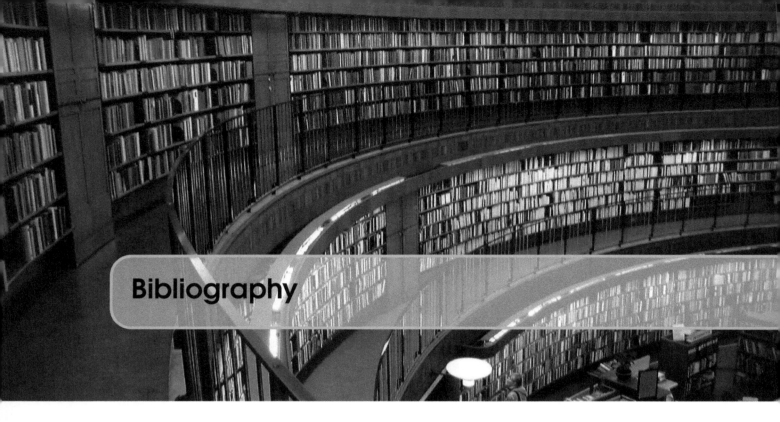

Bibliography

[1] C. W. Churchman, "The design of inquiring systems basic concepts of systems and organization", 1971. [Online]. Available: https://www.jstor.org/stable/1162585 (cited on page 6).

[2] D. T. Hawkins, L. R. Levy, and K. L. Montgomery, "Knowledge gateways: The building blocks", *Information processing & management*, volume 24, number 4, pages 459–468, 1988 (cited on page 6).

[3] A. Newell, H. A. Simon, *et al.*, *Human problem solving*, 9. Prentice-Hall Englewood Cliffs, NJ, 1972, volume 104 (cited on page 6).

[4] R. S. Engelmore and E. Feigenbaum, "Expert systems and artificial intelligence", *Expert Systems*, volume 100, page 2, 1993 (cited on page 6).

[5] H. Zenil, *A Computable Universe: Understanding and Exploring Nature As Computation*. River Edge, NJ, USA: World Scientific Publishing Co., Inc., 2012, ISBN: 9789814374293, 9814374296 (cited on page 8).

[6] C. Adami, "Toward a fully relativistic theory of quantum information", 2011. arXiv: 1112.1941 [quant-ph] (cited on pages 9, 277).

[7] ——, "Information theory in molecular biology", *Physics of Life Reviews*, volume 1, number 1, pages 3–22, 2004 (cited on page 9).

[8] B. L. Van der Waerden, *A history of algebra: from al-Khwarizmi to Emmy Noether*. Springer Science & Business Media, 2013 (cited on page 13).

[9] R. J. Ormerod, "Rational inference: Deductive, inductive and probabilistic thinking", *Journal of the Operational Research Society*, volume 61, number 8, pages 1207–1223, 2010 (cited on page 23).

[10] J. M. Wing, "Computational thinking", *Communications of the ACM*, volume 49, number 3, pages 33–35, 2006 (cited on page 30).

[11] C. E. Shannon, "A mathematical theory of communication", *The Bell System Technical Journal*, volume 27, pages 379–423, 1948. DOI: 10.1145/584091.584093. [Online]. Available: http://cm.bell-labs.com/cm/ms/what/shannonday/shannon1948.pdf (cited on pages 39, 42, 44, 46, 54).

[12] R. Hartley, "Transmission of Information", *Bell System Technical Journal*, pages 535–563, 1927. DOI: 10.1002/j.1538-7305.1928.tb01236.x (cited on pages 39, 41).

[13] F. A. Bais and J. D. Farmer, "Physics of Information", 2007. [Online]. Available: https://arxiv.org/abs/0708.2837 (cited on pages 47, 50).

[14] E. T. Jaynes, "Gibbs vs Boltzmann Entropies", *American Journal of Physics*, volume 33, number 5, page 391, 1965. DOI: 10.1119/1.1971557 (cited on page 50).

[15] E. T. Jaynes, "Information Theory and Statistical Mechanics", *Phys. Rev. Lett.*, volume 106, number 4, pages 620–630, 1957 (cited on page 51).

[16] C. Horsman, S. Stepney, R. C. Wagner, and V. Kendon, "When does a physical system compute?", in *Proceedings of The Royal Society*, 2014. DOI: 10.1098/rspa.2014.0182. [Online]. Available: http://rspa.royalsocietypublishing.org/content/470/2169/20140182 (cited on page 64).

[17] C. Böhm and G. Jacopini, "Flow diagrams, turing machines and languages with only two formation rules", *Communications of the ACM*, volume 9, number 5, pages 366–371, May 1966. DOI: 10.1145/355592.365646. [Online]. Available: http://doi.acm.org/10.1145/355592.365646 (cited on page 123).

[18] D. H. Kaye, "Proof in law and science", *Jurimetrics J.*, volume 32, page 313, 1991 (cited on page 259).

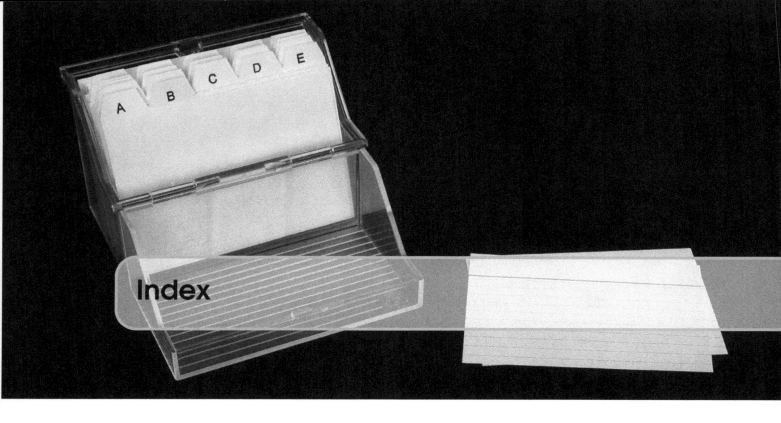

Index

About the author

Ricky J. Sethi is an Associate Professor of Computer Science at Fitchburg State University. Ricky is also Director of Research for the Madsci Network and Team Lead for SNHU Online at Southern New Hampshire University.

Prior to that, he was a Research Scientist at UMass Amherst/UMass Medical School and at UCLA/USC Information Sciences Institute, where he was chosen as an NSF Computing Innovation Fellow (CIFellow) by the CCC and the CRA. Even earlier, he was a Post-Doctoral Scholar at UCR, where he was the Lead Integration Scientist for the WASA project and participated in ONR's Empire Challenge 10.

A completely unrepresentative, decade-old photo.

Ricky has authored or co-authored over 30 peer-reviewed papers, book chapters, and reports and made numerous presentations on his research in machine learning, computer vision, social computing, and data science.

Ricky's work has been generously funded by the National Science Foundation (NSF), the National Endowment for the Humanities (NEH), the Institute for Advanced Study (IAS), and Amazon. He has also served as a panelist on several NSF programs, an Editorial Board Member for the International Journal of Computer Vision & Signal Processing, and an organizer and program committee member for various conferences.

You can find out more at his website http://research.sethi.org/ricky/

Figure Credits

Fig. ToC.1: Source: https://www.pexels.com/photo/businessman-man-desk-working-90333/.

Fig. ToC.2: Source: https://www.pexels.com/photo/close-up-of-hand-holding-pencil-over-white-background-316466/.

Fig. 0.0: Source: https://www.pexels.com/photo/asphalt-blue-sky-clouds-countryside-490411/.

Fig. 0.1: Modified from: https://pixabay.com/en/post-it-notes-sticky-notes-note-1284667/.

Fig. 0.3b: Source: https://publicdomainvectors.org/en/free-clipart/Decorative-glowing-sun-with-spokes-vector-clip-art/30159.html.

Fig. 0.3c: Source: https://pixabay.com/en/clothing-coat-fashion-girl-wear-1298840/.

Fig. 0.8: Copyright © GabrielF (CC BY-SA 3.0) at https://commons.wikimedia.org/wiki/File:Model_of_a_Turing_machine.jpg.

Fig. 1.0: Source: https://unsplash.com/photos/74TufExdP3Y.

Fig. 1.2: R. V. L. Hartley, from "Transmission of Information," The Bell System Technical Journal, vol. 7, no. 3. Copyright © 1928 by John Wiley & Sons, Inc.

Fig. 1.3: Copyright © Htkym (CC BY-SA 3.0) at https://commons.wikimedia.org/wiki/File:Maxwell%27s_demon.svg.

Fig. 2.0: Source: https://www.pexels.com/photo/ideas-whiteboard-person-working-7369/.

Fig. 2.1: Source: https://pixabay.com/en/target-aim-darts-dart-board-297821/.

Fig. 2.3a: Copyright © User000name (CC BY-SA 4.0) at https://commons.wikimedia.org/wiki/File:Values_of_digits_in_the_Decimal_numeral_system.svg.

Fig. 2.3b: Copyright © User000name (CC BY-SA 4.0) at https://commons.wikimedia.org/wiki/File:Value_of_digits_in_the_Binary_numeral_system.svg.

Fig. 2.4: Modified from: https://pixabay.com/en/homer-simpsons-cartoon-comic-155238/.

Fig. 2.5: Copyright © Katakam Venkataramana (CC BY-SA 4.0) at https://commons.wikimedia.org/wiki/File:Simple_electric_circuit.png.

Fig. 2.7: Claude E. Shannon, from "A Symbolic Analysis of Switching and Relay Circuits," Electrical Engineering, vol. 57, no. 12. Copyright © 1938 by Institute of Electrical and Electronics Engineers.

Fig. 2.8a: Copyright © Stefan506 (CC BY-SA 3.0) at https://commons.wikimedia.org/wiki/File:Logic-gate-nand-us.png.

Fig. 2.8b: Source: https://commons.wikimedia.org/wiki/File:NandFullAdder.png.

Fig. 3.0: Source: https://pixabay.com/en/work-typing-computer-notebook-731198/.

Fig. 3.2: Copyright © by Netbeans.

Fig. 3.3: Copyright © by Python.

Img. 3.1: Source: https://www.history.navy.mil/our-collections/photography/numerical-list-of-images/nhhc-series/nh-series/NH-96000/NH-96566-KN.html.

Fig. 4.0: Source: https://pixabay.com/en/math-cube-geometry-structure-shape-1777917/.

Fig. 5.0: Copyright © Christoph Roser at AllAboutLean.com (CC BY-SA 4.0) at https://commons.wikimedia.org/wiki/File:PDCA-Multi-Loop.png.

Fig. 5.1: Copyright © by Python.

Fig. 6.0: Source: https://www.pexels.com/photo/lights-abstract-curves-long-exposure-1944/.

Fig. 7.0: Copyright © Paul Hartzog (CC BY-SA 2.0) at https://www.flickr.com/photos/paulbhartzog/24420377960.

Fig. 7.1a: Source: https://pixabay.com/en/coffee-used-coffee-grounds-2124970/.

Fig. 7.1b: Source: https://pixabay.com/en/kettle-water-boiling-stove-heat-653666/.

Fig. 7.2a: Source: https://pixabay.com/en/coffee-used-coffee-grounds-2124970/.

Fig. 7.2b: Source: https://pixabay.com/en/kettle-water-boiling-stove-heat-653666/.

Fig. 7.3b: Source: https://pixabay.com/en/coffee-used-coffee-grounds-2124970/.

Fig. 8.0: Source: https://www.pexels.com/photo/macbook-pro-908284/.

Fig. 8.1: Copyright © by NetBeans.

Fig. 9.0: Source: https://commons.wikimedia.org/wiki/File:Archive_storage_(Unsplash).jpg.

Fig. 9.3b: Copyright © by Fitchburg State University.

Tbl 9.1a: Copyright © by Fitchburg State University.

Tbl 9.2a: Copyright © by Fitchburg State University.

Fig. 10.0: Source: https://www.pexels.com/photo/architecture-big-ben-blur-building-372038/.

Fig. B.1: Copyright © Marcus Hansson (CC by 2.0) at https://commons.wikimedia.org/wiki/File:Interior_view_of_Stockholm_Public_Library.jpg.

Fig. I.1: Source: https://pixabay.com/en/index-card-box-flashcards-karteibox-2288592/.